W9-AZH-335

THE

SOCIALIST REGISTER 1982

THE SOCIALIST REGISTER 1982

EDITED BY

MARTIN EVE

and

DAVID MUSSON

THE MERLIN PRESS

LONDON

First published in 1982
by The Merlin Press Ltd
3 Manchester Road
London E14

British Library Cataloguing in Publication Data

Socialist register.—1982

1. Socialism—Periodicals
335'.005 HX3

ISBN 0-85036-292-X
ISBN 0-85036-293-8 Pbk

Printed in Great Britain by
Whitstable Litho Whitstable Kent

Typesetting by Heather Hems
The Malt House Chilmark Wilts.

TABLE OF CONTENTS

Page

PREFACE

This year's *Socialist Register* is being edited by David Musson and myself. Through pressure of work Ralph Miliband and John Saville have temporarily stepped aside for 1982, but our intervention from inside the publishing house is for one year only. As befits caretakers, we are making no major changes in direction; readers may find small nuances of difference, but these we have not intended. A journal such as this which has now come of age has a life of its own which tends to resist arbitrary change.

Having said that, there are one or two innovations that have come about. One is that we have a larger number of review articles than has been usual in the past. Peter Sedgwick writes on Alasdair MacIntyre, Paul Kelemen reviews Halliday and Molyneux's *The Ethiopian Revolution*, Huw Beynon contests Jeremy Seabrook's account of changes in the British working class, John Saville reviews developments in Labour History. Along with these is included Valentine Cunningham's answer to a review article last year; the *Register* has always adhered to the principle of the right of reply.

Another innovation this year is the reprinting of Isaac Deutscher's essay on the early history of the Polish Communist Party from his collection of essays *Marxism in Our Time.* Isaac Deutscher contributed to the first two issues of the *Register,* and two posthumous essays appeared in 1968 and 1969, but these were all making their first appearance in the covers of the *Register.* Apart from translations, there has hitherto been no reprinting of articles. Two reasons have suggested to us that we should make an exception in this instance. The first is that this highly apposite piece of historical writing is not now available in any form, nor has anyone else covered the same ground. Deutscher was himself a participant in these early struggles of the Polish CP and was uniquely qualified to write about them. We felt it would be a great loss if this was not made available. A second consideration was that only a small minority of our readers would already be in possession of the original essay; they, we are sure, will be the first to agree with its importance today. To Tamara Deutscher we are grateful for permission to republish and for the Introduction she has written.

For the rest, we begin with British problems. Stuart Hall delivered the first Fred Tonge Memorial Lecture on 'The Battle for Socialist Ideas in the 1980s', and has adapted this for us; Paul Gilroy and Joe Sim have each written around the theme of police power. Roy Green and Andrew Wilson write jointly on the TUC/NEC document 'Economic

Planning and Workers' Control'. Dealing with Eastern Europe, Denis MacShane writes on Poland under military rule and Bill Lomax studies the changing attitudes of opposition in Hungary. From East Germany we have translated the profound and moving speech of the novelist Christa Wolf when accepting the official Büchner prize. Ernest Mandel writes on the problems of the Chinese economy, and David Ruben on Marxism and the Jewish Question. Finally Ralph Miliband contributes a brief obituary on Ruth First, victim of the South African government's terrorism.

In our temporary role as editors we should like to acknowledge our debt of gratitude to Ralph Miliband and John Saville for the help and advice they have given us as well as for the contributions both have made to this volume. We are grateful to Barbara Einhorn who has translated and introduced Christa Wolf's speech, and to Mandel's translators, John Barzman and Gregor Benton. We should also like to put on record our thanks to our colleague Philippa Jones who has shared in all the editorial tasks, and to Heather Hems who for the tenth time has set the entire text of the *Register.* Not least our thanks are due to all those who responded to our pleas for contributions.

October 1982 Martin Eve

NOTE

Until his death in his eighty-fourth year, Fred Tonge was the widely respected President of St Pancras North Labour Party. It was resolved to commemorate his life and work in some suitable way, and it was thought most appropriate to inaugurate a series of annual lectures, of which this is the first.

Leaving Bristol Grammar School at fourteen to earn his living on the railways, Fred volunteered for the army in 1914 and spent four years in the trenches. On his return to the Great Western Railway he became an active union organiser, and in the face of fierce opposition from his employers took part in the formation of branches of the union throughout the West Country. This activity led to him becoming a delegate to the National Executive of his union, then a full-time official; also to his move to London where he became a borough councillor, a London County Councillor and a Parliamentary candidate. These developments in no way modified his socialist outlook and he remained a man of the Left all his life.

In his old age he remained an activist in his branch and constituency party, as well as being a most effective governor of a number of local schools. A generation or two older than most of us, he exemplified the working people who had built the Labour movement from its beginnings.

Martin Eve

THE BATTLE FOR SOCIALIST IDEAS IN THE 1980s

Stuart Hall

I am honoured to be asked to give the first Fred Tonge lecture. I am pleased to be associated with the inspiration behind it, which is to commemorate the link between theory and practice, between socialist ideas and socialist politics, and thereby keep alive the memory of someone who served the labour movement in both these ways throughout his life. Fred Tonge's commitment to socialism did not wane with age, as it has in so many other quarters. His commitment to socialist internationalism did not degenerate into that parochialism which so often besets our movement. He understood the absolute centrality of political education to the achievement of socialism. Those are very distinctive qualities and I want, in what follows to make a small contribution to their continuity. So I have chosen to talk about the struggle, the battle, for socialist ideas in the 1980s.

First, I want to say something about the importance of ideological struggle. Thinking about the place and role of ideas in the construction of socialism, I would particularly emphasise the notion of struggle itself: ideology is a battlefield and every other kind of struggle has a stake in it. I want therefore to talk about the ideological pre-condition for socialist advance: the winning of a majority of the people—the working people of the society and their allies—to socialist ideas in the decades immediately ahead. I stress the centrality of the domain of the ideological—political ideas and the struggle to win hearts and minds to socialism—because I am struck again and again by the way in which socialists still assume that somehow socialism is inevitable. It is not coming perhaps quite as fast as we assumed: not trundling along in our direction with quite the speed and enthusiasm we would hope; but nevertheless, bound sooner or later to, as it were, take command. Socialism, it is felt, remains the natural centre of gravity of working-class ideas, and only a temporary, magical spell could divert working-class consciousness from its natural aim.

One can recognise a certain kind of Marxist 'traditionalism' behind this notion of the 'inevitable triumph of socialist ideas'. But, actually, it is even more deeply rooted in the non-Marxist, 'labourist', traditions. Vulgar economism comes in many disguises. Socialist ideas, having taken root in the culture, will never die; socialism is the true, the 'objective consciousness', of the class; material conditions will always make working people think 'socialism'; once a Labour voter, always a Labour voter; the welfare state is here to stay. And so on. If the 'laws of history' do not, then familial habit and electoral inertia will make 'correct ideas' win through in the end.

I have to confess I no longer subscribe to that view. I think perhaps I once did; but I believe now that, if socialism is not *made* by us, it certainly will not be made *for* us, not even by the laws of history. The alternative which Marx offered: namely, 'socialism or barbarism', sometimes seems to be more powerfully tilted, at the end of the twentieth century, towards barbarism than socialism. The capacity of a nuclear-filled world to destroy itself in the defence of some frozen social system, or some lofty ideal, is as much on the cards as the triumph of socialism in the advanced industrial capitalist world. We have to abandon the notion that socialism will somehow come in spite of how effectively we struggle for it; and I think that is also true for socialist ideas. Since it is possible to conceive of a world without human life, it is possible to envisage a world without socialism.

I want to say something about what lies behind the untenable notion of the inevitable triumph of socialist ideas, and suggest some of the reasons why that is not a socialism in which we can any longer indulge ourselves. There is a strong assumption that, in a class society like ours, where the vast majority of working people are continuously at the negative, the receiving end of the system, the social and material conditions in which working people themselves live will inevitably predispose them towards socialism. And I think that this proposition contains a profound materialist truth—despite the reconstruction job we have had to do on the classical materialist theory of ideology. Marx once remarked that you do not literally have to *be* a shop keeper all your life to have petty bourgeois ideas—an observation demonstrated by our own prime minister. It is true that if you live constantly in a corner shop and try to squeeze a living under advanced capitalism from that particular corner of it, you will be strongly inclined to *think* that that is actually how the world works. Similarly, if you are always at the exploiting end of an economic, social and political system, there is a built-in tendency, in the very material conditions in which the class has to live and survive, to think of socialist ideas as most effectively capturing the interests of the working class and the stake of working people in the future of their own society.

Still, there is no *inevitable* or *guaranteed* link between class origin and political ideas. What matters, Marx suggested, was whether or not, in your thinking you go beyond the horizon of thought typical of the petty-bourgeois—the sort of spontaneous thinking which arises when one tries to *live* one's relation to an advanced capitalist economy as if it were simply the old corner shop writ large. This might be called the 'Grantham' world-view. Undoubtedly, living at the exploited end of a system creates a powerful tendency to see the world in terms of 'us' and 'them': the governing and the governed, the powerful and the powerless, the possessing and the possessed. 'Us' and 'them' is the spontaneous consciousness of all exploited classes and oppressed people everywhere: what Gramsci called their 'good' sense. And, though social struggles have their roots deep in the structural contradictions of a system, they cannot become politically active unless they become articulated through this oppressor/oppressed form of consciousness.

The problem is that even this tendency cannot provide socialism with a permanent guarantee. 'Us' and 'them' can be represented, politically through a number of different political ideologies. It underpins reformism or 'Labourism' just as much as it does more revolutionary positions. Even working class *deference* can feed off this built-in sense of class difference. So, there may be good materialist reasons why, in some circumstances, socialist ideas do win support among the working class. But there is certainly no materialist guarantee that *only* socialism can represent the interests of the working class and their stake in the future. And the addition of 'true' to the word 'interests' only begs the question: an attempt to save our historical face. Interests may be the motor of political action. But interests frequently conflict: the 'interest' in defending one's standard of living against the interest in remaining in employment—a contradiction which Mrs Thatcher, Mr Tebbitt and Mr Michael Edwardes—to name but three—have not hesitated to exploit. Moreover, working class interests do not exist outside of the political space in which they are defined, or outside of the political discourses which give them sense or outside the balance of forces which define the limits of the possible in which they have to be realised. Materialism remains active. But its tendency is not uni-directional. Socialism, it carries no absolute guarantees.

We have to confess that socialist ideas have come and gone among working people in our own society throughout recent history. A significant proportion of the British working class has consistently voted the other way. The deference vote amongst that class is not an insignificant proportion and it is not historically transient. We have to acknowledge that though, of course, material condition may predispose working people to think in the direction of the reform and reconstruction of a system which exploits them in so many ways, they do not guarantee that economic and social position will always be translated into a political project or will and of itself—without political organisation and education—give birth spontaneously to socialist ideas.

The working class, as we know it, is itself powerfully divided and stratified internally. It is not always unified in its origins, though it may become unified through its political practice. It can *become* unified, but it is not unified as it is. As it is, it is sectoralised; impregnated by ideas, interests and outlooks from elsewhere. It is marked by the contradictory conditions in which it came to maturity: for instance by the uneven impact of the social and sexual division of labour under capitalism. The unity of working class political movements, activities and ideas around a common socialist core would not be a reflection of what the class already is 'in-itself' but the effect of the involvement of a 'class-in-itself', in a 'politics-for-itself'. That shift involves something more than merely translating one's every-day, lived-experience into the socialist project. It means qualifying, criticising, interrogating working class 'experience'. It means often, breaking the mould of working class common sense.

I know this idea runs right against the grain of libertarian-socialist received wisdom in the 1980s. Socialists who work as intellectual people have come to understand the costs of their profound separation from the lived, everyday, experience of working people under capitalism. They are also deeply, and correctly, suspicious of setting themselves up as a vanguard to bring socialism to the masses 'from the outside'. In the light of the Bolshevik experience, we know what happens when the party is substituted for the class, and the leadership for the party, and so on. But, in the post-1968 period, such people have been driven to the opposite and equally untenable alternative: Narodnikism. This is the view that 'the people' are *already,* really socialist; and this will come through if we only allow them to speak. The role of socialists is therefore simply to be the 'voice' of this already adequate experience: to flatter the 'authenticity' of working class experience and its spontaneous consciousness by simply *affirming it.*

But this cannot be correct, either. If socialism were simply the flowering of what already exists, and nothing more, why hasn't it defeated its enemies before now? Even more worryingly, if under capitalism the working class is able to live its relation to its conditions of existence transparently, 'authentically', why does it have need for socialism at all? The division of labour has inscribed itself indelibly across the face of the working classes, and nowhere more damagingly than in the division between mental and manual, physical and intellectual labour. But you don't *overcome* the capitalist division of labour by denying that it exists. Only by going beyond it, in reality, in practice. By breaking down some of the divisions, through political education and organisation; by setting—slowly, painfully—in their place, an alternative division of labour. That is why, in spite of all the traps which lie in wait of the attempt to restore the question of 'party' to socialist politics today, the fragmented political scene continues to be haunted by the absent ghost of—not *the* Party (there are plenty of those), but of 'party' in Gramsci's sense. For it is only in the course of political organisation and practice ('party') that the damaging divisions of status between manual and intellectual labour, between the intellectual function (all of us, since we all think) and those who do intellectual work for a living (a very small number of us) can actually be overcome, so that the conditions for genuine political education—learning and teaching beyond the hierarchies of 'teacher' and 'taught', 'vanguard' and 'mass'—can be created. This failure to find an alternative basis for political education—alternative to either the 'vanguardist' or the 'narodnikist' solutions—is part of a larger political crisis: the crisis of political organisation which has afflicted the left since Leninism lost its magic in 1956, and since 1968, when to be 'radical' meant, by definition, to be 'radically against *all* parties, party lines and party bureaucracies': the 'inside—not beyond—the fragments' problem. This problem of 'party' represents an unsurpassed limit in the politics of the left today: a line we seem able neither to return to nor pass across. But we shouldn't mistake this *dilemma* for a *solution!*

It is true that working class experience—the experience of exploitation and of 'secondariness'—is the soil in which socialism takes root. Without it we may have all manner of 'radicalisms'—including the spurious extremisms of 'armed struggle'. But we will not have socialism. On the other hand, if working class 'experience' is the necessary, it is not the sufficient condition for socialism or for socialist ideas today. First, because working class 'common sense' under capitalism *must* be fragmentary and contradictory. It is inscribed with the traces of heterogeneous ideas. It contains in the same thought, as Gramsci remarked, modern and archaic, progressive and stone-age, elements. Experience as such is historically shaped. It is constituted through ideological categories—how can we feel and reason entirely outside the categories of our own culture? It cannot, despite its appearance of immediate authenticity, *escape* its own history. Second, because the lived experience of class exploitation is not the only brand which socialism in the twentieth century must incorporate; it is not the only variant of exploitation which socialism must address, though it may be the *modal* one, the one through which all the other social contradictions are reflected, the paradigm instance. Therefore, other types of social experiences will have to be drawn on, built into socialism if it is to become a politics capable of condensing the variety of social struggles into a single, differentiated one, or—to put the metaphor the other way—if it is to become a politics capable of fighting and transforming life on a variety of different 'fronts'. Once we abandon the guarantee that working class ideas will 'inevitably tend towards socialism' as their given, teleological end, or that everything else follows once socialism begins, it has to be acknowledged that sexist and racist and jingoist ideas have deeply penetrated and naturalised themselves in sectors of working class thinking. Such ideas—frequently drawing exactly on 'immediate experience', and simply mirroring it—are not consonant with socialism. In the name of socialism itself (not in the name of some superior wisdom) they will have to be interrogated, corrected, transformed, *educated*. And, without falling back into vanguardism we must—for all our sakes—find a way of undertaking this far-reaching political and ideological struggle *against* 'working class common sense' *inside* the class itself.

Experience has many diversions, many structures. The 'experience' of the British working class is also the massive historical experience of corporateness, and of the struggle against incorporation. The moment one says this one is likely to be pounced on by the keepers of revolutionary purity as living proof of one's lack of faith in the capacities of the class. This is polemical rubbish. Corporateness is simply an acknowledgement of where, under capitalism, the majority of working people are *positioned.* Otherwise, why would one need the Marxist concept of 'exploitation' at all? Within that, the British working class is also the most 'experienced' industrial class in the history of capitalism, rich in political traditions and culture. It has generated organisation in depth, capable of defending class interests and advancing its cause. It is a class wisdom of the infinite negotiations and resistances necessary for survival within the culture of capitalism. It has immense *depth* in defence. And yet, socialism—of course—requires something more, something that does not arise spontaneously: a class which can transform itself from the secondary to the *leading* element in society. A class which aspires to refashion the world in its image. A class capable of conducting a struggle in areas of civil society, moral and intellectual life and the state, *outside* of its 'immediate' class experience; a class capable of winning the 'war of position' in relation to a whole complex of social movements which do not spontaneously cohere around *the* 'class experience'. We do not yet have a class which is driving to make itself the hegemonic element in society: which sees its purpose, not to defend but to *lead.* Experience of exploitation, alone, will not create a 'class-for-itself' in this sense, though socialism in the twentieth century requires it.

We also have to acknowledge that working people are not 'unified' around *any* single political philosophy or ideology, let alone socialism. There are different kinds of socialist ideas and the labour movement in this country has gravitated for often quite understandable reasons towards reformism. Political reformism represents a strong, indigenous British political tradition: as authentic a working class tradition as the revolutionary one. It represents a different, more adaptive, negotiated, way of struggling for survival inside a system. But it is not an illusion. It is not false consciousness. It is not that working people do not understand the nature of the game in which they are involved. In part, all politics is a form of political calculation; and some people, under certain circumstances will calculate, for themselves, their children, and people they love and work with, that it is better to take advantage of whatever advances you can make rather than cutting off the head of the goose that sometimes—occasionally—lays a golden egg. In a system that usually yields *something* under pressure at the eleventh hour, reformism has its own kind of 'rationality'. All the same, reformism is *not* the same as socialism.

I do not want to make a kind of absolute divide or fetish of the distinction between them. But in the year of the Social-Democratic Party one has to distinguish in a very sharp way between the two. It is certainly important not to fall into the trap of repeating the formal, abstract opposition between reform and revolution—a specious piece of left formalism. Still we must understand the clear line that divides socialists from people who would like to see society more humanely governed, who are more open to progressive ideas, who would like to see people who have not had much out of life getting on a little. Those are all sound, worthy, reformist ideas. They are what you might call socialism without tears. Socialism without all that bother about the working class. They are political change without political power: the great liberal illusion in twentieth-century fancy dress. Well, reformism is not only a long and important tradition. Actually, it has always been the *dominant* tradition *inside* the Labour Party itself. But it is not socialism. I do not want to rely on the rhetoric or received wisdom of the past, because one of the requirements of a socialism without guarantees must be to rethink what socialism might mean in the 1980s and 1990s. But nevertheless, one thing it *has* always meant and that is a fundamental reshaping of the social relations and the institutions in which men and women live.

Socialism has in its past learnt a good deal from progressive people who have contributed in important ways to the labour movement. I expect it always will try to show that only socialism can create the conditions in which *reform* can make a fundamental difference rather than introducing minor modifications. But progressivism can never provide the lure of socialist ideas. Between good reformism and the will to socialism runs what William Morris once called the 'river of fire'. As soon as socialism touches the imagination, people of course do still go on living just as they did before, trying to survive, coming to terms with a society in which they have to make an existence. But their imaginations have been fired by the possibility of an alternative way of making life with other people, and nothing less will do. Socialism may be just half the turn of a screw away from reformist and progressive ideas but it is the final twist that counts. It is what makes the difference between good and humane people and committed socialists: between the logic of one principle of social organisation and another.

Now when that gulf opens, the river of fire dissects people's lives, and they glimpse the possibilities, not of having the existing set of social relations improved a bit, but of beginning the long, dangerous historical process of reconstructing society according to a different model, a different logic and principle that does not come 'spontaneously'. It does not drop like manna from the skies. It has to be made, constructed and struggled over. Socialist ideas win only because they displace other, not so good, not so powerful ideas. They only command a space because they grip people's imagination, or they connect with people's experience; or they make better sense of the world they live in; or they are better at analysing what is happening; or they provide a language of difference and resistance; or they capture and embody people's hopes. Apart from their *effectivity* there is no guarantee that socialist ideas must and will prevail over other ideas. In that sense, I believe that the struggle for socialist ideas is a continuous one. It is something which will have to go on under actual existing socialism itself. I am even quite tempted by the thought of that much discredited leader of the people, Chairman Mao, that the period of socialist construction might be the moment of *greatest* intensity in the battle for socialist ideas.

Why then is the terrain for socialist ideas so stony in the 1980s? One can think of many good reasons but, I refer here to only three. The first I can deal with quickly, though it may surprise you. I think that one of the reasons why the terrain for socialist ideas is so stony is the fact, the legacy, the experience of Stalinism. By this I mean something quite different from the usual simple minded anti-communism. Nevertheless I do think that, when they speak to people drawn and attracted to socialism, socialists today have something to explain, to account for: about why the attempts to transform some societies in the image of socialism has produced this grim caricature of socialism. I know that the transformation of relatively backward societies is a much more difficult and prolonged process than most of us imagine; that 'socialism in one country' is not a particularly good way to have to start; that all is not lost in these societies, that the struggle for socialism is not terminated in them. All the same, people are willing to contemplate pulling up what they know by the roots only if they can have some rational hope, some concrete image, of the alternative. At the beginning of the century, the language of socialism was full of hope, indeed of a perhaps too-naive scientific guarantee about the future. But the actuality of Stalinism and its aftermath has added the tragic dimension to the language of socialism: the stark possibility of failure. The socialist experiment *can* go wildly and disastrously wrong. It *can* produce a result which is both recognisable as 'socialism' and yet alien to everything intrinsic in our image of what socialism should be like. It can deliver consequences against which socialists may have to stand up and be counted. This is a deep and wounding paradox—and a damaging weakness which every socialist has first to dismantle before he or she can persuade people in good faith to come to our side and assume positions alongside us in the struggle. In our struggle to realise a proper kind of socialism, we have first to explain—not explain away—the *other* kind: the kind where, in the name of the workers' state, the working class is actually shot down in the streets, as is happening at this very moment in Gdansk to Polish Solidarity.

Second, there is a problem about the resilience and buoyancy of socialist ideas in our time because of the exhaustion which has overtaken the labour movement, especially under the management of Labour governments in the past two or three decades. I do not want to talk about the record of those governments in detail. But I want to communicate my overwhelming sense that the collapse of the last Labour government in 1979 was not simply the rotation of political parties in government but the end of a particular political epoch. It was the culmination of a period in which, although there were actually Conservative governments in power some of the time, the framework of ideas being drawn on, the dominant ideas, the consensus, was taken precisely from the social democratic repertoire. Those were ideas to which people had become acclimatised; the taken-for-granted welfare state, mixed economy, incomes' policy, corporatist bargaining and demand management. If you stood up at that time, in a debate on the national economy and tried to justify neo-classical economics, or indeed monetarism, you would have been laughed out of court. Everyone who mattered was one kind of Keynesian or another. Good ideas belonged to the 'Left'. In the sixties and early seventies the Right refused to use the word 'capitalism' at all. Bad old capitalism, they insisted had long gone past. In its place we have something else now, which will help people to, as it were, survive through the dark ages of creeping collectivism. This was the epoch of the social democratic hegemony. That is no longer the case. People talk about 'free-market capitalism' again quite openly. When the Institute for Economic Affairs first started pumping out simple-minded monetarism for the one or two experts in the civil service who still read books, they glossed the capitalist ethic by calling it 'social market values'. They could not actually pronounce the word, 'market', in its full, bare, capitalist form. They had, as it were, to colour it over a bit, soften the blow, by calling it 'social market values'. They don't talk about social market values or the mixed economy any longer. The talk about *the market*—the good old, hidden hand, Adam Smith market. There are civil servants in Sir Keith Joseph's ministry who are busy reading *The Wealth of Nations,* for the first time. They actually believe in the invisible hand which draws us all involuntarily into the market, produces what everyone needs and pays us what we all deserve and so on. These ancient, pre-industrial pre-historic ideas are capitalist ideas making a late twentieth century reprise to displace those outdated social democratic nostrums about the benevolent state, the national interest, the 'caring society'. Calculating everything according to its pure market value and measuring the national interest in terms of gross self-interest are back in fashion. Even Mr Roy Jenkins and the SDP can't resist the 'new brutalism'.

I don't deny that social democracy helped to make life more humane and tolerable for many in its hey-day in the 1960s and '70s. We have only to bring to mind the alternative—say, Mr Tebbitt or Mr Heseltine in full flow—to find it relatively easy to think kind thoughts about Mr Callaghan, squalid though his last political hours proved to be. But however we assess the differences, it is clear now that those social democratic ideas which seemed to define the age were trapped in their own contradictions. They proved hopelessly inadequate to the crisis which was already confronting the country and whose dimensions have rapidly increased. They were thin ideas in front of a fat, long historical crisis—some, including me, would say a crisis which began in the closing decades of the last century, the post-imperialist crisis from which Britain has never in fact recovered. The central illusion—the social democratic illusion, Mark I—to which Labour leaders good, bad and indifferent were attached is that the social democratic bandwagon could be hitched to the star of a reformed capitalism: and that the latter would prove capable of infinite expansion so that all the political constituencies could be 'paid off' at once: the TUC and the CBI, labour and capital, public housing and the private landlord, the miners and the Bank of England. Why worry about the size of your slice relative to the next person's if the size of the cake is constantly expanding?

This social democratic illusion was undermined by the fundamental weaknesses in British industrial capitalism and by the logic of capitalism itself. There simply was not enough expansion in the system after a time to pay off everybody. Besides, it was always an illusion that, by taking into the public economy the industrial infrastructure, you had somehow transformed the logic of profitability and accumulation. This illusion was caught by the scissors of capitalist reality. When the goodies stop rolling in, and you have to choose—under the helpful guidance of the International Monetary Fund—between maintaining living standards and restoring profitability and the managerial prerogative, which is it to be? At that point, an incomes policy ceased to be a recipe for 'planned growth' and instead became a strategy by which a government 'of' the working people polices and disciplines the working class. In the end, under capitalism, the interests of capital and restoring the conditions of expanded accumulation must count first, ahead of the wages and living standards of the people.

When caught in the *logic* of a system, there is no need for conspiratorial theories about leadership sell-outs. If you are inside the logic of a declining capitalism, there are not the extra funds in the kitty to pay off the working class. That is a logic which catches governments of the Left, Right and Centre while they operate inside the capitalist logic. That is why I made such heavy weather, earlier on, about the distinction between socialist ideas and other ideas. It is not a distinction between the good and the bad. It is the distinction between two logics. R.H. Tawney—one of those truly progressive minds whom the Social-Democratic Party are trying to hi-jack, once said that capitalism is not an onion, but a tiger:

'You can peel an onion layer by layer; but you cannot skin a tiger stripe by stripe.' Not a particularly SDP sentiment, you may think. Social democracy—I mean, Mark I, when the Labour Party was in power—was no doubt committed, broadly speaking, to improving society in a social democratic way. It chose to reform but not to transform. But British capitalism required not greater humanity but the kiss of life. And, trapped by that remorseless logic, those ideas have gone to the wall. They have disintegrated on us. People are not attracted or powered by them any more. People may be driven back to them because of the horrendous alternative offered by the other side. But that is not a victory for socialist ideas. That is a revulsion against reactionary ideas, which is a very different thing. We could certainly have another Labour government or even a socialist democratic Mark II government next. But whether there will be a government on the basis of a popular and positive mandate for advancing towards socialism is open to doubt. The problem is that the positive commitment to the serious, dangerous and difficult task of unpacking the oldest capitalist system in the world, and beginning to construct some other system without triggering off 'barbarism' will require a great deal of popular will, mobilisation, commitment and nerve. And one of the essential prerequisites for this is the transformation of popular consciousness in a socialist direction. I am not concerned at the moment with prophecies about the exact character and political colouration of the next government. But there is a qualitative difference between advancing towards socialism and another Labour government which comes in on the mandate of the exhausted political ideas of the last two decades.

I have talked about two barriers standing in the way of the advance of socialist ideas. One is the legacy of actual-existing socialism. The second is the historic record of the exhaustion and collapse of the ideas and programmes on which majority Labour governments have taken legitimate power in the state during the post-war period.

But I want to say something about a third inhibition. This is the advance of the Right itself. Since the accession of the Thatcherites to power in the Conservative Party in the mid-1970s, I have taken a more gloomy view of the advance of the Right than most other socialists. It may be that I am overstating the case, in which case I may stimulate you into deeper socialist commitment. I think that the radical Right under Thatcherite leadership is very different from any other conservative power base we have seen in the post-war period. I think its ideological penetration into society is very profound. It has shifted the parameters of common sense. It has pioneered a considerable swing towards authoritarian populism and reactionary ideas. It goes deep into the heartland of traditional labour support: skilled workers; working women; young people. Its success is partly the result of the Right, not the Left, *taking ideas seriously.* The radical Right is not hung up on some low-flying materialism which tells them that, of course, ideas are wholly determined by material and economic conditions. They actually do believe that you have to struggle to implant the notion of the market; and that, if you talk about it well enough, effectively, persuasively enough, you could touch people's understanding of how they live and work, and make a new kind of sense about what's wrong with society and what to do about it.

That is, of course, precisely the nature of ideology. It provides the frameworks within which people define and interpret social existence. Not necessarily in a very learned or systematic way but in terms of everyday practical social reasoning, practical consciousness. Events and their consequences can always be interpreted in more than one ideological framework. That is why there is always a struggle over ideology: a struggle as to which definition of the situation will prevail. This is a struggle over a particular kind of power—cultural power: the power to define, to 'make things mean'. The politics of signification. What matters is, which frameworks are in play, which definitions fill out and articulate the 'common sense', of a conjuncture, which have become so naturalised and consensual that they become identical with common sense, with the taken-for-granted, and represent the point of origin from which all political calculation begins. It has become unfashionable to quote the French Marxist philosopher, Althusser, in polite socialist company in Britain, so since this is a virtual repository of unseasonable thoughts, let me do so now. 'The realities of the class struggle are "represented" by ideas which are "represented" by words. In scientific and philosophical reasoning, the words (concepts, categories) are "instruments" of knowledge. But in political, ideological and philosophical struggle, the words are also weapons, explosives or tranquillisers and poisons. Occasionally, the whole class struggle may be summed up in the struggle for one word against another. Certain words struggle amongst themselves as enemies. Other words are the site of an ambiguity: the stake in a decisive but undecided battle.' ('The Politics of Philosophy', *New Left Review* 64, 1970.) To this struggle the radical Right have devoted themselves with conspicuous success. In the categories of common sense, 'freedom' has not only been separated from but has effectively *displaced* 'equality'. The state, as representative of the 'caring society' and the 'national interest', has attracted to it all the negative connotations of the spendthrift bureaucratic totalitarian machine. In its place there flames once more that spark of hope, freedom and individual choice: free enterprise.

Socialists tend to dismiss the idea that such thoughts could ever really take root again in popular consciousness. They are false, an illusion. But organic ideologies, which are deeply rooted in real practices (as the market, after all, is in our society), which represent the interests of fundamental classes, which have been historically developed and refined and which have mobilised masses of men and women into action, are very rarely pure fabrications in this sense. They may be hideously wicked; but they do touch reality, even if they misrepresent its meaning; they have some rational core. The first thing to ask about an organic ideology is not whether it is false but what is true about it. After all, under capitalism, men and women *do* live their lives and sell their labour, every day, in the market. It has its own materiality; it imposes its gross reality on everyone, whether we like it or not. What Marx suggested was that we cannot unlock the secret of capitalist production, starting from that point: and we cannot supercede the laws of capitalist exploitation until we can surpass the imperatives of market exchange. But he never argued that it does not exist, or that it has no reality or effectivity of its own, or that it is the figment of someone's imagination. Quite the contrary. He showed how—without the concept of surplus value, which had to be introduced into the analysis of capitalism since it did not appear on its surface—the laws of market exchange appeared to work only too well. Also, how simple, succinct, elegant a 'mechanism' it was. Also how men and women came to live their whole relation to capitalism within the categories, the spontaneous consciousness, of market relations: 'Freedom, Equality, Property and Bentham.' And before you jump to the conclusion that this exhausts its 'rationality' as an effective organiser of demand and supply, we had better ask the Hungarians or the Czechs or the Poles whether or not the idea still has some purchase, some rationality, to it; and how it stands up against the superior rationality of 'The Plan' in actual-existing socialist societies, which have attempted to plan everything from tractors to hatpins.

Of course it is possible to reconstruct the market as an ideological construct. Provided—as is always the case in ideology—you play up the good side and repress the negative; provided, that is to say, you do not ask who precisely does, and who does not, benefit from this kind of 'freedom'; provided you do not ask who brings unequal power into the equivalences of market exchange, you can set in motion a powerful cluster of ideas which trigger off a positive chain associations—the market = free choice = Freedom and Liberty = anti-statism = 'put an end to Creeping Collectivism'! Even in the era of corporatism and state capitalism, of giant corporations and multinationals, it is still possible for people to 'make sense' of their experience within the categories of market 'Freedom and Choice'.

One of the most important features of the radical Right in the period between 1975 and 1979 was the degree to which its protagonists grasped the argument that there was no point taking political power with a radical-reactionary programme unless they had already won the ideological terrain. And they set about doing just that. One could contrast that with the Labour policy towards, for example, immigration. Labour's conscience may be in the right place if a little faint, about immigration. But, without the preparatory politics which confronts indigenous working class racism, without the means of ideological struggle which allows you to set your own agenda vis-a-vis racism, without a politics which confronts racism and prepares—educates—people for legislation which will positively favour an anti-racist policy, Labour 'takes office'—a different thing from 'taking power'. Then it sticks the political thermometer into peoples' mouths and its social democratic conscience is shocked and astonished to discover that the fever of racism is actually running quite high in society, not least in local Labour clubs and parties. There is nothing for it but to cut the problem off at the source: thus, immigration controls. If you do not prepare for political power, ideologically you will find the weight of popular ideas stacked against change and your freedom of action constrained by the nature of the existing terrain.

Between 1975 and 1979 an effective ideological crusade was waged by the radical Right. This was not a simple 'Vote for Mrs Thatcher' propaganda campaign. It was an attempt to penetrate to some of the core, root social ideas in the population. They seized on the notion of freedom. They marked it off from equality. They contrasted it against a dim and dingy statism which they chained to the idea of social democracy in power. 'Freedom' is one of the most powerful, but slippery, ideas in the political vocabulary: it is a term which can be inserted into several different political discourses. The language of freedom is a rivettingly powerful one but it contains many contradictory ideas. And somehow the Right persuaded ordinary people that rather than everyone sinking into a morass of social democratic mediocrity it might be better for them to take their chances, as the British people have before now, and make a break for it. Take your chance in the market for education; don't let your children fall behind. Take your chance in the free market for housing; don't wait until the housing list slowly goes down. Take your chance in the market for jobs. The slow wait, the long queue, the people who don't count, the people who don't care, the people behind desks who know how to fill out forms but are uninterested in human problems—that's socialism! Where is the ancient instinct for human freedom which the British psyche has long nourished? The instinct to compete and survive, to get up and go? This ancient instinct is called possessive individualism. I am not so sure that it is printed in the genes of free-born Anglo-Saxons. It is certainly one of the root-ideas of capitalism. Without the ethic of possessive individualism, capitalism would never have taken off. But, old ideas weigh like a nightmare on the brains of the living. At the end of the twentieth century there still are political languages which can bring ordinary working people out into the streets in favour of that notion of possessively individually choosing their own future. Some of these powerful connections have been made active again in the language of the radical Right. They have seized on a number of powerful ideas, indeed positive slogans, which touch deep historical chords. They have transformed them to their own political purposes. They are ideas which have gained once more a powerful currency in our society.

I have talked very negatively so far about what is making it so difficult for socialist ideas. Let me now look briefly at *some* of the areas in which it seems to me a battle has to be joined for socialist ideas. By socialist ideas here you may be surprised to find I am not going to talk about programmatic ideas, like nationalisation and public ownership and so on, important though they are. I am talking about *root* ideas: the social ideas on which the socialist programme or socialist politics must be based. Let me, for instance, talk about the idea of the nation, the people, the British people. No political counter has proved so effective, such a guarantee of popular mobilisation as being able to say 'the people think. . .' Conjuring yourself into 'the people' is the true ventriloquism of populist politics. Political leaders who claim to have no ideas of their own: they just reflect what 'the people', out there, think. . . 'The people' out there are, of course, varied; different; divided by gender, sex, class and race. They are free-traders, rate-payers, low taxers, wild Trotskyists and flat-earth monetarists: they are wife and mother, lover, part-time worker and madonna of the sink all in one and the same person. The politics of *populism* is to construct all of them into a composite political identity so that the divisions of class and interest or the divisions of role and person count for less than the unity, the undifferentiated, unclassed, unsexed, unraced unity of 'the people'. Then you must perform the second ideological trick: which is to project 'the people' back as far as they can go, in a bid for the history of the British people. 'The people', you will find have really *always* existed since at least Anglo Saxon times, or Magna Carta and perhaps before that. These reactionary ideas constitute the essence of 'Englishness'. The British people have *always* been like that. God made them like that and for that purpose, with an instinct for possessive individualism, private property, respect for authority, the constitution, the law and the nuclear family and so on. One cannot go against the grain of history. This ideological construct—'the people'—has been much in evidence since 1975. It was in evidence during the 'winter of discontent', when the discourse of the radical Right successfully counterposed the working class *against* the people. Within this ideological framework the politicised sectors of the working class are represented as nothing more than a narrow interest group. While, out there, are the people—who may well, of course, be the sectional group 'holding the nation up to ransom' in some *other* dispute. Nevertheless, they come to see themselves, to position themselves, as simple, uninvolved, depoliticised commuters: 'the people' who can't get home, who can't bury their dead, who can't shop, can't catch any trains or can't get hospital treatment. Who is causing all this? The workers. The unions. The leadership. Or the Left. The Marxists. The Trots. Somebody. Some other, tiny group of politically-motivated militants is standing in the way of 'what the people want': or, as Mr Heath once felicitously called them, 'The Great Trade Union of the Nation'. Now the astonishing political fact that the people can be colonised by the Right, has in part to do with the fact that there is no alternative vision of what or who the people *are*. On the Left and in the labour movement, we have lost our sense of history. So that, when something like the Falklands crisis blows up, history belongs to the Right. Freedom of speech, of assembly, the franchise etc., the things we took to the high seas to defend have only been won in our society as a result of the prolonged struggle of working people. That is what democracy actually is. But how is it represented in popular history, in popular memory? As the gift of the rulers. Somehow, democracy 'came'. It descended from heaven. It is part of the great Anglo-Saxon inheritance or the Magna Carta decrees or something. There are thousands of young people who do not know that without a civil war and a king walking around with his head lopped off, there would be no so-called parliamentary tradition to speak of, no constitutionalism for Mr Foot to nail his colour to. Without people besieging Hyde Park and Trafalgar Square in a thoroughly extra-parliamentary fashion there would be no such thing as the right of public assembly. Without the radical press there would be no such thing as Mr Murdoch's right to report what was said about him in parliament let alone to command the channels of public communication. Democracy is what working people have made it: neither more or less. Yet the people can only speak and act in history through their representative from Grantham. The Grantham corner shop has become the sum and crystalisation of the whole, so-called democratic process. That is because we have evacuated our own history. We are going to fight Mr Tebbit's anti-trade union Bill without the vast majority of workers knowing when the right to strike was won, or how, or who stood against it, and for how long.

It is not only people in the labour movement who do not know their own history. But, certain absolutely root ideas without which socialism cannot survive have been allowed to wither and atrophy in the past two decades. Consider the notionof equality. What we have at the moment is a phoney argument between freedom and equality which the Right has effectively posed as a choice: if you want everybody to be equal, then that will be at the expense of their liberty. And since, as I have said we are a freedom-loving people at least from Magna Carta onwards, we will not tolerate that, so we have to sacrifice equality in order to defend freedom. Either/or. Against that, where does the notion of equality stand as an unqualified, basic socialist idea with a sense behind it of the deep, persistent, ineradicable inequalities of life in our society? Who speaks today of the way in which capital, wealth, property, status, authority, social power and respect are riven by the divisions between the 'haves' and the 'have nots'? There may be problems about everybody being absolutely equal in the future. I leave that discussion to the future of socialism. But I want to reaffirm that to be ardent for socialism and lukewarm about the notion of equality is a living contradiction. Yet very few people these days speak the radical language of the politics of equality: the politics not just of the redistribution of goods and resources, but of the fundamental equality of condition. The language of equality used to be an absolutely root vocabulary for socialists. Different socialists of different schools spoke it in different ways, but socialism was unthinkable without this notion of destroying the bastions of accumulated privilege of a social and political and cultural kind. The assumption that we could advance the ideas of socialism without rethinking what equality now means in an advanced industrial society is, I think, untenable.

Let me talk about another rather different idea–one that now belongs, as it were, to the other side: the idea of tradition and traditionalism. I remember the moment in the 1979 election when Mr Callaghan, on his last political legs, so to speak, said with real astonishment about the offensive of Mrs Thatcher, 'She means to tear society up by the roots.' This was an unthinkable idea in the social democratic vocabulary: a radical attack on the status quo. The truth is that, traditionalist ideas, the ideas of social and moral *respectability*, have penetrated so deep inside socialist consciousness that it is quite common to find people committed to a radical political programme, underpinned by wholly traditional feelings and sentiments.

This is a movement without a strong republican secularist tradition–socialists without a strong commitment to the ending of the obfuscations of monarchical privilege and ritual. This is a socialist movement which has not committed itself–in general, metaphorical terms, of course–to Voltaire's fond ambition to strangle the last king with the entrails of the last priest. I am not suggesting a witch hunt of Christian socialists or indeed of socialists who believe in the monarchy. But it amazes me that the thrust of the socialist movement should not be pitted unremittingly against a society whose forms are held in place by the rituals of rank, respect and deference. Because our definition of 'the political' is so narrow, restricted and constitutionalist, we do not seem capable of understanding the ideological cement in the crevices of the social system represented by those lines of deference and authority. Already at the end of the eighteenth century, always in the forefront of the programme of the bourgeois revolution–let alone, of socialism–was the notion of 'the bourgeois republic'. Yet here we are, socialists at the end of the twentieth century, jacking ourselves up occasionally, when we are feeling particularly bold, into the odd republican remark. Traditionalism, in the *social* sense, has a deep and profound hold inside the socialist movement, inside the labour movement, inside the working class itself. That is why and where racism and sexism lurk. Traditionalism provides these with the roots on which they continue to feed, inside the minds and consciousness and allegiances of working people. But a socialism which hopes to construct itself on the back of a class committed to the secondary position of blacks and the secondary position of women in the scheme of things, will not transform society. It may reform it, modernise it, and improve it in some ways. But it cannot pick society up by the roots and change the relations in which people live. Indeed, a socialism which has a political programme but does not include in its perspective the questioning of those social and moral ideas and relationships, which does not understand the connection between how people live in families, how men and women relate to one another and what kinds of societies they build, is a socialism which will remain 'backward'. It will remain captured, caught, in the net of the respectability and traditionalism of ancient ideas. For politics are rooted in social relations, not just in a programme of political targets. Socialists must penetrate to the ground, the place, where radical *social* ideas can be brought into connection with the traditional institutions of the labour movement and transform them into a new kind of politics. That is a different sort of struggle for socialist ideas than the labour movement has traditionally had on its agenda.

Let me conclude. I talked first of all about what I think are some of the principal inhibitions to the advance of socialist ideas. The problems that stand in the way of getting socialist ideas rolling again as a popular force in society. I think they are profound. I think one has to confront them head on—but with a socialism which is without guarantees. That is to say which does not believe that the motor of history is inevitably on its side. One has to fasten one's mind, as Gramsci said 'violently' onto things as they are: including, if things are not too good, the fact that they are not too good. . . So that is why I started with the negative. In the more positive part, I have tried to talk about where socialism needs to begin to grow again. Not yet in terms of programmatic demands but, in terms of the root values, the root concepts, the root images and ideas in popular consciousness, without which no popular socialism can be constructed. If you have working people committed to the old ways, the old relations, the old values, the old feelings, they may vote for this and that particular reform but they will have no long term commitment to the hard graft of transforming society. And unless socialists understand the strategic role of this level of struggle—the struggle to command the common sense of the age in order to educate and transform it, to make common sense, the ordinary everyday thoughts of the majority of the population, move in a socialist rather than a reactionary direction, then our hearts may be in the right place but our relation to the task of putting socialism back on the historical agenda again is not all that different from that of the besieging armies at the city of Jericho who hoped that seven times round the city wall, a blast on the trumpet and a quick prayer to the gods would bring that ancient 'Winter Palace' tumbling to the ground.

ECONOMIC PLANNING AND WORKERS' CONTROL

Roy Green and Andrew Wilson

The Liaison Committee Report

'Increased influence and control by workers through their trade unions will be. . . the source from which planning will derive its authority, its knowledge and its power.'[1] This principle is the point of departure for the proposals in the report of the TUC–Labour Party Liaison Committee on 'Economic Planning and Industrial Democracy'. It goes to the heart of the central problem of socialist politics, the relationship between the state and the independent organisations of the working class in the struggle for socialism. The report, however, is a political rather than a theoretical document, the product of political debate and agreement rather than theoretical argument. It reflects, to some extent, varied standpoints. Consequently, there are a number of hesitations and inconsistencies, while some important issues are left unresolved. Nevertheless, the underlying drift and tendency of the report is clear.

The basic principle itself is an essentially practical conclusion, drawn from the political experience under the last Labour government, particularly concerning the attempts to promote 'industrial democracy' through the work of the Bullock Committee, and planning through the 'industrial strategy'. An analysis of these developments, leading to the conclusions drawn by the Liaison Committee, will be given in a further article.[2] The fact that these conclusions have been drawn by the central organisations of the labour movement, and are intended as the basis for the further development of policy, confers upon them a significance which they would not have as simple theoretical insights. It demonstrates a certain degree of development in the actual economic and political conditions, indicating at least the possibility of a further advance. Although the role of theoretical analysis in politics is a modest one, it may nonetheless assist in clarifying the general direction of that advance. Therefore, we intend here to elucidate the issues relevant to an appreciation of the Liaison Committee's report by means of a critical discussion of various conceptions of planning, workers' control and the state.

The replacement of the competitive market economy based upon private production and profit by a system of economic planning organised in the interests of the working class is an essential feature of the transition from capitalist to socialist society. In the millenarian vision of revolutionary syndicalism, this is envisaged as the result of a single act, the general strike or insurrection aimed at destroying the existing political institutions comprising the 'capitalist state', and substituting for them the independent organisation of the working class. Participation in politics is seen as a weakening of this independence and a mere diversion from what should be the true goal of the workers' movement. However, most socialists, and certainly the mainstream of the British labour movement whatever the differences in political ideology within it, have regarded the use of political power as a necessary lever for social transformation. If this commitment to the use of political power is to be anything other than an abstract 'position', it requires the existence of a political party whose purpose is to form a government. Such is the rationale for the formation of the Labour Party and its continued support by the organised labour movement, of which it is the political instrument.

Given this attachment both to the principle of planning or socialisation of production, and to the use of the existing state institutions, the centralised administrative machinery, it is perhaps not surprising that the transformation of the market economy has been seen essentially as a process of extending the power and activity of the state. In fact, the idea that the market on the one hand and control by the state on the other are antithetical poles or principles of economic and political organisation is widely held, and not only within the Labour Party. Those towards the 'right' of the political spectrum tend to defend competition and freedom from interference by the state as economically more efficient and as providing a guarantee for the established parliamentary system. Those towards the 'left' usually stress the advantages of planning over the anarchy of the market, and argue that extending the sphere of state control will actually enlarge the scope of democratic accountability through the representative political institutions by including the processes of economic decision-making.

The 'Socialist Commonwealth' of the Webbs[3]

Advocates of the use of the state as the principal agent for the socialisation of the economy have sometimes acknowledged the dangers involved in granting it monopoly powers over the economy, and have attempted to counter the force of their opponents' criticisms in various ways. The bizarre proposal of the Webbs, who were instrumental in drawing up the Labour Party constitution of 1918 (including the famous Clause IV commitment to 'common ownership of the means of production'), that there should be established two parliaments to represent the people, is in fact such an attempt to meet two basic difficulties inherent in their strategy of gradually subjecting the economy to an increasing measure of determination by the state. First, they admitted the unreality of the idea that parliamentary democracy permitted the people to decide political issues, given the wide range of governmental activity and the period of time between elections. In fact, the only right of the people is to elect representatives, that is, the individuals who will form the government and therefore be invested with a general authority to rule until the next election, when the people will once again have an opportunity, not to govern, but simply to cast judgment on the overall performance of those elected to govern for them. According to Rousseau, under such a system the people are free only at the time of the election, their only opportunity to act for themselves; for the rest, they are enslaved by the state. For the Webbs, the only way in which the political general will could be ascertained was by means of referendum. Alternatively, separate representative assemblies might be established in relation to every issue of importance to be decided by government. Obviously, systematic government would become virtually impossible under such conditions, and both ideas were therefore dismissed as impractical.

By way of compromise, they suggested that the activities of government could be grouped into two 'complexes', the 'political' and the 'social'. These should be the responsibility of separate political institutions, neither having a 'general supremacy' over the other. The reason for this particular division of political power, conjured out of the Webbs' imaginations rather than the likely course of actual political development, reflects a consciousness of a second fundamental difficulty, which arises from the repressive character of the state as an instrument of domination over society. As the Webbs recognised, if the present powers of the state 'were to be applied to the ownership and administration of industrial capital, the individual might easily find himself practically helpless, (p. 140). But the proposal to separate political functions reflects not merely a desire to protect the individual through a system of 'separation of powers' and constitutional 'checks and balances'; it reflects also, at a deeper level, an understanding of the fact that the bureaucratic and authoritarian character of the state machinery renders it 'incompatible with the highest accomplishments in social and industrial administration' (p. 76). However, the Webbs chose to regard this character as inherent, not in the nature of the state itself and its relationship to society, but only in certain of its functions. These functions they identified as the traditional 'political' ones of external defence and the internal administration of justice, which 'inevitably assumed a highly disciplined hierarchical form'. It followed, in their view, that the increase in administrative functions which they proposed in relation to the economy would not necessarily lead to greater subjection to a coercive force since '. . . the organ of the community charged with the administration of things should have no power to use the law for the coercion of persons' (p. 130).

Underlying their argument on the appropriate form through which government control of the economy should be exercised was their concern with the prospects for independent trade unionism, which they considered would still be necessary in their 'socialist commonwealth' to protect the worker from the tendency to drive wages as low as possible in the interests of the 'public' as consumers. 'When a government controlling a standing army sets to work, in its capacity of employer, to "break" a national strike among its own employees, the process is perilously apt to take on the character of the suppression of a rebellion' (p. 141). The difficulties experienced in the conduct of collective bargaining, particularly in the public sector, in the face of various forms of incomes policy over recent years, gives to the reservations expressed by the Webbs the character of prescience. However, the ineffectiveness of their proposed solution is sufficiently demonstrated in their notorious support and approval of the system of 'Soviet Communism'. Here, ever so many constitutionally distinct institutions, guarantees, and personal freedoms are merely the instruments and masks through which the CPSU, drawing its power from the state control of the economy established under Stalin, exercises its ruthless and unmitigated domination over the working class.

Of course, the Webbs were aware that in capitalist society the state is an instrument of domination, serving essentially the interests of the economically dominant force, capital. But, rightly committed to working within existing parliamentary forms in order to bring about the changes they considered necessary, they conferred upon these political institutions an absolute validity, considering them as the ultimate development in social organisation, needing only to be set free from the warping influence of the capitalistic environment. Thus, they failed to see that domination is the inevitable form taken by the centralised power of the community when the members of that community are not organised directly, but are fragmented by the division of labour and private production. The Webbs wanted to abolish private production by centralising control of the economy, not in the hands of the actual producers, but in the hands of the state. This imposed, not the real will of the people, but the illusory 'general will' expressed by representatives of the people, wielding power through political institutions distinct from the other areas of social activity, and immune from direct control by them. The expansion of state activity into these other areas would not, however, lead to any diminution in the authoritarian character of the state, but in the extension of the principle of bureaucracy; this has rightly been termed the system of 'bureaucratic collectivism', contemptuously dubbed by G.D.H. Cole as the 'sordid dream of a business man with a conscience'. The Webbs were sufficiently perspicacious to grasp the problem and recognised the contradiction underlying their political theory, but they conspicuously failed to resolve it.

In order to understand why the development of planning and the creation of a socialised economy was conceived as a process of bringing the economy gradually under the control of the state administration, and, in terms of constitutional 'theory' if not in reality, under the control of parliamentary representatives, we need to consider the reasons given by the Webbs for their rejection of an alternative process of transformation, the bringing of economic activity under the direct control of the producers themselves. In their minds, this problem was but one aspect of the more general question concerning the role to be played by trade unions in a society where collective control of the means of production had eliminated the need for the capitalist employer. This collective control, however, would be exercised, not by workers organised as the collective power of society, but by the 'people' in their capacity as consumers. The idea of consumer sovereignty, a mere apologetic of the economists in capitalist society to justify unplanned competition, would come into its own in a society where the elected representatives of the general body of consumers would control the economy directly through the state administrative machinery. Since consumers, by definition, are not themselves able to control production directly, it follows that consumer control can only be exercised indirectly by means of the state, which would therefore constitute the principal force in the construction of the new society and the axis upon which it would turn thereafter. In the Webbs' view, socialism would see the full flowering of two principles, which although proclaimed, could not be achieved under capitalism where the driving force was not the 'spirit of service' and professionalism, but the interests of private profit. The interests of the consumer, imperfectly protected by the anarchy of capitalist competition, would become dominant through an extension of the principle of representative parliamentary democracy to encompass the organisation of economic activity.

It followed that trade unionism would have to be completely transformed from its function of protecting the interests of particular sections of the workforce against their immediate employers. Trade unions would in future confront, not merely the private interest of employers, but the public interest of society. This would necessarily be accorded a legitimacy and power going far beyond that of the private capitalist. The clear ramifications of this situation for the very existence of independent trade unionism led the Webbs, as we have seen, to the construction of a complex and implausible political structure designed to restrict the power of the state. For they were well aware that the dominant general or consumer interest, expressed by the state, was inconsistent with the interests of workers as producers. To the consumer wages appear simply as a cost of production, an element in the price of the commodity, while to the worker they are his income. Trade unions would continue to be necessary to protect particular groups of workers. Generalising this proposition produces a contradiction between the role of the state in defending the worker as a consumer, and the trade union in defending the worker as a producer. Just as the Webbs attempted an eclectic solution of the contradiction in the nature of the state, that it constitutes the organised collective power of society while, at the same time, it is a repressive or dominating force over society, they attempted similarly to resolve the problem of the relationship between the economic functions they invested in the state and those of the unions. They divided the economic responsibilities between the two forms of organisation by inventing a new and specific function to be performed by trade unions in the new society, the defence of the 'vocational' interests of the workers. The transition to socialism would entail, therefore, the 'transition from the present Trade Union Movement in Great Britain, as now organised both industrially and politically, for its long-drawn-out secular warfare against the capitalist class, to a world of vocational organisations' the purpose of which would be for each the 'elevation of its vocational status in the community' (p. 144). The purpose of trade unionism, being thus defined in terms of a narrow sectional objective, which could only be achieved at the expense of the rest of the community, was unsuited to be an instrument entrusted with power to direct economic activity. The trade union would have influence, expressed through a process of 'bargaining' with the state, over the conditions of employment, but the external power of the state would remain necessary to counteract the inevitable tendency of producers' organisations to exclusiveness, to 'bias. . . as against other sections of producers and the whole community of consumers'.

The Webbs were not unaware that, even at the time they wrote, the trade unions were organised on a much broader basis than that encompassed by the concept of 'vocation', but they considered that this wider unity was merely a temporary phenomenon of capitalist society. Far from representing the beginnings of a truly general class organisation of workers, which could develop in the course of further economic and political struggle to the point where the organised working class itself could direct the whole of economic production, the disappearance of the capitalist would lead to a greater degree of fragmentation. For only the existence of the capitalist employer provides a basis for unity. Producers have no interests in common; '. . . if the capitalist employers are assumed to be eliminated. . . there would be no outside party to attack or to despoil' (p. 312). Once it is assumed that the only interest of the producer lies in the enhancement of his particular 'vocation', then it is indeed easy to dismiss the idea that the carrying on of productive activity throughout the economy in common provides the producers with a sufficient common interest, and that the so-called 'consumer interest' is in reality nothing more than an alienated expression of this common interest of the producers. Where the producers are separated by the division of labour, then society appears as a community of consumers, related to each other through exchange of products in the market. In the absence of direct relationships between the producers in the process of production, the material relationships between them appear only in the form of exchange relationships between the products of their labour. Hence, to each producer the others appear only as consumers of his products, rather than as mutually participating in a process of social production, while production itself appears directly as merely a private affair. The interests of society are expressed economically as 'consumers' through the operation of the market and competition, and politically as the 'public' through regulation by the state.

G.D.H. Cole's 'Guild Socialism'[4]

Perhaps it is not surprising to find arguments such as these put forward by the Webbs, for whom the agency of socialist transformation was to be, not the working class, but the educated and enlightened professionals of the state bureaucracies. It is more remarkable that they were echoed to a considerable extent by such a committed advocate of the principle of workers' control, and political opponent of the Webbs, as G.D.H. Cole. Whereas the Webbs argued for the replacement of capitalist employers by the state administration, Cole proposed that production should be controlled directly by associations of the producers, the so-called 'National Guilds'. However, the emergence of such a system would not, in Cole's view, entail the disappearance or 'withering away' of the state, which had been the mainstay of socialist thought during most of the nineteenth century. By the first part of the present century, that doctrine had come to be identified with anarchism, or with the syndicalists' rejection of parliamentary methods in favour of an exclusive reliance on 'direct action'. Such doctrines were opposed to the political development of the labour movement and in particular to the character of the Labour Party, the purpose of which was to achieve governmental power through the election of representatives to Parliament. To this aim Cole was, no less than the Webbs, committed, differing from them only in his more generous assessment of syndicalism as the 'infirmity of noble minds'.

Marx had defended the participation of the labour movement in the political institutions of capitalist society against the 'political indifferentism' of the anarchists in terms of the necessary development of working class organisation through political struggle. To him, it was obvious that 'as the proletariat still acts, during the period of struggle for the overthrow of the old society, on the basis of that old society, and hence also still moves within political forms which more or less belong to it, it has not yet, during this period of struggle, attained its final constitution, and employs means for this liberation which after this liberation fall aside'.[5] But, generally speaking, the issue was usually seen in more simplistic terms as one concerning the legitimacy of representative parliamentary institutions from a socialist point of view. Those who considered them to be incorrigibly capitalistic in nature spurned involvement on the grounds that it would inevitably be self-defeating. On the other hand, those who supported the formation of a political party as an integral part of the labour movement, and therefore its involvement in existing political institutions, tended to generalise the abstract principle, if not the reality, of these institutions into an imperishable and final form of social organisation. While Cole admitted that 'in the State of today. . . democratic control through Parliament is little better than a farce', like the Webbs, he considered this to be the result of the economic power of capital and corrupting influence of class society. In the society of the future, the state, alongside the trade unions, would, 'radically altered and penetrated by a new spirit', form one of the foundations. To gain a proper understanding of the functions of the state we must, according to Cole, not study it as an historical actuality, but rather imagine it 'as it would be in a democratic community immune from class conflict', that is, in the absence of its real presuppositions. The point of departure for this line of argument is not the interests of the actual working class movement in its struggle against capital, but an imaginary concept of bourgeois political 'theory', the 'general will' and the interests of the 'public' or citizens. Instead of seeing that this illusion would necessarily disappear along with its real basis, the modern state, Cole thought that it would be a logical development if the overthrow of class society produced a real political equality in place of the merely imaginary equality of present society, with the result that the actions of the state would then affect everyone 'equally and in the same way'.

In addition to this political argument, beginning from the absolute validity accorded to the state, there is a second economic argument, similar to that used by the Webbs, to justify the continued domination of the state. For the interests of the producers must be balanced by those of the consumers, the protection of which is the proper activity of the state. The state will own the means of production, but the producers' organisations will control them. The producers will be permitted to determine the conditions under which production is to be carried on, but the division of the national income as well as the 'character and use of the product' will be matters for the consumers to decide through the agency of a 'strong and democratised State'. This division of economic activity into separate spheres of interest, together with the ultimate ownership of the means of production, would appear to give the dominant role in economic planning to the state, necessarily restricting the real scope to be afforded for workers' control of the conditions of production, let alone the actual nature and purpose of production itself. For, if the producers cannot control commodity prices, it follows that nothing else can be within their exclusive control either. Since the attempt to demarcate the respective spheres of authority to be exercised by, on the one hand, the state, and on the other, the producers' associations, has failed, a conflict between the two must necessarily result. Ingenuously, Cole attempted to solve the problem with a simple definition—the relationship between economic and political power in the Guild system would be one of 'equality'. The solution is, of course, spurious. It is in the very nature of political power to exercise a dominant will. The real content of the acts performed by the state may be determined, as Cole saw, by economic power, but in his scheme, the state does in fact wield an economic power based upon its ultimate ownership and control of the means of production. And, since he conceived of the producer interest always as a particular interest, while the 'democratic state' was to be the guardian of the general interest, there can be little doubt about the source of ultimate authority—the producers would be subordinate to the state. Indeed, there seems little reason not to accept the further proposition of the Webbs that production should be directed at enterprise level by managers responsible, not to the workers, but to the government. Cole attempted to abolish the subordination of the worker within industry, but, in effect, maintained a general subordination of workers to the state. It may be doubted whether the prescription of a relationship of 'equality' would create a sufficiently powerful restraint on the tendency to resolve this contradiction in favour of the more powerful force.

Political Power and Class

Both Cole and the Webbs, then, elevated the institutions of parliamentary democracy into an eternal principle to which the working class movement would have to remain subservient, a notion which seems an almost inevitable feature of the political ideology of 'parliamentary socialism', presenting an easy target to anarchists of all varieties. Both were also aware, however, of the repressive character of the state which provides such an important and successful basis for Tory opposition to the 'strong state', and sought various means of counteracting it. However, while the Webbs saw the problem mainly as one of restricting state power by dividing it into an elaborate constitutional structure, Cole aimed at the promotion of an alternative source of power, workers' control of production. But he was unable to develop this idea into a political form. Recognising the weakness of syndicalism, its absence of a realistic political strategy for the transformation of the general conditions of society, and recognising the necessity of using forcible means, governmental power, he fell back upon the political theory of 'Collectivism', the actual performance of an extended range of economic functions by the state, or at least the continued domination of the state in relation to 'political' issues. Far from effecting the 'reconciliation' which he sought between the 'clash of fundamental ideas', Cole produced instead a shallow syncretism, a new set of contradictions. Nevertheless, it is greatly to his credit that he defended, not simply the abstract idea of workers' control, but its concrete manifestations, the developments in 'workshop organisation' stimulated by the economic and political conditions during the First War. In the working class struggle for emancipation from the economic and political domination of capital, this fact puts Cole, politically and theoretically, far ahead of the Webbs.

The root cause of Cole's failure was his inability to conceive of the developing organisation of the labour movement as the process of its formation into a united class, and therefore political, power. Hence he saw workers' control of production as only a principle of economic rather than, at least incipiently, political organisation of society. For Cole regarded the distinction between economic and political power, which rests on the separation of the state from society, or the fragmentation of society by the division of labour, as a necessary and unalterable social principle. The Guild system would not abolish the division of labour, but crystallise it in a new form based upon the separate control of each industry by the producers. The state would therefore continue as the only instrument of political activity; 'the Guilds will be many, the State one'. It is true that in a number of places Cole contemplated the unification of the producers into a 'central Guild Congress', but he appears to have imagined this as some kind of federal body which would represent a variety of diverse and particular producer groups. His insight that 'the workers cannot be free unless industry is managed and organised by the workers themselves in the interests of the whole community' (p. 47) was not developed consistently, but restricted by his conception of the state, and the need for a separate (political) representation of 'consumer' interests.

The underlying reason for Cole's inability to grasp the process of revolutionary organisation of the working class or labour movement was the fundamentally utopian cast of the Guild Socialist theory. Instead of attempting to mark out the most appropriate direction for the class struggle to develop, on the basis of its existing form, in order to promote the most rapid and civilised advance possible, he attempted, like the Webbs, to construct an imaginary form of future society from the various elements, more or less arbitrarily chosen, of the existing one. Instead of developing a strategy to promote the struggle for power, he aimed to prescribe the goal to be achieved. The driving force of social change would be a vision, to be disseminated by education and propaganda, of the future society, rather than the concrete social needs of the working class. Hence, both Cole and the Webbs ignored the real struggle against capital, and therefore the forms through which it passes, in order to speculate on the functions to be performed by the state and trade unions in a society where the capitalist and the class struggle were simply assumed no longer to exist. The consequences of this approach for socialist theory and politics are disastrous, for the central issue, the development of the power of the working class movement, disappears entirely from view. Hence, the changes in the organisation of the labour movement, and the relationship between society and the state, which are a concomitant aspect of the overthrow of capitalist domination, can be left out of account.

This approach has two consequences of central importance to our present inquiry. First, the attempt to construct an imaginary role for trade unionism as the defender of the interests of particular groups of workers has the effect of preserving the division of the working class movement. It is remarkable that the Webbs should have considered it appropriate for unions to advance only the narrow 'vocational' interests of workers at a time when craft unionism among manual workers was already being supplanted by broader forms of organisation, a process which they themselves did so much to describe and explain in their study of trade union structure and government in *Industrial Democracy.* Indeed, the criticisms of producer associations in general put forward in the *Socialist Commonwealth,* concerning job demarcation and restrictions on training, limitations on output, and discouragement of innovations in technique, appear to echo the criticisms made in their empirical study only of the restrictive practices of the craft unions, and which they argued were alien to the methods of the 'new' unionism and to collective bargaining as the predominant method of job regulation. Hence, their views on the future of trade unionism appear to owe less to a study of the actual tendency of trade union development than to the dictates of their political dogma. To the extent that the concept of 'vocational' organisation and interest was based on a real social phenomenon, it appears to have been the middle class professions. To hold up these as a model for future working class aspirations when the necessity for protection against the capitalist employer has been eliminated, due to the reforming efforts of Mr and Mrs Webb (the Sir and Lady Oracle of the Socialist movement, as Cole dubbed them), may be an eloquent testimony to their basic social attitudes, but is unlikely to advance the political interests of the labour movement to any marked degree.

In a similar manner, Cole also attempted to find a fixed principle by which to preserve the division of working class organisation, albeit in a less extreme and reactionary form than the Webbs. The basis of the Guild system was to be industrial unionism, an idea taken ready-made from the syndicalists, dressed up in a political form, and decreed to share sovereignty with the state. The particular or 'corporatist' character of this form of social organisation is sufficiently indicated in the terminology itself, designed to 'link (it) up with the tradition of the Middle Ages'. The medieval guilds were not associations in which the members carried on production in common, for each master was an independent producer, the owner of his means of production. The purpose of the guild was to secure a monopoly over the privilege to carry on a particular trade, and to restrict competition among its members. It was a phenomenon of a society consisting of various 'estates', each claiming its own special privileges, no single one of which could claim to represent the interests of society as a whole. The estate monopolised a particular social function such that the conditions of its existence were peculiar to itself rather than of general validity. The decay of these local and particular forms of community gave rise to universal private property, independent of direct community association and restriction, in turn establishing the foundation of the bourgeois class and the modern state. In contrast to an estate, the conditions under which a particular class is economically dominant are the general conditions under which the whole of social production is carried on, and which are therefore valid for all the individuals of which society consists. The economic domination of a class is necessarily a general political domination, given a practical expression by means of the state. Hence, the domination of one class can only be overthrown by another, by means of political power, not by a congeries of 'producer associations' modelled, however loosely, upon a vanished epoch.

In reality, of course, the growth of the trade union movement has not been confined by the principles prescribed for it by various 'theories'. It is now generally accepted that the traditional classification of union structure in terms of such categories as 'craft', 'occupational', or 'industrial' unions is no longer useful, given the uncertain definition of the categories themselves and the willingness of most unions to organise in a manner that pays scant regard to them. In contrast to the development of unionism during the last century among a fairly distinct stratum of the working class, the skilled workers, the only principle upon which trade unionism can now be said to rest is that of the class position of the worker in relation to the employer. The structure of trade unionism, and the extent to which any particular union can be considered as 'open' or 'closed' to the organisation of particular types of worker, is a purely empirical question.[6]

The second consequence of this approach, which follows directly from the first, is of greater political significance. By constructing an eternal political principle, upon whatever basis, out of the existing divisions and fragmentation of the labour movement, it becomes impossible to conceive of its development into a class, defined not only in the relationship of individual workers to capital, but organised as an independent political force for the advancement of its own interests. Hence, the existing political machinery, the state, is seen as the exclusive source of political power, and the process of creating a planned economy as one of extending the functions of the 'democratic state' to embrace the centralised administration of production. If the labour movement is seen only as an association of sectional organisations, each intent on pursuing its own interest at the expense of the rest, it follows that it is incapable of the concerted activity required for economic planning to meet the needs of the community. It will then appear impractical and 'undemocratic' for the state to promote an extension of the economic influence of trade unions, rather than for it to assume direct responsibility for economic activity itself. The idea of planning assumes the character of an objective distinct from, and even at variance with, the control of society by the working class. In a relatively undeveloped, predominantly agrarian economy, where for particular historical reasons the state has already taken on a dominant economic role, the overthrow of the landlord class by a military force which seizes control of the existing bureaucratic state machinery may lead to a process of industrialisation under its direct tutelage. But in a developed capitalist economy, the economic control over production wielded by capital, and even by the trade unions, far exceeds that which could be developed by the state administration. In these circumstances, only the organised working class provides an alternative force to the sway of capital. To restrict its development on the grounds that trade union organisation is less 'democratic' than the representative state, that the state ought not to 'delegate' functions but perform them itself, is to give so many reactionary guarantees of the continued domination of capital, of the subservience of working people economically to the employer and politically to the state.

The Modern Debate

We have devoted rather more attention than is now customary to the ideas of the Webbs and of G.D.H. Cole, not out of historical curiosity or pedantry, but because the issues with which they dealt recur in the current debates over economic planning and industrial democracy. These debates, however, have been conducted in a more empirical manner, essentially in terms of responses to a political situation, or inquests into the failure of some attempted initiative. While this approach has the advantage of avoiding the more speculative fancies of the theorists, it also entails that the implications of a particular position are rarely worked out sufficiently. However unrealistic a number of the ideas of Cole and the Webbs may appear, they were, nonetheless, attempts to provide a solution to a perceived problem. The more thorough theoretical exposition of their respective standpoints allows these to be analysed without the need for too much extrapolation.

Cole's defence of workshop organisation as a basis for workers' control was very much a minority position at the time within the official labour movement; with the disappearance of an effective shop stewards' movement after the war, the Guild Socialist theory declined along with its real basis. Because of the different political circumstances, the movement did not reappear in quite the same vigorous form during the Second World War, and with the gradual atrophy of the Joint Production Committees and other devices for 'consultation' with the workforce as the controls of the war-time economy were dismantled, it seemed that workers' control was a spent force. In his *New Approach to Industrial Democracy* (1960), which argued that the ability of unions to act as a kind of permanent opposition to management was sufficient to qualify the existing organisation of industry as 'democratic', Clegg pronounced that Cole was, in effect, a dead duck.

Outside the circles of specialists in industrial relations, the Webbs fared little better. They had never been regarded as figures on the left of the labour movement because their alliances were with the predominantly right wing leaders of official labour. In the political climate of the 1950s, determined by the domestic ramifications of the cold war and expansion of the international capitalist economy, their approval of Stalinism was a liability and their attachment to public ownership an anachronism. Neither was it possible to overlook their responsibility for Clause IV, seen as an albatross around the neck of the party by its leaders. Thus, Crosland's *Future of Socialism* (1956) was a 'reaction against the Webb tradition'. Their central battle had been won because now 'we are all incipient bureaucrats and practical administrators'. But state regulation of the mixed economy and advanced social legislation would be sufficient to eradicate the evils of class society without the necessity for a significant expansion in the extent of public ownership. The essence of this approach was to elevate the kind of steps which the Webbs recommended in their section on transitional measures into the alpha and omega of socialism. Cole was right to say that the Webbs were concerned only with the question of a fair distribution of material wealth and the abolition of poverty, rather than with the emancipation of the working class, whose slavery, as Cole saw, was the cause of its poverty. But the Webbs at least understood that a reform of the class system was impossible without the overthrow of its basis, private production. With Crosland, socialist theory 'advances' back to the position of John Stuart Mill.

As it turned out, the epitaphs on the need for planning in the private sector and on the extension of workers' control over the production process were pronounced too soon. Clegg's reservations about the future of work groups, which he saw as a 'constant cause of inefficiency and conflict', were superseded by Flanders' study of *The Fawley Productivity Agreements* (1964). This demonstrated that the most practicable way in which managements could come to terms with the development of powerful shop floor organisation, which had become increasingly prominent during the previous decade, was by permitting the workforce a much greater degree of influence in the actual process of management.

Fragmented pay bargaining and 'wage drift' could only be brought under control by recognising the authority of shop stewards within a more coherent bargaining structure at plant level. And opposition to changes introduced unilaterally by management—in the name of 'custom and practice'—could only be reduced by negotiating reorganisations with the workers concerned. Flanders had correctly identified a trend which has since been given official support and recognition by the trade union movement and the Labour Party, and has provided the foundation for the renewal of interest in 'industrial democracy'. In its current signification, this term goes beyond the forms of collective bargaining analysed by the Webbs, or even the freedom to oppose management decisions over a wider variety of matters. What is at issue now is the extension of the 'frontier of control' to allow a continuing and positive influence in the management process.

Even at the time Crosland wrote, the conditions which induced him to relegate the performance of the economy to secondary status compared with a reform of the divorce laws and the development of 'frivolity' in private life were being undermined by changes in the world economy, the expansion of which had dragged Britain's stagnant and outdated industrial structure along in its wake. By 1961, a recognition of this had percolated through to the Conservative government, whose reaction was to accept the idea of planning as a means of stimulating economic development. The forum in which government, employers and unions were to co-operate in this endeavour was the National Economic Development Council (NEDC), in which the TUC agreed to participate as a means of influencing economic policy. NEDC was conceived as a way of overcoming obstacles to economic growth through planning. However, any practical effect which its proposals might have would depend upon the extent to which the government was receptive to them, since it had no executive powers of its own.

The eclipse of the idea of planning within the Labour Party proved to be only temporary; it came to power in 1964 committed to putting 'teeth' into planning. The chosen method was the incorporation of the would-be planners fully into the normal state administrative machinery by the creation of a new department of state, the Department of Economic Affairs. Although the creation of NEDC as an independent tri-partite body outside direct control of the government had been a defeat for the views of the Treasury, who wanted any new economic agencies to be part of the Treasury itself, by 1964 it was widely felt, and not only within the Labour Party, that this independence from government was also a source of weakness. Although NEDC was free to develop and publicise its own views on the direction of the economy, and therefore act as a kind of pressure group for growth in relation to the Treasury, its influence within government was seen to be correspondingly weaker—too dependent on the good will of the Chancellor. For these reasons, it was concluded that the strengthening of planning would be achieved by creating a suitable agency as an integral part of the machinery of state, which would therefore be represented directly in the government. It would also enable greater intervention of the state in industry.

There was, however, a negative aspect to this transfer of responsibility for planning primarily to the state, and the consequent relative decline in the importance of NEDC in the formation of government policy. Although the plan developed in 1962–3 proved a relative failure, and the method of its preparation could be criticised as superficial, it nevertheless had been agreed by both sides of industry, and was received as a set of economic proposals which carried some authority. The National Plan promulgated by the DEA in 1965 lacked even this advantage. Indeed, the employers complained that the function of NEDC was now to be simply an instrument whereby the government could 'screw a reluctant commitment from industry to a national plan about which industry has serious reservations, and which the Council was given very little time to consider'.[7] The exclusion of NEDC from any real role in the preparation of the Plan was, at the same time, an exclusion of the influence of the TUC, which supported, at least tacitly, the criticisms of the CBI. The result was that the ability of the Plan to influence the activity of employers and unions was effectively undermined, giving it, at best, the appearance of a piece of wishful thinking by government. By withdrawing the planning mechanism completely into the administration of government, the vital links with industry, the real economic power, were destroyed. The effect of this, paradoxically, was probably also to weaken the influence of the planners in the formation of government economic policy.

Prior to 1964, NEDC had emerged as a countervailing influence on the Chancellor to the Treasury precisely because it provided a mechanism for the political influence of industry. The DEA functioned in an entirely different way, neither looking for nor receiving this kind of backing, with the result that its influence within Whitehall was reduced—a point strikingly confirmed by the fact that government policy, following Treasury advice, pursued a rigorously deflationary path as an alternative to devaluation of the currency, in clear contravention of the assumptions underlying the National Plan. These decisions were taken behind the closed doors of the Cabinet Room, while manufacturing employers and unions opposed to this policy looked on from the sidelines. The idea that all this was simply the outcome of some internecine Whitehall struggle which the Treasury won and the DEA lost is superficial and misleading. It gives rise to the mistaken belief, widely held on the left, that the problem can be resolved in the future by some kind of reallocation of administrative functions as between the Treasury and some new 'super' planning department. In reality, it would have made little difference whether the DEA controlled all the Treasury functions or vice versa, or whether they were divided in some other way between them. For the Treasury is simply the mechanism whereby the pressures and constraints of a capitalist economy, and, more particularly, its (in Britain, at least) most politically powerful section, finance capital, are transmitted to the government. The reason for the government's failure to devalue was the effect this would have had on the financial system, and the repercussions on the balance of payments of any flight of 'hot' money. Because of its highly concentrated organisation and the volatility of the monetary system, finance capital, acting through agencies in the City, the Bank of England, and the Treasury, is most favourably placed to exert influence over short-run economic policy. This political power can only be countered by organising those economic forces against whose interests the favoured policies of deflation and high interest rates, which stabilise the financial system at the cost of a massive destruction of the productive forces in industry, work. It is only by strengthening the power of industry, especially the trade unions, through bodies such as NEDC that the cause of economic planning can be advanced. Without the agreement of employers and unions, who must take account of the pressures and interests most closely concerned with economic organisation, it is likely that any policy to promote planning will fail. In the result, the experiment with the DEA and the National Plan was a conspicuous failure, contributing to Labour's defeat in 1970. The crisis measures of July 1966 sounded the tocsin for the DEA and the beginning of a revival in the authority of NEDC—confirmed in the reorganisation of 1967 when the prime minister became chairman and the chancellor was restored to membership of the Council. The DEA detritus was swept away in the 1969 cabinet reshuffle.

The Plan of 1965 was in reality designed to do little more than identify possible 'bottlenecks' which might act as constraints in the context of a general expansion of the economy. Firms were asked, not for their actual plans or views on the way in which their enterprise and sector of industry might develop, but how an assumed rate of expansion of the whole economy would affect them. When the assumed rate failed to materialise, the Plan became irrelevant. It was not a mechanism to co-ordinate what was actually happening in the economy, and was therefore unable to change the underlying trends when these proved to be at variance with its somewhat arbitrary premises. In short, there was no link between the Plan and what actually happened at the level of the industrial sectors and individual enterprises. However, the Party did not conclude that the attempt to impose a 'National Plan' upon industry was fundamentally misconceived, that planning instead should attempt the more modest but realistic task of relating the activities of the individual firms at sector level. This would at least have the merit of providing a secure foundation from which more comprehensive planning might develop, ensuring that planning involved actual decisions about the direction of the economy rather than mere hypothetical exercises. The identification of planning with centralised control by the state, even if this proved illusory, was too strong for that. What was decided upon during the years of opposition after 1970 was a policy of state control of the largest manufacturing firms through the 'planning agreements system'. This would allow a future national plan to be effectuated by influencing the 'medium and longer term strategies' of the dominant firms. There is an obvious difficulty here, for the state clearly does not have the capacity to control the process of production, but would be dependent on the established management structure within the firm to carry out the goals contained within the planning agreement. Without control and knowledge at this level, it is difficult to see how the planners can have the capacity to prescribe a strategy which may well differ in important respects from that towards which the enterprise would otherwise tend on the basis of its existing organisation. In other words, a strategy on investment, location, import substitution etc. can only be taken on the basis of concrete decisions about how much should be produced of each particular product, a matter which Labour's Programme 1973 was prepared to leave to the discretion of the firms as mere 'tactics'. In addition, the problem of how much could or should be decided by the central planning agency, and how much left to be decided by the individual firm, was given a new dimension arising from the need to reconcile the policy on economic planning with another strand of policy, industrial democracy.

The Development of Labour Policy

The seminal report of the Labour Party Working Group on Industrial Democracy (1967) not only advocated the use of state power to promote the extension of collective bargaining to new subject matters—the development of 'continuing processes of joint determination'—but also linked the issue of industrial democracy explicitly to the wider issue of planning. It pointed out that 'trade unions are already established in the various agencies of planning', and that it was 'crucially important not to disconnect plant level participation from a wider concern with economic, industrial and social developments'. Industrial democracy was therefore seen as a means, independent of the state, for making the concentrations of private economic power accountable, not simply to those directly employed in a particular firm, but to society. The starting point for a policy on industrial democracy should be, not the relation of the employee to his particular employer, the idea underlying the various schemes of 'co-partnership' in individual firms, but his position as a worker; in other words, a recognition of the general character of the employment relationship and class position of the worker. Since the domination of capital over the individual worker rests on the subservience of the entire working class, it follows that the amelioration of that domination can only be brought about through an amelioration of the conditions of social domination in general. The essentially political nature of the struggle for 'industrial democracy' is therefore the guarantee against the predominance of narrow sectional interests. The report makes the point brilliantly in the answer given to those who use the concept of the 'consumer interest' to argue against the extension of workers' control as the means of socialisation of production—the position of the Webbs and their epigones.[8] 'The trade union movement as a whole has very obvious consumer interests, and. . . the wider the context of workers' participation and the more connected plant level participation is with industrial and regional planning and development the more influenced by consideration of consumer needs trade union participants will be.'[9] The concern that the extension of worker influence in relation to the particular employer should be part of a broader advance for the trade union movement as a whole also explains why the 'single channel of representation' was treated as an issue of fundamental importance, where it might otherwise appear to make little difference at plant level where strong workplace organisation already exists.

Although the NEC statement on industrial democracy to the Party conference of 1968 accepted a number of the proposals made in the Report, how little the more profound implications of the argument were grasped appears in the statement that 'the aim is to extend into the workplace the constructive power the unions now have in national economic planning. . . . it will require a closer integration of shop stewards into the unions' chain of command'. Whereas the Report saw 'a framework of representation that extends upwards from the workplace', the NEC appear to have imagined the army of labour marching to the orders of NEDC and the government. In reality, the unions do not have influence over the organisation of production at national level, but only influence over the economic policy of the government. The extension of workers' control at plant level involves direct control over their own activity, not merely influence over the activity of an alien power, the state. What the Report proposed was the extension upwards of the direct control which was being enhanced by developments in the nature and form of collective bargaining at plant level, that is, the direct co-ordination of economic activity on a wider basis than the individual firm, the collective organisation of production. The slant given to the proposals in the NEC statement arises from the identification of planning with the activity of the state.

It was this attitude, rather than the novel approach outlined in the Working Group report, which was to dominate the debate within the Party on the future direction of industrial policy. The arguments in the report were criticised on the ground that they confused 'industrial' with 'economic' democracy. The latter concept was concerned with the accountability of firms to the 'public', the community at large, which was the responsibility of the government, while the former was confined to the accountability of management to the workers in the particular enterprise. It was necessary to delimit the concept in this way to avoid getting interests and responsibilities blurred and confused, and to insist that any democratic system of public control over the economy should be the direct responsibility of the government and its agencies. The mistake in the tripartite approach to the extension of workers' influence was that it appeared to reduce the 'public' interest represented by the government to the status of the special interests of the other parties. In other words, the extension of control by the organised working class was to be subordinated to and restricted by—according to the argument which ultimately prevailed—the abstract concept of the 'public interest', the sacred cow of bourgeois politics. The difficulty was how to reconcile the extension of state domination through economic planning with the expressed commitment to 'industrial democracy', for the ability of workers to control the enterprise could not be greater than the degree of autonomy allowed to it under the plan, since the planners were accountable, not to the organised workers, but to the 'public'.

According to Labour's Programme 1973, powers to draw up plans and compel companies to carry them out would only be used 'after the fullest consultation with the trade union movement—and, of course, such powers will always be subject to the control of Parliament'. Clearly, the function of the word 'and' is to disguise what has been made clear by the words 'consultation' and 'control', whereas a previous sentence spoke more vaguely of making industry 'accountable both to the public through Parliament and to its own employees'.[10] Planning by the state is inevitably a restriction on the ability of workers themselves to control production directly. Nor is this conclusion a matter of mere semantics. It follows necessarily from the assumption that the influence of workers over production is limited to the particular enterprise in which they happen to work, while planning is a suppression of the autonomy of that enterprise. If the state is the instrument of planning, then the plan must override the views of workers unless they are in conformity with the plan. Their views may be taken into account, but the ultimate decision is the prerogative of the state. And since the workers themselves are assumed not to constitute a force capable of planning, their direct control over the planning process must be minimal. It will not extend beyond the determination of 'tactics', an idea which, putting aside its purely illusory nature, is similar to those employer-inspired schemes of 'worker participation' which leave the employer to decide what shall be done, but permit consultation with the employees on the best way to do it.

The easy victory won by this point of view within the Party, and the eclipse of the planning aspects of the 1967 Working Party report, reflected a degree of reticence about the extension of workers' control in the private sector. The 1967 report saw 'serious difficulties' in the extension of 'industrial democracy' here, arising from the 'narrowness of its ends' (p. 48). Rather, it was the public sector which appeared to provide more 'important opportunities for a rapid development of industrial democracy beyond its present practice and forms of participation' (p. 53). This had little to do with the relative development of collective bargaining in public and private sectors, however. Productivity bargaining, which the report identified as the main form in which new structures of power were enabling workers to exercise greater influence over the management process, was at the time much more a phenomenon of private manufacturing industry. The decisive factor was the apparent acceptance by the public sector of some idea of 'public service' or 'social accountability', in contrast to the motivation of private profit. It was felt that considerations of this kind might mitigate the conflict which could otherwise develop within the management process itself over the purposes of production. Such conflict, or its possibility, might lead to greater resistance on the part of the employer, making advance more difficult. Or, something which concerned the Working Party, it might induce the employer to 'bypass or emasculate. . . independent trade unionism' (p. 23). This traditional fear on the part of trade unions is an expression of their weakness, although it is often rationalised as a principled refusal to 'associate themselves. . . with the wastes of a destructive competitive process' (p. 23).

The illusory character of the supposed greater compatibility between the 'public' interest and the 'accountability' to the taxpayer on the one hand, and the interests of workers in the public sector on the other, has been sufficiently demonstrated in the pattern of industrial disputes since the report was written. What was important at the time was that this conception required planning and 'industrial democracy' to be related to each other. Hence, planning could be seen as an extension of workers' control. However, the emphasis given to the purposes of production as a basis for 'industrial democracy' gave rise to a different and contradictory conception. By according priority to the public sector, the extension of workers' control was made dependent upon the development of state ownership and planning. Hence, the report concluded that 'it is only as capitalist enterprise is required to work in a more controlled framework that the restraints on a more extensive participation and co-operation in many areas of the activity of firms will be reduced' (p. 23). If the regulation of capitalist enterprise was not to come about through the development of forms of direct control by workers, but was instead to be its precondition, then such regulation could only consist of direct control by the state. Planning in the private sector would be, therefore, primarily the responsibility of the state. The distinction between the private and public sectors in the context of policy on 'industrial democracy' expresses the domination of this idea. As long as it held the stage, further development of a general and political programme for the extension of workers' control remained impossible. The connection between planning and 'industrial democracy' produced the false dawn of a revolutionary insight, but served, at the same time, to inhibit the really progressive side of the relationship.

By moving away from any explicit concern with the purposes of production, the TUC report on *Industrial Democracy* (1974) was able to focus attention exclusively upon the factor common to both private and public sectors, the structures of power within the enterprise. The aim of industrial democracy was now conceived more narrowly as the extension of the influence of workpeople and trade unions over a wide range of managerial decisions which affected their interests directly as employees. These decisions were those on 'investment, location, closures, takeovers and mergers, and product specialisation of the organisation' (para. 85). Without an extension of control into these areas, the ability of unions to protect the interests of their members would remain severely circumscribed in an increasingly crisis-ridden economic environment. Rather than a more cautious approach in the private sector, the need here was considered to be 'particularly acute' because of the limited extent to which collective bargaining had developed at the corporate level, where the important planning and investment decisions were taken. The problem was no longer whether, but how best to secure a greater degree of trade union control over the enterprise. This policy objective was embodied implicitly in the terms of reference of the Bullock Committee—to consider how best to establish a system of worker representation on boards of directors in the private sector.

Party policy on economic planning was formulated during the earlier phase of thinking on the issue of workers' control. The fact that these hesitations had been pushed aside, if not entirely eliminated, was signalled in the 1974 TUC report. Although not overtly concerned with wider questions of planning, the report had noted that the proposed extension of industrial democracy must 'affect the process of national planning itself' (para. 62). The manner in which this would occur was revealed at the November 1975 and January 1976 NEDC meetings, which set in hand special studies in thirty, later increased to forty, key sectors of manufacturing. The studies were to be carried out by the Economic Development Committees, or newly established Sector Working Parties, with the aim of improving the productive potential of industry. Although the TUC continued to call for the conclusion of planning agreements as the mechanism for drawing individual companies into the planning system, the shift in emphasis to the sectoral level cut across the national focus which underlay the conception of the planning agreements system, while the development of independent tripartite machinery cut across direct control by the state. It was this shift in the direction of the industrial strategy which led eventually to the conclusion at the 1978 TUC Conference that 'the next stage of the Industrial Strategy depends critically on full trade union involvement in decisions at company and plant level'. That the extension of 'joint control of decision making at all levels' in the private sector was now seen as the matter of crucial importance for economic policy is indicated in the rider that the public sector ought not to be treated 'less favourably'. These developments in the industrial policy, together with policy on the promotion of industrial democracy, will be discussed in a further article.

The 'Alternative Economic Strategy'

Those who treated the perspective of the 1973 Programme as engraved on tablets of stone condemned this evolution of the real economic forces. Labour's Programme 1976 reasserted the validity of the original conception, criticising the deviation in the government's policy brought about by the combined influence of resistance by the employers and pressure from the TUC for greater trade union involvement (pp. 21–4). While, therefore, 'left' criticism of government economic policy after 1976 overlapped to some extent with that of the TUC, it was also critical of the TUC's connivance in the subversion of the planning agreements strategy.[11] Here is the origin of what has come to be known as the 'Alternative Economic Strategy'. Even when apparently significant verbal concessions are made to some notion of workers' control or 'industrial democracy', the cardinal principle in all its versions is the extension of domination by the state. Although, for example, the CSE London Working Group 'attach an overriding importance to the extension of workers' power—both at the point of production and within the wider democratic process of arriving at economic and social goals', and to the 'extension of organised working class power', these ideas are not developed consistently, but hedged about and qualified by the dependence on the state. The mechanism of the planning agreement is to be 'negotiated between management and government', while the trade unions play only an 'important', but undefined, role. The powers available to the government in this process 'could in theory be used equally against opposition to the government's plans from management or unions' (p. 71). Hence, it is not surprising to find that the argument peters out with weak suggestions for 'progress towards workers' control, set in a local economic context as an integral part of the AES', and 'the involvement of workers at the point of production, and of workers and their families in localities'. It ends on a note of perplexity, wondering 'how to make the institutions of the state more democratic' (p. 84–5).

In his *Road from Thatcherism* (1981), Aaronovitch takes it as axiomatic that 'control of the economy is. . . inseparable from the intervention of central government and of the state'. Accordingly, 'any planning system must take its authority from the elected representatives and the government which is formed on that basis' (p. 69). Of course, there are the usual phrases about the need for the 'government of the left' to be 'backed by overwhelming public support', but the activity of the people is limited to 'becom(ing) involved in a wide ranging debate on policy' on the one hand, and on the other, giving 'loyalty' to the state in the execution of the plan, and acting as its 'monitoring force' (p. 116). Exactly how 'large numbers of people' are supposed to support economic plans which they do not have the capacity to formulate, and which are not even necessarily formulated by their 'representatives', since 'much of the decision making and negotiations between centres of power necessarily takes place outside parliament' (p. 114), is left unclear. To our, admittedly 'inadequate', 'present system of representative institutions', Aaronovitch proposes an alternative 'democratic process'. Since, however, this idea cannot be realised in practice, because it contradicts the essence of state power, namely, its alienation from the people, 'even a thousandfold combination of the word "state" and the word "people" will not bring us a flea-hop nearer the problem'.[12]

What is clear for Aaronovitch is that direct control by the producers is envisaged only 'at the level of the enterprise and the plant' (p. 72), and that 'factory-based workers' councils as the ideal form of organisation is an extremely narrowing and sectarian vision which is bound to be resented by the millions who do not work in such enterprises' (p. 114–5). Of course, as an 'idea', workers' control is equally applicable to all places of work, whether they exist as factories, offices, shops, mines, quarries, or railway premises. It is true that the real basis of this idea, workshop organisation, is developed to the greatest extent in private manufacturing industry where the conditions for collective bargaining over pay and conditions at this level have been most favourable, but it has also become generalised to other sectors of the economy to a greater or lesser extent, particularly over the last decade or so. More importantly, however, Aaronovitch appears to have forgotten that the central issue for economic policy, as set out in his own book, is the revival and development of the industrial basis, production of actual wealth; he admits that the 'issue of accountability and control has arisen mainly for the small number of large firms'. In fact, the planning agreements system is intended, at least 'initially', to cover only about one hundred of the largest firms, controlling about half of manufacturing output. We need only compare this figure with the more than seven hundred enterprises employing over 2,000 workers which, on a conservative view, the Bullock Report on Industrial Democracy (1977) considered to be ripe for a significant extension of worker influence over the management process, to regain a sense of proportion in this regard. It is precisely in the largest, and therefore economically most significant establishments, that union influence in relation to the particular employer is most strongly developed, a point to which we shall return in future.

The consequence of the refusal to allow that those in a position to control production in detail, the workers, must therefore determine the whole process of planning, is that planning can only take the form of bureaucratic domination by the state. In the inability of the state to control production 'in complete detail', Aaronovitch finds a guarantee which 'will limit the need for bureaucratic decision-making' (p. 51). Since, however, this limitation on the power of the state is also a limitation on planning, it follows that 'the market' will continue to play an 'important role'. The 'market' signifies competitive relationships between the producers, that production is still based on the division of labour. Hence, in the absence of direct control by the producers themselves, the control of production becomes a separate function, the prerogative of an external power, capital. Capital is simply the form in which the domination of production by competition becomes a domination over the producer himself. It explains the recurrent failure of producer co-operatives within a competitive environment. Aaronovitch's proposed solution is, predictably, a 'powerful democratic movement' which we can expect 'to have changed the perspectives of many who are in managerial positions' (p. 64). The affinities with the thought of the Webbs are clear. Our guarantee against the anarchy of capitalist competition is planning by the state, but on the other hand, our only guarantee against the bureaucracy of the state is capitalist competition. The only real solution to the oppression of the working class is a more ameliorative attitude on the part of the bureaucratic agents of the state and of private capital. Stalinism and right-wing 'social democracy' are both contained within this approach; in truth, they are simply two sides of the same coin, a reactionary guarantee of continued capitalist domination. Marx's comment is still apposite in relation to the 'state socialists' of the present day.

> Despite its democratic clang, the whole programme is thoroughly infested with [a] servile belief in the state, or, what is no better, by a democratic faith in miracles, or rather, it is a compromise between these two sorts of faith in miracles. both equally far removed from socialism.[13]

NOTES

1. TUC-Labour Party Liaison Committee, 'Economic Planning and Industrial Democracy: The Framework for Full Employment', July 1982, para. 21.
2. See R. Green and A. Wilson in *New Socialist*, No. 7, Sept/Oct. 1982, for a brief discussion of some of this material.

3. S. & B. Webb, *A Constitution for the Socialist Commonwealth of Great Britain* (1920). References are to the 1975 edition.
4. *Self-Government in Industry* (1917). References are to the 1972 edition.
5. 'Conspectus of Bakunin's "Statism and Anarchy".'
6. Hughes, 'Trade Union Structure and Government', Donovan Commission Research Paper No. 5(1).
7. CBI document, cited in Leruez, *Economic Planning and Politics in Britain* (1975), 145.
8. e.g. Sloman, *Socialising Public Ownership* (1978).
9. Report of the Labour Party Working Group on Industrial Democracy (1967), 25–6.
10. *Labour's Programme 1973*, 18.
11. 'The TUC has never taken the idea of planning agreements seriously, and threw its full weight behind the tripartite strategy launched in 1975', CSE London Working Group, *The Alternative Economic Strategy* (1980), 67–8.
12. Marx, 'Critique of the Gotha Programme'.
13. *Ibid.*

The following two articles are written by two members of the GLC's Police Committee Support Unit. The views expressed here are those of the authors alone and not those of the GLC, its Police Committee, or the Police Committee Support Unit. The articles were written in collaboration and the footnotes to both appear on p. 74 ff. We would like to thank Claire Demuth, Paul Gordon, Jenny Pawson, Teresa Sim and Vron Ware for their critical help and support with these articles.

P.G. and J.S.

THE MYTH OF BLACK CRIMINALITY

Paul Gilroy

> The Police must win. . . but we must never be seen to win easily. If policemen all loaded down with special equipment went to a demonstration and arrested 1,000 people and no policemen were injured, why the critics would be coming out of the woodwork. Its like a good cricket match: we must thrash the other side, but our public likes us much better if we come from behind to do it.
>
> (Deputy Assistant Commissioner George Rushbrook)

The last decade has witnessed 'law and order' moving steadily to the centre of the political stage. As the national crisis has deepened, the extension of police power and the recruitment of law into political conflicts have become commonplace. The rule of law and maintenance of public order have appeared in forms which involve a racist appeal to the 'British Nation'[1] and have become integral to maintaining popular support for the government in crisis conditions. Indeed the recent history of 'law and order' is scarcely separable from the growth of popular racism and nationalism in the period following Enoch Powell's[2] famous intervention. Powell's wide-grinning piccaninnies have grown up, and with the onset of their adulthood, potent imagery of youthful black criminals stalking derelict inner-city streets where the law-abiding are afraid to walk after sunset[3] has been fundamental to the popularisation of increasingly repressive criminal justice and welfare state policies.

Beacuse of their capacity to symbolise other relations and conflicts, images of crime and law-breaking have had a special ideological importance since the dawn of capitalism.[4] If the potential for organised political struggle towards social transformation offered by criminality has often been low, images of particular crimes and criminal classes have frequently borne symbolic meanings and even signified powerful threats to the social order. This means that 'crime' can have political implications which extend beyond the political consciousness of criminals. The boundaries of what is considered criminal or illegal are elastic and the limits of the law have been repeatedly altered by intense class conflict. It is often forgotten that the political formation of the working class movement in this country is saturated with illegality. The relation of politics to 'crime' is therefore complex. These points should be borne in mind if socialists are not to rush into the arms of the right in their bid to 'take crime seriously'.

Black Crime and the Crisis

In contemporary Britain, the disorder signified in popular imagery of crime and criminals, to which law and order is presented as the only antidote, has become expressive of national decline in several ways. At best, a lingering environmentalism makes a causal link between crime and unemployment or the deterioration of the inner-cities. At worst, discussion of crime becomes subsumed by the idea that the rule of law, and therefore the Nation itself, is somehow under attack. Here alien criminals[5] take their place alongside subversive enemies within[6] and self-destructive defects in the national culture.[7] Race is, however, always dominant in the way this decline is represented. The left's failure to appreciate how the racism of slump and crisis is different from the racism[8] of boom and commonwealth, has meant that they have not grasped how notions of black criminality have been instrumental in washing the discourse of the nation as white as snow and preparing the way for repatriation. The imagery of alien violence and and criminality personified in the 'mugger' and the 'illegal' immigrant has become an important card in the hands of politicians and police officers whose authority is undermined by the political fluctuations of the crisis. For them, as for many working-class Britons, the irresolvable difference between themselves and the undesired immigrants is clearly expressed in the latter's culture of criminality and inbred inability[9] to cope with that highest achievement of civilisation—the rule of law.

The centrality of race has been consistently obscured by left writers on police and crime, often too keen to view 'racism' as a matter of individual attitudes adequately dealt with under the headings of prejudice and discrimination, and the struggle against it as an exclusively ideological matter far removed from the world of class politics.

In answer to this tendency, it is our contention that recognition of contemporary importance of racial politics allows a number of important analytical and strategic issues to take shape. It is not only that a left movement which makes rhetorical commitment to viewing the law as an arena of struggle can profit from careful attention to the methods and organisational forms in which various black communities have won a series of legal victories whilst simultaneously organising outside the courtroom, though the history of such cases, which span the 12 years between the Mangrove 9[10] and the Bradford 12, does merit careful inspection. It is rather that taking the experience of black communities seriously, can transform 'left wing' orthodoxy on the subject of the police and thereby determine a change in the orientation and composition of the struggle for democratic local control of police services. It is fruitless, for example, to search for programmatic solutions to 'discriminatory police behaviour' in amendments to the training procedure when professional wisdom inside the force emphasises a racist, pathological view of black familial relations, breeding criminality and deviancy out of cultural disorganisation and generational conflict.[11] If this racist theory is enshrined in the very structure of police work, it demands more desperate remedies than merely balancing the unacceptable content against increased 'human relations' training. However, left-wing writers have tended to ignore the well-documented[12] abuse of the black communities by the police which stretches back to the beginnings of post-war settlement in sufficient volume to have made a considerable impact on their critical view of the police. This history not only shows the manner in which police violate the letter and the spirit of the law in their day to day dealings with blacks. It is sufficient to prompt questions about the kind of law which deprives 'illegal' immigrants of their rights of Habeas Corpus, restricts their rights of appeal, operates retroactively, and bids its special branches to round them up whilst sanctioning vaginal examinations and dangerous X-rays of other would-be settlers.[13]

Lack of attention to other important issues has similarly reduced the value of left analysis of police and crime. The continuing war in the six counties of Northern Ireland has had profound effects on the police service on the mainland. These go beyond the simple but important idea that operational techniques, methods of surveillance and even structures of criminal justice refined in that experience are being progressively implemented in Britain.[14] The appointment of Sir Kenneth Newman to the Metropolitan Commissionership indicates the official premium placed on lessons learned there, but the fact that senior policemen routinely study General Frank Kitson's, *Low Intensity Operations*[15] and Colonel Robin Evelegh's *Peace Keeping in a Democratic Society, The lessons of Northern Ireland,*[16] more accurately conveys the transformation of policing theory which has followed the impact of counter-insurgency planning. It has been argued[17] that theories of 'Community Policing' most clearly represent the fruits of this relationship, and though we cannot go into this in detail here, several basic points can be made. Counter-insurgency theory not only stresses the need to combat domestic subversion,[18] but also the annexation and synchronisation of social and welfare state institutions under police control. Though all of Kitson's methods are not readily transferable to the current situation on mainland Britain it is clear that his definition of subversion includes activities which are neither illegal nor alien to the political traditions of the working-class movement in this country.

> It (subversion) can involve the use of political and economic pressure, strikes, protest marches, and propaganda.[19]

General Kitson has recently been appointed Chief of Land Forces in the UK. It is also worth pointing out that it is the liberal ex-police chief

John Alderson who has been credited with pioneering the study of counter-insurgency theory on the senior command course at Bramshill Police College.[20] Kitson's emphasis on the psychological dimension to law enforcement and peace-keeping operations 'psyops' is echoed in Alderson's stress on the imagery and language of police politics:

> We need a climate to be created in which we (the police) are seen not as potential enemies, but as potential friends and, dare I use the word, brothers. You have to start talking like that. You have to use expressions like that. The rhetoric of leaders and administrators is critical.[21]

If policing by consent is the fundamental principle of the British approach, crisis conditions dictate that policemen have ceased to merely pay lip service to this idea, they now recognise that consent must be won, maintained and reproduced by careful interventions in popular politics.

It has been suggested that the use of computers in Northern Ireland has made a considerable impact on the British police in its own right, here too there are lessons which have been learned from maintaining law and order in the six counties.[22]

Popular Politics of Law and Order

Various fractions of the left movement, increasingly marginal to popular concerns, have recently glimpsed in the intensity of feeling around questions of law and order a means to gain proximity to the working class. These theorists[23] take note of the fears of crime and violence which have been amplified by the entry of police chiefs into media politics. But rather than view these fears as themselves produced by a novel situation in which the police have begun to derive their ideological authority from a direct relationship to the people, and their political legitimacy from an increasingly acceptable voice in matters of social policy, this fear is taken as an unproblematic reflection of the reality of crime in working class communities. There is not the slightest acknowledgement that police are in a good position to mould and even create public fear in such a way as to justify an increase in their powers. This is a serious lapse in view of the fact that they state intellectuals have begun to abandon the idea that detecting and preventing crime can be the principal object of police work, arguing instead, that[24] 'the fear of crime. . . is perhaps only marginally related to the objective risk of becoming a victim' and that 'people who feel well policed are well policed'.[25]

One consequence of this is that the public, particularly the black public must be re-educated[26] in more realistic expectations of the police and their capabilities. We shall explore the way in which this shift has transformed the politics of policing below, but it must be immediately related to an understanding of the manner in which Chief Constables have become media personalities and also to the personalisation of their office which has followed Sir Robert Mark's reign at Scotland Yard. It is remarkable that the left has accepted the over-polarisation of debate around the contrasting police personalities of James Anderton and John Alderson.[27] Alderson has himself warned that this simplistic view 'obscures more than it reveals'. There is also evidence to suggest that the police in Devon and Cornwall are as capable of the excesses of 'fire-brigade'[28] policing as their brother officers in Manchester. This makes nonsense of the view of community policing as a miraculous cure-all for urban ailments and the symptoms of economic crisis. Alderson's much publicised solutions to the problems of a society 'in which the only permanence is change' appear attractive when contrasted to the crudities of operation 'Swamp 81', but the reality of community policing is rather more complex in theory let alone in practice, than the optimism and enthusiasm of some left commentators would suggest. It is not always appreciated, for example, that 'community policing' is not planned to be an alternative to other 'more dramatic'[29] modes of police work, but rather a 'complementary strategy' designed to 'bring the reactive and preventive roles of the police service[30] into a balance appropriate to long-term aims and objectives'.

A senior officer from the West Midlands where Alderson's ideas have been put to the acid test of the inner-city, dispels the idea that community policing alters the fundamental orientation of aims of the police officers who practise it: 'We are not always the nice guys. . . these are good sound operational PCs in uniform doing an operational PC's job, but they are doing it more effectively. . . We're not trying to create a force of social workers or make claims we are getting involved in welfare. It's very much policing.'[31]

In his evidence to the Scarman enquiry, Brixton's home beat policeman, John Brown[32] provided further insights into the relationship between the 'criminal intelligence' gained in the practice of 'penetrating the community in all its aspects' and the more reactive and aggressive styles of policing. Brown explains that he not only guided the special patrol group round his own beat during their last tour of duty in Brixton, but also that in the past he aided officers from a neighbouring district in collecting the names of demonstrators engaged in an entirely lawful and non-violent trade-union dispute. When asked if this could be described as intelligence gathering, Brown replied, 'No it is not that.'

Illusions about the nature of policing theory revealed in the naive view of community policing are compounded by an innocent faith in the even-handedness of police practice on the ground. Ian Taylor, for example, criticises the left as conspiratorial in their approach to policing issues and 'proves' this by suggesting that the police have been systematically curtailing the military activities of the fascist right, and calling for bans of their marches. That the gun-running activities of the right can be exposed on prime-time television without the police prosecuting the individuals responsible makes nonsense of Taylor's first claim.[33] The nature of blanket bans which restrict all protest, and which cannot therefore be regarded as victories, invalidates his second. On this last point, it is remarkable how little critical comment has greeted Lord Scarman's recommendation that the Public Order Act 1936 be amended so that the police must be notified in advance of any procession or demonstration.[34]

The left's failings in relation to law, police and crime go far beyond poor analysis of the immediate situation or misunderstanding of the Scarman Report. However, discussion of the conflicts of Summer 1981 and the political responses to them can illustrate more general failings with great clarity.

In a series of influential articles, John Lea and Jock Young[35] have argued that the source of the summer riots lay, not in matters of police harassment and abuse, but in the political marginalisation of inner-city communities. Their analysis is disabled by a startling ignorance of police/community relations. Worse than this, the view of the black communities which they advance shares a great deal with the most conservative explanations of the conflict. They view West Indian life as characterised by pathological family relations and a high degree of generational conflict, but these are not presented as the sole source of black criminality. Discrimination, disadvantage, and economic alienation clash with inappropriate aspirations derived from the internalisation of 'British values' (sic) and this also generates the 'propensity' to crime. Thus the relation between race and crime is secured, not directly, as in the biological culturalism of Conservative explanations, but at one remove which is equally dangerous, particularly as it prompts speculation as to why it is only the black poor who resolve their frustration in acts of criminality. To present 'black crime' as a primarily *cultural problem* whether forged in the economic 'no man's land' between deprivation and restricted opportunity, or secured in a spurious social biology, is a capitulation to the weight of racist logic. This suggests a total discontinuity between the cultures of black and white youth which is inappropriate given the multi-racial character of the riots, and becomes openly visible when Lea and Young trace the roots of urban British street crime to a 'minority and deviant sub-culture within the West Indies'.

The emphasis on black culture legitimates the idea that any black, all blacks, are somehow contaminated by the alien predisposition to crime which is reproduced in their distinctive cultures, specifically their family relations. Police theorists have already made the link between supposedly 'Victorian' conceptions of discipline in the West Indian home and the growth of Rastafarian inspired criminality:

> This unfortunate break-up of family association has seen the formation of

> substantial groups of young blacks leaving home and banding together in numerous squats and communes, unemployed and completely disillusioned with society. Most of them have donned the Mantle of Rastafarianism, or more precisely the criminal sub-cult of the dreadlock fraternity.[36]

Young and Lea do little more than reproduce this pathology in polite social-democratic rhetoric.

Their political solution to police/community conflict is built on the possibility of instituting what they describe as 'consensual policing'. This, they explain, is a situation in which 'the policeman is in and with the community'. They refer to the breakdown of this relationship, implying therefore that it existed in the past, yet are unable to cite a single concrete historical instance of where or when this model of social harmony has actually existed. Their related view of the police officer as a friendly or avuncular figure, acceptable to the urban working-class bears scant relation to the numerous instances of conflict between class communities and the police which appear to have extended well into this century. Their view is also unable to accommodate the practice of forms of social crime in urban working-class communities, particularly by young people,[37] let alone patterns of intra-class struggle which have often involved forms of property crime.[38]

Young and Lea present the militarisation of inner-city policing as a straightforward, if undesirable, response to rising levels of 'street crime' in inner areas. There is no acknowledgement of the possibility that broader imperatives of social control and public order have been transformed by crises of political representation and in the economy. The neat scenario which presents rising street crime as the cause and police militarisation as the effect, places the blame for this state of affairs squarely on the shoulders of minority of deviant blacks. It is posited at the expense of engaging with the history of police/community relations, particularly in so far as this relates to the black communities. Supt. Lawrence Roach,[39] sometime head of the Met's Community Relations Branch has revealed how the development of specialist community relations policing has arisen out of the exigencies of policing the blacks; police theorists' views on the functions of communities in police strategy[40] also suggest that techniques devised in policing black areas can provide a new paradigm for policing cities in crisis conditions.

Significantly, prior to their defeat by black youth at the Notting Hill Carnival in 1976, Metropolitan police evidence to the Commons Select Committee described a situation in London where, during the preceding 12 months, forty incidents 'carrying the potential for large scale disorder' had developed out of police attempts to arrest black youths. The pattern of this conflict dates back to the early 1970s, landmarked by notable cases of police/community conflict in Notting Hill (1970), Brockwell

Park (1973), Stockwell, Cricklewood, Dalston, Hornsey and Brixton (1975). However, London was not unique in the scale of street-level conflict between the police and the black communities. In Birmingham, the massive stop and search operation which sealed off the Handsworth area following the murder of a policeman in July 1975 involved the arrest of 600 blacks though only one was charged. (The officer had been stabbed after setting his dog on a young woman outside the Rainbow Room Club.) In Leeds, the bonfire night confrontations in Chapeltown occurred annually from 1973 to 1975. The summer of 1976 saw well-documented conflict in Manchester, Birmingham and at least four different parts of London.[41]

The combined weight of these 'isolated incidents' is sufficient to transform the picture presented by Young and Lea, restoring in the process a determinancy to the dynamics of police/community conflict which is obscured by their idea of black 'counter culture' or 'unintegrated ethnic culture'. The systematic application of militaristic and reactive policing to black areas the length and breadth of Britain undermines any view of consensual policing—black streets have never enjoyed the benefits of this police policy. Furthermore, the nature of these police operations is not adequately grasped by reference to 'discrimination' or the 'prejudice' of individual officers. They are systematic and, in police terms, rational, as a complex body of specialised policing theory informs them and legitimates the view of blacks as disproportionately prone to criminality.

Black political organisation against police abuses has frequently exhibited a unity between people of Asian and Afro-Caribbean descent,[42] yet most left-wing writers on the subject seem curiously keen to introduce a pernicious contradiction between the interests of the two communities with regard to law and order. Several authors have identified an implicit Asian demand for more rather than less police activity,[43] albeit of a rather different type from that which they have come to expect from the British police. This suggestion, which derives its plausibility from the twin racist stereotypes of the quiescent Asian victim and the criminally inclined West Indian street youth, has been achieved at the expense of historical record. Young and Lea, Taylor and Frith all cite the rioting outside the Hamborough Tavern in Southall last July as an example, and each views this incident as violence of a different order from that experienced elsewhere. Their suggestion that the militant Asian youth did not know what they were doing when they attacked police and skinheads alike is derisory. It is impossible to grasp the meaning of the 1981 riots in Southall without careful attention to previous confrontations there. In 1976, after the death of Gurdip Singh Chaggar, and again in 1979 during the police riot there, Asian youth acquired their own grievances against the local police whose abuse of the black community had been catalogued as early as 1973 by Dr. Stanislaus Pullé. It is therefore more plausible to suggest that their assault on the police was not an inarticulate demand for more bobbies on the beat, but a sign of their deep anger, created by years of harassment and a powerful statement to the effect that like their sisters and brothers in the Afro-Caribbean communities, militant Asians viewed community self-defence as the legitimate answer to racist violence. It is worth recalling that the initial response by officers at a police disco in Hammersmith to the news that rioting had started was to sing 'there ain't no black in the Union Jack'.[44] They were silenced by their senior officers.

The central argument here is that the question of black crime must be approached in a historical fashion, and in a context supplied by the overall pattern of police/community conflict in conditions of deepening crisis. In conclusion, there are several general points about the priorities and structure of police practice which need to be brought into the discussion. There is strong evidence to suggest that emphasis on particular crimes can engineer what appear to be crime waves of these offences, not only because of heightened public sensitivity to these crimes, but also as a result of changes in police practice.[45] It is certainly plausible that 'mugging' has constituted a self-fulfilling prophecy of this type. Blom-Cooper and Drabble[46] have recently shown that the Met's manipulation of the compound categories in which their statistics are recorded can be used to support this view. Young and Lea are not alone on the left in their tendency to take critical crime statistics at their face value.

E.P. Thompson[47] and Ian Taylor, among others, have also been disinclined to question these figures. It is important that the left clarify their views of officially recorded crime rates, particularly as a growing number of police thinkers and right-wing ideologists proceed unimpeded by the idea that they are an accurate reflection of crime actually experienced.

The Police Federation magazine, hardly noted for its radical politics, recently argued: 'no informed person regards the existing criminal statistics as the most reliable indicator of the state of crime'.[48] More significantly, Inspector Peter Finnimore's essay 'How Should Police Effectiveness Be Assessed', winner of the 1980 Queen's police gold medal essay competition, attacked statistics not only as a guide to the level of crime, but also as a measure of police activity:

> It is difficult for experienced police officers to concede that skilful police work has relatively little effect on overall crime levels, but it must be realised that no criticism is implied by such a view.[49]

In addition to this, the fact that official surveys of the victims of crime have consistently returned findings[50] which are completely at odds with the idea that crime itself rises when 'crime rates are soaring', should draw comment from the left. None of these authors appear to be aware of this. Finnimore is correct to insist that the issue of objective knowledge of crime leads directly to whether it is within the capacity of police to prevent or deter. Most recent left thinkers subscribe to what Home Office researchers have called the 'rational deterrent' model.[51] Young, Lea and Taylor, though they are correct to emphasise that the flow of information from communities is the main source of police knowledge, balance this by the idea that in exchange for the information the police will prevent crime. They are particularly concerned with the everyday forms in which it is experienced by working class communities. This view of police capability is debatable to say the least, for two distinct, but related reasons: Scrutiny of the history of policing in Britain,[52] particularly its cities, suggests that everyday crimes in which the working class are the victims have never been of major concern to police; and secondly, the proliferation of private security firms described by Hilary Draper[53] suggests that the police may not even have been very successful in protecting the property of the bourgeoisie. Recognising these limitations to their capacity, Police Chiefs and Senior Home Office researchers have begun to raise the question of whether police are capable of deterring or preventing criminal activity. Assessing recent British research into the effectiveness of policing, R.V.G. Clarke and K.H. Heal from the Home Office Research Unit conclude:

> The crime prevention value of a police force rests less on precisely what it does than on the symbolic effect of its presence and public belief in its effectiveness.[54]

Sir Robert Mark, who uses these arguments to justify a greater police concern with public order and anti-terrorist crime, puts the same point with characteristic bluntness:

> A great deal of crime is simply not preventable. Even the biggest police force that society could want or afford to pay would be unlikely to have any significant effect on the numbers of thefts, burglaries, or on crimes of violence between people who know each other.[55]

This points to the need for more imaginative and bold initiatives from the left on the issue of law and order. Contemporary 'socialist' thinking on crime and police is dominated by pathological and environmentalist explanations wedded to a practice of progressively greater demands of a criminal justice system in which it is often forgotten formal, legal equality sits uneasily on real inequality and relations of power and domination. In crisis conditions, police have increasingly separated the crime detection/prevention side to police activity from its political and ideological requirements.

The implications of this, and the role of representations of black criminality in securing legitimacy for police actions, is explored below in discussion of police responses to the riots in July 1981 and the Scarman inquiry which followed them.

SCARMAN: THE POLICE COUNTER-ATTACK

Joe Sim

On April 14, 1981, William Whitelaw appointed Lord Scarman to inquire into the serious disorder on 10–12 April 1981 and to report with the power to make recommendations. When Scarman reported, everyone—government, police and media—welcomed his report almost uncritically, at least in public. The male, white, seventy-year-old Lord and judge provided, they said, something for everybody. British fair play and commonsense shone through in every carefully written page.

In reality, the issues involved in, and the pressures surrounding the publication of Scarman's report were much more complex, involving a number of different, often contradictory, groups and strands within the British state. From the point of view of the police, for example, any proposals for reform, however liberal, as was the case with Scarman, were regarded as a threat to their power base and autonomy. This power base had been built throughout the 1970s and was constantly being legitimated by their more powerful and often eloquent spokespersons. Any challenge to them was therefore likely to meet with stiff resistance and outright hostility.

At another level, Scarman's report was also overtaken by the announcement, in October, that the police already had new riot equipment including CS gas and plastic bullets available. This process in the militarisation of the police had a long history preceding Scarman and is examined in greater detail below. What it meant was that Scarman's proposal which followed the next month for a greater emphasis on community policing was usurped and became a secondary appendage to the technological imperatives of the force.

Another issue involves Whitelaw himself. Before Scarman reported Whitelaw had made moves to set up voluntary liaison committees between local community groups and the police. Scarman was to recommend that such groups were to be on a statutory basis. Whitelaw did not accept this, hence he moved before the report was published and took the initiative in establishing contacts between police and public. These committees were to be very much on the police's terms. Geoffrey Dear, an Assistant Deputy Commissioner at Scotland Yard was also promoted and put in charge of personnel and training and was expected to put greater emphasis on 'human awareness' training. Whitelaw could point to this the next month when Scarman recommended changes in police training methods.

Much of what Scarman had to say therefore was redundant when he did report, and dead before his document saw the light of day. It is not the intention here to discuss the complexities surrounding the setting up of an inquiry such as Scarman's, nor the power struggles within the state between different interest groups to harness such inquiries for their own ends. Rather we wish to pinpoint the role of the police (despite the contradictions in the force) in undermining Scarman's proposals for limited change in their policing methods and structure of accountability. In doing this they picked up on some of the processes which had been in motion before he reported. They also utilised and emphasised one crucial factor, their belief that black people were disproportionately involved in street robbery. As we saw above, the force had been pushing this line since the early 1970s. Scarman, himself, in the construction of his report, left the door open for the force. It was an opportunity that the police, and in particular the Metropolitan Police (the Met), were not to pass up.

Scarman and Black Crime

Scarman's Inquiry centred on the events of the week-end of April 10–12 1981. During the course of the inquiry, other disturbances broke out throughout the country. In response to this, the government asked Scarman to take these disturbances into account when he came to prepare his report. This request was not evident in the final draft. Scarman mainly concentrated on the first Brixton disturbance and generally ignored those in other areas and regions of the country. Furthermore, although Scarman conducted the inquiry in two phases they were not equally divided in the time allotted to them. The first phase lasted for 20 days. In that time the immediate causes and the events surrounding the first Brixton disturbance were examined. Phase two was to examine underlying social conditions, including the policing of the area. Significantly, this phase lasted for only six days 'and the bulk of this time was spent in cross-examination of two senior police officers responsible for operations, recruitment and training. Once these officers had been cross-examined the Inquiry came speedily to final speeches from represented parties. This bias is reflected in the construction of the Report'.[56]

The bias towards the police evidence was evident in Scarman's discussion of criminal statistics. In paragraphs 4.11–4.15 of the report, Scarman discussed the question of crime in Lambeth, focussing particularly on street crime in Brixton. While he acknowledged some of the methodological problems surrounding the usefulness of official criminal statistics as a reliable measure of the level of crime in a given area, he concluded that the submissions which highlighted these problems 'do not explain away the practical impact nor the seriousness of the crime problem as it presented itself to Commander Adams and, subsequently to Commander Fairbairn'.[57]

According to the police, Brixton was the centre of a particular crime, street robbery, known colloquially as 'mugging'. This crime itself was associated with one group—the Afro-Caribbean male youth. Scarman noted that 'Brixton. . . faced a particularly high level of street crime and one in which black people were disproportionately involved.'[58] In making this statement Scarman ignored the evidence of groups such as Concern[59] and the study by the Home Office based researchers, Stevens and Willis,[60] whose work indicated that black people were not disproportionately involved in street crime. The key to understanding the disproportionate number of black people in the official criminal statistics could be found in the practices of the Met both bureaucratically and on the streets. By concentrating both manpower and resources in areas such as Brixton, the police were likely to pick up more black people, especially the black youth who spent much of their time on the streets. This group then found their way into the criminal statistics thus leading to an even greater police and media concentration on the activities of black people. This, in turn, led again to more of them being picked up. In this way, in an ever-increasing spiral, the racist self-fulfilling prophecy was complete; the black criminal mugger existed, the cold, hard, objective criminal statistics told the public so.

While accepting the police's version about the nature of crime in Brixton, Scarman did have a number of criticisms to make about the policing of the metropolis. It is important, however, to contextualise these criticisms within the overall thrust and tenor of the report. As Nick Blake maintains: 'Scarman seems more concerned with restrained and tactful language than with reflecting the grave consequences of the broken responsibilities of Brixton police officers.'[61] Blake goes on to point out that in a number of crucial areas Scarman failed to make any criticism of police misconduct; the failure to mention the 'ace of spades' tie brazenly worn by certain Brixton detectives; the failure to make any finding on the clearest evidence of three responsible journalists, and of photographs, of 'plain clothes officers carrying barbarous unauthorised weapons from Brixton police station during the disturbances under the noses of senior officers. No comment is made on the later punitive police raids in Railton Road which caused much damage and resentment'.[62]

Scarman recognised that some police officers were racially prejudiced in their dealings with black people. He denied however, the strong evidence that racism was institutionalised in the structure of the Met itself. His answer to individual examples of racist behaviour was to recommend that such behaviour should merit dismissal from the force. Scarman also recommended that there should be a statutory duty imposed on chief officers and police authorities to establish local consultative or liaison committees between the community and the police. This link would, in his view, bring the police and the public closer together. His other major recommendations were made with this objective in mind; the establishment of an independent police complaints procedure, the appointment of lay visitors to visit randomly police stations and the re-examination of policing methods used, particularly in the inner city areas. There should be more emphasis, he maintained, on 'community' and 'home-beat' policing methods. If these recommendations were implemented, then the historical relationship between the police and the public based on consent and mutual respect—an idea which in many areas of Britain was based on fantasy rather than on any historical fact—would, in Scarman's view, return. The benevolent status quo would be restored.

In making these recommendations, Scarman made a fundamental error. He failed to recognise within the police force the institutionalised antagonism towards any kind of proposed change which challenged their power base and autonomy. Even proposals as liberal as Scarman's were a threat. Indeed, the police through spokespersons such as Mark, Jardine and Anderton, openly despised the introduction of liberal police reforms. They were often belligerent in defence not only of their own position but of the criminal justice system in general. Throughout the 1970s they were in the forefront of the argument (often setting the parameters within which the debate was conducted) about the tightening up of both the criminal law and the laws governing moral behaviour. They were, in Stuart Hall's terms 'a sort of vanguard'[63] in this process.

Thus, while Sir David McNee called Scarman's report 'fair and thorough' the Association of Chief Police Officers called it an 'objective study' and the Police Federation said it was 'a historic document',[64] in reality, the police immediately mobilised and set in motion a campaign to undermine Scarman's principal recommendations. The key to their strategy would be to concentrate on the alleged rise in crime particularly street crime in the black areas of the inner cities. They would focus attention on the force's very own folk-devil—the black, male mugger. Scarman himself, by pinpointing black areas as places of criminal activity, had given them the ammunition and legitimation that they needed. It was this spectre—black, violent and unpredictable—which was to haunt the pages of the press in the months after Scarman reported.

Undermining Scarman

Scarman reported on 25 November 1981. By mid-January, Scotland Yard had embarked on the campaign which was designed to undermine the report's major recommendations regarding accountability. The campaign was conducted in collaboration with particular newspapers and selected television programmes. This gave the different senior policemen who spoke for the Yard the platform they needed to put forward their views. Generally, these views went unchallenged.

The basis of the Yard's campaign was an alleged, dramatic increase in the crime rate in general and street crime, 'muggings', in particular. According to the police, it was black youths, living in the inner-city areas, who were responsible for the majority of these crimes. It was on this group that the Yard focussed the attention of the media.

On 21 January, Peter Burden, *The Daily Mail*'s chief crime correspondent discussed violent street crime in London in 1981. The crime rate he maintained, had 'broken all records . His report, *More and More Muggers But The Yard Fights Back,* described how Scotland Yard's Assistant Commissioner, Gilbert Kelland, had held a conference of top officers who came from areas where the Yard alleged that a major increase in crime had taken place—Lambeth, Hackney, Lewisham, Wembley, Tottenham and Battersea. Kelland told those present that there should be no scaling down of operations because of Scarman's criticism of policing operations in Brixton. Burden reported that although, 'Yard figures do not break down the race of muggers senior detectives say case files show that in some areas such as Lambeth and Lewisham most attacks are carried out by young blacks'. Burden also reported that the previous evening James Jardine, the Chairperson of the Police Federation had told a meeting in Guildford that Scarman had failed to provide a satisfactory answer to the level of street crime in the inner city.[65] Two weeks later, *The Daily Telegraph* carried a similar story. 'Muggings of Women Double', said the paper's headline. Citing 'community police sources' the story described how 'the number of women mugged by roaming groups of black youths has almost doubled in many parts of London since last April's Brixton riots'. The report went on to describe how a police squad had been set up in Lewisham 'to trace black youths who mugged 14 people—13 of them women—over a week-end'. Nicholas Bennett, Lewisham Council's Conservative Police Liaison Committee spokesperson, said that reports showed that 'crimes are committed by West Indian youths between 14 and 21 years old against young and elderly, white and Asian women'.[66] The next day *The Sun*'s editorial spoke of Britains 'Danger Street' and two weeks later, on 18 February, it ran a double page spread on 'The Menace of the Muggers'. The next day it was *The Daily Mirror*'s turn. Mugging was 'Britains top crime' the newspaper claimed.[67]

Support for the police's campaign was not confined solely to the pages of the press. Members of Parliament also spoke about the increase in crime in areas populated by black people. In January, Harvey Proctor, the Conservative MP for Basildon, had set the tone for what was to come by arguing that the growth in Britain's non-white population would lead 'within a few years to no-go areas' which would necessitate 'the deployment of army units on the streets of our capital and other big cities and the imposition of night curfews and other profoundly un-English authoritarian measures'.[68] A week later, another Conservative MP, Tony Marlow, asked the Home Secretary, William Whitelaw, whether 'street crime in Brixton had increased since the ending of the riots and if so by what extent'.[69] In February, Alan Clark, the Conservative MP for Plymouth, referred in Parliament to an article in *The Times* which had stated that figures for muggings were up by 50 per cent in certain inner city areas. Clark cited police sources who claimed that 'these offences are becoming increasingly brazen with gangs of up to 50 young blacks looting in broad daylight'.[70]

At the end of the month the police intervened more directly. On 26 February, Deputy Assistant Commissioner Leslie Walker told Independent Television's *The London Programme* that most muggings are committed by blacks. 'That is a fact. . . with street robberies they're disproportionate to white people in the amount of robberies that are committed.' Walker also maintained that the Scarman report had placed the police in a dilemma between the prevention of crime and the preservation of public order. 'What I would like to see his Lordship say is what he thinks we should do when the sheer weight of crime itself is threatening public tranquility.'[71] *The Standard,* one of the newspapers which carried the story informed its readers that there were 80 muggings a week in Brixton. The following day, *The Daily Mail* reported Walker's remarks. The newspaper also devoted space to the comments of two anonymous senior police officers 'operating in London's worst mugging areas'. One officer commented that 'mugging is primarily an immigrant offence. The serious crime undertaken by blacks is out of all proportion to their numbers in the community'. The other officer—a commander—agreed. 'The muggers are in the main black who cause havoc with the crime figures.' Both agreed that the white community 'is screaming at us to do something'.[72]

On 10 March, Scotland Yard were due to release their yearly review of crime in London. This review, which was mainly in the form of statistics, was intended to highlight some of the trends with regard to a whole range of crimes and offences against public order. As usual, this exercise was strictly controlled by the Yard. It was they who decided not only what information should be released and the manner in which it should be presented, but also who was to attend the press conference at which the review would take place. The week before the conference, the press and media campaign became more intense as reporters and commentators continued to identify black areas as major centres and hiding places for the muggers. On 4 March *The Standard* cited, 'confidential figures' which the Yard were to release, 'in a few days time'. These figures showed a 96 per cent increase in muggings. The former Conservative leader of Lewisham Council, Nicholas Bennett, knew where the cause of this increase lay, '97 per cent of the attackers were West Indian', he said. Bennett criticised Scarman, whose report, he claimed, had hampered an effective police clampdown on muggers.[73] In the next few days, several newspapers were quick to pick up the theme. 'Muggings in London Now Top 50 A Day' said *The Sunday Telegraph*,[74] At least 56 'Crimes an hour in London' reported *The Times* on the same day.[76] These reports were also critical of the record of William Whitelaw on law and order. They saw the mugging statistics as indicative of Whitelaw's failure not only to come to grips with the problems of law and order but also to comprehend fully the problem of race relations. On 8 March *The Daily Mail* carried a major article by Andrew Alexander entitled 'Why the public should not trust this man'.[77] Alexander attacked Whitelaw for his record on street crime claiming that this crime had increased from 13,000 in 1980 to 18,000 in 1981. Whitelaw's 'softly softly' approach to crime, he argued, was the root cause of this increase and was tied in with his approach to race, on which Whitelaw was 'not so much soft as positively liquid. . . his desire to appease the race relations industry is at once all consuming and pathetic'. Once again, with the help of some 'anonymous' Scotland Yard detectives, Alexander was quick to make the connection between race and the apparent rise in the level of street crime. 'How can you not be conscious of black crime, it's overwhelming?' one detective had told him. In Brixton, the coloured population was 36 per cent 'yet blacks are responsible for about 80 per cent of crime', the detective went on. The report concluded that 'most reported cases are of muggings by blacks of whites, especially of women'. The next day, at a meeting of the Home Affairs Committee of Conservative MPs, it was decided to summon Whitelaw to discuss the situation. Lord Scarman was in attendance at the same meeting. He was bitterly criticised for himself criticising policing methods in Brixton and for turning 'a straightforward issue of crime into one of race relations'.[78] When Scotland Yard held a press conference the following day, the press and media were primed and ready to hear the news about black muggers. For their part, the Yard were also ready. By using the crime figures, built around the stereotype of the black male mugger, they were about to confront Scarman's challenge to their power and autonomy.

Black Crime: The Alarming Figures[79]

So the *Daily Mail* headlined their front page story on Scotland Yard's press conference. At the conference, the Yard, for the first time, produced a breakdown of street crimes committed by blacks and whites. Of the 18,763 offences of robbery and other violent theft reported by London's police in 1981, the Yard alleged that 10,399 had been carried out by 'non-whites'. Announcing the figures, Assistant Commissioner Gilbert Kelland, commented that the racial breakdown had been given 'to prevent gossip, rumour, and miscalculations and to set the record straight. There is a demand, police feel, for this information from the public and the media'.[80] Kelland omitted to mention that the demand from the media had been instigated by the police themselves. As Gareth Pierce explained, what had preceded the release of the statistics was, 'the strongest weapon in the police arsenal which was not CS gas or plastic bullets, the deployment of which causes some public concern, but effective control of a willing and uncritical press which causes none'.[81]

While newspapers such as *The Guardian*, and to a lesser extent, *The Sunday Times* and *The Observer* attempted to contextualise and critically evaluate the statistical basis[82] of the Met's analysis, the rest of the press and media uncritically accepted their version of events. Photographs of black muggers stared menacingly out of the tabloid's pages. Cartoons depicted them in action. Capital Radio's *London Programme* devoted the first 15 minutes of their early evening show to the figures. William Whitelaw and a senior police officer were the sole contributors. *The Daily Express* headlined its editorial 'Whitelaw the Weak'. 'Crime is not only booming it is becoming racial—just as a great deal of rioting is racial' it commented.[83] *The Daily Mail* used the figures to attack the black community in general. Their report argued that 'the ordinary, decent black citizen of this country will see it as simply not his business that most of the mugging, most of the violence in inner London, is committed by young blacks. . . the reaction to the evidence that the old, the frail and alone among us are living in terror, will include no note of black concern. . . no cry of black compassion'. The *Mail* was clear in its support for Scotland Yard who 'by deciding after so many years to give boldly the facts. . . have ended a conspiracy of silence, compounded of white feelings of guilt, black feelings of persecution, police doubts about their role and Lord Scarman's certainty about nothing'.[84] The next day, the newspaper repeated its call for William Whitelaw's removal to the House of Lords.

Reactions to the statistics from outside the media were equally severe. Jill Knight, the Tory MP for Edgbaston declared that the figures were 'intolerable'. After a meeting with Whitelaw she indicated that she had received a clear assurance that where serious criminals could be deported back to their countries of origin they would be. Her Parliamentary colleague, Ivor Stanbrook, supported this line of action. He commented that 'in the face of overwhelming evidence that instant crime has grown in immigrant areas, the Government has a duty to reconsider its immigration policy'.[85] The day following the publication of the statistics, the Association of British Ex-Servicemen (ABEX) announced that they planned to patrol the streets of Brixton on the following week-end. The organisation maintained that members of ABEX, 'will be patrolling the streets of London as vigilantes and making citizens' arrests on black youths who are seen to be interfering with white pensioners in anyway whatsoever'.[86] It was reported that senior officers from Scotland Yard visited the leaders of the group and had a two hour meeting with them which left the group 'in no doubt that the police would not stand by and let people take the law into their own hands'.[87]

It was difficult to imagine senior policemen meeting left-wing groups to discuss plans for community defence organisations. More fundamentally, it was the police who had clearly defined the parameters within which the debate about crime and law and order was to take place. In presenting the racial background of those alleged to have been involved in street robberies (the identification of whom was based, in the majority of cases, on very quick half-sightings, by the victim), Scotland Yard underlined the racial stereotype that had been built up since the early 1970s and which they themselves had been instrumental in propagating. Every young West Indian male was a potential mugger. Black communities had therefore to be watched and kept under surveillance so that they could be caught. Furthermore, any black person caught committing any crime, never mind a mugging, was to be dealt with severely. At Croydon Crown Court on 12 March, the presiding judge, Clay, duly obliged. Carl Williams, a British-born West Indian was found guilty of stealing from shops during a disturbance at Clapham Junction in the summer of 1981. Judge Clay indicated that he was considering a custodial sentence but when he heard that Williams had intended to go to Jamaica with his family, on a holiday, he bound him over on condition that he left Britain for five years. The judge, had, in effect, imposed a limited deportation order on Williams using powers enshrined in the Justices of the Peace Act 1361 and the Magistrates Court Act 1980. As the National Council for Civil Liberties commented, 'It is inconceivable that such an order would ever be made against a white British-born citizen whose parents had migrated here. The Lord Chancellor must condemn Judge Clay's openly racist behaviour and make it clear that such activities will not be tolerated.'[88] The Lord Chancellor failed to make any such condemnation. On the contrary, the controversy about black muggers, crime and criminal statistics continued and underpinned what became a full-blown debate about law and order. The police, and their spokespersons, were at the centre of the debate. The next stage in their efforts to jettison Scarman was about to happen.

'A Dangerous, Insidious and Ruthless Enemy'

The release of the criminal statistics gave a clear indication of the police backlash to Scarman. In the following weeks that backlash was to intensify. It gained momentum as the force translated its hostility to Scarman's report into a debate about law and order and the integrity of the police. By playing their favourite law and order card, the police were making sure that the deck was heavily stacked against those who questioned their authority and autonomy. This, of course, included Scarman.

On 17 March, the Police Federation launched a £30,000 advertising campaign which called for the return of capital punishment. The Federation placed advertisements in five national newspapers. The advertisements demanded the return of the death penalty for the murder of police people, prison officers and for 'terrorist killers'. More than 80 Conservative MPs signed a Commons motion supporting the Federation's position. Alongside the Federation's campaign, impassioned speeches were made both by MPs and senior policemen describing the horrors of the rising crime rate particularly in the inner cities.

On the same day that the Federation launched their campaign, James Anderton, the Chief Constable of Greater Manchester released the text of a speech that he was to make two days later. In it he criticised the attempts being made by individuals and groups, including Scarman, to make the police force more democratically accountable to local communities. While recognising Scarman's desire for 'responsible communications' between police and public, Anderton nevertheless repudiated many of the proposals which had been put forward as models for accountability. He argued that 'if some of the proposals were introduced the character of the British police would be changed for ever and life in this country would never be the same again'.[89] He went on to say that the police were now a prime target for subversion and demoralisation, that there was a danger that they would be turned into the exclusive agency of a one-party state and that the only defence against this process was to abolish police committees and run a totally independent police force. 'I sense and see, in our midst, an enemy more dangerous, insidious and ruthless than any faced since the Second World War'.[90] To combat this danger Anderton maintained that he and a handful of police chiefs were, 'the just men and saviours of Britain. . . The future of this country will be determined on an economic, racial, social and political basis by what happens in the major conurbations. There is no doubt of that. It is also self-evident that the success or failure of the police forces and chief constables in these crucial areas will determine how well the country survives'.[91] The chairperson of Greater Manchester's police committee, the Labour Councillor Peter Kelly dismissed Anderton's views as 'daft'. However, James Jardine, immediately issued a statement supporting Anderton's position. Clearly for the 100,000 members in the Federation for whom Jardine spoke, Anderton's views were not as 'daft' or unrepresentative of the police as Kelly seemed to think.

In Parliament, the Home Secretary was under daily pressure from his critics to produce something hard and constructive to deal with the problem of law and order. This pressure had increased with the release of the National Crime Statistics, three days after the Met's. These figures indicated that recorded crime in 1981 had jumped by 10 per cent from the preceding year. Some Conservative MPs called on Margaret Thatcher to appoint a 'get tough Minister for Crime'. Their chosen candidate was the hard-line disciplinarian Dr Rhodes Boyson. In one Parliamentary answer Thatcher herself had implicitly backed Anderton's remarks. Clearly, police pressure was beginning to pay off. On 18 March Whitelaw hinted that their campaign was indeed paying dividends. In reply to a question by Eldon Griffiths the Police Federation's Parliamentary spokesperson, Whitelaw intimated that he, 'hoped to be able to bring forward proposals that will implement some part of the plans of the Royal Commission on Criminal Procedure dealing with police powers'.[92] Within two weeks, the nature of these proposals was to become clear.

The police were now on the offensive. In a speech to police officers in Cardiff, James Jardine called on them 'to go to war' with criminals and criticised the abolition of the 'sus' law. In a critique of Scarman's proposals for consultation between police and public, Jardine maintained that genuine consultation was all to the good 'providing the people you consult with are on the same side and there is goodwill and a willingness to cooperate in maintaining the rule of law'.[93] Critics of the police were therefore to be marginalised and omitted from any consultative machinery in favour of those who in taking part in consultation procedures were 'on the same side' as the police. Scarman's proposal for a limited critical dialogue between the police and the public was cast aside. In the same speech Jardine also attacked Paul Boateng, the chairperson of the Greater London Council's Police Committee, which had been set up by the GLC to campaign for a democratically elected police authority for London. Boateng had maintained that the Metropolitan Police was 'riddled with racists' and that he agreed with Lord Scarman that any police officer found guilty of racist behaviour should be dismissed from the force. The Police Federation opposed this recommendation. Jardine was unmoved by Boateng's remarks. On the contrary, they gave him another chance to attack Scarman's report. Thus, he maintained 'that after Lord Scarman's report the accent was on consultation with the public. So far it looks as if all the effort is on one side, the police side, because there has been no let up in the trend of abuse and criticism of the police. We have the chairman of the GLC's so-called Police Committee ranting on about police racism and, at the same time, demanding that he should be put in charge of the Metropolitan Police. God forbid'.[94]

Boateng's speech indicated that the police were not having it all their own way. The General Secretary of the West Indian Standing Conference asked the Commission for Racial Equality about the possibility of taking legal action against the Metropolitan Police following the release of the criminal statistics. They hoped to do this under a section of the 1976 Race Relations Act. The Labour Party, in the form of James Callaghan, broke slightly with the incestuous and bipartisan approach to the policing of London by proposing a new London police authority made up of representatives from local authorities as well as the Home Office. The Met., he said, should no longer be accountable solely to the Home Secretary. The Labour Party's North West regional conference called for a public inquiry into the conduct of James Anderton. Within the police themselves there was conflict. John Alderson, the Chief Constable of Devon and Cornwall criticised Anderton's suggestion that the 43 police forces in England and Wales should be rationalised and collapsed into ten regional forces. These forces would be under the direct control of regional police commissioners. Alderson maintained that such theories about national police forces were 'based not so much on what is good for the people as what is good for the police'.[95]

These criticisms, while important, appeared to make little impact on the thrust of the debate. The police had constructed a campaign which had aimed to outmanoeuvre and undermine those who challenged their authority. At the same time in their speeches and comments they continually legitimated their own position as defenders of the rule of law and as the apolitical guardians of British democracy. They had used the crime statistics, and the public's fear of crime to achieve this goal. In their eyes it was they, and not Lord Scarman who should be dictating the direction and operational duties of the force.

The significance of the events of the previous weeks was spotted by two writers in a contribution to *The New Statesman.* They argued that in what had recently happened 'one can hardly see conspiracy, merely sequence. But there is a certain coherence to it. What we are witnessing is the police backlash against the Scarman report. It comes now because many of the reforms proposed by Scarman, such as an independent police complaints procedure, and police community liaison committees are now close to implementation. In particular, the Met.'s decision to leak its deeply misleading statistics on black crime in London is an attempt to regain the initiative lost by Scarman's imputation of racism in the force'.[96]

It was now up to Whitelaw to act. When he did, the police were not to be disappointed.

Police Powers: The Great Leap Forward

The week beginning 21 March was a crucial one for Whitelaw and, as it transpired, for the police too. The Home Secretary was due to attend a number of meetings where he would face his critics in the Conservative Party. He would have to answer their questions about his apparent failure to control crime and maintain public order. In answering them, he was also answering Margaret Thatcher, who appeared to be asking the same critical questions.

Whitelaw had started the week on a positive note. Sir Kenneth Newman, the former chief of the Royal Ulster Constabulary had accepted the invitation to become the next Commissioner of the Metropolitan Police in succession to Sir David McNee. The appointment was vociferously condemned most notably by Ken Livingstone the Labour Leader of the Greater London Council. Livingstone argued that if Newman employed his Ulster-style policing methods on the mainland then the working class areas of London would be devastated within five years.[97] Whitelaw stood firm. Newman would start on schedule on 1 October 1982. The hard man of Ulster was to be allowed to bring his own brand of policing to the streets of the nation's capital.

The Home Secretary's first meeting was with 115 backbench Conservative MPs, some of whom had been amongst his most severe critics. At the meeting he strongly defended his policies on law and order and ran through the familiar list of programmes which the Tories had introduced into the criminal justice system since their election victory in May 1979. The police force had increased in strength by 8,000. Expenditure had more than doubled in four years. Police pay was at an all-time high. There was to be a £500 million prison building and repair programme. New prisons were to be built at the rate of two per year over the next four years. The short sharp shock in detention centre regimes for young offenders was to become shorter and sharper. All of these, Whitelaw pointed out, were in fulfilment of the Conservative Party's election manifesto. As Home Secretary in the party committed to upholding the rule of law he had not failed—at least, not on paper. By the end of the meeting Whitelaw had pulled the Tory ranks in behind him. Although there were still the odd hard-line dissenters, Edward Gardner, the chairperson of the Conservative Backbench Committee described the meeting as 'the most remarkable demonstration for a Home Secretary one can remember'.[98]

Whitelaw had achieved his success in two ways. First, he revealed that the government and the police were preparing for a renewed outbreak of public disorder which was designed to mark the first anniversary of the 1981 street disturbances. The police, Whitelaw said, would 'go in hard' if such disturbances occurred. They would use the 'Snatch Squad' techniques utilised on the streets of Northern Ireland to identify and pull in those targeted as the ring-leaders. He reminded his audience that he was once Secretary of State for Northern Ireland and that the danger of further disturbances in London and elsewhere lay in what he called the 'anniversary technique' which the IRA employed there to mark significant political events.[99] If this was to be the case on the mainland then the police would react accordingly. Clearly the lessons he had learned in policing Ulster were not to be forgotten when it came to maintaining public order on the mainland.

Whitelaw's second tactic was to indicate that he intended to give more powers to the police. He gave no precise details as to what these new powers would be. His speech, however, was enough for James Jardine to comment that 'we would welcome anything the Home Secretary will do in legislation to strengthen the hand of the police'.[100] Eldon Griffiths, intimated that he had been given 'more than a hint that we will have a bill'.[101] Three days later Griffith's 'hints' had become facts as Whitelaw announced during a Parliamentary debate on law and order the exact nature and extent of the new police powers.

In the debate the Home Secretary said that he accepted the case put forward by the Royal Commission on Criminal Procedure for the extension of police powers. In particular, he proposed to give the police the power to stop and search individuals for offensive weapons. Furthermore, he intended to rationalise existing powers to stop and search for stolen goods. The police would also be able to search premises for evidence in what he loosely described as 'difficult cases'. They would be able to act in cases where they believed that there were 'reasonable grounds' for suspecting that stolen goods were concealed or that suspects had materials, the possession of which involved a criminal offence. These materials included drugs, firearms or housebreaking equipment.[102] Further to this he proposed to give the police power to search premises without a search warrant providing that there was authorisation by a police officer of at least uniformed superintendent rank. This new power overturned the existing law which stated that the police, at least in theory, had to obtain a search warrant before taking action. Finally, Whitelaw proposed to exclude from jury service anyone convicted of an imprisonable offence within the previous ten years. This was to be done even if no immediate sentence of imprisonment had been imposed on the individual accused. This change, which the government was subsequently to postpone until a later sitting of Parliament, had been principally advocated not only by judges who sat in the courts but by police chiefs as well. It meant, in practice, that literally millions of individuals would be excluded from jury service as many minor offences such as stealing a milk bottle or carving a name on a park bench were still liable for imprisonment. As such, 'to have excluded all these people from jury service would have meant disqualifying millions because every year over two million people aged over 17 are found guilty of indictable or summary offences'.[103]

In basing the extension of police powers on the recommendations of the Royal Commission on Criminal Procedure, Whitelaw had done what many critics of the Commission had feared. He had picked up the strand in the Commission's thought which had argued for the extension of police powers. However, as the critics pointed out, the Commission had not provided sufficient countervailing rights for either those accused or those suspected of committing a crime. Here, too, the hand of the police had been at work for the deliberations of the Commission itself have 'been accompanied by a concerted police campaign for further powers. McNee, the Metropolitan Police Chief, argued in his memorandum for a general power to hold suspects for 72 hours before charging, with the option of a further 72 hours with the agreement of a single magistrate'.[104] McNee's other demands had included the abolition of cautionings, an end to the right of silence during interrogation, a general power for the police to set up roadblocks in local areas and the compulsory fingerprinting of whole communities.[105]

McNee's proposals were probably representative of the thinking of the vast majority of police men and women in Britain. When the Commission finally reported in January 1981, many saw it as a triumph for the police. The evidence which the force had presented had won the day. Prophetically, a barrister, Paddy O'Connor, warned that with the publication of the report 'there is much to fear from the future'.[106] Another critic, Paddy Hillyard, was more direct, 'in place of the existing confusion concerning the extent of police powers, the Commission has introduced more confusion but only after extending police powers. . . the package will establish in England and Wales a far more repressive and professionalised and bureaucratised criminal justice system similar to the system in Northern Ireland'.[107]

Whitelaw's implementation of the Royal Commission's proposals was therefore an important success for the police. They were now to add significant new powers to the extensive ones which they already had available. In the Commons the Home Secretary's plans were supported by the Police Federation's Parliamentary voice, Eldon Griffiths. They were, he said, 'welcome steps forward'.[108]

Whitelaw's announcement coincided with the publication by the Law Commission of a working paper which called on the government to toughen up the law on public order. The paper argued that a riot should now be defined as 'three or more persons present together in public or private, engaged in an unlawful course of violent conduct'. The new statutory crime the Law Commission proposed which would take the place of the old common law offence against public order would carry a maximum jail sentence of 14 years. Unlawful assembly and affray would also cease to be common law offences and instead would have a new statutory basis. Any individual convicted of affray would be jailed for ten years; for unlawful assembly the penalty would be five years. At the same time as these proposals were put forward Conservative MP Nicholas Lyell, proposed that the courts should be empowered to order a curfew on young offenders aged between ten and 21. For individuals in that age-group the courts could order them to stay at home, indoors, from 6 pm to 6 am during the week and from noon to 6 am at weekends. This proposal was eventually to receive government backing and was introduced as a clause in the Criminal Justice Bill which was in its committee stage in Parliament. The Bill, itself, was designed to give more powers to the courts. In particular, the courts would be given the power to order parents or guardians to pay fines, compensation and costs incurred by their children or young people in their care. Clearly, the state was now turning the screw.

The success of the police force in their campaign to challenge Scarman meant that the Home Secretary ignored some of his report's most pointed criticisms of police operational practices. This was especially true of their stop-and-search operations. Scarman had criticised the police for their stop-and-search 'Swamp 81' operation in Brixton which was conducted prior to the disturbances. He called it a 'serious mistake'[109] and saw it as a major factor in the escalation of hostilities between the police and the local community, particularly, the black youth. Whitelaw disregarded this criticism. The rising crime rate and the maintenance of public order had taken precedence in Whitelaw's mind over Scarman's recommendations. The police had effectively marginalised Scarman's report through their law and order campaign. In the coming weeks, other proposals made by Scarman in the areas of police accountability and community relations were to receive the same treatment. Where Scarman had recommended statutory liaison committees between the police and local communities as one method of securing, in his view, some degree of accountability, Whitelaw introduced liaison committees in local areas which had no statutory basis. This left the police free to implement critical operational policies, such as the introduction of the Special Patrol Group into an area, without the possibility of any discussions between themselves and representatives of the area.

Scarman had also indicated that riot control equipment such as water cannon, CS gas and plastic bullets should be available in reserve for the police but that such equipment 'should not be used except in grave emergency'.[110] Again, however, the police were putting pressure on the Home Secretary to ignore these proposals. At the Scottish Police Federation Conference police leaders called for riot squads, armed with plastic bullets and armour-plated vehicles to be available in Scotland. While Scarman felt that probationary and in-service training for police officers was both too short and inadequate from the point of view of teaching officers to be skilful and courteous in their relationship with the public, the Federation, in a gross distortion of Scarman's recommendations indicated they would submit training requirements for the riot squads to a committee which had been set up by the Scottish Home and Health Department 'to review police training after the report of Lord Scarman on the Brixton riots'.[111] At the beginning of May, Whitelaw himself told the Police Superintendent's Association meeting in Torquay that they could no longer afford to be without water cannon, CS gas or plastic bullets. In the middle of the month the Home Office invited tenders for a prototype water cannon to be used by the Metropolitan police. At the same time, four West German police officers started a two week training programme for British police officers. The German officers were to instruct their British counterparts how to use the water cannon on board the two vehicles which were on loan from Germany. These officers would then 'instruct forces throughout the country'.[112]

Finally, during this period, the Police Federation in England and

Wales were holding their annual conference at Scarborough. In his final speech before retiring James Jardine gave the Federation's qualified support to Scarman's report. He intimated, however, that there were 'one or two points on which we have reservations'. These reservations, in fact, were substantial and involved some of the central recommendations in the report. The Federation, he said, totally opposed the suggestion that racial discrimination should become a specific offence under the Police Discipline Code.

They were also opposed to changes in the police complaints procedure. While Scarman had proposed an independent element in the complaints procedure, Jardine argued that it would be against the wishes of the Police Federation if an independent assessor was introduced to deal with serious complaints. Jardine supported Scarman's view that there should be better consultation between the police and the local community. There were qualifications here too. The police, he said, would be willing to consult with the public 'provided that the people with whom we consult are genuine representatives of the public and share our wish to maintain the rule of law'. Once again, Jardine had reiterated the force's belief that it was only those who observed the 'rule of law', that is those who were uncritical of police practices, who should be allowed to participate in consultation between police and public.

Basil Griffiths, the Federation's vice-chairperson, supported Jardine's criticisms. Some of the recommendations made by Scarman, he said, were 'arrant nonsense'. He maintained that areas such as Brixton were bound to be criminal because many of those who lived there came originally from Jamaica where, 'it is notoriously the case that it is unsafe to walk the streets alone at any time of the day or night because of the danger of assault and robbery'. Given this situation, Griffiths concluded that, 'amongst any immigrant population there will be imported into the host country, a significant measure of the typical style of criminal behaviour in the country of origin'. As if to back up his claims he also pointed out that 'the overwhelming majority of those who took part in [the] riots were black youths of West Indian descent'.[113]

Finally, the Conference heard from Fred Jones, a Merseyside policeman, who called for a new Riot Act to replace the one repealed in 1967. Jones maintained that the Act was needed to protect police officers in a riot situation. In saying this, he also attacked Scarman; 'It is all right for Lord Scarman to say that there is no need for a Riot Act. Lord Scarman is not out there. He lives in the cloistered seclusion of the Inns of Court.' Once the Act had been read out publicly by a Chief Constable or magistrate then if people got hurt it would be 'their hard luck'.[114] On that note, the Conference ended. The police wheel had come full circle.

Thus, in the six months since Scarman had published his report, the police had successfully conducted a campaign aimed at undermining the challenge to their power base posed by his major recommendations. Together with an uncritical press, an acquiescent Home Secretary and a largely impotent Labour opposition, they had, for the most part succeeded. In the course of this campaign, built around a set of highly dubious criminal statistics, and a readiness to foster the racist stereotype of the black, male mugger, police powers had been extended, riot equipment had been made available on a scale hitherto unknown and the threat of Scarman had been effectively neutralised. His report, from which everyone was eager to quote, was already gathering dust on the shelves of the Home Office by the time the Police Federation met at Scarborough. Scarman's notion that the report would be a blueprint for the future policing of the nation had proved to be fallacious. On the contrary, the politics of policing the future and maintaining social order would be a question to be determined principally by an increasingly authoritarian state mediating its policies through an equally repressive criminal justice and welfare system. The police, it would appear, seem destined to play a pivotal role in that process.

NOTES

1. S. Hall et al, 'Policing The Crisis', Macmillan, 1978.
2. Enoch Powell's speech Wolverhampton, April 1968, reprinted in, 'Freedom and Reality', Paperfront, 1969.
3. *The Sun,* 13 Sept. 1978, is typical of the imagery referred to, there are many other examples.
4. See *Crime and The Law, The Social History of Crime in Western Europe,* eds. Gatrell, Lenman and Parker, Europa, 1980. Especially chapters by Larner, Weisser and Davis.
5. P. Worsthorne, *Sunday Telegraph,* 29 Nov. 1981.
6. James Anderton, *Manchester Evening News,* 16 March 1982.
7. Alfred Sherman, 'Britain's Urge To Self-Destruction', *Daily Telegraph,* 9 Sept. 1976.
8. Martin Barker's excellent, *The New Racism,* Junction Books, 1981, is an exception to the left's failures. See also Errol Lawrence, 'The Roots of Racism' in *The Empire Strikes Back,* CCCS/Hutchinson, 1982.
9. Sir Kenneth Newman's views on the biological base of West Indian anti-authoritarianism can be found in the American *Police* magazine for January 1982 (Vol 5 no. 1). See also speech by Basil Griffiths vice-chairman of the Police Federation reported in *Police Review,* 28 May 1982.
10. See A. Sivanandan, *A Different Hunger,* Pluto, 1982. Especially Asian and Afro-Caribbean struggles, *From Resistance to Rebellion.* Also copies of *Race Today* for the period.
11. Paul Gilroy, 'Police and Thieves' in *The Empire Strikes Back, op. cit.*
12. Gus John and Derek Humphry, *Police Power and Black People,* Pan
    Gus John *Race and The Inner City,* Runnymede Trust 1972. Dr. S. Pullé, *Police/Community Relations in Ealing,* Runnymede/Ealing CRC, 1973. Joseph Hunte 'Nigger Hunting in England', West Indian Standing Conference 1964.

Institute of Race Relations, *Police Against Black People*, 1978.
13. Paul Gordon, *Passport Raids and Checks*, Runnymede, 1981.
14. Paddy Hillyard, 'From Belfast to Britain: Some critical comments on the Royal Commission on Criminal Procedure', *Politics and Power* 4, 1981. K. Boyle et al, *The Legal Control of Political Violence*, NCCL, 1980.
15. Gilroy, *op. cit.*
16. Faber 1971.
17. C. Hurt and co, 1978.
18. Kitson, *op. cit.*
19. Kitson, *op. cit.*
20. *Time Out*, 5 Sept. 1975, p. 3. *Searchlight*, November 1976.
21. *Police Review*, 19 March 1982.
22. Duncan Campbell, 'Society Under Surveillance', in ed. Hain, *Policing the Police*, Vol. 2, John Calder, 1980.
23. The tendency referred to is exemplified by the recent works of Jock Young, John Lea and Ian Taylor. Taylor's *Law and Order Arguments for Socialism* is the fullest exposition of this position, Macmillan, 1981. His article in *New Socialist*, 2 Nov–Dec 1981 also merits attention. Young and Lea also published in *New Socialist* Jan–Feb 1982. See also *Critical Social Policy* Vol. 1, No. 3, and *Marxism Today*, August 1982.
24. R.V.G. Clarke and K.H. Heal, *Police Journal* Vol. LII, No. 1, Jan–March 1979.
25. John Alderson, Chief Constable's Report, 1980.
26. Sir David McNee, Commissioner's Report, 1981.
27. One instance of this is the way in which Alderson was interviewed in *Marxism Today*, April 1982. Also M. Kettle, *Marxism Today*, October 1980.
28. The case of David Brooke is particularly interesting, see *Guardian*, 12 May 1981.
29. See Alderson's evidence to the Scarman Inquiry, 'The Case For Community Policing', p. xii.
30. Supt. David Webb, 'Policing a Multi-Racial Community', unpublished paper, West Midlands Police, 1978.
31. Supt. A. Lievesley, *Police Review*, 7 March 1980.
32. Scarman Inquiry, Day 6, 22 May 1981.
33. 'Guns for the Right', *World in Action*, Granada, July 1981. See also *Searchlight*, August 1981.
34. Scarman Report, para 8.63.
35. See note 23.
36. Webb, *op. cit.*
37. Stephen Humphries, *Hooligans or Rebels, an Oral History of Working Class Childhood*, Blackwell, 1981.
38. Jerry White, Campbell Bunk, 'A Lumpen Community in London Between the Wars', *History Workshop* 8, Autumn 1979.
39. Supt. L. Roach, *Police Studies*, Vol. 1, No. 3, 1978.
40. John Brown, 'The Function of Communities in Police Strategy', *Police Studies*, Spring 1981 and *Police Review*, 31 July 1981.
41. *Race Today* is the best single source of information on these confrontations for Southall see CARF, *Southall the Birth of a Black Community*, IRR 1981.
42. The examples of BASH (Blacks Against State Harrassment) and Southall's People Unite are the most obvious, Sivanandan cites numerous others in his, *Resistance to Rebellion*.
43. All those in note 23, plus Simon Frith in *Marxism Today* (Nov. 1981).
44. *Searchlight*, October 1981.
45. E. Schaffer, *Community Policing*, Croom Helm, 1980, p. 17.
46. *British Journal of Criminology*, Vol. 22, No. 2, April 1982.
47. 'The State of the Nation', reprinted in *Writing by Candlelight*, Merlin, 1979.

48. *Police*, February 1982.
49. *Police Journal*, Jan–March, 1982, Vol. LV No. 1, March 1982.
50. See Home Office Statistical bulletin 12 March 1982. Sparks, Genn and Dodd, *Surveying Victims*, Wiley, 1977.
51. Clarke and Heal (eds.), *The Effectiveness of Policing*, Gower, 1980.
52. For example, David Jones, *Crime, Protest, Community and Police in Nineteenth Century Britain*, RKP, 1982.
53. *Private Police*, Harvester Press, 1978.
54. See note 24.
55. *Police Review*, 12 March 1982.
56. R. Behrens, 'The Scarman Report: A British View', in *Political Quarterly*, Vol. 53, No. 2, April–June 1982, p. 122.
57. *The Brixton Disorders 10–12 April 1981*, Report of an Inquiry by the Rt. Hon. The Lord Scarman, Cmnd. 8427 HMSO para. 4.15.
58. *Ibid.*, para. 4.13.
59. 'The Scarman Inquiry into the Brixton Disturbances: Written Submission by Concern', July 1981.
60. P. Stevens and C. Willis, *Race, Crime and Arrests*, Home Office Research Study No. 58 HMSO.
61. N. Blake, *The Police, The Law and The People*, The Haldane Society, 1982, p. 53.
62. *Ibid.*
63. S. Hall, *Drifting into a Law and Order Society*, The Cobden Trust, 1980, p. 17.
64. Cited in M. Kettle and L. Hodges, *Uprising! The Police, The People and The Riots in Britain's Cities*, Pan Books, 1982, p. 208.
65. *Daily Mail*, 21 Jan. 1982.
66. *Daily Telegraph*, 4 Feb. 1982.
67. Cited in, *Runnymede Trust Bulletin* No. 143, May 1982, p. 6.
68. *Guardian*, 15 Jan. 1982.
69. *Hansard*, 21 Jan. 1982. C. 407–408.
70. *Hansard*, 18 Feb. 1982. C. 399–400.
71. *The Standard*, 26 Feb. 1982.
72. *Daily Mail*, 27 Feb. 1982. At this time the press were also covering the Terry May trial. Seven black youths were accused of murdering a crippled white youth, Terry May, during what the *Daily Mail* described as 'a revenge hunt for skinheads who had attacked black youths at Thornton Heath, South London'. The newspapers graphically described witnesses' accounts of black youths 'swarming' over the dead boy's body. Comparison between this coverage and the coverage given to attacks by white youths on black people is illuminating.
73. *The Standard*, 4 March 1982.
74. *Sunday Telegraph*, 7 March 1982.
75. *The Telegraph*, 8 March 1982.
76. *The Times*, 8 March 1982.
77. *Daily Mail*, 8 March 1982.
78. *Ibid.*, 9 March 1982.
79. *Ibid.*, 11 March 1982.
80. *Daily Express*, 11 March 1982.
81. *Guardian*, 15 March 1982.
82. There are major methodological problems with police criminal statistics. Some policepeople are beginning to recognise this (see above). The Lord Chief Justice and, a bit too late, Lord Scarman also touched upon the problems surrounding these statistics in the House of Lords debate on law and order in March. These serious problems are, however, rarely highlighted, least of all by the majority of policemen and policewomen.

83. *Daily Express*, 11 March 1982.
84. *Daily Mail*, 11 March 1982.
85. *Ibid.*
86. *Daily Mirror*, 11 March 1982.
87. *Daily Telegraph*, 12 March 1982.
88. *Guardian*, 12 March 1982.
89. Anderton's Text Speech.
90. *Ibid.*
91. Cited in *Daily Mail*, 17 March 1982.
92. *Hansard*, 18 March 1982, C. 473.
93. *Guardian*, 18 March 1982.
94. *The Standard*, 18 March 1982.
95. *The Times*, 18 March 1982.
96. *New Statesman*, 26 March 1982.
97. *Guardian*, 23 March 1982.
98. *Daily Telegraph*, 23 March 1982.
99. *The Standard*, 23 March 1982.
100. *Daily Telegraph*, 23 March 1982.
101. *The Standard*, 23 March 1982.
102. The police were already carrying out some of these practices. In January 1982, more than 20,000 police officers carried out a nine week exercise in which every garage in London and the Home Counties was searched ostensibly to look for an alleged cache of IRA explosives. Not a single trace was found (*Sunday Telegraph*, 17 Jan. 1982).
103. *Guardian*, 6 July 1982.
104. A. Friend and A. Metcalf, *Slump City, The Politics of Mass Unemployment*, Pluto Press, 1981, p. 165.
105. *Ibid.*
106. Cited in Blake, *op. cit.*, p. 52.
107. P. Hillyard, 'From Belfast to Britain: Some Critical Comments on the Royal Commission on Criminal Procedure', in *Politics and Power* 4, RKP 1981, p. 96.
108. *Hansard*, 25 March 1982, Col. 1132.
109. Scarman Report, *op. cit.*, para. 4.76.
110. *Ibid.*, paras. 5.72–5.74.
111. *Scotsman*, 30 April 1982.
112. *Daily Telegraph*, 18 May 1982.
113. *Police Review*, 28 May 1982.
114. Police Federation Press Release.

TWENTY-FIVE YEARS AFTER 1956: THE HERITAGE OF THE HUNGARIAN REVOLUTION*

Bill Lomax

'Without the heritage of 1956 there cannot be any real opposition or critique of the regime.'

Mihály Vajda

For many commentators in both East and West, 1981—the year of the crushing of Solidarity and the inauguration of military rule in Poland—was regarded not so much as the twenty-fifth anniversary of the ruthless and bloody repression of the Hungarian revolution of 1956, as the twenty-fifth anniversary of the birth of the Kádár regime, reputedly the most liberal political system in Eastern Europe, or 'the happiest barracks in the camp' as it is often called. At the same time, condemnation of the Polish coup was far more restrained than had been that of the Soviet invasion of Czechoslovakia in 1968.

'The assumption of power by the military', declared the former Hungarian prime minister András Hegedüs, a person often regarded as one of the leading representatives of liberal views in Eastern Europe, on 15 December, 'is both politically and sociologically understandable.'[1] 'General Jaruzelski's intervention', contended an article in the *Financial Times* on 19 December, 'offers the last, faint hope for the reform movement in Poland.'[2] General Jaruzelski, the press of both East and West was at pains to point out, had made clear his commitment to the continuation of reforms, and his willingness to seek an agreement with representatives of the independent trade unions. Even three months into military rule, the East European specialist of the *Guardian* could write, 'The Polish government still considers itself bound by the Gdansk agreements that launched Solidarity.'[3] The best hope for Poland, these commentators suggested, was for Jaruzelski to become a second Kádár, able to obtain for the Poles the optimum possible within the constraints and realities of their given geo-political situation.

*Bill Lomax's study *Hungary 1956* (London, Allison & Busby, 1976) was republished in Hungarian samizdat in 1981 on the 25th anniversary of the Hungarian revolution, together with numerous corrections and additions prepared by the translator György Krassó. The present article is a revised and extended version of the postscript written for a new Hungarian edition published by the author in 1982. The author and the publishers wish to express their appreciation to György Krassó for his considerable and valuable contribution towards the preparation of the present article.

The argument at first looked appealing, until the flaw in it was pointed out by those with a little more knowledge of Eastern Europe than the average British newspaper correspondent. The liberalisation Hungary enjoys today only commenced in the mid 1960s. In the immediate aftermath of the revolution's defeat, the Kádár regime had been installed through the merciless employment of mass terror and repression. Only after their spirit had been systematically broken, to be replaced by apathy, conformism and careerism, was it possible to entice the population with the lure of economic prosperity. The situation in Poland today, however, differs drastically from that of Hungary in 1956. In the present atmosphere of detente, force cannot be employed with quite the same ruthless brutality as a quarter of a century ago. At the same time, the crisis threatening the Eastern bloc as a whole prevents any immediate alleviation of Poland's economic problems. The two main planks of the Kádárist consolidation are thus denied the Polish junta.[4]

An interpretation of Kádárism that stresses the first six years of bloody and merciless repression can, however, be just as misleading as the more common one that pays heed only to the apparent achievements of the last fifteen years. If truth is to be told, then in the immediate aftermath of the Soviet repression of the revolution, the new Hungarian leader János Kádár spoke in terms very similar indeed to those employed by Jaruzelski today—expressing his commitment to the justified aims of the popular uprising, advocating the continuation of both economic and political reforms, and appearing ready to favour the installation, already in the winter of 1956–1957, of the more tolerant regime that came later to be embodied in his now well-known slogan 'He who is not against us, is with us.' Even if the prospects for such a development were heavily constrained by the political and social circumstances of the time, it would be naive to dismiss Kádár's position as one of mere expediency and political Machiavellianism. Indeed, a clearer understanding of the circumstances of the implantation of the Kádár regime, and of the main lines of its subsequent course, as well as the development of popular consciousness both as to the nature of the 1956 events and to the possibilities for future change, may well prove most instructive to any effort to understand what can be expected from the course of events in Poland after 13 December 1981.[5]

The Origins of the Kádár Regime

It is by no means certain that on the morning of 1 November 1956, when the Soviet Politburo took the final decision to invade Hungary and overthrow the government of Imre Nagy formed during the revolution, János Kádár was their first choice to be installed as the new leader of Hungary. After all, Kádár was the man who had already twice in his career disbanded the Hungarian Communist Party—first in June 1943, amid somewhat confusing circumstances following the dissolution of the Comintern, and again on 30 October 1956 at the height of the revolution. Announcing the formation of a new Communist Party, the Hungarian Socialist Workers Party, on 1 November 1956, Kádár had declared his opinion of the previous days' events as constituting 'a glorious uprising of our people' in which the Hungarian Communists had 'fought in the first ranks'. Earlier the very same day, he had told the Soviet ambassador, Yuri Andropov, direct to his face that if the Russians intervened again, he would take his place amongst the Hungarian workers in the streets and fight against the Soviet tanks, 'with my bare hands too, if I have to!'[6]

The Soviets' first choice to head the new Hungarian government was the veteran Communist Ferenc Münnich who, unlike Kádár, was known to them personally from his time as a Comintern functionary in Europe in the 1930s, as an officer in the Soviet army in the 1940s, and more recently as Hungarian ambassador to Moscow. It even seems probable that negotiations were held in Moscow on 2 November to form a government with Münich as prime minister, and that it was only the following day—after pressure from the Yugoslavs—that the Soviets changed their minds and installed Kádár as head of the government as well as Party leader. Even then, however, Münnich remained the main confidante of the Soviet leaders, and in many respects the person who, as minister in charge of the armed forces and state security, held the real power in Hungary in the first months of the Kádár government.[7]

Kádár and Münnich, however, were not the only Hungarian Communists who sought to form an alternative government in November 1956. In a curious and little-known incident, a small group of hard-line Stalinists headed by the Muscovite Andor Bérei and his wife Erzsébet Andics, who had earlier taken refuge from the revolution on 2 November in the Soviet embassy, established themselves in the town of Szolnok to the east of Budapest where, under the protection of the Soviet garrison, they tried to reform the old Hungarian Workers' Party formally dissolved by Kádár on 30 October, hoping that the Soviets would call on them to form the new government. They produced the Party's paper under its old name *Szabad Nép*—published daily from 6 to 11 November and distributed in the town by Soviet troops—even *after* the Kádár government had been installed in Budapest and Kádár's new party had recommenced publication of its paper *Népszabadság.* The Russians appear to have held them in reserve as a possible alternative to the Kádár regime. Only later were they to be arrested by the Soviet forces and deported to the Soviet Union, where they remained for almost one year before being allowed to return to Hungary.[8]

János Kádár had still been a member of the Imre Nagy government on 1 November, and had agreed with its decisions including the restoration of the multi-party system and withdrawal from the Warsaw Pact. In a radio broadcast that night he had called on the newly-formed democratic parties to help in consolidating the Nagy government, and declared, 'Our people have proved with their blood their intention to support unflinchingly the government's efforts for the complete withdrawal of Soviet forces.'[9] After that, however, he was not to be seen or heard from again until three days later, on 4 November 1956, when he returned at the head of a new government that had called for Soviet help to crush the revolution.

The full circumstances of how Kádár came to defect to the Russians, and of just where and how his new government was actually formed, remain shrouded in mystery. It seems established that late in the evening of 1 November he was prevailed upon by Münnich to go with him to the Soviet Embassy, and that he was flown out of Budapest either that same night or early the following morning, possibly to Prague or Moscow.[10] Just how willing he was at first to collaborate with the Soviets is unclear, but it is perhaps significant that the first announcement of the formation of the Hungarian Revolutionary Worker-Peasant Government, assuming responsibility for calling in the Soviet army, was made on the morning of 4 November—over the Balkan radio station of Radio Moscow—not by Kádár but by Münnich. It was only an hour later, and a good two hours after the start of the Soviet attack on Budapest, that Kádár too went on the radio to express his support for the Soviet intervention.[11]

Official Hungarian accounts report the Hungarian Revolutionary Worker-Peasant government as having been formed at Szolnok on 3 November, while Bérei and Andics' *Szabad Nép* reports Kádár's presence there on 4 November. But there is no independent confirmation of these claims and it is now widely accepted that on 4 November Kádár and Münnich were still on Soviet territory, and that their government was assembled at the town of Uzhgorod in the Soviet Carpatho-Ukraine. Some of its members had probably been taken there from Budapest, but at least one, the new minister of commerce Sándor Rónai, only heard of his inclusion over the radio, in the Hungarian parliament building on the morning of 4 November. All that is certain is that Kádár and his entourage did not return to Budapest until three days later on 7 November, when the government was formally sworn in by the Hungarian president István Dobi.[12]

While Kádár's government was established in Budapest under the protection of Soviet tanks, as the Soviet army sought swiftly and mercilessly to crush the remaining centres of armed resistance, there was no question at first of contesting the legitimacy of the revolution. For Kádár, the events had started as a peaceful 'mass movement' with 'noble aims' and 'genuine and legitimate demands'. His government took as its own the demands of this 'popular movement' and in the words of an official

Hungarian publication of February 1957, 'remained true to the government statement of 28 October', in which the revolution had been recognised as 'a great national and democratic movement'.[13] Kádár expressed his readiness to include in his government 'representatives of other parties and non-party persons loyal to our people's democracy', and his government's programme included commitments to 'national independence' and the eventual 'withdrawal of Soviet troops'. It was also declared that, 'the government will not tolerate the persecution of workers under any pretext, for having taken part in the recent events'. While 'the weakness of the Imre Nagy government' and 'the increased influence of counter-revolutionary elements,' were said to have endangered the socialist system and thus necessitated the Soviet intervention, Kádár would still for several weeks seek to maintain a distinction between, 'the popular uprising of 23 October,' and 'the counter-revolution that began on 30 October'.[14]

In this situation not all political freedoms were immediately suppressed, and both the Revolutionary Council of Intellectuals and the Writers Union continued to hold meetings and issue declarations supporting the revolution and condemning the Soviet intervention. New revolutionary journals appeared such as *Elünk* (We Are Alive) produced by the young students who had earlier published the popular paper *Igazság* (Truth), and *October 23* edited by the journalist Miklós Gimes who now became a key leader of opposition to Kádár.[15] Workers' councils also continued, and came to take on a far more political role than they had played before.

On 13 November delegations from several workers' councils met with Kádár who said he recognised them as 'the revolutionary organs of the working class,' and told them he too was in favour of 'the withdrawal of the Soviet troops. . . once order has been restored'.[16] As for the former prime minister Imre Nagy, who had taken refuge in the Yugoslav embassy, Kádár said it was completely up to him whether he returned to political life. He was not under arrest, and neither the government nor the Soviet troops had any wish to restrict his freedom of movement. The following day, when Kádár received a delegation from the newly-formed Central Workers' Council of Greater Budapest, he even told them that he was ready to, 'give up the Party's monopoly of power,' in favour of, 'a multi-party system and clean, honest elections'. Once again he assured them that no-one would be harmed for having taken part in, 'the great popular movement of the past weeks', and that he would be more than happy to meet and seek agreement with Imre Nagy if only the latter would leave his asylum in a foreign embassy.[17]

In these days Kádár met and talked with people of a wide variety of political viewpoints, even receiving the young journalist Gyula Obersovszky—now editing the semi-clandestine journal *Elünk*—to listen to his views on the need for honest newspapers to tell the truth. He continued negotiations with a view to broadening his government by bringing in representatives of the non-Communist parties or other non-party figures. Hints were even dropped that the government was thinking of offering ministerial posts to leaders of the Central Workers' Council.

The limits of Kádár's tolerance, however, were soon to be made clear. While he accepted the workers' councils as organs of factory self-management and was prepared to grant them decision-making powers, he adamantly resisted their requests for authorisation as a national organisation. When despite this the workers' leaders did call a conference for 21 November to establish a National Workers' Council, 400 Soviet tanks were sent to prevent it taking place. The value of Kádár's promises was also put in question when on 22 November, after the issue of a written note of safe-conduct and assurance that no action would be taken against them, Imre Nagy and his colleagues abandoned their asylum in the Yugoslav embassy—only to be seized by Soviet troops and taken the next day, against their will, to Romania.[18]

There must be some doubt as to who exactly was in charge of events at this point. Kádár is said to have been shaken—even desperate—on hearing of the abduction of Nagy, and that night the Hungarian government went into emergency session. But at least one member of his government must have been aware of the fate awaiting Nagy when he left the Yugoslav embassy, for four days earlier three other members of Nagy's entourage—György Lukács, Zoltán Szántó and Zoltán Vas, together with their wives—had left the safety of the embassy only to be seized by Soviet forces and held in custody at the Soviet Military Headquarters at Mátyásföld—where they had been visited on the night of 18 November by none other than the Hungarian deputy prime minister Ferenc Münnich. Is it conceivable that the abduction of Imre Nagy could have been arranged between Münnich and the Soviets, behind the back of the Hungarian prime minister?[19]

Further evidence for the possible insecurity of Kádár's position at this time comes from the report of a meeting he is said to have had a few days later with the Smallholders' Party leader Béla Kovács whom Kádár advised to go to the countryside and 'lie low'. Kádár, it is said, did not want to take action against the leaders of the political parties, revolutionary committees and workers' councils, but he now had no choice but to wind them up. He hoped that later, when the Russians had calmed down, many of the achievements of the revolution—even the restoration of the multi-party system—could be realised, but for the moment he had to do what the Russians wanted.[20]

Certainly in the following days Kádár was to do what the Russians wanted—stiffening his attitudes and resorting to repressive measures to destroy the remaining organised forms of popular resistance. In a radio broadcast on 26 November, he denounced the strikes and continuing resistance, declaring that democracy did not mean anarchy and disorder or freedom for counter-revolutionaries, specifically attacking as 'mindless agitators' Miklós Gimes, the editor of *October 23*, and András Sándor, one of Gyula Obersovszky's young co-workers on *Elünk*, and calling upon the workers councils either to support the government 'or shut up shop'.[21] At the beginning of December a special session of the Central Committee finally pronounced on the events of October as having been from beginning to end a 'counter-revolution of Horthyite fascists and Hungarian capitalists and landlords'.[22]

The Gloves Come Off

In the first days of December, government forces stepped up their efforts to regain control of the factories, arresting some 200 leading members of workers' councils. On 4 December a government decree abolished all revolutionary committees and similar bodies; on 5 December Miklós Gimes was arrested, and on 6 December Gyula Obersovszky. In reaction to this latest wave of repression, calls were raised for a new general strike, and the Central Workers' Council—now meeting in secret—prepared once again to create a National Workers' Council. In reply, on 9 December the government banned the Central Workers' Council, occupied its headquarters and arrested the majority of its leaders.[23]

These days also saw several confrontations in the countryside as government forces sought to restore their authority there too. The most serious occurred at Salgotarján on 8 December when Soviet tanks and Hungarian security forces fired on a crowd of several thousand miners protesting against the arrest of the leaders of their county workers' council—over 80 were killed and at least 200 wounded, amongst them many young workers and schoolchildren. In the following days similar disturbances and armed clashes occurred in other provincial towns, at Eger, Miskolc, Ozd and Kecskemet. On 11 and 12 December Budapest and the entire country was brought to a halt by a 48-hour protest strike against the government's new measures of repression. In reply on 11 December the government declared a state of emergency and banned the Revolutionary Council of Intellectuals as well as all territorial workers' councils. On 12 December a government decree introduced measures of martial law, and on 13 December a further one brought in internment without trial and established special courts of summary jurisdiction with powers that included the death sentence.[24] By mid-December the first summary executions under martial law were carried out.[25]

During November most of the work of repression had been carried out by Soviet military and security forces who took prisoners into custody and interrogated them, and in several cases carried out summary executions. Many prisoners were for a time deported to the Soviet Union, mainly to camps in the Carpatho-Ukraine, but following protests both in Hungary and abroad most of them seem to have been brought back.

From the beginning of December on, however, the new security forces formed by the Kádár regime—the notorious 'R-groups' or 'pufajkások' as they were called after their Russian-style jackets, many of whose members were recruited from the former state security forces as well as from amongst Greek and Yugoslav refugees in Hungary, and the special security force regiments formed from army officers and police units—became sufficiently well organised to take over much of the work of restoring order, and on 15 December the Soviet tank forces were withdrawn from Budapest's streets. By the beginning of January 1957 the Hungarian authorities had completely taken over the tasks of repression.

The more order was restored, however, the tighter the screw of repression was turned. In the first days of 1957 the leaders of the Bulgarian, Czechoslovak, Romanian and Soviet parties (the latter represented by Khrushchev and Malenkov) met with the Hungarian leaders in Budapest and urged them to yet sterner measures. In a speech on 5 January Kádár denounced the Imre Nagy government no longer just for weakness but for 'treachery', and declared that his government's main task remained the defeat of the counter-revolution. The same day a new decree restricted even further the rights of the workers' councils—giving the state the power to appoint factory managers and overrule the councils' decisions. In this situation most of the workers' councils still in existence, feeling they were no longer able to fulfil their duties to the workers, voluntarily disbanded themselves. The workers, however, continued to resist the latest encroachments of the state. On 11 January workers of the Csepel iron and steel works demonstrated against the return of management officials they had kicked out during the revolution. The intervention of the police led to scenes of violence in the streets, until Hungarian security forces and Soviet tanks were called in to restore order, opening fire on the crowd to leave at least one dead and several injured. On the same day a demonstration of 2,000 workers of the Köbánya vehicle repair works, protesting against the introduction of a new wage scheme, was also broken up by state security forces. The Revolutionary Worker-Peasant government replied to these continuing disturbances with a further wave of workers' arrests, and on 13 January issued a new decree speeding up the procedures of summary jurisdiction, widening the provisions of martial law, and extending the death penalty to striking or incitement to strike.[26]

The regime now also started to clamp down on the intellectuals. January 17 saw the suspension of the Writers' Union, to be followed on 20 January by that of the journalists. Then, on 19 January, two of the more well-known leaders of armed fighting groups during the revolution—the swashbuckling József Dudás, and János ('Uncle') Szabó who led the insurgents at Széna Square—were executed. On 26 January several prominent writers and journalists were arrested—amongst them Gyula Háy, Zoltán Zelk, Tibor Tardos, Balázs Lengyel, Domokos Varga,

Sándor Novobáczky and Pál Locsei.

Even at this stage, however, several figures who had played prominent roles in the revolution and in the resistance after 4 November still remained at liberty—such as Imre Nagy's minister of state István Bibó; the leader of the Revolutionary Council of Intellectuals György Adám, and the Central Workers' Council leader Sándor Bali (who had been released the day following his initial arrest together with Sándor Rácz on 11 December), as well as many active writers and journalists. At several places in the countryside, local leaders of the revolution like Attila Szigethy who had headed the Transdanubian National Council at Györ, and Rudolf Földvári at Miskolc who had played a leading role in the Borsod Workers' Council, not only remained at liberty but also continued to take an active part in local affairs. Even Imre Nagy and his colleagues, held under strict security at a Romanian Party holiday resort by the side of Lake Snagov outside Bucharest, were being treated with respect and looked after in quite a lavish way, while continuing approaches were made through Romanian Party officials to win their cooperation with the Kádár regime and their return to public life in Hungary.[27]

January 1957 also saw the appointment by the government of an Economic Reform Committee headed by the director of the Central Statistical Office György Péter with the job of drawing up a programme for the restoration of the economy on the basis of far-reaching economic reforms. In fact the Committee considered proposals for economic decentralisation that had been drawn up by revolutionary committees within the economic ministries in November–December 1956 and adopted by the Central Workers' Council of Greater Budapest, and though its final recommendations were considerably less radical than these, they had much in common with the ideas of the New Economic Mechanism to be introduced several years later in the mid-1960s.

There are thus several indications that at this time Kádár was still hoping to keep open the option of establishing his regime not as the order of open counter revolution that it would now rapidly become, but as one based on the original aspirations of 23 October, seeking to incorporate some of the aims, organisations and even people of the revolution within the post-revolutionary consolidation, and aspiring already in 1957 to the more tolerant and liberal political order that Kádár was indeed to introduce several years later. Such hopes, however, were finally laid to rest by the late spring of 1957.

Order was now returning to the streets of Budapest, production was slowly reviving, and though many feared the possible consequences of a new outbreak of rebellion in March on the anniversary of the 1848 revolutionary struggle against the Hapsburgs—symbolised in the slogan *MUK*: 'We'll begin again in March!'—little more occurred than a few, isolated street disturbances and demonstrations that were easily controlled by the police and security forces. In the last week of March Kádár led a government and Party delegation to Moscow, that negotiated a package of major economic aid to Hungary and agreed to the continued stationing of Soviet troops on Hungarian soil. It seems to have been at this point that the decision to abandon any prospect of a liberal and democratic development in favour of a more hard-line consolidation was finally taken.

April saw the recommendations of the Economic Reform Committee put on one side because the prevailing political conditions, as it was later to be explained, were no longer favourable to their implementation–'Time worked against the reform of the economic mechanism. . . (and thus) the development and introduction of the new economic model was dropped from the order of the day.'[28] On 14 April 1957 in Romania, Imre Nagy and his colleagues were arrested by Hungarian state security forces and brought back to Budapest in obvious preparation for their subsequent trial and execution. In Hungary a new wave of arrests brought a number of writers like Tibor Déry into custody, and in May the first trials of writers commenced. At Györ Attila Szigethy was arrested and later committed suicide in prison, while at Miskolc Rudolf Földvári was taken into custody and later sentenced to life imprisonment. And 23 May saw the arrest of István Bibó who would also, one year later, receive a life sentence.

The consolidation of the Kádár regime was formally confirmed with the parliament session of 9–11 May, and the final seal put on it with the special national conference of the Hungarian Socialist Workers Party of 27–29 June 1957 which issued the Party's definitive pronouncement on the events as having been from start to finish the result of a counter-revolutionary conspiracy.[29]

Arrests, trials and executions continued for another three years. In the course of this repression more than 20,000 people were imprisoned, or interned in the camps at Kistarcsa, Tököl and elsewhere. While intellectuals rarely received prison sentences of more than a few years, several workers' leaders–such as the Central Workers' Council President Sándor Rácz–received life sentences, while the Kádár regime showed least mercy to those workers who had fought with arms in hand against the Soviet tanks. István Angyal and Ottó Szirmai who had led the socialist-inspired fighting group in the Tüzoltó street, where they had continued fighting beneath a red flag against the Soviet tanks on 7 November, were executed in 1958, as was the 'red-capped' János Barány who had formed the Young Workers' League of Csepel and led the fighting group in the Tompa street. László Nickelsburg, a Jewish factory worker who had headed the armed group in Baross Square, was executed as late as 1961. There are even reports of youngsters being held in camps until they were eighteen when–no longer being juveniles–they could be executed. The total number executed, including both those sentenced under martial law and those convicted by civil courts, assessed on the basis of information from court proceedings, press reports and accounts of former prisoners, has been put as high as 2,000–2,500.[30] While the exact numbers are difficult to verify, it is clear that the reprisals were second only to the events in the wake of the Greek civil war in post-war Europe.[31]

The high point of the trials was the condemnation and execution of Imre Nagy, Pál Maléter, József Szilágyi and Miklós Gimes, officially announced on 17 June 1958. (Géza Losonczy had already died in prison while on hunger strike; Sándor Kopácsi was sentenced to life imprisonment and the other defendants received prison sentences ranging from 5 to 12 years.) Imre Nagy's execution, however, did not mark the end of the terror, for trials and executions were to continue up to 1 January 1960. (After that, death sentences for political crimes committed in 1956 were only carried out in 'exceptional circumstances'.) In 1959 in a mass trial of 33 members of the Ujpest Revolutionary Committee, that had played an important role both in the liberation of Cardinal Mindszenty and in the foundation of the Central Workers' Council of Greater Budapest, seven of the accused were sentenced to death and executed, while the remainder received a total of 300 years imprisonment.

Amnesties were announced in 1959, 1960 and 1963. The April 1959 amnesty related only to those who had received very short sentences, while the amnesty of March 1960 only covered persons sentenced to less than six years (most of them were approaching release anyway). While a number of people were released at this time by special pardon, amongst them the writers Tibor Déry and Gyula Háy, and Nagy's colleagues Ferenc Donáth, Ferenc Jánosi and Miklós Vásárhelyi, this measure was also used to free the hated secret police chiefs of the Stalinist Rákosi regime—Mihály Farkas, Vladimir Farkas and Gábor Péter!

In protest against the limited amnesty of March 1960 which was effectively restricted to former communist writers and politicians leaving ordinary workers in jail, and in protest against the release of Gábor Péter and Mihály and Vladimir Farkas, the several thousand political prisoners in the National Prison at Vác entered unitedly into a hunger strike. The strike was put down with most brutal reprisals, and its leaders received further prison sentences. In the so-called 'general amnesty' of March 1963 the majority of remaining political prisoners sentenced for participation in the revolution, reportedly some three thousand, were said to have been released, but in fact several categories of prisoners were excluded from the terms of the amnesty, amongst them all those convicted of murder (which included most of the street fighters), treason or espionage (an almost all-embracing category), and all those with any previous convictions (of whatever nature). At least four or five hundred thus remained in prison after 1963, and while many of these were released towards the end of the 1960s, some remained imprisoned until the early 1970s.[32]

The Police State with a Human Mask

When the Kádár regime launched its much publicised process of liberalisation in the 1960s, culminating in the inauguration of the New Economic Mechanism on 1 January 1968, amid the climate of cultural liberalism, wider availability of consumer goods and rising living standards, which for a time marked Hungary off as significantly freer and more prosperous than most other East European states, there were still political prisoners from 1956 in Hungarian jails. Before long they were joined by political activists of a younger generation, following the establishment in 1956 of an unofficial student committee to oppose the American war in Vietnam, that organised a number of demonstrations outside western embassies in 1966 and 1967. The hard core of the movement was made up of a group of left-wing student activists who were arrested at the beginning of 1968 charged with having formed an illegal Maoist party, and tried and sentenced in May 1968 on charges of conspiracy against the state, their leaders receiving prison sentences of from two to two-and-a-half years.[33]

In 1969 a young poet, György Szerb, was brought to trial and sentenced to eight months imprisonment for writing critical poems. In the spring of 1970 a student commemoration of the 100th anniversary of Lenin's birth was banned before it even took place, when it emerged that it was going to emphasise the 'wrong quotes' from Lenin, and two left-wing student activists, György Dalos and Miklós Haraszti, were placed under police surveillance, then subsequently arrested and sent to a labour camp when they refused to comply.

In 1973 the facade of cultural liberalism was further undermined when the most well-known of Hungary's philosophers and social scientists, amongst them András Hegedüs, György and Mária Márkus, Ferenc Fehér and Agnes Heller, Mihály Vajda, György Bence and János Kis, were dismissed from their academic posts, and Hegedüs, Vajda and Kis expelled from the Communist Party for their revisionist views. In May, Miklós Haraszti was arrested once again, for having written a book entitled *Piece Rates* (later published in English under the rather misleading title *A Worker in a Workers State*) that described his experience working on the shopfloor of the Red Star tractor factory in Kispest.[34] Brought to trial in the autumn on charges of incitement to subversion, Haraszti finally received an eight month prison sentence suspended for three years. In October 1974 the sociologist Iván Szelényi and the writer György Konrád were arrested when the police discovered the manuscript of their study on the intelligentsia as the new dominant class in Communist society, entitled *The Intellectuals on the Road to Class Power.*[35] Speedily released after a wave of international protests, they were immediately pressured to emigrate, which Szelényi eventually did.

But it is not only intellectuals who suffer persecution in Kádár's Hungary. While it is the case that since 1975 the regime has turned away from arrests and imprisonment to the more subtle administrative methods of sackings from employment and blacklisting from work, by the imposition of a *berufsverbot* and increasingly encouraged, when not enforced, emigration as a means of dealing with its dissidents, and while it is probably true that over the last eight years there has not been a single writer, artist or scholar of repute held in a Hungarian jail for political reasons, this does not mean that there are no political prisoners in Hungary any longer. On the contrary, according to official government statements and statistics in the late 1970s some 2–300 persons were brought to trial each year for crimes of an agitational character, the vast majority of them ordinary workers and peasants, of whom about two-thirds received prison sentences.[36] While the number has probably fallen in recent years, in 1981 the Chief Public Prosecutor admitted that sixty-five cases of anti-state crimes, the majority of them involving charges of sedition, had come before the criminal courts the previous year. Even more recently, however, there have been growing instances of young people sentenced to imprisonment for objecting to compulsory military service on religious and conscientious grounds.[37]

All this means that while Hungary today has travelled far from the Stalinist state it was before 1956, while it is by no means accurate to characterise it any longer as a totalitarian society—in which the state seeks to politicise and regiment all aspects of individual and social behaviour—it is still a police state of arbitrary rule, in which the individual enjoys no liberties as of right, and has no means of self-defence against the arbitrary and uncontrolled powers of the authorities. This situation is well-illustrated by the rights of Hungarian citizens to travel abroad, something which the vast majority of them appear to enjoy to a greater extent than the citizens of most other Communist countries. According to Hungarian law, 'Every Hungarian citizen has the right to a passport and to travel abroad.' This right, however, is not quite what it at first appears to be, for the very same law goes on to stipulate, in a later paragraph, that a passport will be denied to anyone 'whose travelling abroad. . . is deemed to be against the public interest'.[38]

Thus, and without further reason, the authorities can deny the right to travel abroad to anyone whom it suits their purpose. Each year in fact over 10,000 Hungarian citizens do have their requests for travel to the West rejected. Moreover, the person so denied his/her constitutional rights and liberties has no right to appeal, nor even to an explanation of in what way his/her travelling abroad is deemed to be 'against the public interest'. Indeed, in a recent judgment, the Hungarian Supreme Court has ruled that it has no authority to examine the lawfulness of such decisions which lie within the sphere of competence of the organs of state security.

The Kádár regime thus presents its human face to those it pleases, or rather to those who please it. The opportunist, the careerist, the conformist and the coward has now learned how best to work the system, how to gain the benefits and privileges that the regime is prepared to hand down to those prepared to play the game according to its rules, to those prepared to stand in the service of the rulers. But those who are not prepared to abandon their self respect, their personal integrity and moral values, or their solidarity with their fellow men and women, those who seek to lead a life of their own making and deny the conduct of self-alienation demanded by the state, or those whom for whatever reason of its own choosing the regime decides not to smile upon, they can be denied all rights and find themselves faced with the total and arbitrary powers of the monolithic police state.

Since the mid-1970s the rise of a wider democratic movement and, in particular, of a new generation of young Hungarians who have grown up since 1956 without personal memories of the revolution or of the terror and repression both before and after it, has led to an ever wider dissent from the consumer socialism and liberalisation within limits of the Kádár regime. Rejecting the conformism of their parents and the compromises made by the older intelligentsia after 1956, this new generation has asserted their right 'to think and behave in a different way' and to enjoy personal freedom and material well-being not on the arbitrary licence of the authorities but as their fundamental and inalienable human rights. As a result the numbers of young persons sacked from their jobs and blacklisted from further employment has grown constantly over the past years while, apart from those particularly well-known in the West, almost all the leading dissidents have been denied the freedom to travel abroad, and many with passports have had them withdrawn.

The number of persons discriminated against in this way has risen significantly over the past two years as a result of the attempt to punish and prevent people from expressing their solidarity with the independent workers' movement in Poland. At the height of the Gdansk strike in August 1980, seven leading dissidents went to Budapest airport in an attempt to fly to Poland and express their support for the strikers. All seven were prevented from travelling and had their passports confiscated. Of others who succeeded in travelling to Gdansk, a further three had their passports withdrawn on their return. Of many more young Hungarians who visited Poland over the following sixteen months, often making contact with *Solidarity,* several had their passports confiscated on their return, and at least one was sacked from his job. Others, who had already made known their support for *Solidarity,* were prevented from leaving Hungary and had their passports confiscated on the border.

On 4 October 1981 another passport confiscation occurred when the 57-year old lawyer Tibor Pákh, a veteran campaigner for human rights, was prevented from travelling to Poland by train. Tibor Pákh had already been imprisoned in 1960 for publicising the cases of Hungarian juveniles executed after 1956, while in spring 1980 he had joined the hunger strike in the Podkowa Lesna church in Warsaw against the imprisonment of the head of the Polish independent publishing house *NOWA*. Returning to Budapest, on 5 October he lodged a complaint with the Procurator General's office, and on 6 October started a hunger strike in the University Church in the city centre. Three days later he was forcibly taken by the police to the National Hospital for Mental and Nervous Illnesses where he was forcibly fed, and given heavy doses of psychotropic drugs affecting the central nervous system. Already in the late 1960s Tibor Pákh had been confined to a mental hospital and given electric shock treatment for his protests against the continuing detention of political prisoners in Hungary. Now he was being administered haloperidol, one of the drugs used to treat political dissidents in the Soviet Union.[39]

After an appeal signed by 57 Hungarian intellectuals, and protests from Amnesty International, Tibor Pákh was released on 26 October 1981. It is, however, a telling comment on the progress made by the Kádár regime since 1956 that on the very twenty-fifth anniversary of the revolution a Hungarian intellectual should be found confined in a mental hospital, being administered drugs more commonly heard of in connection with the repression of political dissent in the Soviet Union, for the crime of having wanted to travel to a neighbouring socialist country.

Beyond the Bolshevik Model

In the immediate aftermath of 1956 the dual impact of imprisonment and emigration resulted in the fact that for several years there was little or no articulate criticism of the regime. The intellectual figures of the revolution, those who were not executed, were either imprisoned or had fled to the West. Even after the imprisoned were released, many were relegated to silence and their names are still largely unknown to the Hungarian public today.

The more radical and far-reaching ideas developed within opposition circles were also for long to remain unknown. It was only in the later 1970s that the ideas of István Bibó, the left-wing political thinker appointed as minister of state in Imre Nagy's final government, began to gain a limited circulation in certain intellectual circles. Even then few knew that in the very midst of the revolution he had produced a critique of the idealist and totalitarian elements in orthodox Marxism that foreshadowed many of the ideas to be advanced twenty years later by the first dissident philosophers to break with the Marxism of the 'Lukács school'.[40] The radical critique of the ideology and practice of Marxist-Leninism developed in the *Hungaricus* pamphlet—written clandestinely in December 1956—was equally unknown, until it was rediscovered and published in samizdat in 1981.[41]

It is thus hardly surprising that the first stirrings of opposition to emerge under the Kádár regime showed little influence of the revolution in ideas that the experience of 1956 had occasioned in many at the time. The first significant opposition to appear was provided by a hard-line student group of Maoist sympathisers in the mid-1960s who set up a clandestine party organised on strictly Leninist lines, condemning in neo-Stalinist terms the revisionism of the Khrushchev era, and charging the Kádár regime with the abandonment of socialism and Marxist principles. Despite its orthodox terminology, student Maoism—as the first and only possible focus of dissent—soon became a rallying point for a far wider gathering of left-wing and rebellious youth. Its radical egalitarianism, and its challenge to the right of a small privileged establishment to monopolise the political process to the virtual exclusion of the rest of society, encouraged exactly those democratic and libertarian sentiments that would later come to challenge many aspects of traditional Marxist thought.

A second oppositional tendency developed in the late 1960s when the more moderate or reformist wing of the student movement came to support the ideas and principles of the Dubcek experiment in Czechoslovakia, looking to the newly introduced Hungarian economic reforms as the first steps in a similar direction in Hungary, and struggled to transform their own student bodies into effective forums of direct democracy. When the Soviet invasion of August 1968 put an end to the reform movement in Czechoslovakia, it was the earlier opponents of the Maoists, the defenders of Marxist reformism, who joined with them in attacking the Brezhnev doctrine and calling for a more radical democratisation of socialist society.

The invasion of Czechoslovakia also had a crucial impact on an older generation of intellectuals who had till then provided a 'loyal opposition' to the Kádár regime—the so-called 'Budapest school' of philosophers and sociologists influenced by the ideas of György Lukács and András Hegedüs—in the belief that existing East European states were essentially socialist in structure, needing only political and economic reforms to turn them into more humane and democratic societies. The crushing of the Czechoslovak experiment, and the halting in turn of the Hungarian economic reforms, undermined the belief that existing East European societies were even capable of further development at all, and cast doubt on the value of the previously favoured ideologies of Marxist humanism and market socialism.

It was two of the younger members of the Budapest school, György Bence and János Kis—the 'Lukács kindergarten' as they now came to be called—who, breaking with the almost unquestioning loyalty of their teachers to the central tenets of Marxism, and challenging some of the ideas of Lukács himself, carried out the most far-reaching critique of hitherto prevailing Marxist orthodoxy. Under the pseudonym Marc Rakovski in a book first published in the West in 1977 entitled *Towards an East European Marxism* they advanced the thesis that existing East European societies were neither socialist nor capitalist, nor even societies transitional between the two, but class societies of an entirely new type unenvisaged in traditional Marxist theory.[42] These societies of 'actually existing socialism'—as they now preferred to call them—had proven capable of stabilising and consolidating themselves, of fragmenting and depoliticising the working class, and even winning a certain degree of popular legitimacy. This view not only ruled out the possibility that these regimes might be transformed into more democratic or truly socialist ones by processes of internal reform; it also rejected any prospect that they might collapse or be overthrown in the immediately foreseeable future. To come to terms with this situation, they argued, the opposition should step down from the heights of theoretical construction and intellectual judgment, and concern themselves more with the practical everyday problems facing people in the societies of 'actually existing socialism'. In a postscript to their book written two years later, Bence and Kis outlined their ideas further and advocated a strategy of 'radical reformism' having much in common with the ideas then being developed in Poland by Adam Michnik and Jacek Kuron.[43]

These concerns were accompanied by a growing willingness to criticise the more utopian elements in Marxism, and to reject the belief in universal truths and real social interests, as opposed to the particular beliefs and actually recognised interests of existing people themselves. The democratisation of thought led in turn to the democratisation of action—to the rejection of Bolshevik-style political practice, of the belief that an intellectual vanguard is justified by its advanced consciousness in acting on behalf of, and in the name of, often indeed in place of, the people. This fundamental reappraisal of Marxism and commitment to the most democratic possible forms of action was most clearly expressed by the philosopher Mihály Vajda who argued that: 'If we wanted to proclaim a programme without being authorised to do so, we would be no better than the men in power now. Intellectuals are only justified in drawing up a programme when a movement emerges whose demands they can express and formulate.'[44]

The 1970s had already seen the growth of a wider dissident cultural movement that in several respects incorporated many of the values now being discovered by the intellectuals. Partly reflecting the late 1960s' youth and student movement in the West, Hungary had seen the development of pop music and experimental theatre, avant-garde trends in the arts, and even attempts to stage 'happenings' and set up communes. Some of the former Maoist students played leading roles in these activities, while it was from the members of the younger generation who participated in them that a wider movement began to develop in opposition to the repressive and conservative social and cultural traditions of Hungarian society that the Communist regime had served, if anything, to strengthen. When the government proposed to introduce a new law in 1973 severely restricting the right to abortion, over 1,500 signatures were collected for a petition against it.

When the young writer Miklós Haraszti was arrested and brought to trial in the autumn of 1973 for his book describing his experiences on the shopfloor of a Budapest factory, his trial provided the common ground on which the various sections of the previously divided opposition—the Maoist leftists, the reformist Marxists, the disciples of Lukács, the dissident sociologists, the counter-cultural youth—could finally come together and publicly express their solidarity in demands for an end to censorship and for greater freedom of expression. The trial also resulted in a step-down by the regime—after several postponements, and owing in part to growing international attention, Haraszti was released, receiving only a suspended sentence.[45]

The Haraszti trial created the unity, and the sense of a common purpose, that provided the basis for the growth of a wider movement concerned less with ideological questions such as had so far characterised the Hungarian opposition, than with the assertion of democratic rights and liberties, and a concern for the existential problems of personal and social life in the actually existing social order. Many of the young people who now became involved in this movement were students who had taken part in the late 1960s and early 1970s in sociological researches directed by leading sociologists like András Hegedüs, István Kemény and Iván Szelényi, in the course of which they had become well-informed about and sensitive to social problems, and in particular to the situation of the most underprivileged members of the existing socialist order. (Many of them would later become involved in the work of *SZETA*, the *Foundation to Assist the Poor,* formed in 1980 to raise funds and campaign against poverty in a country where it is officially declared not to exist, but where their own researches had shown at least a fifth of the population to be living below the poverty line.)

Stimualted by the examples of *KOR* in Poland and *Charter 77* in Czechoslovakia, this new generation of dissidents gave birth to a fledgling samizdat movement that would within five years develop into a fully-grown democratic opposition movement. Less widely known is that one of those who did much to encourage and spur them on was the lifelong revolutionary socialist Ilona Duczynska, who had attended the Zimmerwald conference of anti-war socialists in 1915, and become a founding member of the Hungarian Communist Party in 1918. Half a century later, attending the Haraszti trial in Budapest, she became acquainted with many of the younger oppositionists to whom she served as a moving inspiration, and in many ways she acted as a founding member of the Hungarian democratic opposition too.[46]

The samizdat movement continued the ongoing critique of previously held political and philosophical standpoints, emphasising the need for a radical democratisation of society and the assertion of human rights, for the rejection of opportunism, self-censorship and reformist compromises. In this regard, Miklós Haraszti spoke for many when he declared: 'If a society of free individuals is possible, then at least one thing is certain, that only free individuals can bring it about.'[47]

One question, however, remained as much a taboo for the opposition as it did for the regime and that was 1956, still hardly a topic dear to the opposition's heart. Neither former Maoists, nor reformist Marxists, had stood on that side of the barricades, and many who had opposed the Soviet invasion of Czechoslovakia had not seen fit to condemn the repression of the Hungarian 'counter-revolution'. The members of the Budapest school, just like their master György Lukács, had also been little more than ambivalent towards the revolution. As late as 1978 Mihály Vajda could assert that, 'the events in Czechoslovakia in 1968. . . were more important for us than was 1956', while another young philosopher explained that for many in the opposition '1956 is already history' and represents 'only a fiasco which must be forgotten'.[48]

By the summer of 1980, however, it was becoming increasingly difficult to forget about 1956, for not only was the twenty-fifth anniversary of the revolution approaching but in nearby Poland the spectre of an autonomous working-class movement was rising once again to challenge the right of a small, self-appointed elite to maintain its undemocratic monopoly of power and privilege over and above an entire society. In looking towards Poland in 1980–1981 the Hungarian opposition found itself face to face with its own heritage of 1956.

The Return of 1956

In its pursuit of truth and self-discovery the Hungarian opposition was inevitably to find 1956 continually propelled anew into the centre of its interests and concerns. It is no accident that one of the first authors to be published in samizdat should have been a minister in Imre Nagy's government sentenced to life imprisonment after the revolution, István Bibó, nor that the ideas of this outstanding political thinker, even after his death in 1979, should have continued to provide one of the major sources of inspiration to the opposition movement. Bibó's writings and example, more than those of any other Hungarian thinker, most clearly embodied both the spirit of 1956 and that of the new democratic movement of the later 1970s. His attraction for the younger generation in particular is perhaps best explained by the fact that he was almost the only significant, creative intellectual who, choosing to remain in Hungary after 1956, never made any form of concession to the regime, and never gave way to any form of pressure.

Following Bibó's death in 1979, the samizdat movement undertook its most ambitious project with the publication of a 1001-page *Bibó Memorial Volume* completed in 1980 which assembled articles by 76 authors written in his memory, many of them dealing with issues directly related to the 1956 revolution. Several of the contributors had themselves been imprisoned after 1956 for their actions during the revolution, and one of them, the former Communist politician and close colleague of Imre Nagy, Ferenc Donáth, took the opportunity to argue that Bibó's radical conception of direct democracy, first developed during the post-war democratic coalition period of 1945–48, was also the very essence of the demands of the revolutionary committees and workers' councils in 1956.[49]

By this time, many were coming to recognise that the developing workers' movement in Poland in 1980–1 also had much in common with the more radical features of the Hungarian revolution. As István Kemény, a sociologist who had carried out many studies into the working class in Hungary and emigrated to the West in 1977, now remarked, 'Autumn 1980 is the continuation of 1956,' and in his view, with the independent trade union *Solidarity* the Polish industrial working class had established a sovereign working-class power the like of which had only once before been seen in the Communist world—in Hungary twenty-five years before.[50]

Within this situation an increasingly open interest in 1956 began to find expression in Hungarian samizdat. Already in 1979 the revolution had been one of the topics discussed in a lively political essay by 'Libertarius' on the history of radical alternatives in Hungarian society entitled *Hungary 1984?* March 1980 saw the appearance of the first samizdat journal, the *East European Observer,* which published a collection of eye-witness reports of the revolution written at the time by East European journalists. Writers like Mihály Vajda and György Konrád now also turned their concerns to the issues of 1956, while the revolution came to be a topic inspiring considerable interest and debate in unofficial seminars and at sessions of the highly-successful 'free university' which had been operating in private flats since September 1978. The present writer's study *Hungary 1956* was translated into Hungarian and issued in samizdat, together with many additions and corrections prepared by the translator and other survivors from the revolution. The *Hungaricus* pamphlet, possibly the first ever Hungarian samizdat written clandestinely in December 1956, was also now republished. A new samizdat journal, the *Hungarian Observer,* the first unofficial duplicated journal to appear in Hungary for several decades, had commenced publication in April 1981 and its sixth number in October was devoted to a detailed chronology of the events of 1956.

Finally, on 19 October 1981, the regular free university lecture was followed by the first ever public commemoration of the 1956 revolution. In an introductory address György Krassó, himself an active participant in the revolution who had been imprisoned for eight years afterwards, declared that in 1956 the Hungarian people had overthrown an anti-democratic ruling clique and attempted to build a new society, thereby demonstrating the truth that it lies within people's power to change the course of their lives by their own efforts, and that social action can indeed have value. The historian Miklós Szabó then delivered a short speech in which he argued that, while the demands of the revolution had not been realised, if life was freer in Hungary in 1981 than elsewhere in the Eastern bloc, this was before all else due to the struggles of 1956. The meeting ended with a poem by the popular but banned poet György Petri dedicated to the memory of the revolution.

Hungary 1956–Poland 1980–1

As comparisons were increasingly made between the Polish developments of 1980–1 and the Hungarian events of 1956, the question also came to be raised whether the Polish events would find an echo in Hungary and whether they might lead to a re-emergence of the spirit of 1956.

Unlike Poland, Hungary had not seen any major resurgence of working-class struggles since 1956, this being due not only to memories of the savage repression after the revolution, but also to the undoubted success of the Kádár regime, at least till the mid-1970s, in achieving a gradual, if slow and uneven, rise in living standards. It had succeeded in fragmenting and depoliticising the working class to such an extent that the opposition theorists György Bence and János Kis had been led to conclude that the workers no longer constituted a potential base for social change. At the same time, however, Hungary's economy, highly dependent on foreign trade, had been severely hit by the oil crisis of 1973–4; by 1978 it had attained a record trade deficit, and in 1980 actually experienced negative growth. With living standards starting to fall, the Hungarian working class began to feel the pinch of economic stagnation and the decline of its earning power.

At the time of food price rises in the summer of 1979, workers of the Csepel iron and steel works had symbolically placed a piece of bread and dripping in the hands of the Lenin statue outside their factory. Following the Gdansk strike in August 1980 there were reports in Budapest, 'that there had been some stirrings amongst the workers in Csepel too'. Other rumours spoke of a three-day stoppage, and that, 'Kádár himself went there to put things right'. A month later planned price rises in Hungary were withdrawn at the last moment–in the opinion of one worker questioned about the influence of the Polish events, 'because they were scared that there would be some resistance here too.'[51] The spring of 1981 also saw meetings in several Hungarian universities calling for the establishment of an independent student organisation—again recalling memories of 1956.[52]

Reflection on the Polish events led many people to rethink and reassess the possibilities that might have existed in Hungary twenty-five years before. Though the regime still officially considered the events a counter-revolution, no less a person than the Party first secretary János Kádár had in May 1972, on the occasion of his sixtieth birthday, seen fit to question this official interpretation, declaring that:

> There is another interpretation as well, one which all of us could accept: what happened was a national tragedy. A tragedy for the Party, for the working class, for the people as a whole and for individuals as well. We took a wrong turning, and the result of this was a tragedy.[53]

The obvious implication of this reassessment was that if only the right turning had been taken, the tragedy could have been avoided. If Rákosi had been replaced in July 1956 not by the equally-Stalinist Gerö but by Kádár, and if the way had been prepared for a return to power by Imre Nagy, then 'de-Stalinisation' could have been carried out in a controlled way and the tragedy of the revolution would never have happened. This was certainly the view of Tito and the Yugoslav Communist leaders in 1956, and by some accounts that of the Soviets too.[54]

At the height of the Polish crisis, a similar view came to be advanced from a rather unexpected quarter, from András Hegedüs who had been the Hungarian prime minister at the time of the October uprising—and who at that time had condemned the events as a counter-revolution and supported the Soviet intervention—but who had later become an outspoken critic of the Kádár regime and of the Soviet invasion of Czechoslovakia in 1968. If in July 1956, Hegedüs now argued, the Hungarian leadership had stood down and handed over power to Nagy and Kádár, a compromise could have been reached between the regime and the people, and a peaceful way opened to a more democratic and pluralist society. The Hungarian Stalinists' stubborn resistance to change, however, had led to a polarisation of the situation which resulted in the raising of unrealistic and unrealisable demands for Hungarian withdrawal from the Warsaw Pact and the establishment of a multiparty system, ending in the catastrophe of October and November 1956.[55]

1981 in Poland, for Hegedüs, presented a second chance to realise that 'historical compromise' the opportunity for which had been missed in 1956. If the regime would recognise the necessity for sharing power with society, and if the workers' movement would accept the need to reach a working relationship with the authorities, then the stage would be set for the building of a new model of socialism, avoiding the false alternatives of either the one-party dictatorship or a multi-party system, and creating 'a pluralist political society without a multi-party system.'[56] The main obstacle to reaching such a historical compromise, Hegedüs saw in the collapse of state power and the development of a situation of anarchy that might end either in civil war or foreign intervention. Consequently, when General Jaruzelski declared martial law on 13 December 1981, Hegedüs' first reaction was one of qualified support, declaring that the assumption of power by the army should not be understood as a military putsch but as the necessary restoration of state power that could no longer be assured by the Party.[57]

While views similar to those of Hegedüs may have found a certain echo amongst more than a few intellectuals who had feared a hardening of the regime in response to the Polish events, and amongst those sections of the population who feared most that a spread of the Polish disease might undermine their own recently acquired prosperity, the reaction of the Hungarian opposition to the course of events in Poland, both before and after December 1981, was to be far more radical and uncompromising. For many of them the rise of *Solidarity* showed that the hopes and aspirations of 1956 had not been merely rash illusions, that the demands and struggles of the Hungarian workers and intellectuals were not only justified but realisable too, that, in the words of Mihály Vajda: 'The liberal absolutism of the Kádárist consolidation is not the maximum that can be achieved in Eastern Europe.'[58]

Even after the coup, it is still widely felt that–after sixteen months activity–*Solidarity* will be far less easily crushed than was the spontaneous workers movement in Hungary in 1956, and that the prospects for a Kádár style consolidation in Poland are far from auspicious. 'If we were lovers of the old-time slogans of the Communist International,' declares the opposition journal *Beszélö* (News from Inside) in its first issue since December 1981, 'we could now triumphantly announce that the proclamation of the state of emergency marks not the end of the Polish crisis, but the beginning of the generalised crisis of the East European system.'[59]

After 1956 and 1968, argues János Kis in a considered analysis of the immediate prospects now facing Eastern Europe, it was enough to re-establish forcibly the authority of the one-party state to restore the *status quo,* while economic aid from the Soviet Union and the other countries of the Eastern bloc was sufficient to restore living standards and make up for the loss of production. In 1982 the Polish situation will not be so easily resolved for now the whole region battles with the same crisis. Nothing will ever be the same as before, for with the military takeover of power in Warsaw, the entire post-Stalin epoch is drawing to a close. In this situation, he concludes, the Hungarian opposition will have to prepare itself to face up to new challenges and to assume new responsibilities.[60]

NOTES

1. 'Weder Bürgerkrieg noch Invasionsgefahr—Ein Gespräch mit Ungarns Regimekritiker Hegedüs, *Die Presse,* Vienna, 15 December 1981.
2. Ian Davidson, 'Jaruzelski: Poland's last faint hope', *Financial Times,* London, 19 December 1981, p. 15.
3. Hella Pick, 'How to repair Poland's shattered dreams of freedom', *Guardian,* London, 19 March 1982, p. 8.
4. See Miklós Haraszti, 'Spectre of Kádár may force the hand of Jaruzelski in Poland', *Guardian,* 27 January 1982; and 'On the Deck of the Titanic?' (Editorial to *Beszélö* (News from Inside) No. 2, samizdat journal, Budapest, Jan. 1982) in *Labour Focus on Eastern Europe,* London, Vol. 5, No. 3, Summer 1982.
5. The present essay does not pretend to be a study of Kádárism as a system, but only to deal with certain selected aspects of it. For attempts to interpret Kádárism in the wider sense, see Ferenc Fehér, 'Kádárism as the Model State of Khrushchevism', *Telos,* St. Louis, No. 47, Summer 1979; Mihály Vajda, 'Is Kádárism an Alternative?' in Mihály Vajda, *The State and Socialism,* London Allison & Busby, 1981; and Miklós Haraszti, 'A Belated Introduction into Kádárism', serialised in *Corrierle della Sera,* Milan, June–July 1981.
6. Kádár's behaviour is reported by an eye-witness, György Heltai, 'Imre Nagy au Parlement', in Péter Gosztony (ed.), *Histoire du Soulèvement Hongrois 1956,* Paris, Editions Horvath, 1966, p. 182.
7. It appeared to the Yugoslav ambassador to Moscow who was present at the meeting that took place between the Soviet and Yugoslav leaders on the Adriatic island of Brioni on the night of 2–3 November, 'that the Russians have already formed the government and that Münnich is to be Prime Minister (Veljko Mićunović, *Moscow Diary,* London, Chatto & Windus, 1980, p. 136). Kádár himself later explained that 'it was touch and go' whether he or Münnich would become Prime Minister (*Népszabadság,* Budapest, 29 January 1958), while Khrushchev stated that even after 4 November, 'My own hopes rested with Münnich. I thought I could deal with him better than with Kádár.' (Nikita Khrushchev, *Khrushchev Remembers,* London, Andre Deutsch, 1971, p. 387.)
8. Little published information exists on the Berei-Andics group, but their paper *Szabad Nép* is accessible in Hungarian archives.
9. Kádár's speech is available in Paul E. Zinner (ed.), *National Communism and Popular Revolt in Eastern Europe,* New York, Columbia University Press, 1956, pp. 464–467.
10. Mićunović, *op. cit.,* p. 133, records Khrushchev having said that he had spoken by telephone on 2 November with Bulganin who had told him that Münnich and Kádár had succeeded in fleeing from Budapest and were in a plane 'on their way to Moscow'.
11. In Zinner, *op. cit.,* pp. 474–478.
12. On the occasion of a visit to Uzhgorod with Khrushchev in December 1959, Kádár alleged that it was to this town he had come three years earlier in November 1956 to form his new government (*Népszabadság,* Budapest, 8 December 1959). The account is confirmed by Khrushchev, *op. cit.,* p. 386, though precisely when Kádár was in Uzhgorod remains unclear.
13. Márton Lovas, *Mi történt Budapesten október 23-tól november 4-ig* (What

happened in Budapest from 23 October to 4 November), Budapest, Kossuth, 1957, p. 126.

14. 'Program and Composition of the Revolutionary Worker–Peasant Government announced by János Kádár on 4 November 1956', in Zinner, *op. cit.*, pp. 474–478. See also Kádár's speech of 26 November in *Népszabadság*, 27 November 1956.
15. On Miklós Gimes and his role in 1956, see Igor Cornelissen, 'Boedapest 1958: de tragische terechtstelling van een strijdbaar journalist', *Vrij Nederland*, Amsterdam, Jaargang 42, Nos. 47 and 48, 21 November and 28 November 1981.
16. *Népszabadság*, Budapest, 14 November 1956.
17. *Népszabadság*, Budapest, 15 November 1956. English translation available in Melvin J. Lasky (ed.), *The Hungarian Revolution*, London, Secker & Warburg, 1957, pp. 262–263.
18. The circumstances of the abduction, and the suspicion that there may have been a 'deal' between the Soviets and the Yugoslavs, are discussed in Dick Verkijk, 'Kádár en de Hongaarse Opstand van 1956', *Internationale Spectator*, Amsterdam, January 1981.
19. See Bill Lomax, '25 Years Later–New Light on 1956', *Labour Focus on Eastern Europe*, Vol. 5, No. 3, Summer 1982.
20. See József Kövágó, 'Emlékek, emberek, remények–A Kisgazdapárt a forradalomban' (Memories, people, hopes–the Smallholders Party in the Revolution), *Irodalmi Ujság*, Paris, November–December 1981.
21. *Népszabadság*, Budapest, 27 November 1956.
22. *Népszabadság*, Budapest, 8 December 1956.
23. See Bill Lomax, *Hungary 1956*, London, Allison & Busby, 1976, chapter 5: 'The Workers Councils of Greater Budapest', also published in *The Socialist Register 1976*, London, Merlin Press, 1976.
24. See *Magyar Közlöny*, Budapest, Nos. 100, 101, 102, for 11, 12 and 13 December 1956.
25. See *Népszabadság*, Budapest, for 16, 18 and 21 December 1956.
26. *Népszabadság*, Budapest, 13 January 1957.
27. See Zoltán Vas, *Viszontagságos életem* (My eventful life), Budapest, Magvetö, 1980, pp. 496, 527 and 547; and letter from Ferenc Donáth to Miklós Molnár in Lomax, '25 Years Later', *op. cit.*
28. *Gazdaságpolitikánk tapasztalatai és tanulságai: 1957–1960* (The experience and lessons of our economic policies: 1957–1960), Budapest, Kossuth, 1976, p. 42.
29. *A Magyar Szocialista Munkáspárt határozatai és dokumentumai: 1956–1962* (Resolutions and decisions of the Hungarian Socialist Workers Party), Budapest, Kossuth, 1979, pp. 78–99.
30. Tibor Méray, *Nagy Imre élete és halála* (The life and death of Imre Nagy), Munich, Ujváry Griff, 1978, p. 350.
31. Fehér, 'Kádárism', *op. cit.*, p. 23.
32. See Ferenc A. Vali, 'Twenty Years After: Kádár and his rule assessed: 1956–1976', *The Canadian-American Review of Hungarian Studies*, Ottawa, Vol. 3, No. 2, Special Issue: 'The Hungarian Revolution twenty years after', Fall 1976.
33. On opposition groups in the 1960s, see Bill Lomax, 'A Chronology of Political and Intellectual Opposition under the Kádár Regime: 1956–1978', *Labour Focus on Eastern Europe*, Vol. 3, No. 3, July–August 1979.
34. Miklós Haraszti, *A Worker in a Workers State*, London, Penguin Books, 1977.
35. György Konrád and Iván Szelényi, *The Intellectuals on the Road to Class Power*, Brighton, Harvester Press, 1979.
36. See Marc Rakovski, 'La Hongrie est-elle réelement si différente? ' *Esprit*, Paris, No. 7–8, July–August 1978.
37. See 'Pacifist Movement in the Hungarian Catholic Church', *Labour Focus on*

Eastern Europe, Vol. 5, No. 3, Summer 1982.

38. See György Krassó, 'Wenn einer *keine* Reise tut, da kann er was erleben!' Gegenstimmen, Vienna, No. 5, 1981.
39. See the interview with Tibor Pákh in *Beszélö* No. 2, Budapest, Jan. 1982.
40. Bibó's document will be published for the first time in 1983 in Hungarian in the third volume of his collected works edited by István Kemény and Mátyás Sárközi (István Bibó, *Osszegyüjtött Muvei,* Bern, Európai Protestáns Magyar Szabadegyetem, 1981-1983).
41. The *Hungaricus* pamphlet is summarised in Lomax, *Hungary 1956, op. cit.,* pp. 182-192.
42. Marc Rakovski, *Towards an East European Marxism,* London, Allison & Busby, 1978.
43. György Bence and János Kis, 'On Being a Marxist: A Hungarian View', in *The Socialist Register 1980,* London, Merlin Press, 1980.
44. Mihály Vajda, 'The End of Reformist Thought', *Meta,* Toronto, No. 3-4, 1979. See also the introduction to his political essays: Vajda, *The State and Socialism, op. cit.*
45. The circumstances of the trial are described in a postscript to Haraszti's *A Worker in a Workers State, op. cit.*
46. See Bill Lomax, 'Hungary 1977-1982: The Rise of the Democratic Opposition', *Labour Focus on Eastern Europe,* Vol. 5, No. 3, Summer 1982.
47. Miklós Haraszti, 'What is Marxism? ' in Frantisek Silnitsky, Larisa Silnitsky and Karl Reyman (ed.), *Communism and Eastern Europe,* Brighton, Harvester Press, 1979.
48. Vajda, 'The End of Reformist Thought', *op. cit.,* and Gabriel Becker, 'The Left in Hungary', *Critique,* Glasgow, No. 9, 1978.
49. Ferenc Donáth, 'István Bibó and the Fundamental Issue of Hungarian Democracy', in *The Socialist Register 1981,* London, Merlin Press, 1981.
50. István Kemény, writing in *Magyar Füzetek,* Paris, No. 7, 1980, p. 79.
51. Miklós Haraszti, 'Voices from Hungary', *Index on Censorship,* London, Vol. 10, No. 3, June 1981. See also 'Hungarian Perspectives', *Telos,* St. Louis, No. 47, Spring 1981.
52. See Martin Steinert, 'Versuche zur Gründung einer unabhängigen Interessenvertretung der Studenten in Ungarn', *Osteuropa-Info,* Berlin/Hamburg, 1982, No. 1, March 1982.
53. János Kádár, 'Reflections at Sixty', *New Hungarian Quarterly,* Budapest, No. 48, Winter 1972, p. 5.
54. According to the Albanian Party leader, citing personal meetings with Suslov in the summer of 1956 and unpublished correspondence between the Soviet and Yugoslav leaderships towards the end of 1956, the Soviets had already wanted Kádár, not Gerö, to replace Rákosi in July 1956, and had 'tried, as early as the summer of this year, to ensure that Kádár would become first secretary', while by the end of August 'they were preparing Imre Nagy, thinking they would master the situation in Hungary through him'. See Enver Hoxha, *The Khrushchevites,* Workers Publishing House, London, 1980, pp. 272, 275 and 288.
55. András Hegedüs, 'Ungarn 56', *Gegenstimmen,* Vienna, No. 6, December 1981.
56. András Hegedüs, 'Polen heute', *Wiener Tagebuch,* Vienna, November 1981.
57. *Die Presse,* Vienna, 15 December 1981, *op. cit.*
58. Mihály Vajda, 'Perspektiven der ungarischen Intelligenz', *Osteuropa-Info,* Berlin/Hamburg, 1982, No. 1, March 1982, p. 53.
59. 'On the Deck of the Titanic? ' (*Beszélö,* Budapest, No. 2, Jan. 1982), in *Labour Focus on Eastern Europe,* Vol. 5, No. 2, Summer 1982.
60. János Kis, 'Thoughts on the Immediate Future' (*Beszélö,* Budapest, No. 3, Summer 1982), in *Labour Focus on Eastern Europe,* Vol. 5, No. 5, Autumn 1982.

SOLIDARITY AFTER THE COUP

Denis MacShane

The paradox of Poland is quite straightforward. The workers, intellectuals and activists who formed Solidarity did not know how to convert the gains of August 1980 into permanent change. The generals, security officers and party hardliners who declared a 'state of war' on 13 December 1981 did not know how to convert the locking up of Lech Walesa and other Solidarity leaders into a lasting solution of the country's economic and social problems. The list of problems without easy answers is long enough inside Poland. But the history of Solidarity and the continuing struggle of the Polish working class has presented a number of questions for Western socialists: what is the nature of Russian and East European political systems and what should be the relationships between organisations of the Western labour movement—political parties and trade unions—and organisations with similar names in Comecon countries? Also Western socialists have had to consider what political and economic response would best support Solidarity. The situation has produced some strange bedfellows. Ultra-leftists have joined forces with right-wing reactionaries in demanding a complete economic boycott of Poland and the Soviet Union and a withdrawal of credit that would push Poland into default. Western Communist Parties have stood shoulder to shoulder with bankers in Wall Street, the City and West Germany, in arguing against any interruption in financial and economic relationships with Poland. The paradoxes stretch far beyond the Polish frontiers.

Commentaries appearing not long after 13 December 1981 suggested that Solidarity should have been better prepared. The many warning signs of the authorities' unwillingness to compromise should have alerted the union to adopt a more radical course of action or, at least, to make more careful plans to withstand a probable act of repression. The fact that no such course of action was taken indicates that Solidarity was far more of a trade union than those who dubbed it an embryonic political party or social mass movement would credit. Defining trade unions is an exercise best left to the Webbs. Anyone who has spent a moment examining models of trade unions from Britain, West Germany, France or Scandinavia let alone those from the Americas, Asia or Africa will appreciate the vast differences between forms of trade-union organisation, their declared and achieved aims, and their relationships with other forces in society. Social, political and cultural backgrounds have shaped trade unions in various ways in different countries. But all unions share the common characteristic of organising workers rather than citizens in general, and in presenting demands related to working life as a priority over more general social and political demands. In Britain the TUC Congress debates and formulates programmes on issues that are far removed from the shop floor. Policy issues range from an alternative economic strategy, withdrawal from the EEC and nuclear disarmament to cultural policy and access to the mass media. Yet there is no suggestion that the TUC is seeking to replace the Labour Party. Solidarity put forward a wide range of demands concerning changes in the political, economic and social operation of Poland but it perceived itself, right up to the last moment, as a union with all the limitations that unionism entails. The relative lack of preparation for the December *coup de force* underlines this view. Some preparation had been made, notably in Wroclaw, where all the union's regional funds were withdrawn from the bank shortly before 13 December. In the Lodz region, a traditionally militant area, the idea of workers' guards had been discussed but mainly in connection with proposals for 'active strikes'—syndicalist takeovers of factories by workers who would continue to produce and distribute but without reference to managers or local state representatives. Since 13 December there has been a war of articles and books over the exact nature of Solidarity. This war has been conducted, in part, by people deserving respect because they were locked up in December 1981, and whose articles, interviews and speeches up to that point are available. Their analyses and comments are based on direct experience inside Poland. On the other hand, polemicists sitting comfortably in the West have also engaged in the war of words, moralising about Solidarity's failure in this or that aspect of its troubled existence since August 1980 and earnestly lecturing the union on what it should or should not have done.

Much of this exterior analysis is based on the belief that Solidarity should somehow have immobilised the security services and armed forces, either through agitation and propaganda or forms of mass activity outside barracks and police stations. This would have been as practical a course of action as asking SPG police at Grunwick to lay down their truncheons and link arms with the pickets. Despite the appearance of a quasi-revolutionary situation in Poland the state never lost control over its armed forces and militia. The disintegration of the Polish United Workers Party (PUWP), the collapse of economic direction at central and local levels, and the authoritative presence of Solidarity in so many areas of society hitherto the exclusive preserve of the PUWP, created the illusion that state power had evaporated. That 'the Party equals the State' in Comecon countries, was shown to be a dangerously misleading assumption.

Nowhere in the world have trade unions been able to resist armed state power, ruthlessly applied. The extremely powerful and well-implanted German trade-union movement collapsed the moment Hitler came to power in the face of mass arrests, internments and closure of offices—tactics similar to those used by Jaruzelski. With a complete shutdown of communications, strikes and occupations become atomised. As the Chilean workers found in 1973, working-class resistance is difficult in the face of security forces who can use tanks to break through factory gates and are willing to shoot to kill. There can be little doubt that the spontaneous resistance of the Polish workers was generalised and strong; the sparse picture that we have shows widespread opposition and the use of armed force to smash strikes in the week following 13 December. The full extent of the resistance will not be known until a greater freedom of movement and communication is restored in Poland. But following that unpleasant week there was a return to work albeit a sullen and uncooperative return, punctuated by the Christmas break—but a return nonetheless. Again this follows the pattern of trade-union suppressions in other countries where, following the initial reactive anger, the leaderless working class conforms to behavioural norms and goes back to work.

The state also directed its application of martial law to controlling workplace relationships. The first move was the suppression of Solidarity. The union was suspended, its leaders arrested, its offices shut down and its equipment, including key printing machinery was confiscated. The process of turning Poland into a military dictatorship was achieved by declaring a 'state of war', later ratified by the Polish Sejm (parliament). In addition to being Prime Minister, First Secretary of the PUWP and Minister of Defence, General Wojciech Jaruzelski became Chairman of the Military Council of National Salvation. The term seemed to reflect Latin American language; a hunt through the classic Marxist texts yields nothing which combines the words 'military', 'national', and 'salvation'. The Council's acronym in Polish—WRON—was unfortuantely close to the Polish word for 'crow', *wrona.* This congruence provided an immediate image for underground cartoonists and delighted the sharp-witted Poles whose national symbol is the eagle.

There was nothing funny however about the powers that the Military Council of National Salvation assumed. These included the power to arrest anyone by simple administrative decision and detain them indefinitely; to place under military orders any citizen at any time; to implement direct military control over all industrial, manufacturing and service sectors vital to the economy (notably mines, steel, heavy industry, shipbuilding, cars, transport, post, energy supply, communications and the media); and to shoot any citizen opposing the Council's decisions or found disturbing public order. The Council also issued regulations which prohibited any meetings of groups; being on the streets without identity papers; striking or taking part in any protest action; participating in a banned or suspended organisation (i.e. Solidarity as well as many other associations and organisations stopped from functioning after 13 December); being in the streets between 10 pm and 6 am; and taking photographs.

According to official Polish figures some 6,000 people were interned. Unofficial Polish sources put the figure much higher. It was impossible to find out the exact number. Details emerged quickly enough about the better-known internees and the more notorious internment camps. But information from the more isolated regions was hard to come by even in Poland itself.

The Military Council showed considerable skill in its suppression of information and its control of both Polish and Western journalists. Every mechanism for communication inside the country—television, radio, newspapers and telephones—was either suspended or placed under direct military control. The curfew, check-points, the ban on leaving towns and the shut-down of internal flights successfully atomised the individual pockets of resistance. Western journalists were denied contact with their head offices and when a minimal telex service was restored it was closely censored. Even six months after the coup Western journalists were unable to travel freely around the country. They were still obliged to turn to official spokespersons for most of their hard facts, while using weasel adjectives like 'unofficial', 'clandestine' and 'claimed' when describing information issued by workers and the regrouped Solidarity movement. Poles have never had easy access to *The Times* or *The Guardian* but during the 1970s reports from Poland were broadcast back there by the BBC and other Western European radio services with Polish-language outputs. During the crucial weeks of July and August 1980 when the rolling wave of strikes culminated in the Gdansk and Szczecin occupation strikes, Western reporting and the access of Western television crews increased international pressure on Gierek to concede. Whilst the Polish media ignored the strikes, radio broadcasts from outside Poland provided accurate, up-to-the-minute information. In December 1981 the government dispensed with such liberal measures for foreign journalists. They were put on a very tight leash indeed and have been kept on it ever since. Direct censorship may have been lifted but all the interpreters come from the government Interpress service. It is difficult to get permission to travel outside Warsaw. If the military authorities in El Salvador or Guatemala or indeed, in Vietnam during the liberation war, applied the same ruthless control over internal and external reporting one wonders if Western reaction, especially Western socialist reaction, would have been so strong. We all recall that photograph of the Saigon police chief shooting a prisoner in the head at point blank range and the brutal faces of El Salvador militia in full colour close-up. Had films of Silesian miners being shot dead in December 1981 or stylish photographs of ZOMO security troops tooled up for action been available from Poland, the reaction in the West would have been all the greater. In that sense, at least, the Polish military had learned something from the summer of 1980 and had a more sophisticated understanding of international media relations than their fellow officers in Latin America.

There was a definite attempt to militarise the entire country. Twenty-one officers sat on the Military Council for National Salvation. Below it were two councils, one for economic affairs and one for socio-political affairs. Former ministers and senior PUWP figures sat on these bodies. At the regional level a military officer presided over provincial defence committees which replaced the local *voivods* (provincial governors). Military tribunals dispensed summary justice to Solidarity activists caught distributing leaflets or organising meetings and strikes. These trials continued in the winter and by May 1982 more than 1,000 people had been sentenced to jail terms of up to nine years. These included well-known Solidarity regional chiefs like Slowik from Lodz and Gil from Krakow. The problem of Solidarity members imprisoned following quasi-judicial processes was different from those who were administratively interned. Any acceptable settlement would have to include the release of people serving prison sentences as well as the internees.

The military also installed itself in key factories. Putting workers under military control meant that they could be ordered to do overtime and Saturday shifts. They could be forced to accept changes in their work operations without consultation. Opposition to such orders could be punished under military discipline while being absent from work counted as desertion. As will be seen later this did not significantly improve the economy; the problem with the Polish economy has never been the amount or quality or work performed by Polish workers but the crippling shortages of raw materials, spares, key components and energy. The economy therefore could not be improved by putting factories under military control. But it all added up to the reality that Poland was now governed by a military junta, which tried to present itself in the tradition of the pre-war Pilsudski regime (1926–35) and its successor (the so-called government of the five colonels).

The military authorities launched a series of purges to clear away any other opposition besides Solidarity. 1,200 journalists lost their jobs and others were subject to a 'verification' process. The Polish Journalists Association was disbanded and a new, pro-regime, journalists' association was launched. Dressing newscasters in military uniform in the days after the coup was more than symbolic. The relative freedom enjoyed by the Polish media had been one of the major achievements since August 1980. Broadcasting, the press and publishing were brought firmly back under central control. Similar purges took place in academic areas with, notably, the forced resignation in April 1982 of Henryk Samsonowicz, who had been elected Rector of Warsaw University under democratic procedures in 1981. The students' union was also shut down and condemned as an 'anti-socialist' organisation—its leaders were arrested and interned.

Perhaps the biggest single victim of 13 December, apart from Solidarity, was the Polish United Workers Party. In a tradition that springs from the bowels of history Jaruzelski and the military may have thought they were only taking over for a short period in order to administer a short, sharp shock—they would then hand power back to a refashioned and wiser party. The professed dream of generals who wish to be merely temporary rulers is either hypocritical or stupid. As the snow melted after Jaruzelski's Christmas coup one saw the PUWP fading away as well. Many party members who also belonged to Solidarity handed in their cards. Six hundred provincial and factory party organisations were purged as well as 2,000 branch party organisations. A Central Committee in March 1982 approved retrospectively what its First Secretary, General Jaruzelski, had done. However as a party—a political organism with a genuine base, a set of political objectives and some loose, if not uniformly agreed upon, idea of how to achieve them—the PUWP had ceased to exist. There were said to be two main currents—conforming to the classic Manichean vision of outside observers—a liberal wing grouped around Mieczyzlaw Rakowski and the hardliners headed by Stefan Olszowski. The difference between the two groups was more a matter of debate than practical policy: Rakowski and Olszowski might argue about the extent of the purges but neither could make a deal with the Polish working class. State power had passed decisively out of the hands of the PUWP on 13 December and there was no clear mechanism for getting it back.

We should remember that the official excuse for the Jaruzelski coup was the need to avert a civil war inspired by Solidarity. But the timing of the coup was not fortuitous. Had Jarulzelski not intervened the next major date on the Polish political calendar would have been the local elections. Much was made of Solidarity's proposal in December 1981 to hold a referendum on the possibility of the Sejm suspending the right to strike with a consequent riposte by the union. But such manoeuvring and posturing had been endemic in Poland throughout 1981. The holding of local elections could not, under the constitution, be delayed beyond February 1982. No agreement had been reached on who could be candidates but the old system which allowed a so-called national front list (consisting of the PUWP and its sponsored political organisations) was clearly unacceptable. Even if the compromise proposed by Solidarity of reserving half the seats for the PUWP and allowing free elections for the remainder had been accepted, it would have meant a blow dealt publicly to the position of the PUWP. In addition, the process of selecting the PUWP candidates would have exposed the party to internal conflicts which it could well do without. The arrival of thousands of freely elected municipal councillors, limited as their power might be, would have meant a powerful move towards open elections at other, higher levels. It would have been the first time since August 1980 that liberal democratic processes had operated in an institutionalised way as part of Poland's system of government. To hold elections therefore would have been fatal for the PUWP. It was one of the key, though rarely mentioned reasons for the timing of the military takeover. If now the military were to hand back power to the PUWP, except under conditions of a security police terror, the same political processes would tear the party apart. Like generals everywhere, Jaruzelski will find that taking power is easy: handing it over is extremely difficult.

The one condition that might permit a return to the days before the emergence of Solidarity would be a substantial improvement in the country's economic position. The bleak description of the Polish economy provided by D.M. Nuti in *Socialist Register 1981* 'The Polish Crisis: Economic Factors and Constraints' still obtains today. Except that it has got worse. National income fell by two per cent in 1979, four per cent in 1980, twelve per cent in 1981 and is expected to fall by as much as 30 per cent in 1982. The only economic reform pushed through has been a fourfold increase of prices which had the effect of soaking up some spare zlotys; but it also meant that poorer families are now facing the prospect of real hunger, as opposed to the shortages of the previous years. The militarisation of the economy has entailed a renewed narrow concentration on selected industries–shipbuilding, steel, engineering, automobiles and agricultural machinery. Altogether there are fourteen priority programmes which have privileged access to the dwindling stocks of key imported raw materials (the Warsaw steel works, Huta Warszawa, for example, receives wolfram and vanadium which steel plants in southern Poland are denied. All this has led to a desperate scramble to try and get individual factories into priority programmes. The dislocated Polish economy is still further distorted by the world recession which has destroyed markets for the goods that Poland can produce.

According to official statements there are more than fifty major industrial projects which are starved of components or imported raw materials either because of the Western freeze on export credits for Poland or the simple lack of hard currency. Polish banking officials have juggled to try and reschedule the 27 billion dollar external debt but with limited success. Western banks however have refused to declare a default, using identical arguments to those advanced in favour of maintaining credit lines to countries such as Chile, Argentina and the Philippines.

The lack of credit and the impact of the Western economic and financial sanctions meant that imports from the West in the first half of 1982 were running at 50 per cent below the level of the previous year. In 1981, 57 per cent of Polish exports went to Comecon countries and 62 per cent of imports came from Comecon. Both these figures are expected to increase. Poland has signed a number of new trading agreements with Comecon partners. Czechoslovakia has agreed to increase its supply of raw materials to Poland—an East European irony because Poland was for a long time the raw material purveyor to its neighbouring states. The turn towards Comecon which is also occurring in Yugoslavia (not a Comecon member) and even marginally in Hungary, the most Western-orientated of all the Comecon economies, is not just economically significant but politically significant also. Gierek's dash for growth in the 1970s based on vistas of unlimited Western credit, Western technology and Western markets, was not only economically unsound: it caused contradictions in terms of raised expectations inside Poland and increased political contacts outside the country; it exposed the inefficiency of highly centralised economic control and the clumsiness of appointing decision makers on the *nomenklatura* system (for a list of *nomenklatura* appointments and the system's role in Poland see *Solidarity: Poland's Independent Trade Union,* D. MacShane, Spokesman Books 1981).

Polish economists generally agree that the only way to get the economy moving again is to permit a degree of liberalisation both in economic and managerial decision making and in the market. But all moves in that direction, even if they do not go as far as Solidarity's economic programme and even if they evade the question of self-management and workers' control, carry a political price. The price is the weakening of centralised state power. This may be less important in a country like Hungary where there is no powerful and strongly based opposition to the ruling party but it is vital in Poland which has a suppressed but still massively supported trade union and the powerful Catholic Church. Economic liberalisation also poses the necessity to come to some deal with the working class in order to make workers accept the initial period of austerity, as well as labour redeployment and unemployment arising from such reforms. In short, it is difficult to modernise and improve an East European economy without at the same time modernising and improving political relations. Such a process would threaten to end the Soviet system of political control which has operated in Russia since the late 1920s and in East Europe since the late 1940s. The decision, at least in the Kremlin, appears to be to maintain political security at the expense of economic development (the emergence of Yuri Andropov, the KGB chief for the past 15 years, as a potential successor to Brezhnev underscores this point) and to draw the Eastern European economies back into Comecon again. Given the crisis in Western capitalism such a move, though mainly undertaken for internal political reasons, also has some economic logic behind it.

In Poland, however, a gentle return to the economic practices and managerial style of the 1950s and a goodbye wave to increased Western trading could still not be achieved easily without the cooperation of the working class, and here the continuing existence of Solidarity as an underground union considerably restricts the options available to the authorities. One has to be careful about terminology here. The activities of the independent self-governing trade union Solidarity (in Polish—NSZZ Solidarnosc) were suspended following the declaration of a 'state of war' on 13 December 1981. Its offices were closed down, equipment confiscated and many of its leaders interned. At the workplace and community level managers and regional administrators must no longer negotiate with Solidarity representatives.

Yet six months after the coup all available evidence shows that the union still exists in some tangible form for the industrial working class. In the words of Neal Ascherson reporting a visit to Krakow in March 1982: 'The core of the opposition at present is the extraordinary moral solidity of the industrial workers, taking no extreme attitudes but calmly telling any inquirer that they still support Solidarity. In this sense, the confident mental world which Solidarity created in 1980 still survives.' This process of survival has been helped by the work of union activists underground and the refusal by workers to accept a new union organisation that might be imposed on them from above.

At first sight the military coup was extraordinarily impressive. Four-fifths of the union's national leadership plus its more famous advisers like Jacek Kuron, Adam Michnik and Bronislaw Geremek were swept into internment camps. Lech Walesa was held separately in a villa near Warsaw. Yet as the lists of internees gradually became available, knowledgeable observers of Solidarity were struck by how many were fringe and unimportant people. Apart from the top echelons of Solidarity leadership the kind of people picked on showed that the security police were working from old lists of oppositionists and lists of people no longer active full-time in Solidarity. So a large number of intellectuals were interned while the shop-floor leadership, provided it did not expose itself in the cruel days of resistance immediately following 13 December, was left largely intact. Between September 1980 and December 1981 every single workplace in Poland had a Solidarity organisation. In large industrial plants 95 per cent of the workforce paid dues to Solidarity. Short of taking out and shooting every known Solidarity representative from each factory, office, hospital and print shop it would be difficult to remove the union's presence from workplaces in Poland. In Western countries most trade-union activists carry on a day-to-day work without reference to, or feeling a need for, the physical presence of the top union leadership. The same is true in Poland.

At one level Solidarity has been forced back into the kind of clandestine activities undertaken by those trying to set up independent trade unions in the years before August 1980. But at another level the crucial difference is that hundreds of thousands of Polish workers have had sixteen months of being able to organise freely, hold elections, choose shop stewards, select regional and national representatives and negotiate with employers, local and regional government as well as with national ministers.

Unlike other momentary periods of reform in Eastern Europe (Poland 1956–7, Czechoslovakia 1968) which, in essence, involved a debate within the party and was reserved for an elite, the sixteen months of Solidarity's existence involved nearly every industrial worker. A small example indicates why most workers want a return of Solidarity in order to regain a measure of control over their working lives: since the coup the accident rate in Polish industry has shot up. In the first three months of 1982 the Minister of Mines, General Piotrowksi, reported fourteen deaths and 5,642 accidents. It was concern over unsafe working practices and consequent deaths in mines that led to the creation of one of the first independent trade-union cells in Silesia in 1977. So the reason why Solidarity remains fixed in workers' minds is not the desire to forge a weapon to overthrow the PUWP but, more prosaically, the need for a defence mechanism against the unreasonable demands of management. Of course as the PUWP were interlinked with the appointment and control of managers there was a connection.

The union continues to signal its existence through publishing a wide range of journals, bulletins, leaflets and posters. Solidarity publishes a weekly magazine in Warsaw and even a pirate broadcasting system, 'Radio Solidarity', has managed to transmit irregularly. The authorities' concern about these activities is underlined by the heavy prison sentences imposed on activists who are caught. Even so, Polish conspiratorial abilities combined with wide popular support means that the Polish secret police are simply unable, through the classic mechanisms of informers and fear, to penetrate completely the underground movement and arrest its organisers. If, as seem likely, there is a broad-based underground organisation with mass popular support, this will be an important breakthrough in post-war Eastern Europe with potentially far-reaching implications.

Several key Solidarity leaders including Zbigniew Bujak from Warsaw (unquestionably the most authoritative Solidarity working-class leader apart from Walesa), Wladyslaw Frasyniuk from Wroclaw, Bogdan Lis from Gdansk and Wladyslaw Hardek from Krakow have formed a provisional national coordinating commission and have been able to meet and issue statements. Their call for May Day demonstrations was widely followed (50,000 marched in Warsaw and in Gdansk) as well as token stoppages to commemorate 13 December.

There is a debate about what tactics the underground union should follow. Zbigniew Bujak has argued that Solidarity should be patiently rebuilt by creating a wide network of groups and committees. These would provide aid for internees, discuss problems in the workplace, if necessary organise strikes over workplace issues but without strike leaders, and publish leaflets and bulletins. The loose network of groups and workplace cells would wait for the hopeless economic situation to bring Jaruzelski to the negotiating table. He would then be obliged to release Walesa and accept the existence of Solidarity. Decentralisation is vital to Bujak's tactic which he describes as 'positional struggle'. Bujak's lieutenant, the teacher Wiktor Kulerski, has described what he calls an underground Society: 'Not a centralised organisation with complete allegiance towards it but a multi-centred movement, decentralised, informal, consisting of mutually independent and loosely connected groups, circles, committees etc., with a large scope for independent decision-making. . . Such a movement could lead to a situation when the authorities control empty shops but not the market, workers' employment but not their livelihood, state-owned mass media but not the circulation of information, printing houses but not publishing, the post and telephones but not communications, the schools but not education.'

Jacek Kuron's tactics contrast with Bujak and Kulerski's. Kuron's writings from inside his Bialoleka prison camp have been widely published in the underground Solidarity press. Kuron does not consider that the 'state of war' can carry on indefinitely without a protest or a demonstration erupting into a national uprising that would provoke Soviet intervention in the style of Hungary in 1956. In order to avert this scenario Kuron has called for a highly centralised underground organisation to which activists should give total obedience. Attempts should be made to subvert the army and the security police and at some point a general strike should be called combined with an attempt at taking over radio and television stations. Kuron stresses that the object of such direct action should be to forestall a casual uncoordinated protest undertaken probably by youngsters (an important demographic point is that 60 per cent of the Polish population is under the age of 30 and for them the historic rebuilding achievements of post-war Polish communism are not even a lived-through memory) and its outcome should be a negotiated settlement including the restoration of Solidarity and a pledge that Poland would respect its alliances i.e. stay a loyal Warsaw Pact member. Although according to summaries in the Western media Kuron's position seems adventurist, in his full prison texts he shows great concern that the Polish situation may be slipping dangerously out of control—forces that neither the Church, nor underground Solidarity, let alone the military can handle, could be unleashed causing external intervention and total repression. Certainly there is growing rank-and-file pressure for some sort of action and people are reluctant to give up the idea of having a relatively formal underground union organisation—a shadow Solidarity as it were.

The Church with its memories of the Stalinist repression in the early

1950s is also conscious of the danger. But there is no sign of the Church adopting Kuron's conclusions and supporting a pre-emptive strike aimed at a controlled confrontation. The response of the Catholic Church to the December 13th crackdown and its consequences mirrors uncannily the behaviour of the Church after the Gdansk strikes and the creation of Solidarity in 1980. Just as the veteran primate, Cardinal Wyszynski, initially wavered in the middle of the August 1980 strike and, in one sermon, hinted that a return to work was the best answer, so too his successor, Archbishop Glemp, temporised in the immediate aftermath of the coup. He made a call to do nothing and warned repeatedly against activities that could justify increased violence by the state. The Church later stressed the need for a restoration of human and trade-union rights. But as with all political bodies the Polish Church is divided; the zig-zags in its statements and policy declarations indicate the political debate being waged inside it. A key figure, Archbishop Henryk Gulbinowicz of Wroclaw, is more outspoken in his references to Polish nationalism. Pope John Paul II's external involvement complicates matters. It is a problem for the military authorities and for the Soviet Union who realise that the Pope's nationality and his commanding presence as a world super-star focus world attention on Poland. But it is also a problem for Glemp and the Polish bishops whose ability to take independent decisions is limited by the need to refer to the Vatican. The Polish Church may have one faith but it has two masters, Glemp and Wojtyla. The existence of the Polish Pope further helps to internationalise the Polish crisis.

What has been the strategy of the Church? Like the good Abbot during the French Revolution it wants to survive. Peter Hebblethwaite says that one of the Pope's characteristics is to see things in terms of there being 'a distant goal, a spiritual aspiration, an inaccessible horizon, to be reached God knows when. He reverses the terms of Newman's famous hymn and sings: "I ask not to see the distant scene; I only know what the next step is".' So too in Poland. The Church may have a vague vision of a 'free' Poland in some far-off future but it offers no prescription about how that 'freedom' is to be achieved. The comforting rhetoric about the Church representing Polish nationhood during the centuries of Russian, Prussian and Austro-Hungarian partitions of Poland cannot obliterate the period 1919–39 when the Church was one of the worst landlords in Poland and allied itself with the most reactionary elements in the Polish bourgeoisie and its ruling military junta.

During the 1970s and in the period after Solidarity's birth the Church and the Polish working class developed a symbiotic relationship which has continued since the Jaruzelski declaration of a 'state of war'. As if transported 700 years the Church enjoys a place in Poland unheard of in most other countries since feudalism. It has authority, position, influence and the nation's rulers must always take it into account. But it has no lirect power, no foot-soldiers, and like feudal prelates the Polish bishops nust seek understandings with temporal holders of power to maintain nd advance the Church's authority. In the West we have been mesmerised y the Polish Church; but it is worth recalling that in two areas central to he Catholic Church in other countries—the legal control of female sexualty and fertility and the control of the school curriculum—the Polish riesthood has no power. If priests occasionally fulminated from the ulpit, they have had little effect. Contraception, abortion and divorce re easily obtained and widely practised in Poland and the education rocess from infant school to university is totally atheistic.

The eruption of the Polish working class in August 1980 gave the hurch a powerful new ally in its unceasing struggle for positional nfluence. There is not and has never been a single Polish Church policy owards either Solidarity or the state. If anything the relations between olidarity and the Church betrayed a constant nervousness and vacillation. o be sure, whenever Glemp or the Pope met Walesa they told him to be areful and moderate, which was rather like advising a fish to keep itself vet. The Church lacked a coherent policy for political transformation vhich it could ask Solidarity to try and bring about. There were minor dvances, such as the transmission of mass on the radio and increased ilgrimages to Rome but the Church in Poland was no stronger on 13 ecember 1981 than it had been on 31 August 1980. The problem of ower was always a test that could only be resolved between the Polish vorking class and the Polish state.

In its fight for survival and advancement the Church is not neutral or does it stand apart from the main conflict. It has provided spiritual nd physical shelter for the Solidarity activists operating underground. The isits of priests to internment camps have provided a channel of comunication betwee Walesa, Kuron and Michnik and those outside. One olish army officer, whose remarks were secretly recorded at a party neeting inside Polish television, claimed that the Solidarity leaders workng clandestinely were probably using churches and monasteries as hiding laces. The army officer even complained that it would be impossible to end in ZOMO units to capture people within the sanctuary of church valls because of the national and international outcry. Churches have lso been used, he maintained, as meeting places and for storing paper nd ink used in producing underground Solidarity newspapers. The coninuing flow of charity from the West that has been distributed through hurch channels is a reminder of Jaruzelski's inability to fulfil the first uty of a ruler, which is to feed the ruled.

It is interesting to see that the Church has also provided the launch or some mass protests. One can ban demonstrations and break up rallies ut it is impossible in Poland, to stop people attending a religious service. he major demonstrations that took place in May 1982 developed as people left Churches. Anyone who has attended a crowded Polish mass will know how easy it is to slip through the packed throng standing at the back of the church and pass messages, leaflets and communicate without fear of effective surveillance. The Church is an important organisational tool in the fightback of the Polish working class. The authorities know this but are powerless to do much about it. Glemp has strongly denounced attempts to arrest priests and, even if he wished to, he cannot stop junior clergy from carrying messages or offering their vestries as meeting rooms. In March 1982, the Primate's social Council put forward a ten point plan which amounted to little more than the standard demands of freeing internees, recognising the right of Solidarity to exist and function according to the 1980 agreements and calling for a social dialogue. Solidarity, 'should have defended the idea of a limited social and union programme with more determination and consistency'.

Jaruzelski has been politely indifferent to the Church though his politeness is tactical—he may want to use the Church as a fence-mender at some later date. The presence of the Polish Church limits Jaruzelski's field of operation far more than the rulers of other Eastern European states. A key problem in Poland is agriculture and the Church will resist any reform that weakens private tenure. It is in the countryside that the Church is most strongly implanted. The development of any effective neo-Stalinism in Poland will be difficult, if not impossible, unless the Church is uprooted and destroyed.

In fact, the attempts at pressuring the Church, through classic police state repression in the early 1950s, backfired. The imprisonment of Cardinal Wyszynski, the refusal to permit the building of churches, the desecration of existing churches and the harassment of priests did nothing to weaken the Church's authority or position. The Church has emerged stronger from each of the major post-war crises in Poland. Short of murdering every priest and burning down every church Jaruzelski has to tolerate the existence of a well-organised focal point for opposition as well as a Pole sitting in the Vatican with immense international prestige. These factors complicate the general's options.

Jaruzelski also has to consider the response of the trade-union and labour movements in countries all over the world. Despite the widespread use of the adjective 'inevitable' in left-wing commentaries following the Jaruzelski coup, the Western labour movements were as much caught by surprise as Solidarity itself. The initial reaction was to issue a stream of strongly worded denunciations; but there ensued a lack of certainty and in some quarters, a definite reluctance to develop concrete labour movement opposition to the suppression of Solidarity.

The response of unions tended to follow their previous reaction to the arrival and existence of Solidarity. Right-wing trade-union leaders found themselves on platforms with Conservative MPs protesting against the arrest of Solidarity leaders but reserving their real venom and rhetorical fire for the Soviet Union and communism in general. Union leaderships that were closer to the Communist Party issued token protests and generally kept their heads down. Sometimes craft solidarity transcended the political divide as when the Communist Michael McGahey ordered a minute's silence from the Miners' Union executive in honour of the Polish miners shot down by the militia as they tried to maintain the occupation strike in Silesia.

The different responses inside the British trade-union movement were echoed in other Western countries. In France, the socialist trade-union confederation CFDT, which had developed close ties with Solidarity and had hosted a visit by Lech Walesa, made the organisation of support for Solidarity its number one campaigning issue early in 1982. By contrast, the Communist CGT supported the Jaruzelski coup and despite strong internal opposition to its pro-regime position, played down events in Poland. The confederation accused all those supporting Solidarity in France of trying to whip up anti-communist hysteria for internal political reasons.

There was something in this. As well as the different positions taken up by the two major trade-union confederations (the third French trade-union confederation, *Force Ouvrière,* with its mixture of hardline right-wingers and ultra-leftists, also vigorously condemned the suppression of Solidarity as did the autonomous and extremely powerful teachers union, FEN) the 13 December coup produced a huge public row between the French Socialist Party and the French Communist Party. The former was strongly pro-Solidarity, the latter equally strongly pro-Jaruzelski. Lionel Jospin, the Socialist Party's First Secretary, spoke at public meetings denouncing what had taken place in Poland while Georges Marchais, his Communist Party homologue, went on television to support the Polish authorities. The strains between the two parties over the Communists' humiliating defeat in the French presidential and legislative elections earlier in 1981 and the bickering between the two French union confederations over how to respond to the policies of the Mitterrand-Mauroy government were reflected in the divergent reactions to Poland.

The reaction of the Italian Communist Party was quite different. Enrico Berlinguer, the Italian Communist Party leader, pronounced that the coup in Warsaw heralded the end of an era that had begun in 1917. Again, domestic politics played a part. Since Berlinguer was still clutching onto his 'historic compromise' theses of the mid-1970s and in addition a reinvigorated Socialist Party was snapping at his heels, he found it vital to maintain the pluralist, non-Soviet policies of the past 15 years. The response of the PCI reflected the debate it had initiated on Poland and the more mature analysis it had developed by contrast with the PCF. The Italian trade-union movement, although politically divided, does not suffer the sectarian bitterness that exists between the leadership of th French unions. Indeed, in some industries and crafts (metal-working an journalism) there is a single union, combining the Communist, Socialist and Christian strands—a fusion that would be inconceivable in France Unlike the grudging acceptance of Solidarity by the French CGT in th period after August 1980, the Italian trade-union movement warml embraced their Polish comrades and the Communist CGIL hosted a visi by Walesa to Rome in 1981.

In West Germany, trade-union support for Solidarity was more muted Criticism of the suppression was made but a statement issued by Will Brandt, as Chairperson of the Socialist International, warned agains interference in Poland's internal affairs. This summed up the West Germa labour movement's position though it seemed somewhat illogical for a international left-wing body to absolve itself from concern about th politics of a country which has seen the most decisive working-clas action for many years. For advocates of detente, events in Poland dis rupted the patterns of a slow, cautious movement towards a lessenin of East-West tension and political liberalisation based on increased trad and contacts. Instead, the Polish working class had, through Solidarity- the very antithesis of the official East European unions with which Wester trade unions had studiously developed contacts in the 1970s—suddenl created areas of political, social and cultural liberty for all Poles whic *Ostpoliticians* like Brandt had never considered possible. Furthermor the Jaruzelski coup, which was aimed so directly at working people an trade-union organisation, spat in the faces of Westerners who had argue that improved contacts would prevent repression as seen in Berlin i 1953, Poznan in 1956, Budapest in 1956 and Prague in 1968.

Thus the Polish question became a major problem for the Wester labour movement. The presence of Polish exiles—some from the 1939-4 diaspora, others exiled in the anti-Jewish purges of 1968 as well as handful of Solidarity members stranded in the West on 13 December- was a pressure on the trade unions. But the groups of Poles and the suppo groups for Solidarity could not form one common organisation—the were no less than six separate pro-Solidarity groups in London alone an this dispersed support for Solidarity inside the British labour movemen The demands raised were clear and easy enough to support—the releas of interned prisoners, the resumption of talks with Solidarity and a retur to the August 1980 agreements—but no-one knew how the British labou movement could achieve them. The TUC and several major unions, inclu ing the TGWU, AUEW, GMWU, NUT and NALGO sent protests, an in some cases, delegations to the Polish embassy. Len Murray tried, u successfully, to obtain a visa to visit Poland as part of a delegation se by the European TUC. Some unions contributed to a TUC fund whic was used to buy food and medical supplies; six lorry loads were sent o to Poland in spring 1982. A handful of trade-union leaders were photographed outside TUC Congress House loading supplies onto the lorries. Generous though the gesture was, by the time the charity reached Poland it merged with the immense flow of aid from Catholic sources in the United States and West Europe without any specific trade-union orientation. Several of the British unions and the TUC itself had established personal links with Solidarity leaders and representatives between August 1980 and December 1981 when there had been an exchange of visits. Often in making protests Western union leaders were talking about people they knew personally. The international labour movement links which Solidarity actively developed during its period of legitimate operation now paid off. Since 1945 the British labour movement has made links with Eastern Europe through official bodies like Communist Parties, trade unions, peace organisations, municipalities, which are controlled by the ruling Communist Party. Visits to East Europe were carefully organised. A busy schedule of meetings, factory trips, receptions and a couple of pleasant days beside a Black Sea or lakeside resort, left the impression of cementing contacts across the ideological divide. Unofficial contacts were difficult to arrange and meetings between groups of rank-and-file workers impossible. All this was totally changed by the arrival of Solidarity. For the first time, Western trade unionists could get a real glimpse of workers' problems and hear what the working class had to say. Solidarity, while being welcoming and courteous, wasted very little time on official banquets. A Western union general secretary was likely to find him/herself on a speedy tour of factories and makeshift Solidarity offices with a quick sandwich and a cup of tea as the only refreshment. At the same time, in addition to the well-publicised visits abroad by Walesa, Solidarity sent delegations from the factory floor to visit their equivalents in West Europe and North America. Hardly a LOT flight left Warsaw without a Solidarity delegation on board. These strengthening and increasing contacts between Polish workers and the Western trade-union movements caused some anguish in East Europe, especially in Prague where the Russian-controlled World Federation of Trade Unions is based.

But beyond a public wringing of hands and the despatch of humanitarian aid, the Western trade-union movement and, in particular, the British trade-union movement seemed uncertain in its response. At a rank-and-file level there was a warm response to factory visits and conference speeches made by Solidarity activists in exile. Massey-Ferguson workers in Coventry blacked any movement of goods to and from the Warsaw Ursus tractor factory after an appeal by Piotr Kozlowski, deputy convenor of Solidarity there and who was in England, by chance, on 13 December. On the other hand, Communist Party shop stewards stopped Kozlowski from speaking at other factories in the Coventry and Manchester areas. These blocking tactics were in contrast to the Executive Committee of the

CPGB which had urged a release of prisoners and a restoration of democratic rights and civilian rule.

The TUC wrote to all the national trade-union centres in East Europe protesting against the repression of Solidarity and, apart from the Hungarians, received dismissive responses. So insulting was the reply from the East German equivalent of the TUC that TUC leaders decided to suspend relationships with East Berlin. Although contacts between Congress House and East Europe were effectively frozen in 1982 as a result of the suppression of Solidarity, there was no serious move to reconsider the purpose of TUC-East European union relationships. A motion calling for a severance of such links was decisively rejected by the Scottish TUC in April, 1982. And while the TUC, as a national centre kept its distance from East Europe, there were still bi-lateral visits being made by British unions to the Soviet Union and elsewhere. The events in Poland had shaken but not decisively altered British trade-union policy towards the official trade unions in East Europe.

The Labour Party added its voice to the public outcry in December, though it clearly did not enjoy the embarrassing company of President Reagan and Mrs Thatcher. A very poorly organised Labour Party meeting in March indicated a lack of enthusiasm for Solidarity in Labour Party headquarters. The exuberant support for Solidarity from reactionaries everywhere made the process of building a labour-movement campaign that much more difficult. The growing peace movement, the existence of disarmament as a major issue coupled with the specific British campaign against the United States cruise missiles meant that anti-Reaganism was at a premium. On the whole what Reagan was for it seemed natural to be against. The hopeful and positive initiative of European Nuclear Disarmament, based implicitly on a loosening of East-West tensions and drawing much political comfort from the existence of an independent trade union in Poland also took a severe knock with the suppression of Solidarity. It was clear that Reagan was working for a return to the Cold War. But it was uncomfortable for those who had invested political hope in thawing the ideological divide in Europe to see such a brutal ice-making machine installed in Poland. Both the creation and the suppression of Solidarity should serve as the first point of reference for a major re-evaluation of the labour movement's attitude to Comecon countries and their political institutions. But there is no evidence that such a re-evaluation has yet begun.

When the labour movement does deal with the issue, it will have to take into account several questions. First, what do socialists mean when they talk of economic or financial sanctions? Do we mean a complete blockage of all trade or simply a refusal to extend credit? Who should take such decisions and what procedures for compensation should there be for state- or privately-owned companies and workers who suffer as a result?

What should be our criteria for applying such sanctions? An absence of democratic political rights (Taiwan, the Soviet Union)? An absence of independent working-class organisations (China, Tanzania)? Imprisonment of trade-union leaders (Poland, Turkey)? Persecution of racial minorities (Vietnam, Israel)? Repression of gay rights (Ireland, Cuba)? Or are we only to be moved into making such calls when a particular event seizes our attention (Chile, 1973; Poland, 1981) but ignore the continuing permanent repression existing in many countries? Is it possible to put together a tailor-made set of economic and financial sanctions for a limited period? Or, is it not more likely, that economies can survive indefinitely against such external sanctions and that, if anything, the application of sanctions can make the people of the victim country more determined to resist what is seen as external interference?

Does the labour movement really know how contemporary international financial operations work and how they can be controlled, not just in a theoretical sense but in terms of day-to-day operations? Should the Labour Party not pay more attention to what possibilities exist for a socialist government intervention in the overseas operation of the City? Instead of the false trail of sanctions should not the labour movement concentrate on providing effective political and material support for organisations seeking to introduce democratic, progressive change inside their own country? Is it possible or honest to expect a clear division between 'political' and 'trade-union' demands in countries (South Africa, Brazil, Poland) where working-class political pressure can only be channelled through trade-union organisations? What relationships should labour-movement organisations have with their equivalents in East Europe? What are the possibilities of building links at a rank-and-file level? Did the almost *communard* internal democracy of Solidarity also present a challenge to Western trade-union systems of operation?

Why did the British labour movement (in common with other Western labour movements) not campaign in the hopeful period after Solidarity's birth for a massive package of Western aid to Poland so as to support a secure economic base for the political gains made by the working class? Is it not too late even now to make the offer of substantial Western aid to Poland—to replace an ineffective stick by a juicy carrot—in exchange for the release of interned prisoners and the restoration of Solidarity? What are the long-term implications of the militarisation of Poland? Are we to see more examples of generals becoming party leaders and then cementing their position by military *force majeure*? What has happened to the post-1917 communist political principle (and practice) that has the army and security forces firmly subordinate to the party?

The list of questions can continue and to attempt an answer from a socialist perspective is a daunting task. But it is a task that needs to be undertaken. The 1945 European settlement is no longer acceptable to an increasing number of workers in East Europe and to an increasing number of socialists, including many in Communist Parties in West Europe. After the heroic early phase of industrialisation, accumulation and rapid social, educational and cultural improvements in East Europe the atrophy of personal freedoms (it was Marx and Engels after all who pointed out, 'that in no social order will personal freedom be so assured as in a society based on common ownership') and the absence of political dialogue has brought about deteriorating economic relationships that finally ended in the absurd and alarming sight of generals taking power in an advanced north European state.

The events in Poland mark a decisive break in European socialist history. The rupture came because the country's working class, almost unconsciously, made a fumbling bid for power but the Polish state was not ready to tolerate the dual power which existed for 16 months between September 1980 and December 1981. Poles talked fondly of sharing power but they were chasing a will-o'-the-wisp: the phrase 'power-sharing' is one of the phoniest additions to the modern political vocabulary. Power cannot be shared. It can only be transferred. And Solidarity, like all trade unions, was not the instrument for securing in a decisive fashion that transfer of power.

NOTE

For anyone interested in following events in Poland through reading original documents two indispensable sources in English are *Labour Focus on Eastern Europe*, Box 23, 136 Kingsland Road, London E8 and the bulletin of the Information Centre for Polish Affairs, 115 Redston Road, London N8.

INTRODUCTION

Tamara Deutscher

The Tragedy of the Polish Communist Party dates from 1957, when K.S. Karol asked Isaac for a brief outline of the history of Communism in Poland. It might be worth recalling that shortly after the dramatic Twentieth Congress of the Communist Party of the Soviet Union, in February 1956 (at which Khrushchev in his famous 'secret speech' revealed for the first time to a Russian audience some of Stalin's crimes and misdeeds), a communiqué from Moscow announced the 'rehabilitation of the Polish Party and its leaders,' who, it was stated, had fallen victims to 'provocations and slanders' during the period of the 'cult of personality'. This short announcement, hardly noticed in the West, was in fact a strange epilogue to one of the greatest tragedies of Communism, in which a whole party had been annihilated. In 1938 the Comintern announced the dissolution of the Polish Party under the pretext that it was corroded by 'Trotskyist and Pilsudskist influences' and had become merely an agency of fascism and the Polish political police. Yet all the members of the Central Committee, threatened by the very same police, escaped from Poland to seek refuge in Moscow. On Stalin's orders they were imprisoned and executed as traitors. Among them were Adolf Warski (Warszawski), the founder of the party and friend of Rosa Luxemburg; Lenski (Leszczynski), a veteran of the October Revolution and a former member of the Executive of the Comintern; Wera Kostrzewa (Koszutska), a most militant woman revolutionary. At the time not much was known about the fate of the victims: Stalin did not bother to stage even a mock trial and at the height of the terror his dealings with the 'fraternal party' were enveloped in murky silence. In Poland the remnants of the illegal party, persecuted by the police, led a precarious existence.

Isaac, himself a former member of the party—he was expelled in 1932 for 'exaggerating the danger of Nazism' and 'sowing panic' in Communist ranks—traced the circumstances of its wholesale destruction. He was fully aware that 'the views expressed here must. . . provoke opposition'. 'I do not pretend,' he wrote, 'that what I have to say is a revelation of infallible truth. I would be quite satisfied if my work were to bring new elements into a discussion about the history of the Polish Party and if it helped to a more thorough understanding of its tragic fate.' This wish was fulfilled in a rather unusual manner. The interview, which was recorded, was translated from Polish into French and appeared in *Les Temps Modernes* in March 1958. Soon afterwards the editors of the Warsaw *Polityka,* the official organ of Gomulka's party, planned to reproduce it, but had to abandon the idea after protracted negotiations with the censors. Then the more esoteric theoretical quarterly *Zeszyty Teoretyczno-polityczne* intended to publish it, but did not succeed either. The problem 'to publish or not to publish' came before the Polish Politburo. There was no clear majority either for or against, so a compromise was reached: it was decided not to publish the text, but to duplicate it and distribute it among party cells. Nicknamed 'Isaac Deutscher's secret speech', it soon became the subject of passionate debate. By 1980–81 the 'secret speech' was largely forgotten, and if it was known to a handful of people of the younger generation, it was in its French, German, or English version.

Exactly a year ago, on 18 May 1981, I received a letter from a Dutch scholar from Utrecht University: 'I spent recently a week in Poland', he says *inter alia,* 'and had the opportunity to speak amply with people of KOR, Solidarnosc, the Independent Students Organisation. They try very hard to be informed about their own past, the history of the Soviet Union, and related subjects, but they have up to now no good literature. The works of your husband (with one exception among the people I spoke with) are unknown.'

It is undoubtedly true that young people have tried 'very hard to be informed about their own past'. After all, defying danger, they flocked to the 'flying universities' to acquire knowledge which was denied them at official schools and universities. In setting up the flying universities the organisers followed a tradition going back to the times of the struggle for national independence when such clandestine schools contributed to the preservation of Polish culture against efforts at Germanisation or Russification by the occupying powers. In the curriculum of the underground study groups in the late 1970s more stress was laid on the teaching of the national history of Poland, on risings and insurrections in the 18th and 19th century than on social history and class struggles of the 20th century; more time devoted to the achievements of Pilsudski's Legionaries than to the activities of the Polish Communist Parties, and the shafts of the opposition were aimed more sharply against foreign totalitarianism than against the domestic quasi-fascist pre-war regime of the Colonels. To the heroic Polish Communists, martyred by both, not much attention was paid.

While in 1958 Deutscher's 'Tragedy of the Polish Communist Party' was discussed at the politbureau and then circulated in a duplicated form as if it were the rulers' own 'Samizdat', 22 years later the essay was, so to say, *non grata* either with the ruling party or with the opposition. Both sides had their particular reasons for consigning it to oblivion.

There was, of course, great pressure from the intelligentsia for the publication of literature which hitherto, through the fiat of the government, was on the index. Among the books which the opposition wanted to see published openly were those of Gombrowicz, Milosz and Kolakowski. (Solzhenitsyn, in a clandestine edition, sold well in the forecourt of the Warsaw University.)

It is true that Polish society is intensely interested in its own past, but it is not eager to learn about the past which it does not consider its own, while the ruling party has no wish to learn about the past which it is still determined to disown. Neither *raison d'être* nor *raison d'opposition* should prevent the independent Left in the West from learning about the tragedy of the Polish Communist Party.

THE TRAGEDY OF THE POLISH COMMUNIST PARTY*

Would you throw some light on the key problems of the history of the Polish Communist Party, which I am at present studying? I am particularly interested in the ideological and political currents within the Party, in the background to the formation of its various factions, in the Party's policy during the critical periods of the two interwar decades, and, finally, in its tragic end.

Let us begin with some general reflections and with a remark of a personal nature. When you ask me to speak of the history of the Polish Communist Party you are surely aware of the particular point of view from which I reply. In June 1957, exactly twenty-five years will have elapsed since I was expelled from the Party as an oppositionist. I shall not analyse now the reasons for my expulsion: they have been stated clearly although tendentiously—and with the passage of time their very bias becomes more and more self-condemnatory—in the documents and statements published at the time by the Party leadership dealing with the 'Krakowski affair'. (Krakowski was one of the pseudonyms which I was then using.) From 1932 until its dissolution I was in sharp conflict with the Polish Communist Party. Nevertheless, at the time of the dissolution and of the accusations made against its leaders, I stigmatised these actions as an unparalleled crime committed against the working class of Poland and of the whole world. The opposition group to which I belonged was in fact the only group of members or former members of the Polish CP which denounced this crime then and protested against it vehemently.[1]

It was unquestionably the Polish Communist Party which had the greatest influence on my intellectual and political development. I never doubted that it would be 'rehabilitated'—though even the term 'rehabilitation' is out of place here. It was a great and heroic party, the only party in Poland which represented the interests of the proletarian revolution, the great Marxist tradition, and a true and living internationalism. In this respect no other Polish party could be compared with it. Unfortunately, up to this day the history of the Polish Communist Party still remains a

*This interview was originally published in French in *Les Temps Modernes*, March 1958.

closed and sealed book. The most recent publications which I have had an opportunity to read are on the whole rather pitiable. They note the Party's rehabilitation, but do nothing more. There is no real attempt to depict the great periods in the Party's existence—the high flights and decline. What is striking is a tendency—the result of habits acquired in the course of many years—to be satisfied with clichés and writings in the manner of *Lives of Saints.* The only party in Poland which was worthy of bearing the name of a proletarian and Marxist party deserves to have its record studied in a serious, realistic and critical manner. The Polish CP was once buried under a pile of outrageous slanders. Let us not bury it again, wrapped in shrouds of golden legends to the accompaniment of senseless hymns.

I should like to add a remark of a general methodological character. In order to understand the history of the Polish Communist Party, every important phase of it must be considered from a double point of view: from the angle of the class struggle within Poland itself, and from that of the processes which were taking place within the Communist International and the Soviet Union. These two groups of factors acted upon each other continuously. An investigator who restricts himself to an analysis of only one of these will be unable to grasp the essence of the story. As years went by, the processes occurring in the Soviet Union played a more and more important role and weighed more and more disastrously on the fate of the Polish Party. Therefore to see clearly the policy of the Party and its ideological tendencies and also to understand the factional struggle, we must be continuously aware of the class relationship within Poland and of the processes of development taking place within the Russian Revolution.

What were the main internal divisions in the Polish Communist Party at the time it was founded, that is to say, at the end of 1918 and the beginning of 1919?

These divisions followed from the fact that the Polish CP was born from the fusion of two parties: the Social-Democratic Party of the Kingdom of Poland and Lithuania (Rosa Luxemburg's party, the SDKPiL) and the Polish Left Socialist Party (the PPS Lewica).[2] Each of these two parties had its own traditions. The Social-Democratic Party grew in opposition to the nationalism and patriotism of the Polish nobility harking back to the insurrectionist romanticism of the nineteenth century, and placed its main emphasis on proletarian internationalism. The Left Socialist Party had at first adhered to the patriotic-insurgent tradition, and the restoration of Poland's independence had occupied a central place in its programme; but later on it came closer to the internationalist attitude of the Luxemburgist Party. The Left Socialist Party had its affinities with the Left

Mensheviks; only under the influence of the October Revolution did it move closer to Bolshevism. The Social-Democratic Party adopted—as the proceedings of its Sixth Congress show—an attitude very close to that of Trotsky, remaining independent both of the Mensheviks and the Bolsheviks. At the time of the revolution, the Luxemburgist Party—again like Trotsky—identified itself with Bolshevism. Here we must take note of the differences within the Party between adherents of the Party's official leaders (Rosa Luxemburg, Marchlewski, Jogiches) and the so-called 'splitters' (Dzerzhinski, Radek, Unszlicht). This was, however, a discord, not a genuine split. The 'splitters' represented a certain opposition to the centralism of the Executive Committee, which operated from abroad. Furthermore, they were somewhat closer to the Bolsheviks. In the Polish Communist Party the SDKPiL tradition was predominant from the beginning. Nevertheless the importance of these differences should not be exaggerated. They were in actual fact restrained and even obliterated by the real unity of the newly founded Party and the conviction of its members that the old divisions were a matter of the past. The Party's ranks were further united by a sharp awareness of their common and unyielding opposition to the nationalist and reformist Poland, to the Poland of the landlords and petty nobility.[3]

Is it not true that the Communist Party began its political life in independent Poland with a certain moral disadvantage arising from its Luxemburgist tradition, which was opposed in principle to the struggle for national independence?

There is a little truth and a great deal of exaggeration in that. The proof that this is so is seen, for example, in the relative strength of the different parties within the Soviets of the Workers' Deputies which were set up, at the end of 1918, in Warsaw, in Lodz, and in the Dabrowa coalfields. In Warsaw the forces of the Communist Party and of the Socialists were equally balanced and, if I am not mistaken, the Bund[4] tipped the scales. There was a similar situation in Lodz, although there the Communists had a certain superiority. In the Dabrowa mining district the Communist Party was incomparably stronger than the Socialist Party, and with this is connected the episode of the Red Republic of Dabrowa. One could say that on the eve of independence, the influence of the Polish CP over the working classes in the main industrial centres was certainly not smaller than that of the reformist and 'patriotic' PPS—it was probably larger.

The situation was complicated. On the one hand, events had *to a certain degree* refuted the assumptions on which Rosa Luxemburg and her comrades had dissented from the 'struggle for national independence'. On the other hand, however, Luxemburg and her followers had been alone in placing their hopes on revolutions in Russia, Germany, and

Austria, the three empires that had subjugated Poland, rather than on an unending repetition of Polish nineteenth-century insurrections. Pilsudskism—and the Polish Socialist Party which in 1918 was almost inseparable from Pilsudskism—had above all proclaimed its scepticism and distrust of the reality of revolution in these empires. Events had given the lie to this scepticism and distrust. Contrary to Rosa Luxemburg's expectations, Poland had regained her independence; but contrary to the expectations of her opponents, Poland had received it mainly from the hands of the Russian and German revolutions. History showed itself to be more cunning than all the parties; and that is why I do not believe that, in comparison with other parties, the Communist Party entered the phase of independence with any particular 'moral handicap'. Moreover, while the 'Luxemburgists' were rotting in tsarist prisons and in exile, the Polish bourgeois parties (especially the 'national democrats', who opposed all movements for national independence, but also Pilsudski and the Socialist 'patriots') placed themselves at the service of the occupying powers and collaborated with them; after the fall of these powers, this did not prevent the bourgeois parties from adopting hypocritical, ultranationalist attitudes and from seizing power.

After the foundation of the Polish Communist Party did the old controversy over Poland's independence go on within the Party?

Only at the beginning, and to an insignificant degree; later it stopped altogether. The Party was concerned with other problems—its position in the configuration of social forces; the elaboration of its political line; and, of course, the problem of the Russian Revolution and the prospects of world revolution.

Did not the question of boycotting the Constituent Assembly of 1919 mark the appearance of a new division within the Party?

Unless I am mistaken, this question did not give rise to much discussion. On this matter the Polish and the German parties took similar stands, considering elections to the Constituent Assembly as a diversion which had as its aim the liquidation of the Soviets of Workers' Delegates. The Polish *Seym* and the Weimar Constituent Assembly were regarded as the foundations of a bourgeois parliamentary republic, erected on the ruins of the workers' Soviets—the potential organs of the socialist revolution. Undoubtedly, the two parties made a mistake in proclaiming the boycott of the bourgeois parliament, and in both cases this mistake was a result of the ultraleft mood of the period.

How did the Communist Party react to the Polish-Soviet war of 1920?

The Polish Party treated this war—as it had every reason to do—as a war of the Polish possessing classes (or of their decisive elements) against the Russian Revolution, and as an integral part of the capitalist powers' intervention in Russia. The Party felt it was at one with the Russian Revolution and obliged to defend it. The situation became complicated after Pilsudski's retreat from Kiev and at the time of the Red Army's march on Warsaw. The state of siege and the existence of military tribunals reduced to a minimum the Party's open activities; and it was difficult for both leaders and rank and file to express the various nuances of Communist opinion. Nevertheless I should like to draw attention to characteristic differences which appeared among the numerous groups of Polish Communists living in Moscow. When the question of the march on Warsaw came up, this group split in a rather paradoxical manner. On the one hand, the old 'Luxemburgists', the 'opponents of independence', Radek and Marchlewski,[5] spared no efforts to convince Lenin and the Russian Politburo that the march on Warsaw should not be undertaken, but that peace should be proposed to Poland as soon as Pilsudski's armies had been chased out of the Ukraine. (They succeeded in winning to their point of view only Trotsky, who was then the People's Commissar for War.) On the other hand, the old supporters of independence, former PPS men like Feliks Kon and Lapinski,[6] favoured the Red Army's march on Warsaw; they maintained that the Polish proletariat was in a state of the utmost revolutionary ferment and would welcome the Red Army as its liberator. I should like to report yet another episode: in 1920 the paper *Rote Fahne,* the organ of the German Communist Party, published a protest against the march on Warsaw signed by Domski, one of the most eminent 'Luxemburgist' members of the Central Committee of the Polish Party. By the way, under the conditions of internal democracy, which existed at that time in the Party, the right of a member of the Central Committee to publish such a protest was considered as something quite natural. Domski remained a member of the Central Committee and played a leading role in it for many more years, until 1925 precisely.

You asked whether the Luxemburgist tradition was not a moral embarrassment for Polish communism. I have no intention of defending *post factum* Rosa Luxemburg's ideas about national independence. I shall simply say that the Red Army's march on Warsaw was a much more serious and more damaging moral handicap for the Polish CP than had been all of Rosa Luxemburg's real or imaginary mistakes taken together; about these mistakes both her bourgeois opponents as well as Stalin (the latter misusing, in his characteristic manner, quotations from Lenin) have made an enormous amount of noise. However, the mistake made by Lenin in 1920—let us call things by their proper name—was a real tragedy for the Polish CP, because in effect it pushed the Polish proletarian masses towards anti-Sovietism and anti-Communism.

Nevertheless, after 1920 the Party rapidly regained its strength—didn't it?

Yes, to a certain extent. That does not alter the fact that the march on Warsaw also had certain permanent effects: it undermined the trust of the Polish working masses in the Russian Revolution. However, after 1920 the workers recovered fairly quickly from their first enthusiasm for Polish national sovereignty, and from the illusions that went with it. In the relatively freer atmosphere which followed the war, the working class had the opportunity to view the events more calmly. It became known that Lenin's government had done everything possible to avoid war between Poland and Russia and that without Pilsudski's march on Kiev there would probably never have been any Soviet march on Warsaw. The Polish working class came to understand that Pilsudski, in 1920, was not fighting so much for Polish independence as for the estates of the big Polish landowners in the Ukraine, and also to satisfy his own dreams of grandeur. The early years of the twenties marked another increase in the influence of the Polish Communist Party, an influence which reached its peak in 1923, particularly in November, at the time of the general strike and the rising of the Cracow workers.

This was the time of the 'three W's' leadership, wasn't it?

It was. One of them, Warski, was a former Luxemburgist, and the two others, Walecki and Wera (Kostrzewa), were former Left Socialists. Nevertheless, they formed a united leadership which proved that the old divisions within the party had been overcome. Now, however, we are approaching a particularly critical period, when the development of the class struggle in Poland was complicated once more, and to a certain extent distorted, by the influence of events taking place in the Soviet Union. For many years, I personally believed that in Poland, as well as in Germany, the year 1923 was one of a 'missed revolution'. Now, after an interval of thirty-five years, I can no longer be so sure that the historical evidence bears out the correctness of this point of view. In any case, we certainly had many elements of a revolutionary situation: a general strike, the rising of the Cracow workers, the army going over to the side of the working class, and more generally, the country in a state of utter ferment. The only factor, it seemed, which was lacking was the initiative of a revolutionary party which might have led the revolution to success. The Polish CP did not show that initiative. In accordance with the resolutions of the International, the Party was then following a policy of united front with the socialists. Up to a certain moment, this policy had produced excellent results, enabling the Party to widen its influence, and introducing more vigour into the class struggle. But at the same time, the Party leadership left the political initiative to the Socialists; and in the critical days of November 1923, this produced unfortunate consequences. The rank and file felt that the Party had allowed a revolutionary situation to pass by without taking any advantage; and they reacted, not without bitterness, against the 'opportunism' and the lack of revolutionary initiative of the 'three W's'.

As I have said, the situation became even more complicated because of events taking place in the USSR. At that time the struggle between the so-called triumvirate (Stalin, Zinoviev and Kamenev) and Trotsky broke into the open. At once it took on extremely violent forms unknown hitherto in the movement. The European Communist Parties were deeply disturbed, all the more so as until then Trotsky, like Lenin, had been the International's inspirer and greatest moral authority. In the autumn of 1923 the Central Committees of the Polish, French and German parties protested, in one form or another, to the Central Committee of the Soviet Party against the violence of the attacks on Trotsky. Those who protested had no intention of associating themselves with Trotsky's specific policies. They were simply warning the Soviet leaders of the harm which the campaign against Trotsky was doing to the Communist movement, and they appealed to them to settle their differences in a manner worthy of Communists. This incident had serious consequences. Stalin never forgot or forgave this protest. Zinoviev, who was then president of the International, viewed it as a vote of no confidence in himself. Immediately, the Communist Parties of Poland, France and Germany became involved in the internal Soviet conflict. The leadership of the International —in other words, Zinoviev and Stalin—dismissed from their posts the principal leaders of the three parties who had dared 'to come to Trotsky's defence'. A pretext was provided by the mistakes committed by these leaders, notably by the group of the 'three Ws' in November 1923; they were expelled for 'opportunism, right deviation, and failure to exploit a revolutionary situation'.

Does it not follow from your account that those who criticised the 'three Ws' were justified?

Even if they were justified, that did not authorise the leadership of the International in Moscow to intervene in such a drastic manner in the internal affairs of the Polish Party. I must add that the leadership of the German and French parties was changed in the same way.[7] In all these cases the changes were brought about as a result of orders from above, and not as a result of decisions taken by the members of the Party in a way corresponding to the principles of internal democracy. This was the first dangerous attack on the autonomy of the Communist Party, the first act, as it turned out, of 'Stalinisation,' although this was done not only by Stalin, but by Zinoviev also. Both played demagogically on the feeling of disillusionment which existed among the rank and file of the Polish and German parties. This feeling was understandable and it turned violently against the 'three Ws' in Poland (as it did against Brandler in Germany). It is possible that if the Party had been free to decide for itself, it might have changed its leadership. Nevertheless, more important than the fact of the change itself was the manner in which it was carried out: the way was opened to further unscrupulous interference by Stalin in the affairs of the Polish Communist Party, an interference which was to end in the Party's assassination.

How did the Party react to this first act of deliberate interference?

Passively, unfortunately. Many of its members were more or less in favour of the 'three Ws' being replaced. And even those who weren't did not oppose it. The operation was mild in comparison with the expulsions, purges and forced recantations which were to follow. Stalinism was only in its formative period, and could not yet show its claws. The attack on the displaced leaders was carried on with relative moderation and correctness of form—and this facilitated its acceptance. What was decisive, however, was the Party's psychological attitude—its misguided conception of solidarity with the Russian Revolution, its belief that any conflict with Moscow must be avoided, no matter at what cost. The moral authority of the Soviet Party, the only one which had led a proletarian revolution to victory, was so great that the Polish Communists accepted Moscow's decisions even when Moscow abused its revolutionary authority. Stalinism was indeed a continuous succession of abuses of this kind, a systematic exploitation of the moral credit of the revolution for purposes which often had nothing to do with the interests of Communism but served only to consolidate the bureaucratic regime of the USSR. During the years 1923–4 it was vital for Stalin to attack Trotskyism in the whole International. Warski and Kostrzewa tried to safeguard their own position by dissociating themselves from their own protest against Moscow's anti-Trotsky campaign. Their motives were understandable. In Moscow the majority of the Politburo and of the Central Committee had come out against Trotsky. In view of this, Warski and Kostrzewa decided that they could not support the minority in the Soviet Party and thus expose themselves to the charge of interfering in the internal affairs of the Party. That did not, however, protect the Polish Party from Soviet interference. Thus, although the 'three Ws' had some sympathy with the views of the Trotskyist opposition, they came, in fact, to support Stalin and Zinoviev and to proclaim their loyalty to them. For this moment of weakness they had to pay dearly later on.

What was the change in the Party's policy after 1923?

What was called 'the left' took over the leadership: Domski, Zofia Unszlicht, and Lenski. Both in the International as a whole and also in the Polish Party the new policy presented a sharp reaction from the orientation of the preceding period. This was, in fact, the time of an 'ultraleftist' policy. If, in 1923, the Party did not show enough revolutionary vigour, its policy during the years 1924 and 1925 was marked by a false excess of that vigour. This was all the more harmful because after the crisis of November 1923 the objective possibilities of revolutionary action had decreased. During this period the Polish CP rejected the united front tactic completely and dispersed its efforts in futile adventures. The result? It lost its influence and cut itself off from the working masses.

It is worth recalling that, at the beginning of 1924, in local elections, the Polish CP was still stronger than the Socialist Party. This success, however, was no more than a delayed echo of the radicalisation of the masses which had taken place in 1923 and it did not foreshadow the rise of a new revolutionary wave. In the following years the Communist Party's influence declined drastically. The Party was unable to lead any mass action. This was not only a Polish phenomenon. The same fluctuations could be seen in all the Communist Parties of Europe—all were, in fact, pursuing the same ultraleftist policy with similar results. This was the time of the Fifth Congress of the Comintern; it was called the 'Bolshevisation Congress,' but actually it was the 'Stalinisation Congress'. Henceforth, all parties were subjected to the same treatment; all followed the same 'line'; all had recourse to the same tactical tricks; all launched the same slogans without taking into account differences in the class relationships of different countries, in the level and form of class struggle, etc. The movement had reached the stage of bureaucratic uniformity. The Polish Party was affected by this even more painfully than were other European parties because its revolutionary tradition had been deeper and stronger, and it operated in conditions of complete illegality,[8] appealing continuously to the spirit of revolutionary self-sacrifice and to the heroism of its members, which never failed. Bureaucratic uniformity and revolutionary enthusiasm are a contradiction in terms.

Nevertheless, at the end of 1925, Warski, Walecki and Kostrzewa returned to the leadership of the Party, didn't they?

Yes. The ultraleftist policy was soon discredited in the eyes of the Party, and that of the 'three Ws' was almost automatically vindicated. Whatever might be said against Warski and Kostrzewa, they had the gift of feeling the moods of the working class and the ability to strengthen and widen contacts between the Party and the masses. The periods when they led the Party were, in general, those when the Party expanded and conducted its activity on a grand scale, although it frequently lacked—how shall I put it—a revolutionary edge. The return of Warski and Kostrzewa to the leadership of the Polish Communist Party was, again, due more to what was then happening in Russia than to the change of climate in the Polish Party.

In Russia, a new political situation had developed. The triumvirate had broken up. Zinoviev and Kamenev had turned against Stalin, and shortly afterwards they were to ally themselves with Trotsky. Stalin formed a bloc with Bukharin and Rykov and followed what has been called 'a rightist line' in the Soviet Party and in the International. What was called the 'Polish right', the 'three Ws', came back into favour for the time being because they had lent support to Stalin and Bukharin. On the other hand, a part of the ultraleftist leadership, Zofia Unszlicht and Domski, sided with Zinoviev; it was for this reason, more than for any mistake they had committed in Poland, that they were removed.[9] Once more, calculations connected with the struggle in the Soviet Party were decisive. Lenski, in spite of his ultraleft policy, remained in the leadership, sharing influence with the 'three Ws'; Lenski, unlike Domski and Unszlicht, had come out against the Zinovievist opposition. More than this, he became the leader of the Stalinist nucleus within the Polish CP, whereas Warski and Kostrzewa, although completely loyal to Stalin, maintained a certain reserve towards him and were closer to Bukharin's group. Later this division within the Polish Party was to be crystallised in the formation of a 'minority' faction led by Lenski and a 'majority' led by Warski and Kostrzewa. At the beginning of 1926 these two factions shared the leadership and both were responsible for policy, in particular for the 'May mistake', that is, the support the Polish CP gave to Pilsudski at the time of his *coup d'état* of May 1926.

Could you say something more about the 'May mistake' and explain its background? Among old Party militants I often find the following thesis: at the time of the coup the Party could not avoid supporting Pilsudski, who had the confidence of the Polish Socialist Party and of the entire left, and whose 'putsch' was directed against the so-called Chjeno-Piast government (a coalition of the right-centre). The Party, they say, considered that the coup constituted in a certain measure the beginning of a bourgeois revolution, and as such was relatively progressive, because during the previous period only the semifeudal landed proprietors had held power, to the exclusion even of the bourgeoisie.

The 'May mistake' is clearly of fundamental importance in the history of

Polish Communism. I cannot attempt to give you here a detailed explanation of its background. This would require an analysis of the most complicated class relationships and political forces.[10] Therefore, I shall simply try to sketch in certain broad historical outlines. Again, it is essential to examine the situation on two levels: on the level of the class struggle in Poland and on that of the internal development of the Soviet Party and the Comintern.

Let us begin with the purely Polish aspect. Poland was going through a crisis of the parliamentary regime. No stable government could be formed on a parliamentary basis, and this reflected the breakdown of the social and political equilibrium outside parliament. All the possibilities of parliamentary alliances had been exhausted. The masses were utterly disillusioned with their regime, which proved incapable of providing employment and of protecting workers from the catastrophic results of the currency devaluation, had deceived the peasants' expectation of land reform, had condemned the national minorities to oppression and despair. On the other hand, the propertied class were equally opposed to parliament and to the 'omnipotence of the Diet'. They were afraid that the feeble Polish parliamentarianism, unable to ensure stable, let alone 'strong' government, might expose the existing social system to the danger of violent attack and revolution. Objectively, the situation was ripe for the overthrow of the parliamentary regime. Theoretically, there were three possibilities. The parliamentary regime might have been overthrown by a fascist mass movement, similar to Nazism or the Italian prototype. This, however, was not the actual prospect. For reasons which I shall not examine here, all attempts to launch such a movement in Poland, attempts repeated more than once both before and after 1926, failed. Our native varieties of fascism or Nazism were little more than comic-opera creations.

The second theoretical possibility consisted in the overthrow of the bourgeois-parliamentary regime by proletarian revolution—for this, one might have thought, the Polish CP should have been preparing. However, during the months preceding the May coup the CP had been preparing for almost everything except revolution. Up to a point, this fact reflected the ebb of the militant mood among the working class, the shock the 1923 disaster had inflicted on them, and, finally, the exhaustion of the movement by the pseudo-revolutionary, sterile 'activities' of 1924–5. The Communist movement lacked self-confidence; and when there was little self-assurance in the vanguard, there was, naturally, even less of it in the working class as a whole. Not believing in its own strength, the working class was inclined to place its hope in external forces and to calculate the benefits which it might obtain for itself through the activities of other classes or social groups. Such was the objective political background to the 'May mistake'.

A remark in passing—the Polish Communist Party's 'May mistake' began even before 1926. If my memory does not mislead me, it was Warski who, on behalf of the Communist group, offered an emergency motion in the Diet in the autumn of 1925 on 'the dangers threatening the independence of Poland'. The motion was as unexpected as it was amazing. It was astonishing that a friend of Rosa Luxemburg should suddenly raise an alarm about the 'dangers threatening Poland's independence'. In the situation of 1925 it was difficult to see what justified the alarm. The conclusion of this emergency motion was even more amazing. In it, Warski—to meet the 'threat to independence'—demanded the immediate return of Pilsudski to the post of commander-in-chief of the armed forces (this at a time when Pilsudski had left the army and was sulking in his retreat in Sulejowek).

The spectacle was tragicomic indeed! Hardly five years had elapsed since Pilsudski had marched on Kiev, mainly in order to return the Ukrainian estates to their landowners, and the Communist Party was now calling back this man of destiny to head the army, in order to safeguard national independence. It is enough merely to describe the situation in these terms—and these are the only realistic (though grotesque) terms—to dipose of the theory according to which the comeback of Pilsudski was supposed to mark the beginning of the bourgeois revolution in Poland. How could the defender of the feudal estates of the *szlachta* (nobility and gentry) have become transformed suddenly into the inspirer of the bourgeois revolution, the main task of which is usually to destroy feudalism, or what is left of it?

I have mentioned three possible solutions to the crisis of the parliamentary regime in Poland. The third solution consisted in the setting-up of a military dictatorship. Pilsudski was clearly the candidate, the pretender. He had this advantage over other generals: he enjoyed a high reputation. A legend surrounded him as a fighter for national independence, as former chief of the Polish Socialist Party, as the anti-tsarist terrorist of 1905, and as the founder of the Polish legions in 1914. By clamouring for his return, the Polish CP blindly and in spite of itself wove a few of its own purple threads into the fabric of this rather phoney legend. The Party helped to create illusions in the working masses about the 'Grandad' *(Dziadek)*, as Pilsudski was called familiarly, and so to prepare the way for the May *coup d'ětat*. How much more correctly did Adolf Nowaczynski, the talented clown of the National-Democratic petty bourgeoisie, grasp Pilsudski's role when he nicknamed him 'Napoleon IV, the very smallest'! How much more appropriate it would have been for Marxists, who should have learned the art of political analysis from Marx's *18th Brumaire*, to take this view of Pilsudski!

It is, nevertheless, true that Pilsudski was opposing a centre-right government, presided over by Witos, which represented the interests of the petty nobility and gentry. Is it not true that it was precisely this government which had abolished parliamentary liberties and begun to set up a fascist regime? Do not these facts—independently of what happened in 1920—indicate that the Party was right to a certain extent to support Pilsudski?

It is undeniable that this is how the situation now appeared to very many Communists—and even more so to Socialists. Nevertheless these were optical illusions; and their spell was broken only when it was too late. In any case one could not, without simplifying things too much, define the Witos government as one representing the interests of the large landowners. Witos represented a compromise between the interests of the landed gentry and those of the rich peasantry, a compromise that had been reached at the expense of the poor peasants, robbing the latter of the benefits of an agrarian reform. This compromise was clearly the result of the aspirations of the landlords and the kulaks. Moreover, it was not true that the danger of fascism came from this government. The government coalition represented the most reactionary combination of interests and forces that was possible *within the framework* of the parliamentary regime, but it worked precisely within that framework. Outside parliament it did not possess a political force strong enough to be set against the 'omnipotence of the Diet'. This was the insoluble dilemma of the Polish propertied classes and their traditional parties: they were incapable of maintaining their class domination either by a stabilisation or by overthrowing that regime. As in Marx's description of the *18th Brumaire,* only the executive, the state machine, could solve this dilemma, at least for a time. Throughout the twenty years between the two wars, the objective conditions favourable to the rise of a real fascist dictatorship did not exist in Poland, if by 'fascist' we understand a totalitarian dictatorship based on a strong and clearly counter-revolutionary mass movement. There was no lack of candidates for the role of Hitler or of Mussolini, but in Poland the counter-revolution never succeeded in setting such a mass movement in motion. The counter-revolution could only offer a 'dictatorship of the sword'. And once again, as in Marx's classic description, we are witnessing the quarrels and the coarse rows between our own pseudo-Napoleon and our own Changarnier, quarrels which were concerned with the question of whose sword was to rule the nation—Pilsudski's or Haller's.[11] (There are probably few in Poland today who realise that Haller was at one time Pilsudski's most important rival.) And because of the role that the 'independence mythology' played in our political life and also in our political thinking, the choice of the sword depended on the sheath. Only Pilsudski's sword, sheathed in the legends of the struggle for independence, was considered worthy of exercising power over the people and capable of beheading the feeble body of Polish parliamentarianism.

In other words, Pilsudski expropriated the Polish landlords and bourgeoisie *politically* in order to preserve their *social* domination over the proletariat and the peasantry. When, in May 1926, we saw President Witos, with his trousers half-buttoned, scuttling through the courtyard of the Belvedere Palace in Warsaw, pursued by detachments of Pilsudski's forces, we were witnessing, in fact, an act of political expropriation. To the working class and to its parties this looked like the beginning of economic and social expropriation. But Pilsudski saved the Polish propertied classes in spite of themselves and in spite of their traditional representatives; and he did this with the help of the workers' parties.[12]

All of this does not yet explain fully the origin of the 'May mistake'. Even before the May coup, the leaders of the Polish Communist Party had a premonition that Pilsudski was getting ready to seize power and that this augured nothing good for the working classes. Warski, it seems, said so publicly. Indeed, even some of the leaders of the Polish Socialist Party had few illusions on this score. I remember how, as a novice journalist of nineteen, on the first night of the putsch I found myself by chance in Warecka Street, in the office of Feliks Perl, editor of *Robotnik,* the historian of the Polish Socialist Party, and one of its most eminent leaders. Perl was very worried and indignant. Every few minutes he grabbed the telephone and demanded to be put through to Pilsudski's headquarters, to General Tokarzewski, if I am not mistaken, and with a sweet-and-sour look on his face asked: 'Any news of *our* front, comrade general? How are *our* troops getting on?' Replacing the receiver, he paced nervously up and down, and forgetting that I was there, grumbled to himself: 'This adventurer has landed us in the soup ['adventurer' applied to Pilsudski]. If he fails, things will go badly, but if he wins, he'll thrash us.' This scene repeated itself several times during the night. Meanwhile, the presses in the *Robotnik* printing shop were turning out an appeal 'to the toiling people of the capital' in which the 'adventurer' was hailed as a firm friend of the working class and of socialism.

But let us come back to the Polish Communist Party. Its leaders were too good Marxists to be, in normal circumstances, taken in so easily by optical illusions, even when these illusions originated in the peculiar class relationships in the country. There was another and perhaps a weightier reason for the 'May mistake', and it should be sought in the ideological atmosphere and in the policy of the Soviet Communist Party and the Comintern. The Polish Party was not alone in making such a 'mistake': a similar one on a gigantic scale, which was to have tragic consequences, was committed by the Chinese Communist Party when it blindly supported Chiang Kai-shek and the Kuomintang. And in nearby Roumania, almost at the same time—I think this was also in May 1926—the extremely weak Communist Party supported a similar military putsch carried out by General Antonescu.

This was, we remember, the time of the Stalin-Bukharin bloc. Trotskyism had already been routed; the bitter struggle between the Stalin-Bukharin group and the so-called Leningrad opposition led by Zinoviev and Kamenev was in full swing. Bukharin for reasons of principle, and Stalin for tactical reasons, had both declared themselves the defenders of small peasant property and of the peasantry in general, which was supposedly threatened by the Leningrad opposition. The actual disagreements were over domestic, economic and social policies but, as usual, Stalin transformed a discussion on specific policies into a great dogmatic battle in which the issue at stake was allegedly the fundamental attitude towards the 'middle strata'—the peasantry and the petty bourgeoisie. Stalin and Bukharin accused the Leningrad opposition of hostility towards the 'middle strata' and of failing to understand the importance for the proletariat of the alliance with these strata. This discussion formed a sequel to the anti-Trotskyist campaign of 1923–5, during which the most serious accusation made against Trotsky had been that in his theory of the permanent revolution he too had not 'appreciated at their true value' the importance of the middle strata, their progressive role, and the need to form alliances with them. Trotsky, it was said, had not understood in 1905 the necessity for a bourgeois revolution in Russia (and in the other backward countries) or had underestimated it; that was why he had proclaimed that in the twentieth century the bourgeois-democratic revolution and the socialist revolution would merge into a single one ('permanent revolution') to be accomplished under the leadership of the proletariat throughout. To try and 'skip' the bourgeois stage of the revolution, so the argument ran, was the characteristic aberration of Trotskyism.

I cannot enter here into an analysis of these extremely complex problems; I am concerned now with their repercussions in Poland. The Comintern was just then busy eradicating the Trotskyist and Zinovievist heresies. The distinctive marks of these heresies were defined as an 'ultra-leftist' and negative attitude towards 'alliances with the middle strata', a fundamental unwillingness to make such alliances, and an unwillingness to recognise that bourgeois revolution, especially in the underdeveloped countries, formed a separate stage of the historical development, in which the bourgeoisie played a progressive and even a revolutionary role. The Comintern was as if seized with an obsessional cult of 'alliances'. Any sign of scepticism with regard to this cult was stigmatised as Trotskyism. The cult of alliances served a double purpose: within the Soviet Union it justified the 'rightist' line of Bukharin and Stalin; internationally it justified Soviet policy in China, which subordinated the Chinese CP to the Kuomintang and placed it under Chiang Kai-shek's orders. The principles and the methods of this policy were soon applied, automatically and bureaucratically, to all the parties of the International, and among them obviously to the Polish Party. Translated into the terms of Polish politics, this line implied an 'alliance' with Pilsudski as the representative of the 'progressive' forces of the 'bourgeois' revolution. Pilsudski suddenly appeared almost as the ideal ally—and only the Trotskyists and the Zinovievists could spurn the ideal.

At this time were there any Trotskyist or Zinovievist groups within the Polish Communist Party?

As I have already mentioned, Domski and Zofia Unszlicht had ideas which brought them close to the Zinovievist opposition. However, by that time, they had been removed from any activity in the Polish Party. Nevertheless, the Party leadership was fully aware of the practical and political questions as well as of the doctrinal issues which had been raised; and it worked under the pressure of the ideological conflicts in Moscow. At this time Warski and Kostrzewa showed a quite extraordinary docility towards Stalin. They cherished the illusion that by paying the price of submissiveness they would buy for themselves freedom of action in their own Party. Handicapped as they were by their double 'mistake' of 1923 (their intervention in Trotsky's favour and their 'opportunistic' policy in Poland), they were anxious to provide every possible proof of their conversion to the new 'Bolshevism' that spoke of the two *distinct* stages in the revolution, the bourgeois and the socialist, the 'Bolshevism' that attached so much importance to its alliance with 'progressive bourgeois' elements. The whole Party propaganda was carried out in this spirit; and it created certain conditioned political reflexes within the Party which definitely contributed to the 'May mistake'.

In addition we must examine the effect on the Party's state of mind of the campaign which was carried out with the aim of liquidating what was called the 'Luxemburgist heritage'. This, by the way, is a problem which so far has not received the attention it deserves in Poland, probably because those who study the Party's history have not been equipped sufficiently to tackle the problem—they lack both method and factual knowledge. The most extraordinary myths have multiplied around the 'Luxemburgist heritage'. I do not want this statement to give rise to misunderstandings: I do not claim that Rosa Luxemburg was infallible, and I am not a Luxemburgist. Undoubtedly, she made some mistakes, but they were no more serious than those committed by Lenin or even by Marx, and in any case they were in quite a different category than Stalin's 'errors'. It was, and still is, necessary to analyse these mistakes rigorously and objectively, and to see them in their true proportions. This, however, was not the kind of analysis in which Stalin was interested—nor was Zinoviev in the years 1923–4, when, in the name of the 'Bolshevisation' of the Polish CP, they declared a holy war on Luxemburgism—that is, on the main ideological tradition of Polish Communism. In order to realise what really mattered to Stalin it would be enough to reread his notorious 1931 letter to the editor of *Proletarskaya Revolutsya.* Instinctively, Stalin detected Rosa Luxemburg's affinity with Trotsky. And, even though there had been no Trotskyist opposition within the Polish Party during the 1920s, that party reeked to him of 'Trotskyism'; Stalin considered Luxemburgism as the Polish variety of Trotskyism. This provoked the *furor theologicus* with which the Comintern set out to crush the Luxemburgist heritage.

It is undeniable that this heritage was not above criticism. Lenin's attitude on the question of national independence, or rather of the self-determination of oppressed peoples, was more realistic than that of Rosa Luxemburg. As far as the agrarian question was concerned, Rosa Luxemburg and her disciples did not go beyond advocating the socialisation of farming, without understanding the necessity, in Russia and Poland, to share out the land of the semi-feudal latifundia among the peasants. This attitude did not allow Polish Communism to exercise revolutionary influence over the peasantry in 1920, particularly in the eastern marches. At the time of the anti-Luxemburgist campaign, however, it was not enough to analyse these mistakes critically. The whole way of thinking, which belonged both to Luxemburgism and to Marxism—the traditions of true internationalism, the Party's specifically proletarian and socialist orientation, its healthy suspicion of the leaders (genuine or self-appointed) of the so-called middle strata—had to be rooted out. Thus the Polish CP began to atone for the Luxemburgist 'sins' against national independence by belated and absurd demonstrations of its reverence for the fetishes of patriotism; and it began to pay undeserved homage to the 'Legends of Independence'. From this there resulted the paradoxical spectacle, which I described above, when, in 1925, Warski sent out a cry of alarm at the dangers which faced national independence and demanded the return of Pilsudski to the post of commander-in-chief. On the one hand Warski was prey to the qualms of his own political conscience, and on the other hand he echoed the anti-Luxemburgist exorcisms that came from Moscow. As if to expiate the 'antipatriotic' sins of his youth, Warski—and in his person Polish Marxism at large—went to Canossa. On this pilgrimage the Party was once more torn and tormented by bitter misgivings: it paid homage to the would-be dictator, of whom Rosa Luxemburg had said, at the beginning of the century, that his whole 'patriotic' ideology was but the sublimation of the dream of a déclassé petty nobleman who, even under tsardom saw himself as the future gendarme-in-chief of his 'own' independent Polish state. Rosa may have been mistaken about the chances of bourgeois Poland regaining independence, but she was not wrong about Pilsudski's ambition and the nature of Pilsudskism.

Finally, Luxemburgism, like Trotskyism, was charged with the mortal sin of failing to understand the Party's tasks in a bourgeois revolution. In their enthusiasm to fight and defeat the Luxemburgist tradition, the Party leaders suddenly discovered that in Poland history had put on the agenda the bourgeois democratic revolution, and not, as they had thought hitherto, the socialist revolution, which would complete our overdue and unfinished bourgeois revolution. But if the bourgeois revolution was on the agenda, who could be its chief and its leader? Neither in its youth nor in its maturity had the Polish bourgeoisie produced a Danton or a Robespierre. How could it produce one in its old age? But an offshoot of our petty gentry, our 'frontiersman-gentry',[14] could still produce our own parish-pump edition of the *18th Brumaire.* It was in him, then, that our Marxists, misled and hopelessly confused by Stalinism, discovered the hero of the bourgeois stage of the revolution. The situation was grotesque precisely because this *bourgeois* revolution was designed to overthrow a government presided over by Witos, the leader of the kulaks, backed by the largest section—the peasant section—of the Polish bourgeoisie. And in retrospect the vicious circle in which the Polish CP moved under Stalinist guidance can be seen even more clearly: in 1926 the Party saw in Pilsudski an ally against the 'fascism' of Witos; and a few years later, in the Popular Front period, it greeted in Witos a fighter and an ally in the struggle against Pilsudski's 'fascism'. Incidentally, without any Stalinist promptings, the Polish Socialist Party was floundering in the same vicious circle.

You have recalled the analogy between the Polish CP's 'May mistake' and the support the Chinese CP was giving to Chiang Kai-shek at the same time. Did the Polish CP give its support to Pilsudski on definite orders from Moscow in the same way as the Chinese supported Chiang Kai-shek?

No. Not at all. Stalin's and Bukharin's attitude towards Pilsudski was different from that towards Chiang Kai-shek. In Chiang Kai-shek, then an honorary member of the executive of the International, they saw an ally of the Soviet Union and of Communism. In Pilsudski they saw the enemy of the 1920 war. Not only had Moscow not advised the Communists to support Pilsudski, they immediately took an unfavourable view of the CP's stand in the May *coup d'état.* Moreover, when the Communist group in the Diet decided to vote in the presidential election for Pilsudski, it was prevented from doing so by the veto of the executive of the Communist International. It was not 'orders from Moscow' which were responsible for the 'May mistake', but rather a certain political fetishism which spread from Moscow and which was inseparable from that stage of the Stalinisation and bureaucratisation of the Comintern. Stalin did not prompt Warski to report to Pilsudski's headquarters during the May coup. Yet Stalinism was responsible for the 'May mistake', because it had confused the Polish CP, as it had confused other Communist Parties, because it had made it impossible for the Party to analyse situations and problems in the Marxist manner, because it had terrorised the Party leaders with cults that did not allow them to work out policies in accordance with the demands of our class struggle and our ideological tradition. One may say what one likes against 'Luxemburgism', but within the framework of this 'ism' there was certainly no place for anything even remotely resembling the 'May mistake'. Can anyone imagine Rosa Luxemburg reporting docilely at Pilsudski's GHQ and declaring her Party's support for his coup? It took a luckless disciple of hers, a disciple whose backbone was already hopelessly deformed by Stalinism, to perform the feat.

How long did the Party maintain this policy?

For a very short time. On the day following the *coup d'état* or very shortly afterwards as far as I can remember. Communist Party proclamations were circulating in Moscow, branding Pilsudski as a fascist dictator. Pilsudski himself did not allow the Party to cherish any illusions; he refused straightway to grant an amnesty to the thousands of imprisoned Communists, he boasted loudly of the 'strong arm' government he was going to set up, he repudiated all 'social experiments' and reforms, and he sought at once to come to terms with the big landowners.

There are some mistakes which are committed in a few days or even hours, but which cannot be repaired in decades. The 'May mistake' was of this kind. In fairness to the Communist Party leaders it must be said that despite Pilsudski's reactionary and dictatorial manners, the Polish Socialist Party backed him for two years or more, while the Communists recovered quickly from their May 'intoxication' and began at once to wage an active struggle against Pilsudski, continuing to do so until the end. Disoriented and knocked off balance as it was, the Communist Party was still the only one to defend the cause of the proletariat and of the poor peasantry, and to stand up for democratic liberties, while the declared upholders of democracy—the socialists—helped Pilsudski to strengthen his position and to undermine all democratic institutions. Warski tried as best he could to make good the 'May mistake'. On this occasion he showed great dignity, militancy, and personal courage. In the name of the Party, he hurled accusations in Pilsudski's face and for this, on the dictator's orders and in the dictator's presence, he was dragged out of the National Assembly by Pilsudski's guards. In order to realise the effect that Warski's cry, 'Down with the dictator' had, one must bear in mind the cult which surrounded Pilsudski at that time. Pilsudski himself was as if taken aback by this cry: this was the first attack on his legend, the first attempt to tear it to shreds. I also remember the image of Warski at the Theatre Square on May 1, 1928. He was marching in the forefront of our huge and illegal demonstration, through the hail of machine-gun fire and rifle shots with which we were greeted by the Socialist Party militia,[15] while tens and hundreds of wounded were falling in our ranks, he held up his white-gray head, a high and easy target visible from afar; unyielding and unmoved, he addressed the crowd. This was the image of him I had in my mind when, some years later, it was announced from Moscow that he was a traitor, a spy, and a Pilsudski agent.

What responsibility had the different 'majority' and 'minority' factions for the 'May mistake'? Did this split exist even before 1926?

As far as I know these divisions did not exist before 1926. It was, in fact, the 'May mistake' which brought them into being; if my memory does not betray me, these two factions first came to the fore at the plenary session of the central committee in September 1926. And, as it happens, the new split was traced back to previous dissensions. Lenski, the leader of the minority, belonged in 1924–5, after the 'three W's' had been dismissed, to what was called the 'left'. Most of those who had belonged to it were now indeed on the side of the minority; and many of those who had belonged to the 'right' were now on the side of the majority. Even older antagonisms played a role, for two of the leaders of the majority, Kostrzewa and Walecki, had come from the Left Socialist Party; as for the opposition between Warski and Lenski, an attempt was made to trace it back to the conflicts within the Social-Democratic Party (the Luxemburgists) before the First World War. Nevertheless, it seems to me that these were artificial genealogical trees, and that they were dragged in quite gratuitously. Their irrelevance to the situation of 1926 is proved by the fact that both factions, the majority as well as the minority, were responsible for the 'May mistake'. At the critical juncture both behaved in exactly the same way. Both supported Pilsudski. Both equally recognised their responsibility for the blunder—the question they quarreled about was which of the factions had contributed more and which had contributed less to the 'May mistake'.

The majority was particularly identified with the theory of the 'two distinct stages of the revolution' and the tactic of the united front, in which the Communist Party marched, or limped, behind the Socialist Party. It was a little more difficult to define the attitude of the leaders of the minority, who themselves did not go to the trouble of defining it. To a large extent they represented a mood of 'radicalism' in the Party rather than any precise theoretical concepts. In no instance did they fight against the fetishes which were being imposed on the Polish Party from the Comintern, and which had contributed to the 'Bolshevisation', or in other words to the bureaucratisation of the Polish CP. To that extent they contributed in a greater measure, perhaps, to the moral disarming of the movement. Both factions shared responsibility and each tried, not very effectively, to shift the blame to the other. This was a difficult period. The Party was split from top to bottom and indulged in mutual and sterile recriminations.

The recriminations were sterile because neither of the two factions was in a position to reveal the true sources of the mistake; neither was capable even *post factum* of making a Marxist analysis of the May putsch and of the regime which came out of it. Each faction sought in its adversary the cause for the Party's moral-political disaster; neither dared to look for the cause in the Comintern; neither had the courage to attack the fetishes of Stalinism; neither had the courage to challenge the false 'Bolshevisation' of the Party. Neither dared to submit to a critical analysis the methods by which the 'Luxemburgist heritage' had been fought; neither had the nerve to try to save what had been and still was great and valid in this heritage. Let us hope that the Polish working class will now rediscover this heritage at last. It will find there its own past and its own forgotten greatness. However, it is quite possible that habits of thought, formed not just in these last years but for a good thirty years, will make it difficult for the young as well as for the old generation of Polish Marxists to find a key to that heritage. I should like to add that this cannot be a question of using, for some tactical purposes, a few isolated fragments of Rosa's thinking, such as, for example, her initial doubts about 1917—there is no lack of such attempts to 'use' Rosa Luxemburg in present-day Poland. No, the task of Polish Marxists is to assimilate the sum and substance of the ideas of our greatest revolutionary, the ideas which are in full harmony with the enduring achievement of Lenin.

But let us come back to the Polish CP. The Party was then searching exclusively within itself for the causes of its political errors. The leaders hoped to remain at the helm with the support of the ruling circles in the Soviet Union. Warski and Kostrzewa relied more, perhaps, on the support of Bukharin, who was then the moving spirit in the International. As for Lenski, he staked his future on Stalin. The two factions were desperately afraid of the possibility of a conflict with the Russians; they feared that this would amount to a break with the revolution and with the international Communist movement. I am not making here any indictment of the men who led the Polish Party. They had their reasons for behaving as they did. I know from my own experience, as the former member of an opposition which was not afraid of conflict with the Soviet Party and which undertook the struggle in 1932 with full knowledge of what was involved—I know from my own bitter experience that in fact all the groups which did not recoil from this conflict condemned themselves to isolation and political impotence. But the fact that the leaders of the

Polish Party had submitted to Stalin did not save them from political impotence either. And it did not save them from leading the working class into a blind alley; it condemned them to intellectual and moral sterility, and the Party—to death.

The conflict between the majority and the minority already presented a sad spectacle of that sterility. It was like a quarrel of damned souls imprisoned within the enchanted circle of Stalinism. There was no endeavour to find an explanation of the situation and to investigate the mistakes made and the tasks ahead; all were merely anxious to display Stalinist orthodoxy and loyalty to the bosses of the Comintern. Each faction used the latest orthodox formula to whiten itself and blacken its adversary. Any student who would now immerse himself in the Party literature of this period would be struck by the scholastic methods of this controversy, by the obsessive repetition of some magic formulas, and by the queer violence of a debate, the object of which remains altogether elusive.

Did you yourself belong to the majority or to the minority?

I did not belong to either, probably because when I joined the Party, at the age of nineteen, the dividing line had already been drawn and I did not really understand what it was all about. However, I remember clearly that in 1926–7 I had a very sharp sense of the futility of the dispute. It seemed to me that the majority carried the burden of a certain opportunism, and that the minority had the more revolutionary dynamic. What disturbed me about the latter was its intellectual crudity and inclination towards sectarianism. It seemed to me that the majority represented a more serious school of thought and a deeper Marxist tradition. This was the predominant view among the group of comrades with whom I mixed, young Communist as I then was. This may have induced me to keep aloof from both factions and to search in a different direction for a way out of the impasse. I am convinced that the history of the Polish Party must be tackled afresh; to approach it from the angle either of the old minority or of the old majority would lead nowhere and would bring no positive result, intellectually or politically.

Which of the factions was dominant in the Party after May 1926?

At the time of the *coup d'état* the two factions shared the leadership, and this state of affairs lasted almost until the end of 1928. At the beginning of this period, Warski's and Kostrzewa's ascendancy was more marked, if only because the Bukharinist line still predominated in the Comintern. As usual, their influence showed itself in a more 'organic' activity of the Party, in a closer link between the Party and the masses, in a greater realism of its agitation, and in its stronger pull on the left elements in the Socialist Party, and also on the rural population and on the national minorities. In spite of the mutual recriminations which weakened it, the Party had in certain respects recovered quickly from its 'May mistake'. The working class had 'forgiven' that mistake. Hadn't the Communists admitted their error sincerely and unambiguously? After all, they all shared the same illusions. The Party was now gaining strength. This was proved, for example, by the results of the municipal elections in Warsaw, where, in 1927, more votes were cast for the CP's illegal list than for the list of any other party. The electors knew that their pro-Communist votes were lost, that none of our candidates would get into the municipal council, but they nevertheless demonstratively voted Communist. This was again a period when in the main industrial centres–Warsaw, Lodz, the Dabrowa coalfields–the CP was stronger than the Socialist Party, in spite of severe police persecution and wasteful inter-factional struggle. In 1928 the Communist Party really was leading the working class in its struggle against the Pilsudski dictatorship. The fear which seized the Pilsudskists and a section of the Socialist Party explains the bloody repression of May 1, of which I spoke earlier. (The illegal Communist demonstrations were very often larger than the demonstrations of the Socialist Party, which marched under the double protection of the police and their own armed militia.) In spite of all the handicaps and difficulties, the Party had some chance of going over to the offensive again. Just at this moment, however, it suffered a new blow, which knocked it off its relative balance and rendered it powerless.

Are you referring to the change in the leadership and to the elimination of Warski and Kostrzewa?

Yes. And once again it was not *what* happened that mattered so much as *how* it happened. Whether Warski and Kostrzewa or Lenski was at the helm was less important than the fact that the change was brought about solely from 'above', that it bore no relation to the logic of the class struggle in Poland. Once again, the Russian Party and the International weighed on the fate of Polish Communists and the Polish working classes.

At the Sixth Congress of the International, in the summer of 1928, the struggle between Stalin and Bukharin, previously confined within the Soviet Politburo, had burst into the open. Acting under the pressure of the USSR's internal crisis, Stalin was reviving his policy towards the peasantry and preparing the wholesale collectivisation. A huge social drama was being enacted in the Soviet Union, and it entailed another drama, less obvious but in its consequences equally grave, for European Communism. Having broken with Bukharin on domestic issues, Stalin set out to eradicate all Bukharinist influence in the Comintern and to change international Communist policy. Automatically, this involved th condemnation of the 'majority' in the Polish CP. Warski and Kostrzew were deprived of all influence. The steering wheel was violently turne 'left'. In 1929 Molotov put forward the ill-fated conception of a 'thir period' which, briefly, consisted in this: the capitalist world was enterin a directly revolutionary situation, and consequently the Communis movement must go over to an offensive struggle for power; social democracy, otherwise 'social-fascism', was Communism's main and mos dangerous enemy; moreover, the left wing of the social-democratic partie was more dangerous than the right wing; the Communists should direc their main fire against that enemy; they were forbidden to enter into an agreements with Socialists, they should set up their own Red Trad Unions (breaking away from the general trade unions) and, with thei help, organise general strikes and armed insurrections. The policy o the 'third period' was in force from 1929 to 1934. This was the tim when Nazism was growing like an avalanche in Germany, and in the fac of this threat, to which the Social-Democrats were surrendering anyhow the Communist Party found itself disarmed. When the Party was tol that its main enemy was not Hitler but 'social-fascism', and that it ha no right to ally itself with social-democracy against Nazism, Germa Communism, tied hand and foot, was delivered over to the heroes o the swastika.

In Poland the *direct* results of this policy were not yet quite as tragi but they were grim enough. The simmering conflict between Pilsudsk on the one hand, and the Socialist Party and the peasant movement o the other, was nearing the boiling point. These were the years of the Left Centre opposition. Pilsudski seized the leaders of this opposition an had them imprisoned and tortured in the fortress of Brzesc. The ant Communist terror, too, had grown more intense and reached a clima with the tortures inflicted on Ukrainian Communists imprisoned in Luck In these conditions the policy and the slogans of the 'third period', dil gently translated into Polish by Lenski, had all the characteristics of malignant political diversion. The Party member had to 'concentrat the fire' on the victims of Brzesc and not on their executioners; he ha to believe that the Party's gravest sin would be to support the struggl of the Left-Centre against Pilsudski, or to turn this struggle into a fierc revolutionary contest, which the leaders of the Left-Centre neither coul nor wished to do.

In conditions incomparably more serious, the Polish CP repeated th whole series of ultraleft mistakes which it had committed in 1924–5 It indulged once more in ultra-revolutionary acrobatics, which consiste in launching revolutionary activities with great energy into an empt space—activities the aims of which became less and less real. Loud an big words were not followed by deeds. The Party operated exclusivel within its own ranks—and these were melting away. It cut itself off from the working and peasant masses who had been first aroused and then confounded by the half-hearted struggle of the Left-Centre. It lost common language with the mass of workers and found itself driven more and more towards the fringe of politics, towards radical but politically impotent déclassé petty-bourgeois elements (mostly Jewish). The leaders did not, and would not, see the vacuum around the Party and the moral ravages in the rank and file. In the long run a revolutionary party cannot tolerate with impunity a divorce between word and deed; nor can it turn its back on reality and feed on the conventional fictions of a pseudo-revolutionary 'line' without having one day to pay for all this with the distortion of its own character. This indeed was the price the whole Comintern paid for the policy of the 'third period'. The Polish Party, in addition, laboured under the dictatorship of a faction which—following Stalin's example—dragged its inner-party opponents in the mud, gagged them, and thus stopped all the processes of opinion-formation within the party. These characteristics of the Stalinist inner-party regime, with which Poland was to become so thoroughly acquainted in the 1940s and 1950s, existed by the end of the twenties and had become fully developed in 1932–3. The phenomenon was all the more paradoxical because it did not result from the 'corruption of power', which to some degree may be expected in a ruling party, nor did it come about through the growth of a bureaucracy jealous of its social and political privileges. The Polish Communist Party remained the party of the oppressed and the persecuted. Its members and followers continued to crowd Pilsudski's and Rydz-Smigly's prisons. The dream of proletarian revolution and socialism still animated them. It was this dream precisely that made them inclined to accept blindly everything which came from the Soviet Union—the fatherland of the proletariat. Instead of being true to itself, the Party was becoming false to itself. Guided by its devotion to the cause of revolution, it was losing itself as the party of revolution.

In the middle 1930s there took place in the Party a turn in favour of the Popular Front. How did this influence the Party?

At this time, I was already out of the Party. Cut off from it, I could judge the facts from the outside only. Whatever else may be said about it, the policy of the Popular Front undoubtedly rejuvenated and refreshed the Party, which came into contact with reality. This brought new elements within the Party's sphere of influence. The intellectuals, who were then attracted by the Polish Party, now play, it seems to me, an important role in Poland's political life. That is why to the young generation they present this period as idealised and enveloped in a beautifying mist. Nevertheless, we must examine it coolly and objectively.

The Popular Front was the extreme opposite of the policy of the 'third period'. Yesterday's 'social-fascists' turned out to be anti-fascist fighters. Even the right-wing leaders of the peasant movement, like Witos, were recognised as knights-errant of democracy and progress. By comparison with the moderation of the Party's new tactical line, the 'opportunism' of Warski and Kostrzewa looked like exuberant, ultra-radicalism. Yet the slogans of the Popular Front were, in 1935 and 1936, launched by the same leaders (Lenski and Henrykowski) who in the previous year had directed their main fire against the 'social-fascists' and who had considered 'united front from below' as the only admissible policy, and who had expelled hundreds of militants simply because they had dared to doubt whether social-fascism was really 'the main and most serious danger'. Once again, what is important is not so much *what* policy was applied as *how* it was applied. No inner party discussion had preceded this violent change of line, which only followed the change of line of the Comintern, a line based in its turn on the calculations of Stalin's foreign policy. The effect which the reversal of policy had on the Party itself was therefore full of contradictions. On the one hand, the break with the 'third period' had a stimulating and reviving influence on the Party, and allowed it to escape from its vacuum. On the other hand, the mechanical character of this turn, coming entirely from 'above', increased still further the atrophy of political thinking among the cadres of old militants, who had already become accustomed to replace one set of political rituals by another at a single word of command and to consider all political notions and all watchwords as so many conventional phrases with no living content. Cynicism and ideological apathy made serious inroads. The young, who began their political life under the banner of the Popular Front, greeted the new slogans much more seriously and threw themselves with enthusiasm into the thick of anti-fascist activity. Nevertheless, this period was not conducive to the formation of Marxist consciousness in the young; they absorbed only very little of the Party's specifically Communist tradition. The Party propaganda, disseminating the vaguest of 'democratic' and antifascist slogans and the most insipid 'let's all get together' proclamations, was jettisoning all the criteria of proletarian interest and class struggle. It hardly differed from the routine propaganda of right-wing socialists, except that it markedly lacked any genuineness. Ideological shallowness and a patriotic-democratic vulgarity characterised the Party which once drew its inspiration from Rosa Luxemburg's flaming thought.

I am dwelling on this not in order to tear open old wounds or revive lapsed controversies, but in order to show the state of spiritual weakness in which the Party found itself on the eve of its assassination, and so to explain the passivity and the silence with which in 1938 it received its own death sentence and endured the unparalleled slaughter of its leaders.

A picture presenting the Polish CP as a flourishing, intellectually healthy body, brimming over with strength, which suddenly fell a victim to Yezhov's provocation, would be false and unhistorical. There is no need to resort to such a myth in order to rehabilitate the Party. Moreover, this would transform the very act of rehabilitation into a magic ritual. How did it happen, we must ask, that a Party which had to its credit decades of underground struggle and a long (seventy years long!) and proud Marxist tradition submitted meekly to this horrible outrage—without a protest, without making any attempt to defend its martyred leaders and fighters, without even trying to vindicate its honour, and without declaring that in spite of the death sentence Stalin had passed on it, it would live on and fight on? How could this happen? We must be fully aware of the moral corrosion to which Stalinism had for so many years exposed Polish Communism in order to understand its complete collapse under the blow.

At the time of its dissolution, the Polish CP was charged with being 'infected' with Trotskyism and of being an agency of the Polish political police. What in fact was the influence of Trotskyism on the Party?

The Trotskyist opposition in the Party was formed in the years 1931–2. It grouped comrades who had formerly belonged both to the minority and to the majority, and others who had not been connected with either faction. The opposition did not *a priori* take up a Trotskyist stand. It was formed on the basis of a critical view of the policy of the 'third period', the slogans about 'social-fascism', the 'united front only from below,' etc., and also of the bureaucratic inner-party regime. Demanding the right of self-determination for the Polish Party, the opposition adopted a critical attitude towards the regime that was prevailing within the International and the Soviet Party. Consequently, the ideas of the Trotskyist opposition in the USSR and particularly the magnificent, though fruitless, campaign which Trotsky waged in exile for a united front against Hitler, had a powerful and decisive impact on our group. At the beginning, the opposition exercised a fairly large influence. In Warsaw, where the Party counted at that time, it seems, hardly more than a thousand members, the opposition had about three hundred members (most of whom had played an important role in the movement), not counting a large circle of sympathisers in the Party organisations. Unfortunately, the deplorable condition in which the Party found itself affected the opposition too. The Party was cut off from the workers in large industry and was relegated to a petty-bourgeois fringe, and this weakness was reflected in the opposition. Although we had attracted many militants in the capital, our influence was much weaker in the provinces, where the pulse of Party life in general had been rather feeble. The bulk of the militants viewed the opposition with much sympathy so long as they did not realise that not only adherence but even mere contact with the opposition would be punished by expulsion from the Party. The new grouping, which did not simply continue the old and sterile quarrel between minority and majority but posed the problem of Party policy on a new plane, was at first greeted with relief. The Party leaders retorted by expelling and slandering us in the best Stalinist style. The same leaders who, a few years hence, were to be liquidated as police agents now branded the opposition as the 'agency' of 'social-fascism', then simply of fascism, and as a gang of 'enemies of the USSR'.

By the use of such methods, the leadership succeeded in stifling all discussion and terrorising Party members to such an extent that they began to shun us with the superstitious fear with which faithful members of the Church used to shun excommunicated heretics. The opposition was hermetically isolated from the Party, and by 1936 had almost no contact with it. Thus the charge that the Polish CP had become a Trotskyist 'agency' was sheer invention. But nevertheless, the doubts and ideas that the opposition had sown in the Party continued to germinate. Even while Party members remained conformist, many of them never ceased to listen to the voice of the opposition, and they were influenced by it to a greater or lesser degree—at any rate sufficiently to be sceptical about the holy writ of Stalinism. And since nothing in nature is ever lost completely, the Luxemburgist tradition had not vanished completely either, in spite of the years which had been spent on uprooting it. The opposition's influence and the effect of that tradition was such that even after years of 'Bolshevisation', the psychological profile of even the most orthodox Polish Communist left much to be desired from the Stalinist point of view. Thus it was in the 1930s; fortunately it was like this also after the Second World War: during this whole period a certain law of continuity had never ceased to operate.

Nevertheless, a question must be posed. We know that Pilsudski had his agents in all the left-wing parties. Surely he must have tried to introduce them into the CP as well?

The theory of these networks of agents which Pilsudski supposedly had created in various left-wing parties is again a crude simplification. No network of secret agents could have enabled Pilsudski to exercise on the Socialists and on a part of the peasant movement the influence he did exercise as a result of his long and above-board connections with these parties. He was one of the founding fathers of the Polish Socialist Party and was for many years its chief leader and inspiration. He had been the Commander of the Legion, to which men of the patriotic left had rallied. Even after he had left the Socialist Party, he continued to represent something that belonged to its essence: social-patriotism pushed to the xtreme. It was that which formed the basis of Pilsudski's 'magical' nfluence. The worship of Polish 'statehood', the dreams of the 'One and overeign' Poland, old loyalties, friendships, and ties of sentiment—these ave birth to those Pilsudskist 'networks' in parties of the moderate and atriotic left, which at times of conflict he attempted to destroy from vithin. There was not, and there could not have been, any similar basis or a Pilsudskist network in the Polish CP. The left-wing socialists who, fter 1918, found themselves in the ranks and in the leadership of the ommunist Party, had to their credit more than ten years of bitter struggle gainst Pilsudski. As for the old Luxemburgists, it is hardly necessary to well on their attitude towards him. However, even in the moderate, atriotic, left parties (PPS or *Wyzwolenie*) Pilsudski's 'agents' achieved ery little. Very quickly these parties overcame the confusion and splits rovoked by the 'networks'. Only the Polish CP, if we are to believe talin, was *completely* in the hands of Pilsudski's 'agents'. In 1938, when his accusation was made and one wanted to refute it, one felt overvhelmed by the sheer nonsense of it all. It is true that during the 1930s he Polish Party had suffered particularly from police provocations. The all in the ideological level of most of the militants, the bitterness of the actional struggles, the ultra-revolutionary policy of the years 1929–35—ll this had facilitated to a certain extent the penetration of police agents nto the Party. It would in any case have been surprising if the police ad had no agents whatsoever in the Polish CP in the same way in which he tsarist Okhrana had had its Azefs and its Malinowskis in nearly all he illegal Russian organisations. However, no one would have had the dea of dissolving the Bolshevik Party or the Socialist Revolutionary arty for that reason. The Stalinist provocation was a much more serious anger for the Polish CP than all the *agents provocateurs* of the Polish ecret police.[16]

Vhat, then, in your opinion were the reasons for which Stalin ordered he dissolution of the Polish Party? The view which prevails now among ld Party militants is that Stalin was already preparing the ground for his 939 agreement with Hitler and that he liquidated the Polish Party and ent its leaders to their death because he feared that they might obstruct hat agreement.

his motive no doubt played a part in Stalin's decision but does not xplain it fully. Warski and Kostrzewa, for years cut off from all contact vith Poland (and the world), were no longer in a position to offer the lightest resistance to Stalin, even if they had wished to do so. As for enski and Henrykowski, I am convinced that they would have remained aithful to Stalin even in a situation as critical for Polish Communism as hat of August and September 1939, in the same way as were the leaders of the French Party, not to mention the Germans and others. But here we are dealing with hypotheses. It seems to me that no single motive or sober calculation can explain Stalin's behaviour in this matter. His irrational impulses were quite as important as his 'rational' calculations; and he was impelled to act as he did by old grudges and ancient phobias, all intensified to the utmost by the persecution mania which gripped him at the time of the great Moscow trials, when he was settling his final accounts with the Leninist old guard. In this frame of mind, Stalin saw the Polish CP as the stronghold of hated Luxemburgism—the Polish 'variety of Trotskyism'—which had defied him as long ago as 1923; the Party in which some leaders were close to Bukharin and others to Zinoviev; the Party of incurable heresies, proud of its traditions and of its heroism; the Party, finally, which might well in certain international situations become an obstacle on his road. . . And so he decided to remove that obstacle by the blade of the same guillotine which, working furiously, was already destroying a whole generation of Bolsheviks.

The historian will not end his account of the fortunes of the Polish CP on the act of its annihilation. The epilogue of the story is, in a sense, its most important chapter. The 'posthumous' fate of the Polish CP will remain the most striking testimony of its greatness. Crushed, decimated confounded and outraged, the Party's old cadre was still the spearhead of all of Poland's revolutionary forces. It was that remnant of the old Party which at the end of the Second World War, in the peculiar international situation which favoured social revolution, carried this revolution through. The survivors of the Polish CP came forward as the executors of their Party's will, although they had to do so in conditions and by methods that no philosophers dreamed of. And nearly twenty years after the massacre of the Polish CP, its spirit and, if you like, something of its old Luxemburgist tradition, showed themselves in October 1956.

Not only the historian, but also every militant Marxist, must draw certain conclusions from the tragic history of the Polish CP. Here I must of necessity confine myself to one rather general idea: if the history of the Polish CP and of Poland at large proves anything at all, *it proves how indestructible is the link between the Polish and the Russian revolutions*. This has been proved both negatively and positively. For her attempt to place herself athwart the international revolution which had begun in Russia—the attempt made in 1918-20—Poland had to pay with twenty years of stagnation and backwardness, of provincially narrow and anachronistic social life, and, finally, with the catastrophe of 1939. On the other hand, the revolution, isolated in old and backward Russia, isolated by the world's anti-communist forces (with Poland's eager help), underwent a distortion which affected tragically not only the peoples of the USSR but revenged itself on Poland as well. Already in 1920 Poland had felt something of that revenge. Subsequently, it led to the deformation of the working-class movement in Poland, condemning it to sterility and impotence. Then there came 1939. After the Second World War, the Russian Revolution, in spite of all its distortions, still showed itself to be sufficiently alive and dynamic to stimulate new revolutionary processes in Europe and Asia. Poland once again absorbed from the Russian Revolution its shadows as well as its lights and took over from it, together with the blessings of a progressive upheaval in social relationships, the curse of bureaucratic terror and the Stalin cult. Poland had to pay a heavy penalty for the 'miracle on the Vistula' of 1920,[17] in which she had gloried for twenty years. Having spurned the Russian Revolution in its heroic stage, she had to humble herself before the same Revolution after it had degenerated. Having scorned Lenin and Leninist internationalism, Poland had to prostrate herself before Stalin and Great Russian chauvinism. Only as the Soviet Union was beginning to awaken from the nightmare of Stalinism could Poland free herself from it, and by that very act stimulate processes of recovery in other socialist countries. But only as the Russian Revolution emerges from the sidetracks onto which history had driven it and at last enters the highway of socialist democracy, will the perspectives before People's Poland clear up definitely. At every step history demonstrates *ad oculos* how indissoluble are the bonds between the Polish and the Russian revolutions. But whereas hitherto history has again and again demonstrated the indissoluble nature of this bond in a negative manner—by inflicting the most cruel lessons on Poland—in October 1956 it has begun perhaps to demonstrate it in the positive, that is, in the only effective manner. History so far has not always been a good and sensible teacher. The lessons in internationalism which it attempted to teach the Polish masses were singularly involved, badly thought out,and ineffective. During almost every one of these 'lessons', history mocked and insulted Poland's national dignity and, in the first place, the dignity and independence of the Polish revolutionary movement. Is it surprising then, that the 'pupil' has not been very receptive, and, trying to escape the peculiar 'teacher', has sought refuge in the jungle of our nationalist legends? The Polish masses will understand that the bonds which unite their destiny with that of the Russian and other revolutions are indissoluble, but only after they have recovered from the blows and shocks inflicted on them in the past, and when they feel that nothing can ever again threaten their independence and national dignity. Marxists, however, must rise above the shocks and the traumas from which the masses suffer; and they must even now be deeply and thoroughly aware of the common destiny of Poland and other nations advancing towards socialism. Marxists have no right to nourish themselves, nor to feed others, on the spiritual diet of stale and warmed-up myths and legends. Socialism does not aim at the perpetuation of the national state; its aim is international society. It is based not on national self-centredness and self-sufficiency, but on international division of labour and on cooperation. This almost forgotten truth is the very ABC of Marxism.

You may say that what I am proposing is a new edition of Luxemburgism, slightly amended and adapted to the needs of 1957. Perhaps. You may tell me that this is merely a new version of the theory of 'organic incorporation'.[18] Perhaps. But what is at stake this time is the 'organic integration' of Poland, into international socialism, not her incorporation into a Russian empire.

NOTES

1. It is said that at one of the meetings of the Central Committee which took place after October 1956, when Gomulka was relating the story of the Party's dissolution and of the slanders made against its leaders, he was asked whether at that time, in 1938, he himself believed them. Gomulka answered: 'No.' Why, then, had he not protested? he was asked. 'I was not brave enough to do so, or I had not enough self-confidence,' he is said to have replied, 'but if Lenin had been living in Poland, he would certainly have protested in such circumstances.' We must acknowledge Gomulka's sincerity and modesty. Nevertheless it was not necessary to be a Lenin in order to dare to protest. I knew ordinary workers who had no ambitions towards leadership and who understood that their duty was to protest, and acted accordingly.
2. The Social-Democratic Party of the Kingdom of Poland and Lithuania was formed in 1893 as a Polish party; the Lithuanian Social-Democrats attached themselves in 1900. From the beginning this party was led by Julian Marchlewski, Leo Jogiches-Tyszka, and Rosa Luxemburg. The Left Socialist Party was formed in November 1906, as a result of a split in the Polish Socialist Party (PPS) and of an opposition, stimulated by the 1905 revolution, to Pilsudski's reformist, terroristic and nationalist leadership.
3. It is a curious fact that the 'splitters' and particularly Dzerzhinski and Radek should have made almost the same criticism of Rosa Luxemburg as the latter made of Lenin during the division of the Party into Mensheviks and Bolsheviks. They accused her of applying a policy of ultracentralism in the Party, of enforcing too much discipline, etc. In fact, Rosa Luxemburg's Party was led in a manner very similar to that in which Lenin led the Bolshevik Party. This was due essentially to the fact that both parties were operating illegally.
4. The Bund was the Jewish socialist party, which then maintained an intermediate position between socialist reformism and communism.
5. Julian Marchlewski, one of the closest friends of Rosa Luxemburg, was an eminent writer and Marxist theoretician who played an important part in the German socialist left and in the Polish movement. After the October Revolution he stayed in Russia.
6. Feliks Kon, a veteran of Polish patriotic socialism, was one of the founders of the Communist Party and with Marchlewski and Dzerzhinski was a member of the 'Provisional Communist Government', set up during the Red Army's march on Warsaw. Lapinski belonged to the same group as Feliks Kon, and in the twenties played an important role in the Comintern.
7. In France, Monatte, Rosmer and Souvarine were dismissed from the leadership of the Communist Party.
8. The Polish CP was made illegal at the beginning of 1919, only a few weeks after the proclamation of Polish independence. It remained illegal until 1944.
9. At that time, too, Treint was eliminated from the leadership of the French

Communist Party, of which he had been general secretary.

10. Shortly before the war I wrote a large-scale study of the history of working-class movements and class struggles in Poland; unfortunately this manuscript was lost.
11. General Jose Haller, the commander of the Polish divisions in France during the First World War, was the hero of the extreme right in Poland, and was Pilsudski's antagonist during the 1920s.
12. The western reader will see clearly the analogy between this attitude of the Polish Communists and socialists and the illusions which Proudhon, for example, entertained for a time with regard to the person of Napoleon III, or Lassalle with regard to Bismarck. Polish Marxists—especially Rosa Luxemburg's followers—had adopted a very critical attitude towards the traditions and methods of Proudhonism and Lassallism.
13. *Robotnik* was the main newspaper of the Polish Socialist Party.
14. Pilsudski came from the eastern borderlands of the old Poland, famous for the fanfaronades and feuds of its Falstaffian gentry.
15. Shortly afterwards this militia was to break with the Socialist Party and enter Pilsudski's service.
16. Azef was a well-known *agent provocateur* who led the terrorist organisation of the Russian Social-Revolutionary Party. Malinowski, who was Lenin's friend, a deputy of the Duma, and an influential member of the Bolshevik Central Committee, was finally also exposed as an *agent provocateur.*
17. The 'miracle on the Vistula' was the name given to the battle of Warsaw, in which Pilsudski's armies inflicted defeat on the Soviet army. At the time of this battle, General Weygand was Pilsudski's adviser.
18. In her theory of 'organic incorporation', which she formulated in her doctoral thesis, Rosa Luxemburg stated that the struggle for Poland's independence was hopeless and in essence even reactionary because of the 'organic' economic ties that linked Poland and Russia; neither the Polish bourgeoisie nor the Polish proletariat were interested in the restoration of a sovereign Poland: the bourgeoisie because Russian markets were more profitable to it, and the proletariat because it strove for international socialism. This conception formed the theoretical basis of the Luxemburgist politics.

INTRODUCTION

Barbara Einhorn

'. . . now they share the dreadful secret, the taboo of taboos: that Leonce by his many names is incapable of loving.'[1]

The theme, in Büchner's play *Leonce and Lena,* of men's inability to love as a result of their entrenchment in reason–rationality seen as an escape from the reality of social relations and human emotions–recurs in Christa Wolf's more recent writings. What is new in this speech is that she explicitly links this theme with disarmament. 'Literature today must be peace research.' Wolf implies that scienticism gone wild has brought us to the brink of self-destruction. Christa Wolf is one of the, if not *the* most important literary figures in the GDR (East Germany). Her writing is both innovative and exciting, thought-provoking and deeply reflective, with a profound impact both within and outside the GDR. The particular interweaving of feminism and disarmament which she achieves in this speech is of great significance for our own situation.

Wolf first elaborates the problem of men's inability to love in a short story entitled 'Self-Experiment'; the main character, a woman scientist in an institute for genetic research, consents to be the human guinea pig in a sex-change experiment.[2] Though successful the experiment is broken off prematurely by the subject. At first, she is elated by the increased power, autonomy, status and consequent ease of living as a man. But she discovers that the professor whom she had previously admired and loved from a distance and now sees in the bosom of his family from a man's perspective, is incapable of loving. Her professor has become a workaholic. His only concern is with his career. He is entrenched in the dispassionate scientific mode in order to hide his basic complacency, lack of caring and perhaps even regret at being so incapacitated. He is unable to involve himself fully in real-life relationships, which he experiences as a moving picture show–'like at the cinema'. As a man, the central character also experiences what Wolf refers to in this speech as the partial blindness which all men acquire as the only way of sustaining a privileged position. The blindness of science to the needs and the future of humanity is one of the central themes in Christa Wolf's Büchner speech.

The same themes are elaborated in her introductory essay to Maxie Wander's *Guten Morgen, du Schöne,* a collection of women speaking about and for themselves.[3] In this essay Wolf portrays pragmatic 'rationality' as an emotionally debilitating mode of being. In the GDR no less than in capitalist economies, where there exist hierarchical social structures in which the division of labour in social production is increasingly dominated by scientific and technological considerations, men have become severely crippled. Women, in the view of Wolf and other women writers in the GDR, have been spared the worst effects of the division of labour between mental and manual work precisely because of their oppression; the fact that women have been forced into manual tasks has freed them from the mould of 'dispassionate' rationality.

The GDR is almost unique in having introduced almost all the material preconditions for the emancipation of women. As a result, GDR women have made tremendous gains in status and self-confidence.[4] Factors such as economic independence from men and real autonomy in reproductive choice have enabled women to pose new questions, extend their horizons and attempt to formulate in humane and emotional terms and the needs of the society of the future. However, since the necessary social, legal and economic preconditions for women's liberation do not necessarily constitute sufficient conditions, the dilemmas around the issue of gender which arise in the GDR today and are reflected in literature written by women must be of particular interest to feminists in the West. Christa Wolf, although not a self-defined feminist, is able in this specific historical context to explore in her characteristically subtle and nuanced manner the social and psychological relations of gender.

Wolf envisages a future socialist society as one in which non-alienated social relations will enable individuals to develop their full potential. Thus in the Büchner prize speech, Rosetta, woman by her many names, raises her voice, albeit at the eleventh hour, to warn of the earth's dangerously thin crust and the need to halt, indeed to reverse the processes tending towards the extinction of life on earth.

It is also evident in the Büchner prize speech that this is not a separatist feminist view based on biologistic 'inherent difference' and hence irreconcilable antagonism between men and women. Wolf explores the problem in the historical context of the age of reason. She implies that the Enlightenment aspiration of education for responsibility was quickly distorted and finally crushed in the Restoration of the early 19th century. She also stresses the necessity for men and women to find a united solution, especially in view of the urgency lent to the more general problem of social relations by the ever present threat of nuclear devastation. 'How can we women be "liberated" so long as all humanity is not?'[5] she asks in the Wander introduction, referring to the continuing alienation of both men and women in social relations dominated by production and the need to increase productivity in order to compete on the world market, sharply intensified in the present recession. The wider question of how to achieve emancipation for all is formulated more despairingly in the Büchner speech. Wolf's (last) hope is that Leonce, the man, will hear Rosetta's plea and take it (and her) seriously. Only then would he be able to avert the disaster he has constructed and whose victim he has become. He may be able, just in time, to come out of his entrenched position and to 'see' what is necessary for the maintenance of life.

With bitter irony Wolf refers to the distortions which allowed Oppenheimer whilst 'blinded' literally and emotionally by the first atomic explosion—the outcome of his research—to cite a classical work of literature, and to reveal through the quotation the manic delusion of god-like power over life and death. Goethe's Faust also aspired to divine power and was duly punished with death for over-reaching himself. The lesson should have been clear; but Wolf is saying more, that we must go beyond the fascination with death expressed by Oppenheimer and by Büchner's dramatic figures. The survival of life on earth must outweigh all other issues. Women must stand up and make themselves heard, they can no longer afford to remain mere onlookers in a man's world. Indeed they must change the terms of the debate. What is needed for there to be a future for 'civilised' society, in Wolf's view, is an entirely new set of values which would start afresh and not simply formulate the opposite to the dominant male 'scientific' ideology. Women were peripheral to the debates on the Revolution which cost Danton and Camille their heads; Lucile lost her sanity and Julie her life for 'mere' love of their men. Marie too was a victim, murdered by her lover Woyzeck who was himself driven insane by a cruel, unfeeling, grotesque 'scientific' experiment to which he was forced to consent in a world of harsh social inequalities and hierarchical military structures of subordination and control.[6]

It is the so-called scientific approach, an approach divorced from the real issues of social relations, rationality gone mad, which could make Woyzeck eat nothing but peas for forty days to 'see what would happen' to his reason. The same 'scientific rationality' has lead humanity to the brink of mass suicide, against which women must take a stand, hopefully together with men.

Büchner's works illustrate his early awareness of the problems of language as communication in the proximity of life and death, sanity and madness, and the absurdity of too high-sounding idealistic discourse in a context of dire social problems. One of Christa Wolf's dominating concerns has always been with the process of writing itself, literature as an act of communication between writer and reader. This is evident in the intricate narrative structure and fabric of her novels. It is the central issue confronted in a collection of her essays entitled *The Reader and the Writer.*[7] Linked to this is the theme of the relationship between literature and reality, fiction and reality, fantasy and reality.

Wolf focuses on the operation of the unconscious and its expression in creative fantasy. The dilemma of giving voice to this process in language is decisive in forming Wolf's writing. Her style is allusive, opens up questions for the reader, is *about* ambivalence and the attempt to come to terms with ambivalence through the process of writing itself.

It is in this context that Christa Wolf makes a plea for literature to find a new language beyond the screech of words destroyed by the media—words such as 'freedom' in whose name armaments for the multiple destruction of humanity are justified by both Super Powers. Christa Wolf's language is beautifully lucid, even translucent, and yet at the same time exposes the reader to a myriad of levels of meaning and reflective dimensions. The simplicity, the unassuming phrases which she sees as the task of literature committed to peace research, are evident in her own writing. Initially, the development of her style was possibly influenced by the demand of socialist realism in the GDR for a literature easily accessible to ordinary people. In this respect, the cultural/political ambience from which Christa Wolf's works have emerged may have had an enabling effect on her writing. However, the way in which her literary language has developed is unique to her work and is an ingredient which makes her one of the most outstanding writers in the German language today. Whilst the earlier demand of socialist realism for 'truth to reality' in an optimistic perspective tended in the 1950s to result in naturalistic realism of an unimaginative kind, it led in Christa Wolf's case to an exploitation of and experimentation with this relationship in a very differentiated and nuanced manner throughout all her works. In her novel *Nachdenken über Christa T. (The Quest for Christa T.)* the narrator, concerned to establish the elusive 'reality' of a friend who has died (and with whose identity her own is both subtly and intentionally blurred at times), stresses the importance of fantasy and creative imagination in speaking of 'what it is that one has to invent, for the truth's sake'.[8]

In the Büchner speech too, Christa Wolf is making a plea for imaginative literature to be heard, in the name of the preservation of humanity. The moral commitment of the author must be to help establish a new set of values based on cooperation, not domination and subordination, before it is too late. Wolf's plea for literature to be heard in this quest is based on the achievements of literature in both Germanies in the last decades. She evaluates this achievement in terms of the way it has been able to grieve for and confront squarely the horrors wreaked by fascism in recent German history. To this past history and the future threat of nuclear holocaust she counterposes life-asserting literature, literature as oral history. Leonce's ennui and the modern writer's disgust with tarnished words emptied of their meaning must be overcome in the name of the 'truth of the here and now',[9] as well as of a humane future.

At this moment in history, when millions in the West are mobilising in the cause of disarmament, there is an urgent need for fresh formulations of what is at stake. The potential for feminist intervention to alter the terms of the debate is great indeed. It is in this context that Christa Wolf's voice from 'the other side' with its particular blend of socialism and feminism, its breadth of understanding and its vision of a viable future against all odds, resounds with a powerful vibrancy, setting up multiple and urgent reverberations in the consciousness of the reader.

CITADEL OF REASON

Christa Wolf's speech on receiving the Büchner Prize in October 1980

Translated by Barbara Einhorn

I would like to thank the German Academy for Language and Literature in Darmstadt for awarding me the Büchner Prize this year. Such an occasion tends to increase dramatically a writer's dissatisfaction with her own work; self-doubts continue to grow about one's chosen way of life. I shall pass over my endless agonising on this subject as futile or perhaps even vain. I shall also put aside those pages which reflect the difficulty I feel about speaking here and now. With Büchner's example before me, I feel more uneasy than ever about the undercurrents which weave together writing and living, responsibility and guilt, and which simultaneously bring forth and threaten to tear apart the person who lives by writing, writes by living. These contradictory currents must, I now believe, be not merely endured, but accepted. To be innocent and without responsibility is wishful thinking which arises at times of weakness; it is escapist thinking. There is no room for a state of innocence without responsibility in the concrete circumstances in which we live, write and become mature—which also implies having one's eyes opened. For these are circumstances in which we intervene, fail, protest anew and become obsessed with new experiences. Here and now! is the order of the day and the masks are torn from our faces as we go. *Will our faces come away with them?*[10]

Rereading Büchner makes us see our own situation in sharper focus. *I accustomed my eyes to the sight of blood, but I am no guillotine blade.*[11] The Germans' arduous, frequently dislocated, often halting or violent and at times desolate progress through history could be paved and punctuated by the words of their great writers. I intended to give a speech in Büchner's words which would sound as if it were written today. But it is impossible to make up for what remained unfinished in his time.

Büchner himself would never have had to face the embarrassment of delivering a public speech of thanks. By what right do we refer to the phenomenon and the work of this very young man who—as a revolutionary, poet and scientist—risked everything to prise a bearable alternative from the bleak circumstances of his era, whose feverishly sober dialogues and clearsighted, urgent prose must have been dragged from him by the most terrible suffering. *The pain began bringing him to his senses. He spoke rapidly but was in torment.*

The consciousness which emerges from the pain of insanity is not his former consciousness. The tortured language it has to use in order to find itself is alien to him. Lenz[12] goes mad as a result of losing touch with common sense. Disillusioned through and through, we stand dumbfounded in the face of the reified dreams produced by that form of instrumental thought which still calls itself rational, but which has long since lost sight of its emancipatory Enlightenment origins in the notion of education for responsibility. This 'rationalism' has entered the industrial age in the form of an unmitigated mania for expediency. The metaphor of the magic broom, now a harmless fairy tale,[13] was at first sufficient warning. Later, once the profit motive merged with technical progress, acts of violence became masked by the motto: 'All's fair in love and war'. Bourgeois literature, seriously disorientated by this, crafted the image of blind old Faust, who in a grotesque act of self-deception adapts the sound of spades digging his grave to fit his beatific vision of the future.[14] This metaphor has only now really chilled us to the marrow—we who are the contemporaries of that civilisation which with the most insanely short-circuited vision is directing everything it values most highly—money and technological perfection—to the production of its own destruction. We, who are the contemporaries too of that new Faust, the 'father of the atom bomb', whose humanistically shaped memory—even whilst he is blinded by the light brighter than a thousand suns—triggers lines from a sacred Indian epic poem: 'I am Death who robs all/Destroyer of the worlds.'[15]

What further misuse of literature must we witness? What more can happen before words fail us completely? To what lengths, into what manner of death will literature follow mankind as its official mourner? No longer giving counsel for life, but only for death? Fettered by a past which remains in large part not understood, spellbound in a present to which there is practically no alternative, filled with foreboding for the future—how should we speak? In the context of 'overkill'[16] will there be time for a new cycle of historical contradictions now just beginning to develop fully? What are the options for a literature whose language and forms express Western patterns of thought and behaviour, a literature whose structures, albeit formed in the portrayal of contradictions, yet are predicated on a productive relationship between human beings, a productive relationship that we can no longer count on: Whichever way it twists and turns, however much it may torment itself and rack its brains, must not this literature remain an accomplice to the process of increasing alienation and loss of touch with reality? Is its only choice one between crude and cunning deceptions? In the age of their mechanical reproduction, do not words themselves turn against their producers? And doesn't this age express what there is to be said about it in plastics, concrete and steel? Monstrous, forbidding, self-deceptive, this age exhibits a sheer force to which language cannot aspire. Should then the language of literature fail us?

'May humanity be noble!'[17] and: 'A mistake was made in our creation.'[18] Fifty years separate Büchner's phrase from Goethe's. Büchner realised that paradox was the symbol of the dawning age. Hence his century, acting consistently, since it was ready to accept anything but that stigma, punished him with silence. He was confronted at a very early stage with that dearth of an opinion, that loss of certainty with which we are afflicted today and which brings in its wake revulsion at language. We have been deprived of a large body of words which we thought were indispensable, words of the category 'freedom', 'equality', 'fraternity', 'humanity', 'justice'. These words have been taken over by the press, since they express nothing, not even a belief corresponds to them any more. In terms of the logic of language, this means their opposites must also be dropped, since words like 'horrific', 'frightful', 'atrocious', 'ominous', 'barbaric' no longer suit the circumstances. Into their place, replacing all the well-informed, words, the judgmental, loud-mouthed or resigned words steps the quiet, unassuming phrase: out of joint.[19]

The times are out of joint, we say tentatively, and we feel: it is so. We could rise to defend that phrase. It's not a pretty one, it's simply right, and so gives our shattered sense of hearing a welcome break from the screech of big words. It also provides some measure of relief for our conscience, which is disturbed by too many false and misused words. Is it possible that it could be the first word of a different language, an appropriate language which already resounds in our ears but is not yet on the tip of our tongue? Perhaps it could lead to the development of a whole chain of further, similarly appropriate words—without our forgetting for a moment that naming is not rectifying, does not of itself redress or change anything—words which ought to express not merely the reverse of the old values, but a new and different sense of values, suited to the times. So that we would have something to say. We could talk to one another again without feeling ashamed.

Those who wish to embark on the search for this language would, however, have to be prepared to suffer the almost total loss of their sense of self and self-confidence. They would no longer have at their disposal a single familiar pattern of speech, conversation, thought or poetry. Indeed they would experience what it really means to lose your cool.

We are not the first. In the disjunctures between different eras much of what is a necessary part of the ability to speak is broken: courage, backbone, hope, immediacy. Fear springs into the resulting vacuum. Literary precursors nearly always anticipate a fear which later overcomes many.

Dance, Rosetta, dance, so that time may tick to the beat of your dear little feet. . ./My feet would rather take me right out of time.

A rhythm which pounds its way into sleep, into dreams, which can transfix and obsess you. My feet would rather go right out of time.

Dance, Rosetta.

Rosetta dances. Sings: Oh, dear grief. Goes off, since Leonce simply doesn't love her, indeed is only capable of loving the corpse of their love. Tears, Rosetta?–Must be diamonds, they are piercing my eyes–Leonce, left alone, pronounces: *It's a strange thing, love is.*[20]–Meanwhile his brother Danton proclaims on the neighbouring stage: *I will retreat into the citadel of reason. I shall break forth with the cannon of truth and crush my enemies.*[21]

Where does that leave the women–Rosetta, Marie, Marion, Lena, Julie, Lucile?[22] Outside the citadel, of course. Unprotected, in the direct line of fire. No thought construction encompasses them. They are made to believe that the only mode of rational thought is the entrenched one! And it is not just that they lack the education to think in this way; they simply don't wish to. From below, from outside they watch the man's strained mental activity which becomes, over time, increasingly directed towards strengthening his fortress by measurements, calculations, ingenious numerical and diagrammatic systems. It is intellectual activity which feels at home in the iciest abstraction and whose ultimate truth is the formula. How could Rosetta have the slightest idea that fear of being touched is what makes him withdraw from the fullness of reality; that it is his vulnerability and the fear of becoming aware of his vulnerability which drive him deep into his insane systems. Or that, robbed of his wholeness by the merciless division of labour, wounded and torn to shreds, he pushes himself at the most breakneck speeds solely to avoid embarking on precisely that 'hellish journey to self-knowledge' without which, according to Kant, there can be no reason. And that he who does not know himself is also incapable of knowing a woman.

Hence their ways part. Rosetta is silent. Loves. Suffers. Is murdered, as Marie. As Julie, follows her husband into death. Is driven mad, as Lucile. Sacrifices herself. Laments–now her name is Lena: Am I then like the defenceless pool which must reflect in its still depths every image which leans over it?[23]–One of them, Marion the woman of pleasure, has obeyed the dictates of her own nature: that is the extent of Büchner's realism.

People were unable to read him. They did not want to know that the progress they were in the process of launching on a grand scale, comprised the stuff of new myths. That it could provide pleasure, but not love. And that its most powerful motivating force would be fear of its own inner emptiness. Büchner realised so very early–and I think with horror–that the pleasure the new age derived from itself was fundamentally linked with pleasure in destruction. But he did not live to see the fully-formed caricature of the paradox coupling creation with destruction. He was not acquainted with a word like 'mega deaths'. He endowed his characters with a love of death, but even he could not have imagined that a perfect, if murderous, technical solution would be called 'sweet', or that women's names would be inscribed on the rumps of rockets. Büchner could not have conceived of the lengths to which his Leonce would go—once his hall of mirrors became too confining for him[24]—purely in order to avoid being without a reflection. For the fear of death grips them—Leonce and his more powerful and more active descendants—the instant there is no mirror—a woman's eyes or body, a theatre, a corporation, a powerful organisation, a state of apparatus, the globe, the universe!—to throw back a larger-than-life reflection of them.

Oh, to be able to see oneself upside down.[25] Büchner, if anyone, must have known the desire to achieve the impossible: to make visible the blind spot in this culture. He circumscribes it with his characters, whom he pushes to the limits of what can be said. On one occasion he tries to express this with a scream—when Lucile loses her sanity at Camille's death. But 'that doesn't help, everything is just as before.'[26] A dramaturgy of screams is an absurdity in the theatre of relatively resolvable contradictions. It is impossible to portray on the stage that which would adequately convey the actual terms of existence. This was another issue Büchner had to confront. Consequently he created space in his 'either/or' dramaturgy—a dramaturgy he links loosely to the old dramatic structure so that people can go on believing they understand what they see. He made space for those phrases which are to be spoken tonelessly, a single breath before the scream: My feet would rather go right out of time.

Rosetta's fate is to remain invisible both to herself and to Leonce, to be speechless, deprived of substance, occupying precisely that disowned, soundproofed space which has been manipulated out of sight and which the world, to which after all she also belongs, is unable for the life of it to perceive. She becomes definable by that which she is not.

She allows herself to be robbed of her history. Lets her claim to a soul be disputed. Her claim to reason. To being a person. To having responsibility for herself. She allows herself to be married off. Serves her husband. Gives him heirs. Is made to believe him when he claims that the sensual pleasure he enjoys is denied her once and for all. She conceals her unhappiness. Dances. Hears his reproach: I want to sleep, but you insist on dancing.

Rosetta allows herself to be deprived of her rights. Of her right to speak. Of her right to grief. To joy. To love. To work. To art. Lets herself be raped. Prostituted. Imprisoned. Driven mad. Allows herself, as Rose, to be overworked, exploited: 'doubly', so it has been said.[27] Lets herself be forced into bearing children. Made to abort children. Allows her sexuality to be analysed away. Becomes enmeshed in nets of powerlessness. Becomes a pain in the neck. The hussy. The vamp. The housewife. Leaves the doll's house, as Nora.[28]

Finally, when she is called Rosa, she begins to fight back. In return, she is beaten to death and thrown into the canal. Persecuted, her rights are equal to those of the oppressed and persecuted man. Dance, Rosetta. She dances. Now her name is Marlene.—You want me to laugh? Sure, I'll laugh then./You want me to dance? Of course, any time./You want me to turn your heads? Don't mention it! It's my pleasure.[29]

It's a strange thing, love. Rosetta under her many names allows herself to be utterly destroyed rather than admit to herself what is happening to her: namely that when the philosophising Leonce says: 'subject', he never ever means her, the real woman. That for him she has become just another object. That he therefore. . .

Here she stops herself. Is in no hurry for the final insight. Prefers self-effacement. Suppresses her talents. Succours under many names, some of which you will know well, the genius of the philosophising, poetising, painting man.—*You do love me, don't you, Leonce?—Well, why not?*[30]— Whereupon she can become strange, hard as well, jealous, bitter. Cries out, screams at him. Becomes hysterical. Starts drinking. Turns on the gas.

After the wars, during which she took the man's place and proved her worth in his machinery of production and destruction, she gets to hear as the ultimate concession: that she is like him. So now she's out to prove it to him. She works like a man, that's progress. And it *is* progress of a kind. Stands beside him at the machine day and night. Sits beside him in the lecture theatre, in advisory and executive bodies (in the minority of course in these). Writes, paints, writes poetry like him—*almost* like him: for the first tiny cracks are beginning to appear, which they blame on her hypersensitivity; or not, as the case may be. To a certain extent she keeps within the grid for thinking and seeing drawn up by him. And to the forms in which he expresses his feelings about the world and his world-weariness as well. In this way she emerges from the blind spot and is discovered. Becomes printable. Review-worthy. A 'talent'. A name. Possibly even merits a prize.

Will anyone believe that she feels ambivalent? It did after all take a long time for her to understand herself. Why does she still feel so out of place; why can't she shake off the feeling that in their praise and criticism it is not her who is meant, but still someone else, the false picture of her, the 'other' woman. And that they have scarcely mentioned her at all so far.

Paradoxically—yes: for on entering the citadel she becomes subject to its laws!—paradoxically she herself had to foster this failure to see her for what she is. In order to become free, she has accepted new restrictions. For her to be able to come to herself, new forms of self-denial were appropriated from her. She had the best will in the world. Set her hopes on the scientific age. Trusted its rationality and now sees herself at the mercy of the irrationality it is cornered in and which it renders unassailable by means of expert scientific reports. Never, she now admits to herself, never ever did time tick to the beat of *her* feet. Yet in a strangely insistent and at times even uncanny way she is now prepared to take herself seriously. It is at this point that she meets with opposition.

Up until now, whenever things became serious, she was always protectively sheltered from seriousness. They didn't bother her with the construction of weapons systems, additional and super weapons systems, which spell the end for old-fashioned individual death. In its place, in the fantasy of nuclear planning bodies, these weapons systems have already irradiated, incinerated and reduced each of us to ashes seven, eight, twenty times over. They didn't initiate her–Rosetta by her many names–into the secret purpose of their global economic, political and military strategies. She sees the preserver of the balance of terror sitting washed out in front of the television every evening, observes the planner of distorted economic growth drifting towards a heart attack, watches the distributor of worldwide hunger reaching for the bottle, exhausted. They're working not only themselves to death.

Dance, Rosetta, dance.

But now–admittedly late, perhaps too late–she raises her voice. Asks: gentlemen, friends, colleagues, comrades: Don't you think the earth's crust has become rather thin even for light feet by now?[31]

She shouldn't have spoken like that. Now she has become really ungrateful. She's dancing out of line. Letting herself slip through the net of her powerlessness–as if this were a pleasure trip which she could indulge in or not, as the fancy took her!–out through the net whose stitches were after all very finely meshed, of stuff such as dreams are made of: the nightmares of alienated thought processes.

The fear which sets in at this point.

Hers *and* his fear: for now they share the dreadful secret, the taboo of taboos: that Leonce by his many names is incapable of loving, that he is no longer able to love anything but dead matter. *(Beautiful corpse, you rest so sweetly on the black bier cloth of night that nature abhors life and falls in love with death.)*[32] Does that leave her, Rosetta by her many names, only the choice of being pushed back into the dead space or becoming like him? Doesn't each step she takes towards her liberation increase his fear and thus his resistance? Should *she* now entrench herself and shoot from the citadel of her reason 'with the cannon of truth'? Regard him as her enemy, to be 'crushed'? And: together, bringing each other to their senses: shouldn't that be possible? Couldn't the two of them, locked in the same paradox, take a single step towards one another? Was this historical moment also to be lost?

This is where the old beat starts up again, particularly in the night, loudly, very loudly indeed: My feet would rather go right out of time. That's when fantasies are sparked off, under the threshold of consciousness, where the constant threat triggers a constant alarm, constantly seeking viable alternatives—fantasies fed too by the moral dilemmas of him or her who is compelled to write. Writing on this paper-thin crust? No longer 'in hope' but only in preparation for the 'state of emergency'?

'Nothing pleases me any more'—thus begins Ingeborg Bachmann's last poem.

> Should I
> Embellish a metaphor
> With an almond blossom?
> . . .
> Should I
> Fetter a thought
> Imprison it in a well-lit sentence cell?
> Titivate eye and ear
> With first-rate tit-bits of words?

The poem ends:

> (Should. The others should.)
> My part should be lost.[33]

That is language beyond belief. But it is still language nevertheless. A metaphor is used to renounce metaphors, the lines which dissociate themselves from first-rate tit-bits of words are themselves of the highest quality. The poem which renounces art is itself of necessity a work of art. Almost every product of this era carries within itself the seed of its own destruction, or at the very least within the counter-product invented to complement it. Art is unable to cancel itself out as art, literature can not do away with itself as literature. A person who expresses herself fully is unable to rid herself of art or literature: the wish to be rid of them remains as testimony. Her part will not be lost.

Books can burn: the lesson has sunk in deep. Literature, despairing and weary of itself as it may be, must yet persist, indeed must overcome this despair and self-disgust. Assuming it is not lost by its authors going away: to another country, into another profession, taking on a different name, retreating into illness, into insanity, into death—all of these metaphors for silence when they happen to writers: Being silenced. Choosing silence. Having to be silent. Finally, being permitted to be silent.

But—and you should visualise a long silence before this but, a silence whose colour, if it had one, would be black—despite the fact that the three languages of politics, science and literature which Büchner managed to combine in his one person, admittedly by a super-human exertion of body and soul, have since then drifted hopelessly far apart from one another: the language of literature appears, strangely enough, to be the one which most closely approximates the reality of humanity at this time, however much this may be disputed by statistics, numerical codes, standardisation and performance tables. Perhaps this is so because moral courage on the part of the author—the courage to risk self-knowledge—is an ingredient in literature. Or maybe it is an outcome of the consensus reached and firmly established in literature—although laboriously attained, constantly at risk and repeatedly violated—which has nonetheless created over the centuries the stuff of what we call 'civilisation'. Our antipathy to this outmoded word may serve to make us realise how threatened is the continued existence of what it stands for. And yet this word, unlike political and scientific terms, has its admirers, emits an aura, as do other words which occur to me randomly such as: 'peace', 'moon', 'city', 'meadow', 'life', 'death'. Do we really want to give them all up? Do we seriously mean to replace them with the concepts: 'nuclear stalemate', 'earth satellite', 'settled conurbation', 'fertile area', 'kinetic form of matter' and 'expiry'?

The natural scientists have managed with the help of scientific jargon to protect their inventions from their own feelings; apparently logical linguistic constructions support the politicians' idée fixe that the salvation of humanity lies in the possibility of its multiple destruction.

Literature today must be peace research.

Writing hasn't been made any easier by the knowledge that our two countries, once called 'Germany', a name they forfeited when they corrupted it with Auschwitz—that the land on both sides of the Elbe would be amongst the first to be blotted out in the event of a 'nuclear conflict'. There are sure to be geographical maps already drawn up which have charted the stages of this obliteration. Cassandra, it seems to me, must have loved Troy more than she loved herself when she dared prophesy the downfall of their city to her fellow citizens.[34] Have these two countries perhaps been insufficiently loved by their inhabitants, I ask myself, and hence display a tendency—like a person who has not been loved and hence is unable to love—to destroy themselves and others? I ask this in order to be able to strongly contradict myself and, absurd as it may seem, as proof of the contrary I take literature itself. It would not be enough, I know, for a people to possess a homeland only in their literature. And yet, I suggest—in the present situation any suggestion, even the most eccentric one, should be granted—literature should be permitted to confront that map of death with its own map'. Every place and landscape, everything about human relationships which literature has described minutely, exactly and partisanly, painfully, critically, devotedly, fearfully and joyfully, ironically, rebelliously and lovingly, should be erased from this map of death and count as saved. It's about time literature written by Germans was not ineffectual; the efforts and achievements of literature in both German states over the last three decades in grieving and rejoicing, this literature's confrontation with the 'truth of the here and now' ought to count for once, to the benefit of both countries. After such a long time literature should be consulted and taken at its word for once, just this once, in order to help safeguard the survival of life on earth.

She's stark raving mad, you say. Fine. So I lack—to use the language of psychiatry—insight into my illness, and I'm succumbing to this sheer madness to avoid falling prey to the darker side of reason. It is conceivable that a military command really would find it harder to mark out for destruction a city described in precise and intimate detail than one which no-one knows very well, or one which affected no-one so deeply that they had felt compelled to describe it as the place they grew up, the place where they had been humiliated or first fallen in love.

Now you are smiling at my naiveté. At my irrationality: *He seemed perfectly rational, spoke with people,* Büchner said of Lenz. *He behaved just like the others; yet there was a terrible emptiness in him, he no longer felt fear or desire, his existence was to him a burden to be endured.*[35] In that land beyond belief too, there of all places, people will talk, albeit softly. A conversation about trees, about water earth sky man—in an attempt which seems to me more realistic than the strictly crazy speculation about the end of the world. After exhaustive exploration of the truth expressed by the phrase 'out of joint', other words would be sure to pop up which we would wish to use cautiously and not in a loud-mouthed manner. Because we would know: none of them, not even the most honest, would be the last word. We would hope that none of them would be the *last.*

This skin too will be peeled off and torn to shreds.[36]

NOTES

1. 'Taboo of taboos'. This is a quotation from the speech which follows and refers to two characters from a comedy by Büchner entitled *Leonce and Lena* (transl. by Victor Price, Oxford, O.U.P., 1971). In the speech, Christa Wolf uses 'Leonce by his many names' and 'Rosetta by her many names' as generic names for men and women both in literature, life, and history.
2. *Selbstversuch—Self Experiment*—Wolf (1972)—see attached bibliography for works by Wolf available in English. This story was originally commissioned for a volume entitled *Blitz aus heiterm Himmel (A Bolt from the Blue)* in which an equal number of men and women writers contributed a story around the theme of how it would feel to wake up one fine morning and find oneself transformed into the opposite sex. Ed. by Edith Anderson, Rostock, Hinstorff Verlag, 1975.
3. Maxie Wander, *Guten Morgen, Du Schöne* (Berlin, Buchverlag Der Morgen, 1977). Christa Wolf's interpretative essay on this volume, entitled 'Berührung', first appeared in the GDR literary journal *Neue Deutsche Literatur,* No. 2, 1978, pp. 53–62. In the West German edition of Wander's work which followed, Wolf's essay was included as an introduction.

4. The German Democratic Republic is one of the few countries in the world to have instituted almost all the material preconditions for women's emancipation. Women are legally guaranteed equal educational opportunity and equal pay for equal work. Since 86 per cent of them work in social production, they enjoy economic independence from men. There are also several schemes for women to improve their qualifications whilst on the job, to raise their level of skills and hence income in relation to men's. Women have entered many formerly male-dominated sectors of the economy, (although the converse is not true). Child-care facilities including after-school clubs are provided by the state for all children over three and for about 65 per cent of those under three. Contraception and abortion are freely available on the women's decision alone, to all women over sixteen regardless of marital status, and paid maternity leave is extremely generous (six months for the first, one year for the second and subsequent children). With such reproductive control, maternity leave provisions and childcare facilities, women in the GDR enjoy an area of real choice and autonomy over their lives–whether and when to have children, whether and when to return to work after having them–which is available only to the privileged few in the West. This is not to say that these necessary preconditions are sufficient conditions for the full liberation of women, as indeed is manifest in the Wander volume, in which women of varying ages, family and professional status speak frankly of their aspirations and disappointments in the personal, work and political arenas. The contradictions faced by women in their daily life are also the subject of stories appearing in the GDR in the last few years written by a younger generation of women writers, who see themselves (as one of them, Helga Schubert said) as no longer hampered by Wolf's difficulty in saying 'I'.
5. Wolf, 'Berührung' (1978), *op. cit.*, p. 62.
6. The references here are to plays by Georg Büchner to which Wolf refers in the text of the speech and which are detailed in the biographical information on Büchner given below.
7. Wolf, *Lesen und Schreiben* (*The Reader and the Writer*, 1971/1977). See bio/bibliographical details below.
8. Wolf, *The Quest for Christa T.*, 1982, Eng. ed. p. 23.
9. Wolf, Büchner prize speech, see below (p. 178).
10. See Büchner, Danton in *Danton's Death* (Price ed.) Act 1, Sc. V, p. 20. See below for bibliographical details of Büchner's plays available in English.
11. Büchner, Letter to his fiancée Minna Jaeglé, Spring 1834, in Werner R. Lehmann's edition of Büchner's complete works in 4 vols., Hamburger Ausgabe, Wegner Verlag, 1967, Vol. 2, p. 426.
12. Büchner, *Lenz* (Harrap's German Classics, p. 39, or: Mermaid, pp. 143, 144).
13. The 'magic broom' refers to a ballad by Goethe, entitled *Der Zauberlehrling (The Sorceror's Apprentice)*, which was set to music by Paul Dukas.
14. Johann Wolfgang van Goethe, *Faust,* Part II, Act V, pp. 326, 327. (Vol. 3, Goethe's *Works* in 4 vols., Frankfurt a.M., Insel-Verlag, 1965.)
15. Wolf is alluding here to Robert Oppenheimer, 'father of the atom bomb', and to the book about him and other nuclear scientists involved in the development of the atom bomb, *Brighter than a Thousand Suns* by Robert Jungk (1958, first appeared 1956 in German). Robert Jungk has written several further books dealing with the implications for humanity of this discovery (amongst them *Children of the Ashes*–1961, about the survivors of Hiroshima, *The Everyman Project: Resources for a Humane Future*–1973, *The Nuclear State*–1978) and is an active campaigner for peace. He was a speaker at the October 1981 mass peace demonstration in Bonn and was present at the Congress for European

Nuclear Disarmament (END) held in Brussels in July 1982. He also participated in the Writers' Congresses on questions of peace held in Berlin, GDR in December 1981 and in the Hague in May 1982, as did Wolf herself. The sacred Indian epic poem Jungk quotes Oppenheimer as reciting in the face of the first atomic explosion is the *Bhagavad Gita*—see Jungk, *Brighter than a Thousand Suns,* New York, Harcourt, Brace and World, Inc., 1958, p. 201.

16. The word 'overkill' appears in English in the original German text.
17. Goethe, 'Das Göttliche' ('The Divine'), in Goethe, *Werke,* Vol. I: *Gedichte (Poems),* Frankfurt a.M., Insel-Verlag, 1965, pp. 85, 86.
18. Büchner, *Danton's Death, op. cit.,* spoken by Danton to Camille, Act II, Sc. I, p. 28.
19. This appears as one word in the original German: 'verkehrt'.
20. Büchner, *Leonce and Lena,* (Price ed.), Act I, Sc. III, pp. 81, 82.
21. Büchner, *Danton's Death, op. cit.,* Act III, Sc. IX, p. 58.
22. Rosetta and Lena are the main female figures in Büchner's play *Leonce and Lena,* Marie the female lead in *Woyzeck* and Marion, Julie, Lucile the female characters in *Danton's Death.* All of these characters are no more than foils to or appendages of the male protagonists as Wolf's speech both exemplifies and generalises for women's role in history.
23. Büchner, *Leonce and Lena, op. cit.,* Act I, Sc. IV, p. 88.
24. Leonce says: 'The world is. . . a hall of mirrors, so narrow I hardly dare stretch my arms for fear of smashing them. . . I'd be left standing in front of the bare naked walls.' Büchner, *Leonce and Lena, op. cit.,* Act II, Sc. I, p.
25. Leonce, in ibid., Act. I, Sc. I, p. 75. In a similar vein, Lenz regrets being unable to walk on his head. (Büchner, *Lenz, op. cit.,* p. 37).
26. Büchner, *Danton's Death, op. cit.,* Act IV, Sc. VIII, p. 70.
27. An allusion to Engels, *Origin of the Family, Private Property and the State.*
28. An allusion to Ibsen's play *The Doll's House.*
29. Marlene Dietrich in one of her songs.
30. Rosetta in Büchner's play *Leonce and Lena, op. cit.,* Act I, Sc. III, p. 80.
31. In Büchner's *Danton's Death* (*op. cit.,* Act II, Sc. II, p. 33) a citizen remarks: 'The earth is a thin crust. I always think I might fall through where there's a hole like that. . . You've got to step warily, it might break under you.'
32. Leonce to Lena, Büchner, *Leonce and Lena, op. cit.,* Act II, Sc. IV, p. 95.
33. Ingeborg Bachmann, 'Keine Delikatessen', in Bachmann, *Werke (Collected Works),* Munich, Piper & Co., 1978, Vol. I, pp. 172, 173.
34. Christa Wolf gave five lectures in Frankfurt, West Germany in May 1982 on the Cassandra theme, entitled 'The Genesis of a Story' (culminating in a Cassandra story).
35. Büchner, *Lenz,* Harrap, p. 61, or Mermaid, p. 166.
36. Alludes to Büchner's *Leonce and Lena, op. cit.,* Act III, Sc. III, p. 100, where Valerio, court jester, ponders while taking off a series of masks: 'Am I this? Or this? Or this? I'm getting frightened; I shall peel myself away to nothing.' This closing sentiment reiterates the theme raised at the beginning of Wolf's speech with the allusion to roles played as against true identity in *Danton's Death,* referenced above in note 10. The concept raised by Büchner and Wolf of the face becoming the mask, the person becoming the role, the face coming away with the mask or the mask sticking to the face is graphically illustrated by the mime Marcel Marceau in his 'Mask Builder'.

BIOGRAPHICAL DETAILS

Christa Wolf (1929–)

Born in 1929 in Landsberg, Wartha (now Gorzów Wielkopolski in Poland), Christa Wolf studied German literature at Jena and Leipzig universities from 1949–1953. Between 1953 and 1962 she worked variously as research assistant to the Writers' Union of the German Democratic Republic (GDR), reader, journalist, literary critic and editor for the literary journal *Neue Deutsche Literatur* and for the Mitteldeutscher Verlag, one of the largest publishing houses in the GDR. Since 1962 she has been a freelance writer.

Wolf's main works are the novels *Der geteilte Himmel (Divided Heavens),* 1963, *Nachdenken über Christa T. (The Quest for Christa T.),* 1968, *Kindheitsmuster (Imprint of Childhood)* 1976 and the story *Kein Ort. Nirgends (No Place, Nowhere)* 1979. In addition, she has written numerous film scripts, stories and essays. Some of the latter appeared in the important collection *Lesen und Schreiben (The Reader and the Writer)* 1971, and three of what Wolf calls in a subtitle 'improbable' stories, including 'Selbstversuch' ('Experiment in Identity') were published under the title *Unter den Linden* (a street name in Berlin) 1974.

Prior to winning the Georg Büchner prize for literature in 1980, Christa Wolf had been awarded the Heinrich Mann prize in 1963, the National Prize of the GDR for Art and Literature in 1964 and the Bremen literature prize in 1978. Christa Wolf has participated in both the recent Writers' Congresses concerned with questions of peace–the first between writers from the GDR and West Germany, held in December 1981 in Berlin; the second a wider European gathering which took place in the Hague in May 1982.

Christa Wolf's portrayal of the relationship of the individual to society has always been dominated by the exploration of subjectivity and the possibilities for the full development of individual human potential within a humane socialist society. She sees the writer's task as reflecting these deliberations transparently to aid the understanding and personal growth of present and future generations, a process she calls in her motto for *Christa T.* (in a quotation from Johannes R. Becher, Expressionist and GDR poet and man of letters) 'Dieses Zu-sich-selber-Kommen' ('This coming-to-oneself').

Christa Wolf's writing is also deeply influenced by her experience of a childhood under fascism, an experience she attempts to confront and come to terms with *Christa T.* and especially *Kindheitsmuster.* In her writing she refers to her generation as being deeply marked by the violent break between this influence on their formative years and the idealistic aspirations and partial disillusionment of their commitment as young adults to socialism. It is the split between these two 'eras' in her life which leads Christa Wolf to speak in *Christa T.* (a theme echoed in the narrative structure of *Kindheitsmuster*) of the 'Schwierigkeit, "ich" zu sagen' ('The difficulty of saying "I" ').

Georg Büchner (1813–1837)

Born in 1813 near Darmstadt, Büchner studied science and medicine at the universities of Strasbourg and Giessen. Fired by the ideals of the French Revolution, Büchner became involved in political struggle, forming an illegal revolutionary organisation called 'Society for the Rights of Man'. In 1834 he wrote *Der hessische Landbote (The Hesse Country Messenger)*, a flaming denunciation of the poverty and miserable feudal living conditions of the peasants in his home state, the Grand Duchy of Hesse. He combines his attack on the rich for their exploitation of the peasants with an incitement to the peasants to rise up in revolt.

Büchner was forced to flee the resulting police search in 1835, first to Strasbourg, then to Zürich, where he completed his doctorate at the university and began work as a lecturer. In 1837 he died suddenly at the age of 23 of typhoid fever.

In 1835 Büchner wrote his first play, *Danton's Tod (Danton's Death)* which deals with the tragic failure of the French Revolution, the internal struggles, Danton's ultimately fatalistic pessimism and the real conditions of the poverty-stricken masses, for whom neither Danton and Camille, nor the Jacobins under Robespierre and St. Just provide bread. *Lenz,* also written in 1835, is a novella about the 18th century poet of that name. It suggests the style and themes of Expressionism in Lenz's despairing emptiness, his chaotic visions of nature gone wild and his failure to maintain a grip on everyday reality. With *Woyzeck*, the drama fragment of 1835/36, Büchner returns to the attack on social injustice of his first work. Based on a documentary case of a poor army barber who was hung for killing his wife, *Woyzeck* illustrates the origins of such events in the social circumstances of poverty and exploitation. Finally in 1836, Büchner wrote his satirical comedy *Leonce and Lena,* which in its parody on the boredom and emptiness of court life and its comic portrayal of meaninglessness prefigures the theatre of the absurd.

Bibliography

Büchner, Georg, *The Complete Plays.*
Translated by Victor Price, Oxford, O.U.P., 1971.

Büchner, Georg,
1. *Lenz*
In German, but with introduction and notes in English, edited by M.B. Benn, London, Harrap's German Classics, 1963.

Büchner, Georg
Complete Plays and Prose
Translated with an introduction by Carl Richard Mueller, New York, Hill and Wang, A Mermaid Drama Book, 1963.

Büchner, Georg
The Complete Collected Works
Translated and ed. by Henry J. Schmidt, New York, Avon Books, 1977.

Wolf, Christa, *Divided Heavens*
1. Berlin: Seven Seas, 1965.
2. Translated by Joan Becker, New York, Adler, 1976.

Wolf, Christa, *The Quest for Christa T.*
Translated by Christopher Middleton, London, Virago Press, 1982 (first appeared New York, Dell, 1970).

Wolf, Christa, *The Reader and the Writer*
Translated by Joan Becker, Berlin, Seven Seas, 1977.

Wolf, Christa, 'Self Experiment'
Translated by Jeanette Clausen in *New German Critique,* No. 13, Winter 1978, pp. 109–131.

Wolf, Christa, *A Model Childhood*
Translated by Ursule Molinaro and Hedwig Rappolt, London, Virago Press, 1982.

CHINA: THE ECONOMIC CRISIS

Ernest Mandel

Ever since the victory of the Chinese Revolution in 1949, the different factions and coalitions of factions that have succeeded each other at the head of the Chinese Communist Party (CCP) and governments have faced a series of strategic problems rooted in the country's backwardness. They include:

1. How to feed a population that grows by between ten and fifteen million people a year, when China's traditional agriculture is already among the most productive in the world and it will not be possible for a long time yet to resolve the problem through a radical modernisation. Related to this question is the attitude towards population growth as such: should one favour it (as Mao did), oppose it by crude material disincentives or repression (as Deng does) or adopt some third road?

2. How to reduce the enormous extent of rural underemployment and urban unemployment caused by demographic growth and the inevitable rural exodus.

3. How to divide national income between consumption and accumulation, and the accumulation fund between agriculture, heavy industry and light industry; and how to deal with the consequence of these decisions for feeding the population, providing employment and stimulating productivity.

4. How to organise planning and management and to gauge the implications of the techniques chosen for the rate of growth, the satisfaction of basic food needs, and the degree of social equality and social tension; as well as the repercussions of these implications on the relative efficiency of planning itself.

5. How, and at what pace, to industrialise and modernise China, for whatever the idealists may say to the contrary, modernisation cannot go without industrialisation. This modernisation is indispensable not only for national defence, but also for satisfying the population's most basic needs, including literacy, universal medical care and the raising of the general cultural level.[1]

6. What position to take up in relation to the world market that avoids autarchy on the one hand and total integration on the other, since total integration would mean that China's forms of development would be determined by the logic of capitalist profit and imperialist super-profit.

To be schematic and overly simple, one might sum up the choices a follows. *Grosso modo* the Chinese peasant family produces one ton o cereal per work-year. How much of this ton of rice or wheat should it kee for its own consumption (which presently fluctuates between 300 an 350 kg per year) or for that of the village as a whole? What proportion o it should stay in the village for agricultural accumulation? If this pro portion is changed, relatively or absolutely, what effect will that chang have on the productivity of agricultural labour, on the rate of growth o agricultural production and on the peasantry's degree of tolerance fo the regime?

How much of this ton of rice should go to the cities to feed worker and bureaucrats, or to be exchanged for foreign capital goods? Wha would be the implications of the decision made here for the rat of industrial growth, the pace of industrialisation, the productivity o industrial labour and the lowering of unemployment? In what form shoul the agricultural surplus be extracted from the village? By forced levy By manipulating market price mechanisms? And what would be th consequences of the method of extraction for the satisfaction of basi food needs and the degree of inequality within the peasantry itself?

Changes in Economic Policy since 1949

After 1949 the CCP leaders at first committed themselves to a Sovie style policy, although they behaved much more cautiously than th Soviet bureaucracy towards the peasantry. But it soon became clear tha China was too underdeveloped to follow Stalin's path to industrialisatio In ten to fifteen years some 200 million young people could be expecte to leave the villages for the cities. To give each a job would cost at leas $2000 in investment (at 1955–65 prices). This would have meant invest ing $400 billion in industry. But such an amount was clearly beyond th purse of an economy whose annual national revenue was calculated a only $50 billion in 1957.[2] Moreover since traditional Chinese agricultur is already highly productive, to increase that productivity so that it wa capable of feeding 200 to 300 million more individuals would be impossib without massive mechanisation. Already the marginal productivity o Chinese agriculture is falling disastrously because the Chinese peasan (who throughout large parts of the country is better described as a gardene than a farmer) can no longer increase output without huge amounts o new investment in chemical fertilisers.[3] It is hard to imagine a mo vicious circle. There could be no big increase in industrial productio unless there were one too in agricultural output. But agricultural outpu would only rise quickly if investment in it were greatly increased, whic required a big increase in industrial output. Clearly a change of cours was necessary. And so one after the other the following economic polici were adopted.

During the Great Leap Forward of 1958–62 the focus was on 'labour-investment', i.e. mobilising the peasantry's underemployed labour on projects designed to raise agricultural production (including irrigation works, backyard blast furnaces and workshops to produce simple agricultural tools). The original idea was not wrong. But it soon became coupled with an excessive extraction of agricultural surplus and even of the agricultural necessary product by the state, and with bureaucratic methods of leadership. The peasants became dissatisfied, and output dropped disastrously.

In 1962–66, during the period of 'rectification' and cautious modernisation under Liu Shaoqi and Deng Xiaoping, the centralisation of agricultural labour in giant communes was abandoned. Brigades incorporating several villages and even work teams (incorporating one village) became the basic units of production. The communes retained only a few of their functions. Peasants were allowed to dispose of a limited part of their farming surplus on the free market. Plans were laid for the modernisation of some branches of industry. At the same time, China embarked on a policy of autarchy as a result of the simultaneous Soviet and Western blockades.

In 1966–71, during the Cultural Revolution, the private sector was hard hit but it was not completely abolished (especially not in the countryside). During this period the strategy of 'labour-investment' was followed in industry as well as in agriculture, particularly in the oil industry, which made its first important advances thanks to the extensive application of labour (the Daqing experiment). Autarchy was stressed more than ever before or since, and modernisation stopped. There was probably even some disinvestment.

In the period 1971–76 Zhou Enlai and Deng Xiaoping succeeded in putting an end to autarchy by making overtures to Japan and the West. China began once more to import modern technology, although these imports were still only on a limited scale. A free market for the agrarian surplus, which was left in the hands of the peasants, was partially re-established. But this 'new course', which oscillated between the policies of the Cultural Revolution and those of the period 1962–66, was constantly challenged, and it scored no striking successes.

After Mao's death in 1976 the Deng Xiaoping leadership committed itself more wholeheartedly to the Four Modernisations and speeded up China's reintegration into the world market, the search for capitalist credits, the dismantling of the People's Communes, and the full rehabilitation of material incentives. But the very magnitude of the turn threw the economy off balance again in 1979. A new adjustment became necessary.

For nearly two decades workers' wages and real income had stayed practically frozen, and the communes' 'surplus' labour was hired out to industrial enterprises at wages well below the official rates. When these 'coolies of Mao' demonstrated against their conditions during the Cultural Revolution, they were accused of 'economism' by the extremist Maoist faction and harshly repressed.

Bureaucratic privileges were slightly reduced during the Cultural Revolution,[4] and the technocratic layer lost out to the political cadres and the military. But despite Mao's promises and the Red Guards' demands, there was no workers' power in the factories, let alone in the country as a whole. After 1968 the more militant layers of youth and workers were harshly repressed by the 'Gang of Four', which explains why the Maoist leaders got no mass support when they were finally removed from power.

Since 1976, workers have had their wages raised and their conditions improved. Between 1978 and 1980, around 60 per cent of urban wage-earners were said to have received a modest increase of 10–15 per cent. But at the same time the power of the technocratic wing of the bureaucracy has grown rapidly. Social inequality has widened, so that wealth and poverty mingle in the cities more than at any time since the early 1950s.

The Four Modernisations

The decision to strive towards the Four Modernisations was taken above all because the Chinese leaders came to see that China could never be transformed into a modern great power before the century was up if they continued with their policy of relying mainly on 'labour investment'. Such a policy would have brought social tensions to the point of explosion. To freeze (or, even worse, cut) living standards over the next quarter century would raise neither industrial nor agricultural output. It would also have made it impossible to integrate the mass of unemployed (in the cities) and the underemployed (in the villages) into modern industry in the foreseeable future.

And so a more pragmatic strategy was developed. This strategy foresaw combining accelerated development of modern industry through applying foreign aid with the development of the private or the cooperative sector, which despite its low productivity would at least absorb some workless.

So this is not a return to the Stalinist model: for Deng's economic policies have no more in common with Stalin's line than did Mao's in their time. If Deng's policy has any precedent at all, it is rather in Tito's Yugoslavia (but without the workers' self-management) or better still in the 'Hungarian reforms'. Rehabilitating the market economy and material incentives is the foundation of Deng's strategy (or rather, of the strategy of Hu Qiaomu, Zhao Ziyang and Chen Yun, who are the reform's true initiators).

According to the new strategy, it is the market that will connect the various economic sectors: the 'leading industries' from which modernisation of the country's entire infrastructure is to proceed; the 'export industries', i.e. mainly oil, coal and textiles, but also many industries competing with Hong Kong and Taiwan; agriculture (which is to be stimulated by increased supplies of chemical fertiliser[5]); industrial consumer goods; and the rapidly expanding private and cooperative sector.

China's new prime minister, Zhao Ziyang, had already tested this new strategy extensively in the country's most populous province, Sichuan, which he administered from 1975 to 1979. In Sichuan he dismantled the People's Communes more vigorously than anywhere else in China. The peasant family (rather than the brigade or production team) was made responsible for achieving production goals, and got the 'three freedoms': bigger private plots; a bigger free market on which to dispose of its surpluses; and the chance to form private non-agricultural enterprises (mainly in handicrafts and commerce). According to the *Neue Zürcher Zeitung* (5 December 1980) private activity today procures on average 40 *yuan* per year per peasant household, i.e. some 30 per cent of their total income, but with great differences between 'rich' and 'poor' communes, villages and households.

But at the same time Zhao Ziyang returned to one of the main themes of Mao's economic policy during the Great Leap Forward and the Cultural Revolution (although Mao himself had more and more clearly abandoned it after 1970): the idea that rural industry should be developed to serve the needs of the peasants and of agriculture, and that this industry should be mainly financed by agricultural expansion (or even by 'labour investment' in the villages). But Zhao, unlike Mao, is trying to reach this goal by crude but effective 'material incentives' rather than by political mobilisation, indoctrination or coercion.[6] However, the basic premiss stays the same (and in this sense the fundamental difference with Stalin and Khrushchev remains): that China's cities and her modern industry cannot absorb the labour surplus of her villages, and that another way must be found.

Overheating and Skidding

After a fine start–industrial output is said to have risen by 14.3 per cent in 1977 and 13.5 per cent in 1978–the Four Modernisations soon came up against some intrinsic obstacles.

1. Exports did not grow at the same rate as imports of modern technology. Oil extraction in particular has stagnated, mainly because of bad management and lack of modern technology. One illustration of the problems facing this industry was the oil-rig disaster in the Gulf of Bohai, when 72 workers died.[7] Oil exports to Japan seem to be falling. They are expected to drop from 9 million tons in 1981 to 8.3 million in 1982, whereas the original contract foresaw increases of 9.5 and 15 million tons respectively.[8]

Had China maintained the pace of modernisation projected since

1975–76, she would have accumulated a colossal debt on the level of Poland's or even Brazil's. The trade deficit with the imperialist countries rose from $1.2 billion in 1977 to $3.5 billion in 1978 and $4.5 billion in 1979 (although it is true that this was partly offset by a favourable balance with Hong Kong of $1.7, $2.2 and $2.6 billions over the same period). The US Department of Commerce forecast in July 1980 that China's gross external debt of $3.5 billion in 1980 (with an annual debt service of $2 billion) would grow to a minimum of $16 billion in 1985 (with an annual debt service of $3.2 billion).

This the Chinese leaders were not prepared to accept, so they cut back heavily on their original plans, cancelling some of the more expensive projects and slowing down the overall pace of expansion. In particular they cancelled various plans to import whole factories.[9] In his speech resigning as head of the government, Hua Guofeng officially announced that the 1976–85 Ten Year Plan, which had incorporated the most ambitious goals of the Four Modernisations, would not be carried out.[10]

2. Many modernisation projects set up since Deng returned to power have failed or fallen short of the desired results because of lack of qualified staff, planning errors, bureaucratic negligence and workers' indifference. These problems were similar to those facing Poland under Gierek, but the comparison is hardly useful, since China is so much larger and less developed than Poland.

Two scandals symbolised these failures: the Wuhan Steelworks, which was supposed to produce four million tons of steel and was bought in West Germany at a high price, was without enough electricity had been overlooked in the plan; and the Baoshan Steelworks near Shanghai, ordered from Japan with a capacity of six million tons, was assigned a construction site in the middle of quicksands.[11]

More generally, output targets in steel, oil and agricultural machinery were greatly scaled down. Priority was no longer to be given to steel ('cereals and steel' were the two axes of economic expansion under Mao); the goal of 60 million ingots of steel by 1985 seems to have been reduced to 45 million. Also abandoned was the hare-brained scheme to achieve 'rural mechanisation in the main' by 1980, which had been reconfirmed as late as January 1978 and would have meant manufacturing the equivalent of 3.5 million units of fifteen-horsepower tractors and motorised implements in the space of three years (as opposed to a more realistic target of six to eight years).[12]

Coal, by contrast, will get high priority, and may make up for declining oil exports to Japan, as well as cover China's energy deficit (which threatens to get worse in coming years).[13]

3. It was impossible to reconcile concessions to peasants in the form of increases in the purchase price of agricultural products and to workers in the form of higher wages. As a result, inflationary pressures built up and

there were shortages of some staple goods.

In mid-1980, the rate of inflation was put at 6–7 per cent;[14] by the end of the year there was talk of a 15–20 per cent inflation.[15] The main cause of this inflation is China's large budget deficit—her first ever since 1949. This deficit has been put in the $10 billion range, representing 15 per cent of the entire budget expenditure for 1979. (Other sources give the figure of $12 billion.)[16] It was mainly to cut this deficit that austerity was introduced and investment policy was readjusted.

4. Covert resistance to the Four Modernisations by part of the political leadership—especially the military—has delayed, curbed and even prevented reforms and has further increased the imbalances. But this 'resistance' probably stems as much from the incompetence of officials selected in the course of factional struggles as from genuine political disagreements.

5. There have been less joint ventures with foreign capital than was originally expected. At first most of those capitalists who entered into joint ventures were Overseas and Hong Kong Chinese. They were granted important concessions in exchange for participating in these schemes, including the recovery of all bank accounts expropriated during the Cultural Revolution and the restitution of various compensation payments suspended between 1966 and 1976. The new policy got off to a bad start when output fell instead of rising at the Jiang Sho Spinning Mill in Guangdong Pronvince, which was the first of these joint ventures set up with a Hong Kong and a Macao firm.[17] By late 1980, only thirteen of the 800 joint venture projects submitted had been definitively approved and were operational.[18] To make up for lost income the Deng regime has even begun to export cheap labour,[19] but here too the results have been meagre, at least up to now.

To summarise, one could say that Deng's modernisers have committed the same sin as Mao and his supporters: that of immoderation. They have set out to do too much too fast, even though the means they used were different from those used by the Maoists.[20] Of course, this was hardly a coincidence. When the same mistakes are made so frequently, it is not enough to put them down to the innate defects of the bureaucracy alone. One should seek their roots also in objective problems. For a poor, backward country like China to feed, house and provide even a minimal level of welfare for one billion human beings is a colossal task that will need a Herculean effort to resolve.

Any government in power in Beijing that does not serve the interests of a possessing class subordinated to foreign interests would face the same drama. Its historical villains are not the Chinese Communist leaders, but the foreign imperialists who plundered China, dismantled her economy and mired her in underdevelopment; Stalin, Khrushchev and Brezhnev, who did their best to subordinate the Chinese Revolution to their own state interests; and the leaders of the American, European and Japanese workers, who refused to lessen the colossal weight of China's underdevelopment by broad, generous and disinterested aid. World revolution will make up for these shortcomings. But in the meantime, while we wait and fight for its victory, those billion mouths must be fed. Here and nowhere else lies the main source of the twists and turns of the CCP's economic policy since 1949.

Social Tensions

Alongside problems connected with the modernisation drive, important social tensions have appeared at all levels of Chinese society. These tensions are not new. They also plagued earlier phases of China's economic development. But economic 'liberalisation' unquestionably sharpened them, while the limited 'democratisation' of 1978–79 and the growing scepticism of workers and youth towards all factions of the Party allowed them to be displayed more openly. Among these social tensions we should note the following.

1. The rise of youth unemployment in the cities. Youth unemployment was already an important factor in the emergence of the Red Guard movement. It was resolved in a particularly cruel way when Lin Biao and the 'Gang of Four' liquidated the Cultural Revolution and deported huge numbers of these youth to the countryside. Even though ideological indoctrination at first softened the impact on some of the victims, most soon changed their minds, especially when they saw that the peasants' welcome was less than lukewarm (for the one thing that Chinese agriculture needs least is more labour).

As a result, great masses of young people returned illegally to the cities, where they started a crime wave. They had to live mainly by their wits, since they had neither residence permits nor work permits. It seems likely that the terrorist incident at Beijing Railway Station on 29 October 1980 was the work of a young desperado of this type.[21] The authorities' response to the youth troubles was surprisingly mild. This is because the Deng faction does not (as yet) want to be associated with the massive deportation of youth in the years 1968–70.[22]

In September 1978, 50,000 young people working on state farms in Yunnan went on strike, and in December thousands of unemployed youth staged demonstrations in Shanghai. In early 1979 some youths rioted in Shanghai, blocking rail traffic for twelve hours. Two 'ringleaders' went to prison for nine and five years.[23]

It is therefore obvious why the Chinese leaders are concerned about the problem of youth unemployment, and cautious in how they treat it. The size of the problem is staggering. Some twenty million young people are thought to have been deported to the countryside in the late sixties and early seventies. Of the twelve million urban young people who left school in 1979 and were looking for jobs, only seven million got them.[24]

The Chinese leaders have tried to bring down this unemployment in two ways that combine typical features of the Deng approach. One way is to use material incentives and the free market to channel the problem out of the public sector. Young people are now allowed to set up small retail businesses and workshops, or to enter the repair trade. China is experiencing a rapid expansion of the 'service sector', as have many underdeveloped capitalist economies. Of course the authorities tend to favour cooperative enterprises, but even private initiatives are tolerated.

Another way is by encouraging resettlement in the countryside, although the coercion used under Mao has been replaced here too by a system of material incentives. One million young people are reported to have organised 30,000 collective farms where they can earn twice what they would in a People's Commune and almost as much as in the cities.[25]

2. Increased differentiation in the countryside. The gradual dismantling of the People's Communes and the key role that the market is increasingly playing in the rural economy can only accentuate social differentiation in the countryside. As in the Soviet Union in the 1940s and 1950s, the difference between rich and poor areas (communes and brigades) and even between rich and poor peasants is growing now that the old levelling drive (which led to a dangerous slowdown in the rise in food output) has been abandoned.

Zhao Ziyang's flatterers stress that Sichuan peasants now take their (private) pigs by (private) bike, (private) motorbike or (cooperative) truck to be sold on the free market. The watchword is familiar: Enrich yourselves! But for how many People's Communes, or for that matter how many Chinese peasants, is this prospect realistic?

I have already mentioned that according to official sources the average farmer's income is half that of the average urban worker's, which is 75 *yuan* a month. It is easy to picture the poverty in which a great part of the Chinese peasantry still languishes–especially that part of it which carried the Revolution to victory thirty years ago. Vice-Premier Yao Yilin recognised that ten per cent of peasants do not eat enough to still their hunger. Here too the discontent has acquired political form. In January 1979 tens of thousands of peasants demonstrated in Beijing under the slogan 'Down with famine!'

The average income per peasant household is said to oscillate between 30 *yuan* a year in poor communes and 400 *yuan* a year in rich ones (45 and 450 *yuan* if you add that part of the grain harvest that the peasants consume.) Average income per peasant household is estimated at around 100–120 *yuan* a year. One leader of the Deng faction has even claimed that the average peasant consumed less cereals in 1978 than in 1957.[26] But this claim is not too credible, and was probably intended to paint the Maoist years in the worst light. The American journalist Felix Butterfield reported that according to Chinese government sources, life expectancy in China has risen from 32 years in 1949 to 68 years in 1978.[27] Since average consumption in 1957 or 1937 was below 2000 calories per day per person, any further reduction in calorie intake would have ruled out a rise in life expectancy in a country where 80 per cent of the population still live in the countryside. The same point could be made about Nicholas Lardy's claim that per capita food intake was lower throughout the years 1958–78 than it was in the 1930s.[28]

The Deng faction's policy of encouraging the free market has led to reactions that Mao foresaw and feared: rich communes, rich brigades and even rich work teams are more interested in growing crops that sell well on the market than cereals to be delivered to the state at fixed prices. As a result cereal output has stagnated and even dropped, while agricultural production as a whole has risen.[29] According to official sources 14.6 per cent of farm products were sold on the free market in 1978.[30] The government's dilemma is cruel: either raise the price of the cereals it buys from the communes (which would increase the budget deficit and quicken inflation) or return to a system of fixed quotas, i.e. severely restrict the newly granted 'market freedom'.

3. Growing urban inequality. This is the combined result of various factors, including salary rises for top officials; the restoration of the privileges of the 'national patriotic bourgeoisie'; the extension of the private sector; and the massive reappearance in China after thirty years' absence of well-to-do foreign tourists, businessmen and technicians, and Overseas Chinese. Things like luxury stores, luxury goods, luxury restaurants, the black market, prostitution and the like, which were cut to a minimum or discretely hidden from view in the decade before Mao's death, are now openly flaunted.

Foreign currency plays a key role in widening and consolidating social inequality, just as it does in the Soviet Union and Eastern Europe. China now has a sprawling black market in Hong Kong dollars, Japanese yen and other strong currencies, where domestic and foreign luxury goods (including illegally imported ones) are up for sale. Tourists are considered one of the main supply sources for this market, and the authorities now require them to exchange their currency for Chinese 'special money' in an effort to prevent the black market getting out of hand. But this has merely led to a new black market in 'special money'.[31] Like Eastern Europe's 'foreign currency stores, this alternative money circuit has led to protests and demonstrations by some Chinese.[32]

The regime is trying to make the politicians who came to power through the Cultural Revolution into scapegoats for the growing inequality. Official propagandists have exposed amazing cases of corruption among the 'Gang of Four' and their supporters. The corruption of the Party bureaucracy under Liu Shaoqi and Deng (which was no less genuine) was similarly denounced during the Cultural Revolution. But when jobless youth and low-paid workers see privilege flaunted once again and on an even wider scale under the present regime, it must occur to them that the various trials and purges of the last few years were none too effective. The conclusion must be that grave social tensions are accumulating in China, and that a Polish-style explosion is not to be ruled out in the coming years.

The New Management Model

During the second session of the Fifth People's Congress, Deng explained that factory life was to be democratised in the framework of overall 'economic liberalisation'. But he emphasised that 'democracy' was to be firmly wedded to 'centralised leadership'. Just as the Party is centralised at national and provincial levels, so should firm management be centralised in the hands of a director. Workers would gain the right to elect team and workshop leaders, but not directors.

As for the various Western comments about the 'rehabilitation of profit' and even the 'return to a market economy', they are as wrong now as they were about the Liberman-Trapeznikov reforms in the Soviet Union. What the debate in China is really about is what criteria central authorities should use in judging an enterprise's performance. Should they look at gross product, total transactions (sales figures), 'added value', or profit? Profit is far from becoming the autonomous motor of economic development, but is simply an instrument for achieving the plan. Firms have been granted neither the freedom to fix (or change) prices nor, where essential products are concerned, the freedom to change the assortment they have been assigned to manufacture. In one sense (as Thierry Pairault rightly noted),[33] the central institutions' control over large institutions is even stronger under the new management system than it was in the past. For although firms may now choose their suppliers and contract relations are therefore established between firms, all expenditure must now pass through the banking system, which has become—as in the Soviet Union—the main instrument through which the implementation of the plan can be checked. Any expenditure outside the framework of the plans for producing and supplying the main products will not be authorised by the banks and is therefore impossible. The role of profit (apart from its use in accounting) is reduced to that of a small 'material incentive', in the sense that workers get increased bonuses that average out at some ten per cent of wages. (No doubt bureaucrats will benefit more from it, but as yet there is no evidence of this.)

On the whole one gets the impression that the big changes have taken place not so much in large industry as in local and rural industry. During the Cultural Revolution when (partly for defence reasons) the idea of provincial self-sufficiency was pushed very strongly, it was above all small-scale local and rural industry that was affected by decentralisation. At the same time efforts were made to develop a parallel basic industry (mainly steel, but also energy) in each province, to be managed by provincial and local authorities.

Once again, despite appearances, the change brought in by the current reform moves more towards centralisation than decentralisation. The idea of 'backyard blast furnaces' has been abandoned once and for all, as has that of provincial self-sufficiency. The emphasis is now on the diversity of natural resources and the need for a greater division of labour between local industries on a national scale. This has inevitably reduced the weight and power of local authorities in favour of that of managers on the one hand and central branch administration on the other, although it has not meant a return to the old Stalinist system in which ministries in each branch controlled everything from the top. It is possible that these administrations will be replaced by national 'trusts'. In the new climate the government encourages local and provincial units to develop new resources in whatever ways they see fit; but these local and provincial initiatives must stay within the broad framework and under the ultimate control of the central authority.

I should stress that this does not mean that the weight of the market has not greatly increased under China's new management system, or that 'Hungarian-style reforms' did not really take place. There is no doubt that the cooperative and private sector, i.e. that sector of the economy outside state control, has broadened greatly in recent years, both in the cities and the countryside. Moreover the new self-management system, which was introduced cautiously and in the most profitable firms first, gives the managers a wider margin of manoeuvre and uses rivalry and competition between firms to improve productivity. But there has been no challenge to the general framework of top-down centralised planning or to the bureaucratic determination of priorities in distributing and developing national resources by a small handful of top bureaucrats.

But here a problem arises that already became apparent in the Soviet Union during the Liberman-Trapeznikov reforms. Although profit is 'in command', the firms (i.e. the managers) are not able to influence the essential determinants of profit, i.e. the price of raw materials and machines; the wage fund; and the sale price of finished products. No wonder the technocratic wing of the bureaucracy, like its counterparts in Hungary and Poland, would like to extend the reforms in the direction of granting directors the right to fire workers. (The director of a Chongqing steelworks that currently employs 40,000 workers would like to see his workforce cut by half.)[34]

Moreover growing inflationary pressures and recent budget cut-backs have now been translated into what is clearly a policy of austerity. Wages will not be raised by 15–20 per cent as promised, and the whole question of bonuses will be reexamined in the light of the need to 'tighten up'.

General Balance Sheet

A balance sheet of China's economic evolution since the Great Leap Forward, and even more so since 1949, leads to two general conclusions.

First, it is now clearer than ever that socialist revolution in China was necessary and historically justified. The Chinese Revolution matches the Russian one as the most important and progressive event of the century. It brought about changes that benefited huge numbers of human beings—this despite inordinate costs and sacrifices, some avoidable, others not.

Today this positive assessment of the Chinese Revolution is challenged not only by pro-imperialists and by Moscow, but also by some anti-Maoists in the Chinese leadership. But facts are stubborn. Contrary to a current legend, China's economic progress over the last thirty years has easily outstripped that of India. Official statistics of the present leaders show that if China's per capita output is stated as 100, India's stood at 68 for cereal production, 60 for electricity, 48 for steel and 46 for cement.[35] The area of Chinese farming land that is irrigated has grown from 60 million acres in 1949 to 110 million in 1980. Nothing of the kind has happened in India.

Social conditions vary greatly from one area of China to the next, and even from one village to the next. There is still terrible poverty in China. But that she has progressed enormously is beyond dispute. Felix Butterfield summarised the progress made as follows:

> Every day, just after noon, in the office buildings of Beijing many employees carefully clear away their desks and unfold sleeping bags. They prepare for one of the most important and satisfying rites of Chinese life, the long noon nap, the *xiuxi*.
>
> . . . An American engineer who visited an oil-prospecting platform in the South China Sea was surprised to see that the workers stopped drilling at lunch time. They stopped all the machines and went to sleep. . . The *xiuxi* is one of the comforts brought about by the Communist revolution. It is even codified in the Constitution, whose Article 49 states: The labouring people has the right to rest.
>
> Instead of the constant threats of famine, banditry and pestilent epidemics which haunted the country before 1949, the Communists have created what sometimes looks like a giant welfare state.
>
> In addition to a generous rest period, there is guaranteed employment for life, a system called the 'iron rice bowl'. It is almost impossible for a factory to fire a worker if he is not a thief or a murderer. Medical care and education are free. Urban housing is heavily subsidised; the average rent is about $2.70 per month.[36]

One might object—and one would be right—that this leads to a very low level of labour productivity. But it was no higher under the old regime, and then it went coupled with intolerable physical effort and unconscionable misery for the mass of the producers.

What are the causes of China's progress? The main one is that China's labour power is no longer a commodity, that there is no longer a labour market in China, that workers have job security and a guaranteed minimum wage (despite the enormous mass of unemployed), and that the means of production are collectively owned (although the state that controls them is highly bureaucratised). This shows that capitalism has not been restored in China, and that China retains an economic structure comparable to that of the Soviet Union, the 'people's democracies', Yugoslavia, Cuba and Vietnam, which sets in motion the same long-term dynamic and similar economic problems.

Second, the enormous weight of underdevelopment has imposed rigid constraints on China's economic development. These constraints have remained remarkably unchanged over the last thirty years, despite violent political convulsions. Rhetoric apart, what strikes one about China's economic policy over the past thirty years is not so much its change as its continuity. When it came down to fundamental choices, all leadership factions gave priority to developing heavy industry and systematically neglected light industry (see Table 1), even though light industry is the most developed part of Chinese industry and extremely important both for satisfying immediate needs and for exports.

TABLE 1

Light industry's share in total investment

First Five Year Plan, 1953–57	5.9%
Second Five Year Plan, 1958–62	3.9
Third Five Year Plan, 1966–70	4.0
Fourth Five Year Plan, 1971–75	5.4
1978	5.4
1979	5.8

(The figures for the Five Year Plans up to 1975 are from *People's Daily*, 25 May 1979. The figures for 1978 are based on reports by You Jiuli and Jiang Jingfou in *People's Daily*, 29 and 30 June 1979.)

Faced with the problem of a modern industry that constantly threatened to go under in an ocean of archaic production, all factions maintained and tried to strengthen central tutelage over large-scale industrial enterprises, although the means they used to do so differed greatly. This is true not only of Deng's faction but also of Mao's (although many of Mao's Western admirers blithely ignore this).

Faced with the problems of satisfying food needs and the threat of famine, all factions have regularly imported large amounts of cereals, ranging from 3 million tons in 1971 to an estimated high of 10.5 millions in 1981.

But it would be wrong to assume that this basic continuity is an automatic result of the constraints of underdevelopment. The only inevitable

TABLE 2

Economic growth, 1952–79

	1952	*1959*	*1979*
Steel (millions of tons)	1.3	13.3	35
Coal	66.5	347.8	635
Crude oil	0.4	5.5	106
Cement	2.9	6.0	73.9
Chemical fertilisers	0.2	2.0	53.5
Cotton thread (millions of bales)	3.5	8.2	14.7
Bicycles (units)	80,000	?	10.1 million
Radios	–	?	13.8 million
Watches	–	?	17.1 million
Electricity (billions of KWh)	7.3	41.5	282
Cereals (millions of tons)	164	185–200	332
Cotton	1.3	2.4	2.2
Sugar	0.45	1.1	2.5
Pigs (millions at year's end)	90	140	319

(The figures for 1952 and 1979 are from Chinese official sources. The figures for 1959 are from Jacques Guillermaz, *Le Parti Communiste Chinois au Pouvoir*, Payot, 1972.)

outcome of these constraints is that the choice range is narrowed. No economic policy could give one billion Chinese a level of consumption and culture comparable to that of industrialised or even semi-industrialised countries. But precisely because the range is narrow, the consequences of bureaucratic management and planning, wrong policies, bad investments, wasted resources and the smothering of mass initiative have been far worse in China than they would have been in more developed countries.

The crisis of the Chinese economy is a crisis of its bureaucratic management and not of its socialised nature, and in this sense China is basically no different from the Soviet Union and Poland. It is a crisis of the under-production of use-values, not a crisis of the over-production of exchange-values as in the capitalist countries. It is a crisis of the under-utilisation of resources (material and human), not a crisis of the over-accumulation of capital.

The Chinese case confirms that socialist democracy is not a 'luxury for rich countries'. It is not an ideal that can only be achieved after the final elimination of imperialism, but that in the meantime must be subordinated to the imperatives of *Realpolitik.* Socialist democracy is a material, immediate requirement in *all* the workers' states, the indispensable condition for a minimally rational use of material and human resources, the only framework that can permit a minimally harmonious planning, and the only means to cut waste, incompetence and fraud in the management of the collectivised means of production to a minimally acceptable level. Without socialist democracy how can one know the true needs and priorities of consumers? And how can one know the true productive capacity of enterprises and check that it is efficiently used? It is impossible to plan effectively as long as bureaucrats have a material interest in hiding some of their firms' resources. The whole of economic life becomes opaque.

In this sense China's main dilemma, as a country that is far less developed than the Soviet-bloc countries and Yugoslavia and where the proletariat is far less developed and skilled, is that socialist democracy is much more difficult to realise. But by the same token socialist democracy is all the more necessary. It is precisely because China lacks many of the safety valves of other countries that the absence of this democracy imposes such serious imbalances on the economy and such intolerable sacrifices on producers. Luckily, one can expect growing numbers of workers, young rebels and critical Communists in People's China to draw the necessary conclusions. A sign of the times is that China's unofficial democratic movement has made 'The Fifth Modernisation' its watchword: democracy, upon which depends the realisation of the other four modernisations, the scientific and the economic.

15 January 1981

Post Scriptum

Throughout 1981 the general trend of the CCP's economic policies continued to centre on readjustment, retrenchment and austerity. Economic growth seems to have fallen to 2 per cent; total industrial output rose by only 0.8 per cent in the first semester, as against the 2.7 per cent planned.

Inflation remained rampant, its main source being the cumulative budget deficits of 1979, 1980 and 1981. But the budget deficit was cut from 20.6 billion *yuan* in 1979 to 13 billion in 1980 and an estimated 3 billion in 1981. These budget deficits in their turn originate from an explosion of capital construction outlays, triggered off by the Four Modernisations. These reached 48 billion *yuan* in 1978, 51.5 billion in 1979 and 53.9 billion in 1980. It is true that central budget capital expenditures were cut in 1980 and in the first half of 1981 were even cut by 22 per cent compared with the first semester of 1980. But these cuts were more than offset by a huge rise in local investment of 25 per cent in 1979, and a significant new rise above target in 1980. The target for 1981 is to reduce capital construction outlays by a full 45 per cent, from 54 to 30 billion *yuan* (*Far Eastern Economic Review*, 25 September 1981).

Currency in circulation rose 26.3 per cent in 1979, and again 29.2 per cent in 1980. In 1981 inflation fell markedly and part of the excess liquidity was mopped up the sale of government bonds to enterprises. But industrial profits, which provide a large part of the state budget's revenues, were down 12 per cent on 1980 in the first half of 1981 (*Financial Times*, 30 September 1981). In spite of retrenchment, negotiated with Japan for large loans and 'joint ventures' were apparently restarted.

Foreign trade continues to grow. Exports gres by 28.7 per cent in 1980 and by 15 per cent in the first half of 1981 (*FEER*, 25 September 1981). China's main exports continued to go to Hong Kong, Japan and the EEC, while its main imports came from Japan, the USA (especially grain) and the EEC. China is now a member of the International Monetary Fund and has extensively used Special Drawing Rights to cover conjunctural deficits in her balance of payments.

A main development in 1981 was the loosening of the 'right to work' rule. According to the *International Herald Tribune* of 4 September 1981,

> For several months China's leaders have been experimenting quietly in dozens of factories with notions that workers who do not work should be subjected to pay cuts and, if that fails, be dismissed. These ideas were put forward last week in a front-page article in the *People's Daily*, which leaders often use to signal policy changes. The newspaper reported that since April (1981) 30 factories in Shanghai have been experimenting with forms of 'labour discipline' in which unproductive workers receive a range of warnings, demerits and pay cuts eventually leading to dismissal.

As a result of retrenchment, thousands of factories have been idled or shut down, and urban unemployment is currently estimated at a minimum of ten million. (Officially unemployment is said to have grown from five million in 1980 to seven million at the end of 1981.) So the threat of dismissal now hangs over the heads of 100 million wage-earners in China.

But the Chinese leaders are acting cautiously here, fearful of 'Polish-type' developments. In scattered but recurrent slowdowns, demonstrations and strikes, industrial workers are protesting against low pay, poor working conditions and lay-offs. Dissident journals report continuing efforts to form independent trade unions.

The Chinese bureaucracy's flirtation with Yugoslav-type self-management has been quietly abandoned and replaced by purely advisory 'workers' congresses', which now function in 120,000 of China's 400,000 industrial enterprises. But only a quarter of these congresses are said to function in a satisfactory way:

> The trade unions, now under Party instructions to represent the workers more effectively, complain that they are frequently frustrated by government officials who side with enterprise managers. 'The production-at-any-cost-mentality still blinds many leading cadres to the real dangers in worker resentment', a union leader told a Peking conference. . . Chinese officials appear to have dealt successfully with most of last year's protests through conciliation. These involved coal-miners, tool-and-die makers and chemical industry workers who have demanded unions independent of the Party and the government. Young steelworkers in Taiyuan west of Peking have demonstrated for better living conditions. Other actions involved a two-day strike at the large Anshan steelworks in northeast China. . ., another two-day strike at a Shanghai glass works and half a dozen reported protests over lay-offs when old plants were shut. The latest reported

strike was by workers of an electrical transformer plant in the southweatern Chinese city of Kunming to protest the plant management's allocation of new apartments to the director, Party secretary, trade union leader and their friends, instead of the workers for whom they were built (*International Herald Tribune*, 30 October 1981.)

For this same reason the Deng faction seems to have changed its position on Poland, giving *de facto* support to Jaruzelski's counter-revolutionary coup.

The other main economic development concerns the broadening of the private sector in agriculture, the service sector and retail trade. This broadening is linked to the problem of unemployment. A joint decision of the Party's Central Committee and the State Council on 23 November 1981 explains that increases in employment are more likely to be found in the retail trade, and over the past three years are said in Beijing, Shanghai and Guangzhou to have come from private businesses and urban cooperatives.

The decision authorises private businessmen to hire up to seven wage-earners rather than the two previously permitted. The Dazhalan Multi-Service Centre in Beijing is said to employ 223 workers, to have a gross turnover of $780,000 a month and to make thirteen per cent profits (*US News and World Report*, 23 March 1981). Some private businessmen make profits as high as ten times the average industrial worker's wage.

In agriculture, private land has been extended from seven to fifteen per cent of the cultivated surface (*Le Monde*, 17 November 1981). In 40 per cent of China's villages the Commune work-points system has been abolished and replaced by a family contract system, enabling the peasants to sell their surplus on the country's 40,000 free markets (*People's Daily*, 5 November 1981 and *Time*, 16 November 1981). Here again, the main pressure is hidden rural unemployment, estimated at 50 per cent of the 300 million agricultural producers.

Some rich farmers could make as much as $6000 a year (nearly 10,000 *yuan*); in Shandong Province, 2000 families were able to buy private tractors (*Newsweek*, 19 October 1981). This now poses a further problem: the need for a flow of industrial consumer goods into the countryside, without which material incentives for the peasants will not work, even in the medium term.

At the end of 1981, prime minister Zhao Ziyang predicted four per cent economic growth in 1982; while the finance minister spoke of a budget deficit of around three billion *yuan* for the same year. The goal is to quadruple the country's gross output by 1999 (*Neue Zürcher Zeitung*, 2 December 1981).

All these developments clearly explain why the Deng faction put a rapid damper on the modest political 'liberalisation' of the previous years, and has again embarked on a course of sharpening repression.

10 January 1982

NOTES

1. Sixty per cent of school-age children cannot attend school; twenty per cent of primary school graduates cannot enter lower middle school; half of those who graduate from lower middle school cannot enter upper middle school; and only five per cent of those qualified to do so can enter university (*People's Daily*, 11 August 1979).
2. Jacques Guillermaz, *Le Parti Communiste Chinois au Pouvoir*, Payot, 1972, p. 198.
3. In the famous Dazhai model brigade the immense earthworks undertaken by thousands of peasants between 1970 and 1974 only extended the area of land sown with wheat by 3 hectares and the average yield by one per cent (Pierre Péan, *Après Mao: Les Managers*, Fayolle, 1977, p. 113). It has (almost) been forgotten that one of the first charges against the 'Gang of Four' was that they had 'sabotaged Dazhai'. Hua Guofeng (following Mao) was a great propagandist of the Dazhai model, whose achievements are now said to have been falsified. We leave aside the question of the–very real–ecological risks of applying massive amounts of chemical fertilisers to irrigated areas.
4. Around 1975–76, the average monthly industrial wage was about 30 *yuan* (36 *yuan* in the Guangzhou Paperworks). The most skilled workers earn 120 *yuan*, the highest-paid technicians and engineers 200 *yuan*, a few economic executives and political leaders 300 *yuan* (to which one should add important benefits in kind) and talented artists 400 *yuan* (Péan, *op. cit.*, p. 53). These figures had stayed unchanged for ten years.
5. Importing factories and petro-chemical technology was aimed at rapidly developing the production of chemical fertiliser, which was to rise from 8.7 million tons in 1965 to 28 million in 1975 and 53 million in 1979 (Thierry Parault, *Les Politiques Economiques Chinoises*, Notes et Etudes Documentaires, La Documentation Francaise, 1980, pp. 100 and 173). At the same time the irrigated surface grew from 16 million hectares in 1949 to 35 million hectares in 1957 and 45 million in 1977.
6. The Western press gave wide coverage to the Sichuan 'pilot scheme'. (e.g. *Far Eastern Economic Review* (hereafter *FEER*) 21 November 1980). *Christian Science Monitor* of 13 October 1980 reports how the Sichuan press discussed the case of the 'rich peasant' Luo who, having saved 1000 *yuan* and got a bank loan of 300 *yuan*, bought a two-and-a-half ton truck which he then rented to his commune for 400 *yuan* a month.
7. *FEER*, 10 October 1980.
8. *FEER*, 26 September 1980.
9. See especially *Neue Zürcher Zeitung*, 7 November 1980; *Financial Times* (hereafter *FT*), 4 December 1980; and *Le Monde*, 10 January 1981.
10. *FEER*, 12 September 1980.
11. Parault, pp. 84 and 86.
12. *Ibid.*, p. 112.
13. *Christian Science Monitor*, 21 April 1980; and *FT*, 17 September 1980.
14. *FEER*, 6 June and 26 September 1980; and *Businessweek*, 19 January 1981.
15. *Le Monde*, 17 December 1980.
16. *The Times*, 29 September 1980.
17. *FT*, 10 October 1980; *Businessweek*, 19 January 1981.
18. *FT*, 26 November 1980.
19. Those sent abroad are mainly building workers, 1200 of whom were recruited by two Japanese companies working in Iraq (*Business Week*, 28 Janaury 1980). According to *Newsweek*, 14 September 1980, the Chinese government reportedly committed itself to 40 contracts to provide labour in exchange for $100

million in wages.

20. Pairault, p. 75, makes an interesting historical review of the origins of the concept of the Four Modernisations. It was first used by Liu Shaoqi at the Eighth Congress (1956), and then by Mao in his 1957 speech on contradictions (when culture took the place of technology). One has the impression of an alternation of feverish spurts and readjustments: the Great Leap Forward, then the readjustment of 1962–65; the Cultural Revolution, then the readjustment of 1971–74; the Four Modernisations (with overinvestment and overheating), then the readjustment of 1979–81 (or even 1979–82).
21. *Libération*, 14 November 1980, reports the bomb attack in detail.
22. Two books describe the poverty, bitterness, revolt and disarray of Chinese youth: *Avoir vingt ans en Chine à la campagne*, Le Seuil, 1978; and *Le printemps de Pékin*, Archives Gallimard, 1980.
23. *Keesing's Contemporary Archives*, p. 30, 491.
24. *Ibid.*, p. 30 941–2.
25. *New China News Agency*, 2 November 1979.
26. *Jingji yanjiu*, No. 12, 1979, quoted in Pairault, p. 97; *Neue Zürcher Zeitung*, 5 December 1980.
27. *New York Times*, 1 Janury 1981.
28. *New York Times Magazine*, 28 December 1980.
29. Between 1977 and 1979 cereal production only rose by an average of 8.5 per cent a year, while oil-seed rose by 16.5 per cent, sugar-cane by 10.5 per cent and sugar-beet by 12.5 per cent. Grain production is said to have stagnated or even fallen in 1980.
30. *FT*, 1 October 1980.
31. *The Guardian*, 9 October 1980.
32. AFP (2 January 1981) reports that the Chinese press denounced the black market dealing on the train between Guangzhou and Beijing (Guangzhou being the transit-point for Hong Kong). Fifty per cent of travellers are said to board the train for the sole purpose of illegal trading. Between January and September 1980, 410 cases of precious coins, gold and silver jewellery and gold bars were reportedly seized by police.
33. Pairault, fn 11.
34. *FEER*, 21 November 1980.
35. Pairault, pp. 13–16.
36. *The New York Times*, 1 January 1981.

Translated by John Barzman and Gregor Benton.

MARXISM AND THE JEWISH QUESTION

David Ruben

> Deep down in the soul of each of us, revolutionaries of Jewish birth, there was a sense of hurt pride and infinite pity for our own, and many of us were strongly tempted to devote ourselves to serving our injured, humiliated and persecuted people.
>
> Rosalia Bograd, wife of Plekhanov

A number of interrelated questions about Jewry, collectively referred to as 'the Jewish question', have been discussed by many Marxists, beginning with Marx himself in his essay, 'On the Jewish Question'. Perhaps the phrase has been forever discredited by those who not long ago offered the world its final solution. Names aside, the substantive issues are still of great importance for historical materialism. For example, we still have no plausible comprehensive account of the causes of anti-Semitism, an account without which we cannot fully understand the nature of the Soviet Union today. In this paper, there are two other questions that I wish to discuss. The case of the Jewish people provides an extremely interesting test for the explanatory and political adequacy of historical materialism, and it is in this fact among others that one can find more than a merely parochial interest in the Jewish question. There is at least a *prima facie* inability to account for the survival of Jewry in terms available to historical materialism, for historical materialists explain in terms of classes and class relations, and Jewry does not appear to constitute a class. So the first of the two questions I shall discuss is this: (1) Can historical materialism show that appearances here, as so often elsewhere, are deceptive, that the Jews do constitute a class, and that it was as such that they were able to survive as a distinct grouping?

Marx said that, as the truly universal class, the emancipation of the proletariat was necessarily universal human emancipation—for women, blacks, oppressed nationalities, all categories of the exploited and downtrodden. The claim itself has numerous ambiguities hidden within it, but, leaving them aside, it gives rise to the second question I want to ask: (2) How, in the case of the Jews, might this claim that their emancipation is included in the emancipation of the proletariat be made good, and in what, for the historical materialist, does the emancipation of the Jews consist? The answers given to (1) and (2) are not independent of one another. I shall not only look at how historical materialism answers the two questions, but also at how it derives an answer to (2) from its answer to (1). In answering these two questions, I think we shall be able to learn a great deal about the nature of historical materialism itself.

Zionism offers a non-Marxist answer to (2)—the idea of Jewish emancipation, in terms of a bourgeois nation state. I do not, in this essay, want to discuss Israel in particular or even Zionism more generally; there are many other aspects of the Jewish question which have as much claim to our attention. Even if Israel ceased to exist and Zionism became discredited in the eyes of world Jewry, the need to answer the questions I have posed would be greater, not less. Some of what I do say has implications for Zionism. The remarks I make at the end of the paper concerning an acceptable historical materialist answer to (2) have consequences about the ways in which Marxists ought to reply to Zionists.

Historical Materialism: The Classical Approach

The most complete statement of what I call the 'classical' historical materialist approach is to be found in Abram Leon's *The Jewish Question,*[1] although almost every Marxist without exception who has written on the Jewish question has adopted the same line of argument. I have selected Leon's book for discussion, because it is the most complete statement of a view about Jewry that informs nearly all of the classical Marxist writers; Lenin, Kautsky, and the Austro-Marxists, to mention but a few. The outlines for such a position go back to Marx's essay, 'On the Jewish Question', but it is best to consider Leon independently of those origins. Marx's essay is very much a Hegelian work, in the sense that there Marx is speaking of the idea of Jewry, an idea developed in almost complete ignorance of the empirical reality of the Jewry of his own day or of any other epoch. His idea of Jewry is drawn, in the main, from the not very complimentary image of the Jew then current in German literature and philosophy.[2] I do not say that Marx's essay has no value as an analysis of demands for formal emancipation made by a group under pre-parliamentary democratic conditions. What I assert is that it has no value as a scientific work into the nature of Jewry in central Europe in the early nineteenth century, nor do I believe that Marx ever imagined that it had.

Turning now to Leon, I want to look at the way in which he answers the first of the two questions that I posed earlier, and how an answer to that first question suggests an answer to the second. Why is it, according to Leon, the Jews were able to survive as a distinct group of some kind? Sometimes it is said that Jewry survived only because of anti-Semitism. I shall want to return to this thesis in much greater depth later, but it is important to point out that this reply is not the one Leon gives, nor is it the one that the classical historical materialist takes to be central. Leon opposes his account to all accounts (like the one mentioned) which place the explanatory onus on the human will—for example, on the will of the Jews to retain their identity or on the will of the anti-Semites to oppose Jews. Leon quotes disapprovingly the great Jewish historian Simon Dubnow, murdered like Leon himself by the Fascist anti-Semites: Jewry survived because of its 'attachment to the national idea' (p. 65). Leon rejects this explanation, and ones structurally similar to it, because he seeks to 'reject the fundamental error of all idealist schools which consists of putting under the hallmark of free will the cardinal question of Jewish history, namely: the preservation of Judaism'.

To this idealist mode of explanation, Leon opposes what he regards as the historical materialist mode: 'It is precisely by studying the historical function of Judaism that one is able to discover the "secret" of its survival in history' (p. 67). Briefly, Leon's 'functionalist' account is this: (1) 'The Jews constitute historically a social group with a specific economic function. They are a class, or more precisely, a people-class' (p. 74). Conversely, 'Whenever the Jews cease to constitute a class, they lose, more or less rapidly, their ethnical, religious, and linguistic characteristics; they become assimilated' (p. 81). (2) Their function is to serve as agents of exchange in a predominantly natural economy. 'So long as a natural economy reigned, the Jews were indispensable for it' (p. 132). With the decline of the natural economy in western Europe in the eleventh century and after, more serious persecutions of the Jews than they had hitherto experienced began. 'With the development of exchange economy in Europe. . . the Jews are progressively eliminated from the economic positions which they had occupied. This eviction is accompanied by a ferocious struggle of the native commercial class against the Jews' (pp. 135–7). By the end of the long lead-up to the emergence of capitalism in western Europe, the Jews had, by and large, either assimilated into the Christian bourgeoisie, or been driven eastwards, or remained only in small, impoverished pockets in the interstices of western European society. (3) Eastern Europe, to which numbers of Jews had fled in order to escape persecution in the west, lagged behind western Europe in economic development. Thus, the Jews retained there an economic function long after their economic usefulness in the life of western Europe had ended. In eastern Europe, the Jew 'represented exchange economy within a purely feudal society' (p. 183). By the middle of the sixteenth century, 'with the end of the feudal state of things in Poland the privileged position of Judaism is likewise finished' (p. 193). (4) 'Contrary to western Europe, where their assimilation was favoured by capitalism, in eastern Europe capitalism uprooted the Jews from their secular economic positions' (p. 124). Because of the 'degenerate' nature of eastern European capitalist development, assimilation of the Jews into the Christian merchant and allied classes proved to be impossible. It is this unassimilatibility of Jewry in late capitalism for economic reasons, both in eastern Europe (Leon is writing before the Holocaust) and in the other places to which large sections of eastern European Jewry immigrated, often resuscitating a dying local Jewry, that constitutes the heart of the Jewish question today. Leon's thesis is not held only by historical materialists. In an important article, Toni Oelsner traces the theory through the tradition of German sociology, and especially through the writings of Roscher, Sombart, and Weber. This view on the historical function and nature of Jewry is very widely held indeed.[3]

Leon's thesis on why the Jews survived leads naturally to an answer to the second question that I posed: In what does the emancipation of Jewry consist? Leon himself did not draw this obvious implication, although other writers in this classical historical materialist tradition have done so. According to Leon, Jewry survived only to the extent that it had a specific economic function to perform. In western Europe, when this function no longer existed, Jewry was well on the way to extinction. If capitalism had developed a more progressive character in eastern Europe, the same pattern of events would have asserted itself there. The disappearance of Jewry once and for all was blocked only by the nature of capitalist development in eastern Europe. Under socialism, where there can be no question of exchange functions, or any specific economic functions permanently allocated to specific groups of individuals, Jewry cannot be expected to survive as a distinctive grouping. The emancipation of Jewry then means the liberation of Jewish individuals from Jewry, as Marx himself had made clear in his original essay. Along with all the other witherings to be expected under full communism, one should also speak of the withering of Jewry.

It is not uncommon to hear Jews accuse Marxists or Marxism or both of anti-Semitism. I have no doubt that there are individual Marxists who are anti-Semitic, but beyond this obvious point, I do not think that there is any truth in the accusation. Still, I think that it is true that this classical historical materialist perspective on the Jewish question tends to encourage a kind of theoretically-induced blindness to the goals and aspirations of Jews as Jews. It should not be wholly unexpected that a theory which regards a group as in the advanced stages of dissolution is unlikely to evolve a political programme sensitive to and understanding of the desires and wishes of that group.

So What's Wrong with the Classical Approach?

Before we begin to assess the empirical evidence for and against Leon's classical thesis, we first need to address a conceptually prior question: What evidence is relevant to the assessment of Leon's thesis? That is, we must be clear about what in principle one would have to demonstrate in order to show that Jewry survived because of some function that it had.

Leon believes that he is required to show that most Jews have actually been engaged in occupations associated with the performance of an exchange function: 'The overwhelming majority of Jews in the Diaspora unquestionably engaged in trade' (p. 69). Weinstock, in a spirited defence of Leon, weakens this to the claim that there was merely a tendency for this to be so, that there was a tendency which increasingly pushed the majority of Diaspora Jews into these occupations.[4] In fact, I do not think that Leon, in order to make good his functionalist account, would have to show either of these two things. It is no requirement of the thesis that the Jews survived because of their economic function, either that a majority of them performed that function or that there was a tendency for this to occur. Rodinson, in his introduction to the French edition of Leon's book, cites a great deal of evidence about the occupational differentiation of numerous Jewries that renders both of these spatially and temporally unrestricted claims unsupportable.[5] Rodinson's evidence, and much other evidence, is incontrovertible. In almost every historical period and in almost every place, there have been a great number of different occupations which Jews entered, from which there was no tendency for them to be pushed, and in which they were perfectly able to survive as Jews. The idea that the majority of Jews have engaged in some specific occupation is so oblivious to the realities of Jewish history that one can understand the remark made by one non-Marxist writer that there appears to be a direct relation between ignorance of Jewish history and willingness to embrace this idea. When we consider examples as wide apart as the Byzantine Empire,[6] the Yemen, the Falashim of Ethiopia, the Jewish farming communities of Daghestan and Kurdistan, the Jews in Babylon under Persian rule who were an agriculturally based community, and the Jews of Cochin in India, it is clear that one cannot show that *most* Jews in those communities that were able to retain their identities for extended periods were engaged in trade or allied occupations, nor can it be shown that there was a tendency for this to be the case. The evidence we have about western Europe, and especially about France, in the earliest period of the Middle Ages, suggests widespread Jewish land ownership. Spanish Jewry, until the Expulsion of 1492, seems to have been remarkably differentiated in terms of its occupations. There is far too much evidence to the contrary to take seriously the idea that the majority of Jews were, or tended to be, engaged in occupations connected with exchange in those places where they were able to preserve their distinctive identity. Leon assumes that such evidence, if true, would refute his functionalist account since its truth requires the idea that the majority of Jews were connected with exchange. Rodinson thinks that such evidence, since true, does refute Leon's thesis as an unrestricted generalisation about the survival of all Jewries. My view is that such evidence, although true, does not refute Leon's thesis, since his functionalist account does not require the idea that there was a connection between the majority of Jews and exchange-related occupations.

The evidence of occupational differentiation may simply be irrelevant to the classical account of the survival of Jewry, at least if that account is plausibly formulated. Leon could argue, if he wished, that Jewry survived only because of those Jews, whatever numerical proportion of the community they might have been, who were in occupations connected with exchange. Jews not in these exchange occupations might have been able to survive as Jews only because of those Jews who did have exchange-connected occupations, however few of the later category there were. Exchange-connected Jews may have had a 'coat-tail' effect in assuring the survival of the other Jews only because their own exchange connections may have guaranteed their own survival as Jews. Leon's thesis could be stated in such a way as to make it compatible with almost unlimited evidence about occupational differentiation within Jewries, as long as one could always find evidence of some group of Jews engaging in exchange-related occupations in each Jewry.

If Rodinson's evidence is incontrovertible but irrelevant to the classical thesis as most plausibly formulated, one might wonder what empirical constraints there then are on the classical theory. Surely, it would be insufficient for confirmation of the theory merely to find some group of Jews engaging in exchange-connected occupations. For example, there is a group of rabbis and other ecclesiastical authorities in every Jewry, but no historical materialist would accept the thesis that Jewry survived because of them.

One empirical requirement of Leon's thesis arises as a requirement that every functional explanation must meet. The idea of a functional explanation is this. In some specific set of circumstances, some system is functioning adequately or properly. The system in question might be a social system, or a biological organism, or an artefact. What is meant by 'adequate' or 'proper' function will vary, depending on the sort of system in question, but usually it is not difficult to see what is intended once the system has been specified. Moreover, the system may function properly in the circumstances only if some condition is satisfied. Now, suppose that we find some part of the system, such that the effect of that part is to ensure that the condition for proper functioning is satisfied. It is common (but, as we shall see, ultimately mistaken) to attempt to explain functionally the existence, or continued existence, of that part of the system, on the grounds that it ensures that a necessary condition for the proper functioning of the system is met.[7] Two examples might help to make this rather abstract account comprehensible. First, the system in question might be the human body, in normal circumstances. A human body can function properly only if an adequate blood supply is pumped around the body. So we might try to explain the existence of the heart functionally on the grounds that it is the part of the body that ensures that this necessary condition, the required distribution of the blood supply, is satisfied. Second, the system in question might be a society. A society can exist only if at least some minimum level of social cohesiveness exists. We might then attempt to explain functionally the existence of some specific practice or ritual in the social life of the society on the grounds that its effect is to ensure that at least this minimum level of social cohesiveness is achieved. Those who defend the legitimacy of functional explanation need not rule out the possibility that, when we have more knowledge, these functional accounts might be replaced by, or supplemented with, more satisfying causal accounts of the origins of the heart or the ritual. What they would claim is, that at least at a certain stage of human understanding, they offer some genuine understanding of the existence of parts or items like the heart or the ritual, or whatever part of a system we are seeking to explain.

Although functional explanations might be a perfectly respectable form of explanation in general (at least at a certain stage of human knowledge), it is important to see why, in both of the examples that I have used, the functional accounts are incomplete as they stand. If we know that a body or a society are functioning adequately, and if we know that, for that to be the case, blood must be pumped or a level of social cohesiveness achieved, we can conclude that there must be something in the first system which is in fact pumping blood and that there must be something in the second system actually achieving the minimum level of social cohesiveness. But this falls importantly short of explaining the existence of the heart or the ritual, even when we know that the heart is the body's blood-pumper and that the ritual is the society's cohesiveness-achiever. This is because we may not yet know why it is the heart or the ritual which are the parts which ensure that the necessary conditions of blood-pumping and cohesiveness-making are met, rather than some organ or part which could do the same thing ('functional alternatives', as it is often put in the literature). In order to explain functionally the heart and the ritual rather than just the existence of some blood-pumper or cohesiveness-maker or other, we must show that, in the circumstances, only these things and nothing else were able to fulfill these functions, viz, that nothing else was able to pump blood or achieve the minimum level of cohesiveness. To summarise then: If there is some system which is functioning adequately or properly, and if some condition must be met in order for this to be so, we can demonstrate that there must be some part or some item or other that is actually ensuring that the condition is met. But if we wish to go further and explain the existence or continuing existence of a specific part or organ, then we must additionally show that in the circumstances the existence of that specific part is *necessary* for the condition being met or satisfied—that in the circumstances, nothing else could have done so. One can easily extend the functional account in the case of the heart so that its existence can be functionally explained, since in the circumstances nothing else could have pumped the blood. It is doubtful whether the functional account could plausibly be extended in the required way in the case of the ritual, so that we could functionally explain its existence. Most commonly, if the ritual had not been ensuring that the requisite level of social cohesiveness was achieved, something else would have done so. In these cases, one does not yet know why it is that the ritual is achieving this rather than the possible alternative to it.[8] To show why the heart or the particular ritual exist by reference to their function, each must be necessary in the circumstances for ensuring the proper functioning of the system in which it is located, and that entails the absence of functional alternatives in the system. I do not say that there cannot *be* systems in which there are functional alternatives. There can be systems in which two parts do exactly the same thing. The point is that when this is so, there can be no functional explanation of the existence of either of the alternatives.

It may not always be easy to determine whether or not two things have the same function. Sometimes, one item or part of a machine is intended as a backup or failsafe device for another, and when this is so, these parts have different functions. In social reality, the situation is often far more complicated even than this. One ritual may provide some social cohesiveness and another ritual may provide some *more* social cohesiveness. The level of social cohesiveness they jointly provide may be in excess of what is necessary for the adequate functioning of the system, although every increment in social cohesiveness makes the system function still better. In these cases, since functional accounts depend on what is necessary for adequate functioning of the system and not on what is merely necessary for improving the system's operation, we can say that both rituals are useful for the system but neither is necessary, since in the absence of either the other would provide the minimum social cohesiveness necessary for the adequate functioning of the system. There are problems, too, in defining what adequate or proper functioning is for a social system, whereas it is a clearer notion when applied to artefacts and natural organisms. But leaving all these complications aside, for they are further complications with any functional account and hence with Leon's classical thesis on Jewry, we can say this: there may be many systems which exist with parts that are functional alternatives to one another. But one cannot explain the existence of a part of a system in terms of its function in that system if there are functional alternatives to it in that system.

With this in mind, it is easier to see what are the empirical constraints that Leon's thesis must meet. The constraints are not, as Rodinson and Leon himself imagined, that most Jews be in exchange-related occupations. Nor need it be the case that there was a tendency for this to be so, as Weinstock argues. Rather, even if only a few Jews in each Jewry were engaged in occupations connected with exchange or exchange value, and the other Jews were able to retain their Jewish identity only because of these former Jews, being in exchange-related occupations (in an otherwise natural economy) must be an *exclusive* function of the Jews, one which no other group did or could do, if Leon's thesis is to be confirmed. We are meant, on Leon's functional account, to think of the societies in which Jewry found itself as the system, whose proper functioning must include some circulation of commodities or use of money, even when the dominant mode of production in the society was a natural economy. Leon's account purports to explain the existence of Jewry as a part of that system in terms of its function of ensuring that this necessary condition for the adequate working of the society is met, coupled with the additional claim that when the Jews no longer have the function of being representatives of exchange in a natural economy, because the system itself changes to one in which exchange is dominant, Jewry as a distinct grouping tends to die out. It is important to see that this last claim is additional to the functional explanation itself, because one might otherwise argue that even though the existence of Jewry in a natural economy can be explained by the role they play in the process of circulation of commodities or money, there is some other role they play in an exchange economy which can also functionally explain their continuing existence within exchange economy.[9]

But consider just the first part of Leon's claim: the Jews were able to survive within a predominantly natural economy because of the role they played in the processes of exchange. If we are able to explain the survival of the Jews in a natural economy on these grounds, then the Jews must have been *necessary* in the circumstances for this exchange to have taken place. That is, it has to be something that no other group than the Jews did do or could have done. Leon in fact implicitly recognises this requirement when he says, 'So long as a natural economy reigned, the Jews were indispensable for it' (p. 132). Leon must show not only that at least some Jews were in exchange-related occupations, but that they were indispensable for these occupations—i.e., there was no other group that did or could engage in these exchange-related activities. It means that Leon must show that those individuals who were Jews could not have continued to engage in exchange-related activities had they ceased to remain Jews, for Leon's thesis attempts to account for the continuing existence of a group of individuals not *qua* the individuals they are, but *qua* members of a specific group to which they adhere.

The failure to appreciate fully or make explicit this indispensability-in-the-circumstances requirement might arise through a conflation of two distinct though related questions about Jewish survival: an internal and an external question. I do not think that much progress can be made in unravelling the problems that arise in understanding the nature of Jewry unless these two questions are clearly demarcated from one another.[10] The external question is this: under what conditions was Jewry tolerated or permitted to survive and under what conditions was it eliminated by some means or other? Sometimes at least the answer might be that they were merely economically useful or advantageous. They might not have been indispensable in order for their usefulness to count as an appropriate answer to the external question; usefulness by itself might provide a perfectly comprehensible motive for explaining why some rulers permitted the Jews to survive as Jews. The internal question on the other hand is this: why was Jewry able to renew or reproduce itself, why did the Jews themselves tend to continue as or remain Jews? Leon does not separate very carefully these two questions. Some of the things he says are addressed to the external question. But when Leon says that Jewry tends to die out when it loses its specific function, he is certainly addressing the internal question of Jewish survival. Insofar as he is answering this internal question, usefulness by itself is insufficient; indispensability is required. I have argued this on general grounds about the nature of functional explanation, but I would like to add some further arguments about this, drawn not just from such general considerations but rather from considerations specifically about functional explanations of social phenomena. I think that it is these further considerations which will lead us to see something important about historical materialist explanations.

Perhaps one can never 'reduce' functional explanations involving social categories to explanations couched only in terms of individuals and the decisions they take. But, in spite of what some historical materialists say, the decisions taken by individuals could hardly be irrelevant to those explanations. Put it this way: even if the survival of Jewry cannot be reduced to what individual Jews did or decided, the survival of Jewry (in terms of the internal aspect; I ignore the external aspect for the present) must in some way be related to the decisions of individual Jews to remain Jews or at least to their failure to decide to cease being Jews. It is perfectly compatible with what I am saying that these individual Jews may have been unaware of the real motives or reasons for which they decided as they did. They may have mystified their decisions, enshrouding them in all sorts of theological or moralistic conceptions. It is no part of my claim to deny this. But a decision taken for real reasons hidden from the decider is a decision nonetheless. If we focus on the internal question of Jewish survival my point is that Jewry can persist only if a sufficient number of individual Jews decide to remain Jews, or at least refrain from deciding to abandon Jewry. However, if other groups in the society were also performing the same, non-exclusive exchange functions, functions shared between the Jews and those other groups, or even if other groups were not performing those functions but could have done so and hence individual Jews could have continued their economic activity while ceasing to be Jews and joining those other groups, in such cases economic function cannot explain the persistence of Jewry. In cases of non-exclusive function, the economic activity of the Jews provides no obvious rationale for understanding why individual Jews did not cease being Jews and affiliate themselves to these other groups, since there was usually at least some pressure on Jews to do just that, all the while continuing the same economic function as before the change of group affiliation. Although it is true that some rulers at certain times established economic disincentives for Jews to cease being Jewish, due to the loss of their tax revenue, on balance, throughout almost every period of Jewish history, there were overwhelming economic disadvantages in remaining Jewish. If so, then any non-exclusive economic function of the Jews will not permit us to explain why Jewish merchants and traders did not continue in the same economic role while at the same time becoming non-Jews. There is simply no way in which the fact that the Jews had some economic function that was or could be carried out by other groups as well could provide a motive, whether conscious or unconscious, for a Jew in such an exchange-related occupation to remain Jewish. But, if the fact that Jews had some non-exclusive economic function cannot explain why any individual Jews did not decide to cease being Jews, then it cannot explain why Jewry survived, since the survival of Jewry must be in part at least a consequence, whether intended or not, of those decisions taken by individual Jews.

On the other hand, if Jews were indispensable in the economy in the sense that they performed some economic function that no other group did or could perform, one can see why at least that section of Jewry which engaged in such exclusive occupations remained Jews, since for them to have abandoned Jewry would have been for them to abandon their economic means of existence. They could not have continued doing what they were doing as non-Jews. Thus, unless the function in question is an exclusive function of the Jews, unless the Jews or some section of them are indispensable, the economic facts of occupation are motivationally irrelevant to understanding the survival of Jewry.

Did the Jews have an exclusive economic function, were they 'indispensable', in the natural economy or indeed at any other time when they managed to survive as a community? It seems plain that Leon's thesis fails the empirical test, once these constraints on the acceptability of the classical historical materialist thesis concerning the survival of the Jews are made clear. Let us recall that Leon's own thesis is meant to be true unrestrictedly for all historical epochs in which Diaspora Jewry existed, whatever the mode of production. Crudely, either the mode of production is a natural economy, in which case they survive because they are the representatives of exchange, or the economy is an exchange economy, in which case they tend to die out, having lost their saving function. Leon himself cites evidence from the classical period of antiquity. Consider, then, the Jews of the Roman Empire outside Judea. We know that there was great occupational differentiation among Jews in the Roman Diaspora[11] (they were in great demand at certain periods as mercenaries) and that, among the range of occupations, trade and commerce were certainly important. But I have already agreed that evidence of occupational differentiation will not by itself refute Leon's thesis. However, we also know that Jewish merchants and traders had at all periods a great number of non-Jewish commercial rivals. A class within almost all of the other civilised nations engaged in trading—the Egyptians, the Syrians, and others. Leon plays down the extent to which the Greeks themselves engaged in trade, since they 'despised trade and industry'.[12] This may have been true of upper class Greeks in Greece itself, but it cannot be true of the large Greek or Hellenised colonies in the towns outside Greece. Relations between the Jews and the Greeks, or other Hellenised populations, were atrocious in the period of the Roman Empire, often leading to riots and physical extermination of the one side by the other. Josephus, in *The Jewish Wars,* gives a grim picture of the state of relations between Jews and the Hellenised populations amongst whom they lived in the period just prior to and during the revolt of the Jews of Judea in 66–70 A.D. Nowhere were the relations worse than in Alexandria, which had the largest Jewish population outside Judea in the first century A.D., a population entirely exterminated by the Romans and the native non-Jewish population after the Jewish uprisings there, and in North Africa and Cyprus, in 115–7 A.D. Although 'ideological' factors such as the unpopularity of the Jewish religion and the refusal of the Jews to engage in emperor worship played a minor role in arousing this hostility, the hostility took a racial (in the classical sense of that term) form. Commercial rivalry and jealousy must have played no small part in these developments; no other explanation has ever been offered for these deep social tensions. If so, one cannot say that Jewish merchants and traders had any exclusive function in the period of the Roman Empire.

In Byzantium from the division of the Roman Empire until its fall to the Turks, in Spain until the Expulsion of the Jews in 1492, in Babylon under first Parthian and then Persian kings, in North Africa, Arabia, and the Middle East from the coming of Islam until the modern period, in India from their arrival in the second century B.C., in Oriental centres such as Bokhara and Afghanistan, we find large Jewries able to maintain and reproduce themselves, sometimes over a span of two thousand years, often it is true with the Jews either concentrated into a few professions or especially important in a few professions, but almost never in such a way that an exclusive economic function is accorded them. Where the Jews were merchants, there were other, non-Jewish merchant groups. Where the Jews were artisans, there were other, non-Jewish groups of artisans. And where the Jews were money-lenders, there were almost always non-Jewish groups of money-lenders, with the latter groups usually being far more important in the economy. Where Jews were important in some particular industry, as were the Jewish silk workers in Byzantium, other groups worked in those industries as well, and the Jews could have continued in those industries had they apostatised. Where Jews worked the soil, as they mainly did in Babylon, other groups were also agricultural. In none of these examples that I have mentioned had the Jews an exclusive economic function, and hence there were no reasons arising from their function, whether conscious or unconscious, which could explain why Jews continued to be Jews and hence for Jewry to reproduce itself. Jews could have continued in their occupations, usually more successfully, as non-Jews.

Some may find this claim of non-exclusive function surprising with regard to the granting of loans on interest in the Middle Ages, but the claim is nonetheless true. The Church's opposition to usury itself only developed and hardened over time, but even when it finally hardened against usury, it was never able to control it effectively. In the early middle ages, the chief moneylenders appear to have been the monasteries and the secular clergy, but later, with the rise of a merchant class, usury increasingly fell into the hands of the merchants who had money which could be lent, some of whom then became specialised in the lending of money on interest. Commentators agree that the Jews had rivals in this occupation, and that their rivals were far more important economically than were they. Parkes, in his important study of usury in the Middle Ages, claims that, 'The rivalry between Lombard or Cahorsin, burgher and Jew, extended over the whole field and the whole period'.[13] Both Pirenne and Parkes agree that the Jews played a subordinate role in this rivalry: 'Compared with the effectiveness and ubiquity of Italian credit, that of the Jews appears a very small affair and the part which they played in the Middle Ages has certainly been much exaggerated.'[14] '. . . Throughout the period the chief moneylenders were Christian, and . . . apart from short periods and particular localities, the Jew never played more than a subordinate part.'[15] Pirenne even explains the expulsions of the Jews from England and France in the thirteenth century and after as arising from the intervention of their Italian and other rivals in the granting of loans at interest. The Mosque also disapproved of usury, but Rodinson similarly describes the merely occasional and local ability to prevent Muslims from engaging in usury, and the Jews appear to have had no more of an exclusive economic activity of usury under Islam than they had under Christendom.[16]

In fact, Leon's thesis of an exclusive economic function fits precisely one case, that of international trade in western Europe in the period of about 700–1100 A.D., although even this has been disputed by some writers. In that period, western Europe had been forced back into a natural economy. One important reason for this was the capture of the Mediterranean by the Moors and the consequent cutting of normal trade routes between western Europe on the one hand and Byzantium and Asia on the other. In this period, the Jews were, almost without exception, the sole representatives of an exchange economy in western Europe.

It is easy to see why this should have been an exclusive function of the Jews in western Europe in this period, one that they could not have performed at all or at least not well had they ceased being Jews. The Radanites, as these traders were called, had available to them, as Jews, an international network which they could use for trading purposes, in an otherwise extremely fragmented economic situation in which the trade connections normally available to non-Jews had been broken. Moreover, being neither Muslims nor Christians, they could be considered neutrals in the state of war that existed between Islam and Christendom. These two facts, when taken together, made them not only ideal, but the only available, agents of international exchange in this period and conferred on them an exclusive (or near to exclusive) function in western Europe for this limited time. We know that these Radanites developed routes for trading goods between the Frankish and Chinese kingdoms via Jewries in India, central Asia, Persia, and Byzantium. But this exclusivity of function never existed anywhere else at any other time. As soon as conditions permitted the generalised resumption of trade, non-Jewish merchants competed with, and soon surpassed, their Jewish trading rivals.

Leon's account is not only Eurocentric. It is western Eurocentric because it obtains no confirmation from the course of events in eastern Europe. It is true that the Polish kings welcomed Jewish immigration in the latter half of the thirteenth century and after, since they saw that the influx of Jews would help Poland develop economically by encouraging trade and finance. This fact can help us explain the external aspect of Jewish survival, for it explains why Jews were permitted to live in Poland. But the same reason which drove the Polish kings to welcome Jews also drove them to welcome the more general settlement of Poland by German merchants and traders. Almost from the first years of significant Jewish settlement (Baron estimates a Polish Jewish population of only 30,000 in 1500), the status and fortunes of Polish Jewry resembled that of the Jews of western Europe in the period *after* they had lost their economic indispensability. The reason for this is quite simply that the Jews in Poland never had an indispensable economic function. Their function was non-exclusive; they always had rivals. Dubnow and Baron[17] chronicle the extensive economic rivalry between the Jews on the one hand and both the German and native Polish merchants on the other, a rivalry that existed from the earliest period of significant Jewish settlement in Poland, and which almost invariably resulted in new restrictions against the trading rights of the Jews—hardly evidence for the indispensability of the Jews to Poland. Not only was there no tendency for them to be pushed into exchange-related occupations, but rather, due to this economic rivalry in which they were fated to be perpetual losers, there was a tendency for them to be pushed out of such occupations. One cannot hope to explain the near thousand-year history of Polish Jewry by their function, for Jewish merchants and traders and bankers co-existed, more or less peacefully, with their Polish and German rivals who did precisely the same things. There was no obvious economic motive for a Polish Jew to remain a Jew, that arose from his function in society, as there may well have been for the Radanite. Leon's classical thesis will not work even for the case of Poland.

I suspect that some are attracted to Leon's thesis by the following pattern of thought. The essential class relation in feudal society is that between lord and serf. There is no place in this essential relational structure for the Jews, for a variety of reasons, so the Jews alone had to find some other economic niche in which to fit. This they did by uniquely assuming the functions relating to exchange, functions for which the other elements of the society, lords and serfs, were unfitted. Now, although it is perfectly true that the lord-serf relation is the essential class relation of feudal society, it is a caricature of actual feudal society to think that it was so homogeneous that only the Jews stood outside that relation. In all but very limited periods, other groups existed alongside the Jews which also stood outside that social relationship. In the earlier discussion of money-lending, I mentioned Lombards and Cahorsians—foreigners were an especially noticeable group outside the feudal relations. And there were always small native merchant classes, even in the Radanite period, when they still had available regional and local trade even if cut off from long-distance trade across the religious boundaries. There was never an absence of groups in actual feudal societies which could or did provide the Jews with occupational rivals.[18]

An Alternative Historical Materialist Approach

The classical historical materialist approach to answering the first question, why Jewry survived, in terms of the survival of a class with a specific function, fails. Its account of the emancipation of Jewry in fact means the emancipation of Jews from Jewry, which is itself to disappear. With the failure of the classical approach on which it is based, the idea that Jewry is bound to disappear under socialism loses whatever support this classical thesis was thought to give it.

I stress that it does not follow from any of this that historical materialism, using a different approach, cannot provide an answer to the question of why Jewry survived. Insofar as there may be an alternative approach available to historical materialism even if not specific to it, our view of in what Jewish emancipation consists may have to be modified from what it was on the classical approach. I do not think that it is a fault in this alternative account that it can also be used, in whole or part, by non-Marxists. The point is that it is usable by Marxists who want to go beyond the classical view. After all, we do not need to insist that women must constitute a sex-class, or blacks a race-class, in order to say that historical materialism can accept these divisions and advance a programme for liberation. Of course, the analogy is imperfect. There is some sort of biological differentiation between men and women, blacks and whites, however much one comes to see that many if not all of the consequences of these biological differences are culturally superimposed on the facts of sex and skin pigmentation. No one but a Fascist would think that there is any significant biological difference between Jews and non-Jews. The point is only that a mature historical materialism can accept that there are important differences between people that are not themselves economic ones; in this way, a different sort of approach to the question of Jewish survival might be possible other than the insistence that the Jews must form a 'class, or more precisely, a people-class'. Of course, some alternative to a biological principle of differentiation would have to be found, and this I now intend to provide.

Marx tells us: 'It will be seen how in the place of the wealth and poverty of political economy come the rich human being and rich human need. The rich human being is simultaneously the human being in need of a totality of human-life activities—the man in whom his own realisation exists as an inner necessity, as need.'[19] We can say that historical materialism is a theory about how all human needs become satisfied, thwarted, expanded, and restricted in the course of human history, in different modes of production. It may be that human beings must eat before they theorise, but this is not to deny that theorising is itself a need. Marx speaks of the need for human life-activities. One such human life-activity that Marx has in mind is labour, but he is thinking of many other activities beside labour. 'Man does not live by bread alone', says the theologian, and this is surely right. If we try to think about the various sorts of needs people have, and the activities in which they need involvement, we will think of such things as love, affection, a personal sense of worth, a sense of identity and belonging, culture, and communal activities. Why do people need cultural settings in which to act and communal activities? No doubt for numerous reasons, amongst which is the need to provide their lives with a structure or form that gives shape to the routine of their daily existence, and that provides them with a means of coping within a public context with the major events of life: birth, pubescence, love and death. In part, a sense of significance in one's own life comes through the social identity and significance of one's actions. This structure and form that gives the shape to what one does is achieved by such things as a calendar, a cycle of holidays and festivals that recur throughout a lifetime, historical memories at the level of collective existence, a certain recognisable rhythm and tempo to life itself attained through the observance of customs and ceremonies, the celebration of the changing of the seasons, public occasions on which to mark events of significance to the individual and the community.

We can sum this up in an overworked metaphor from Wittgensteinian philosophy: people need a form of life. No social thinker has appreciated this more than Herder: 'It was Herder. . . who first drew wide attention to the proposition that among elementary human needs. . . is the need to belong to a particular group, united by some common links. . .'[20] Far from being some sort of contemporary middle-class penchant, championed by those who feel the need for community politics, this need identified by Herder is a universal need that has found expression in every human society, but found expression in countless different ways. Often, professional revolutionaries say that these things are luxuries at best, frivolities at worst. Frankly, if there really were people who could do without these things, and not just say that they could, their inhumanity would frighten me. These are neither frivolities nor luxuries for human beings, as they face life and try to collectively come to terms with it. No historical materialism should neglect these truths, truths not only consistent with historical materialism but actually part of what it should understand by 'rich' human need. It may seem strange that, as an exponent of a variety of historical materialism, I should cite the views of a reactionary thinker like Herder. But of course the same insights are available in Hegel himself. Hegel, more deeply than anyone since, appreciated the essential involvement of the individual with the community in which he was placed.[21] The relations between individual and society are not just relations of production; they involve a whole nexus of relations that extend beyond production and embrace many other aspects of life.

The need that each person has is a need for some culture or other. This is an unspecific need, which in principle can be satisfied in an indefinitely large number of ways (I say more about this in what follows). However, there is not the slightest reason to expect, let alone hope, that sometime in the distant future of full communism, there will only be one such human culture or form of life. Of course, I speak of cultures and forms of life, not bourgeois nation-states. Full communism would be impoverished without a great plurality of traditions and cultures. Historical materialists are not obliged to sing the praises of Esperanto. Surely this, if anything, is the reconciliation of the universal with the particular, the cosmopolitan with the distinctive; this is the concrete universal which was the great insight and advance of Hegelian philosophy over the abstract conception of humanity that he found in the philosophy of the Enlightenment. One humankind, one planned economy with everything that that entails, but one humankind realised in ever so many cultures, languages, traditions, differences, ways of doing things. This seems to me what Marxists should understand by the rich human being—the need for culture and community being satisfied in countless different ways. A person is richer if other persons, as members of other cultures and traditions, do things differently.

Leon called an explanation 'idealist' when it referred to free will in its explanatory principles. I think that we need to rethink the place of the will (I do not say 'free', because in the sense in which Leon means this, I do not think that the will is free) in historical materialist explanation. I said earlier that even if we are not methodological individualists who reduce the survival of Jewry to the decisions taken by individual Jews, it would be absurd to say that these individual decisions (even if they are unfree in Leon's sense) were irrelevant. Jewry could survive, as any other socio-cultural grouping, only because of the decisions taken by individuals, however little they may have been aware in making those decisions of their real meaning or significance. Now, in every period apart from western Europe from 700–1100 A.D., in those places where Jewry did survive (it did not always do so, even in the absence of external reasons mitigating against survival), this was accomplished only insofar as a sufficient number of Jews chose to remain Jews, in spite of the economic advantages that would usually have come their way by becoming Muslim or Christian. Many of course did convert, or otherwise made their exit from Jewry. Jewry survived where it did (apart from external causes of extinction) only because some significant number, for whatever reasons, did not convert or assimilate, and this is quite compatible of course with extensive conversion and assimilation. None of this presupposes free will in Leon's sense, but it does invoke in the explanatory account the concepts of human choice and deliberation. And so much the better it is for so doing. Finally, this is in no way incompatible with historical materialism as I understand it, since what no doubt made vast numbers of those Jews who chose to remain Jewish do so, was that, for them, their Jewishness was the mechanism by which their need for culture and community, a significance to their lives, was given to them. For many of them the idea of a life as a non-Jew would have presented itself as a horribly deprived life, one hardly worth living, for they would not have been able to see how some of their deepest needs could have been met. I do not think that the point is merely speculative; Jewish history books provide us with innumerable examples of this choice being made essentially for these reasons, although the language the choosers use to explain those choices to themselves is often (but not invariably in the modern period) theological.

A requirement that all functional explanations must meet and that I have continually stressed in my discussion of Leon is indispensability in the circumstances. The need that human beings have is a need for some culture and community, but not for some specific one. Chinese are not born with a specific need for Chinese culture, nor Jews for Jewish culture and community. But, given the biography of an individual, the circumstances in which he is placed, and the memories and patterns and norms of behaviour he is taught, the general need can attach itself to a specific object. Jewry survived because a significant number of Jews found, for the satisfaction of these needs on their part, that specifically Jewry was indispensable in the circumstances of their life as it had been lived. Surely if this had not been the case, then given the slightest reason to abandon Jewry (and there have nearly always been far more than merely slight reason to do so), any sane Jew would have done so. It is a long and complicated story, hidden from sight in the vagaries of personal biography but explicable in principle, why each individual did or did not find Jewry indispensable in the circumstances of his life. Of course, it is not an all-or-nothing affair; Jews will find it of varying significance in their lives, and hence will resist varying amounts of pressure to abandon Jewry. Many Jews chose to abandon Jewry because their cultural needs and sense of belonging were satisfied by the prevailing culture. This was true of many Hellenised Jews of the classical period. It was also true of Marx's father, for example, who converted for opportunistic reasons, but he was, well before his conversion, thoroughly at home in the culture of the European Enlightenment, a man who drew none of his emotional sustenance from traditional Jewish sources. Historical materialism is not obliged to discover the reasons why each individual Jew chooses one way or another, although often the reasons are perfectly obvious at the level of ordinary observation. But even though we are not required to offer a theory that can account for every individual case, there are some considerations which have a general bearing on the question, and that I discuss in the next section.

Why Did Jewry Survive and Other Cultures Fail To Do So?

Cultures and ways of life generally meet certain needs and desires of those who belong to them, but Jewry is distinguishable from most other examples by its extraordinary ability to survive and continue. There must be some other characteristic of Jewry that differentiates it from those other cases, since it has outlasted most of them. What feature did Jewry possess that gives it this remarkable longevity?

I introduced earlier, and will continue to work with, the distinction between internal and external factors making for cultural survival. There is some measure of arbitrariness in this distinction, and some problematic cases (as we shall see), but roughly the internal aspect of the question concerns the choices and decisions taken by members of that culture (and of course these choices and decisions are themselves grounded in objective facts and anchored in the reality of external circumstances, if the chooser is at all rational), whereas the external aspect concerns those features of the objective situation (like physical extermination, forced conversion, expulsion) which do not manifest themselves in the choices and decisions of the participants but are conditions forced upon them whether they will it or not. A borderline case would be a situation in which a Jew was faced with a choice of expulsion or conversion (as was the whole of Spanish Jewry in 1492). Here, the Jews had a choice, but one narrowly circumscribed by external constraint over which they were powerless.

I believe that a major factor (perhaps not the only factor) that made for the differential survival of Jewry when compared to so many other forms of life was the Diaspora of the Jews. This may seem surprising, since the Diaspora of the Jews is usually thought of as an unmitigated disaster for Jewry. It had, naturally, its disastrous side. But it also made for the preservation of Jewry as a whole. The point is not novel; Leon himself makes it. Had the Jews remained in Palestine, there is no reason to believe that they would be different from the Palestinian Arabs today, many of whom are descended from the Jews who remained in Palestine and succumbed to Islam over the course of the centuries. Most cultures or ways of life that become extinct become extinct for external reasons, such as military conquest, the forcible introduction of another culture, mass immigration of peoples, and so on. History is replete with examples of the waning and waxing of cultures for these reasons: the coming of Norman culture to Anglo-Saxon Britain, of Greek culture to the world of the Greek Empire, of Aryan culture to the pre-existing peoples of the Indian subcontinent. There are very few examples of what I would call territorialised cultures that have survived in a single continuous line of development for the length of time Jewry has survived in the Diaspora (Chinese and Japanese cultural traditions seem an exception to this claim). It is true that Judaism changed, but it is remarkable how great a line of continuity there is between Jewish life in 200 A.D. and today. It is also something of an abstraction to speak of *a* Jewish culture or way of life, for there were differences between Jews of various areas in their cultural practices. There were not only the Ashkenazim and Sephardim, and important subdivisions in these categories, but other groups of Jews who were neither: Yemenite, Persian and Indian for example. But one should not overestimate these differences. Except for a few cases in which Jewish communities were cut off from world Jewry (the case of Chinese and Ethiopian Jewry comes to mind), there were continual contacts between these communities, and a Jew would have recognised any other group of Jews as participating in a common form of life.

A main factor making for Jewish survival when compared with other cultures was, then, the external factor of Jewish dispersion, de-territorialisation. But it was not only the fact that they were dispersed, de-territorialised, but the pattern of this dispersion. Religious Jews say that God never prepares for chastisement of the Jews until he has also prepared the remedy, and there is a sound point hidden in this theological expression. Simmel argued[22] that Jewish survival was enhanced by the spatial distribution of the Jewish people in the Diaspora: 'By dispersing throughout the world the Jews insured the survival of the group because no single persecution could hit them all; at the same time the Jews in any given city assembled in ghettoes in order better to defend themselves.'[23] The first point of Simmel's thesis is correct: Jewish life was spread sufficiently thin so that it was highly improbable that all of Jewry could ever be eliminated in a single blow. As one Jewish centre waned, another arose to take its place: Spain from Babylon; Turkey and North Africa from Spain; Germany from France and England; Poland from Germany; the United States from Poland and Russia. The second part of Simmel's thesis can be accepted with a modification. It is true that the dispersion was also not too thinly spread, not because the Jews needed some population concentration to defend themselves, but because without a sufficient concentration of population, the conditions do not exist either for establishing and maintaining a communal structure, or to make intra-group marriage a realistic possibility. In conclusion, it seems to me that the main feature that differentiated Jewry from other cultures in terms of longevity relates to the external factors of both the fact of and the spatial distribution of the Diaspora. Territorialised cultures were less able to resist external threats than were the Jews.

I have said that the main causes of cultures ceasing to exist are external causes. Although there are exceptions to this, it is in the main true. I am in substantial agreement with Rodinson on this point: 'Dans ces conditions triomphait la tendance normale des communautés à persister dans l'existence et à défendre au niveau communautaire les intérêts et les aspirations de leur membres.'[24] That is, if we abstract away from external conditions that work for the disappearance of cultures, the normal condition for any culture is persistence rather than disappearance. Newtonian physics does not provide an answer to the question: why do objects remain in motion? It reverses the way this had been thought about previously, for the law of inertia asserts that unless an object is subjected to external forces, it will continue its motion or rest indefinitely. Something like this is true for cultures, although once again I admit the imperfection of the analogy. Any culture, if not interfered with by external intervention, will tend to reproduce itself. In the case of a de-territorialised culture such as Jewry, the organisation of the culture into institutional forms becomes especially important. If cultures like Jewry are numerically strong enough, and are permitted, to organise themselves and evolve institutions such as schools, universities, law courts, meeting places, and other institutions for the transmission of its culture and values across the generations, it will hardly be surprising that sufficient Jews remain Jews to speak of the survival of Jewry. The 'tendance normale' for cultures to persist if not externally interfered with is not to postulate some hidden, mysterious force. It rests on the way in which it answers needs in the lives of its participants, and hence their making it survive through their choices and decisions. In the case of de-territorialised Jewry, in which, as I have said, the necessity of institutions to guarantee that that culture is available to each generation becomes so important, since it is not available in the larger social context, there is a connection between the degree of participation in that organised cultural life and the maintenance of the way of life itself. Although everyone knows of examples of Jews with an orthodox background who effectively leave the Jewish people, available statistics show that there is a high correlation between depth of involvement in Jewish life and facts like probability of inter-marriage.[25] This is of course not surprising, in the case of a de-territorialised culture. Since the need for a specifically Jewish life cannot be acquired effortlessly in society at large but must be acquired by participation in Jewish communal life (not necessarily in religious spheres), it is not surprising that Jewry can survive only if there are, in any place, sufficient Jews to establish such institutions, and that Jewry's survival is, in part, a function of the degree to which Jews participate in them.

Rodinson agrees with Otto Heller's expectation of 'la fin du Judaisme. . . comme mode particulier de vie', and speaks of the resurgence among Jews since the establishment of the state of Israel of a certain attitude of particularism which 'manquait le plus souvent de toute base culturelle, sociale, ou même religieuse.'[26] In this, I think he greatly exaggerates. Of course, the extent to which Jews today outside the state of Israel rely on Jewish culture does not begin to approach the near total reliance many Jews of Poland and Russia had on Jewish culture before the Holocaust. On the other hand, this situation is not unlike other historical examples where Jews were members of both a Jewish and a more general culture simultaneously (pre-exile Spain for example). In the case of today's relatively assimilated 'Yahudim of the West', as Deutscher so contemptuously called the Jews of western Europe and North America in one of his essays, today's Jews rely on as many different combinations of Jewish and general culture as there are Jews. Most Jews, outside small, compact, orthodox communities, find at least some of their needs met by the prevailing general culture. Other Jews find their need for Jewish tradition only at crucial times in their lives—birth, circumcision, marriage, death. Others avail themselves of synagogues, law courts, Jewish education.

Importantly, there are a large number of non-religious Jewish institutions—Jewish sport, camps, youth clubs, charities and hospitals. It is estimated that 80 per cent of British Jewry actually belong to a synagogue (this is not to be confused with attendance). In most Diaspora countries, the overwhelming number of Jews, although they find many of their cultural needs answered by the prevailing culture, have not, as a matter of fact, arrived at that point where so few of those needs are met by Jewry that they have left organised Jewish life entirely. Diaspora Jewry will survive, I think, as far as any historical materialist can see into the future. Otto Heller's 'untergang des Judentums' seems very hasty prognosis.

On Anti-Semitism

It may seem strange that thus far, in a paper on the Jewish question, I have said nothing whatever about anti-Semitism. That I have not done so reflects the fact that I give it much less importance in the question of Jewish survival than is usual. However, I want now to say things about anti-Semitism, not in connection with what its causes are, but rather about what its effects are on Jewish survival.

To begin with, there is something obscene about speaking of anti-Semitism as if it were merely a cause of Jewish survival in the Diaspora. Some say (I do not count myself among them) that if it had not been for anti-Semitism, Jewry would have disappeared. Whatever truth there may be in this, looked at from the external point of view, anti-Semitism has led to Jewish destruction. Even if we were to accept that there was some connection between anti-Semitism and Jewish survival, these effects would have to be balanced by the ways in which anti-Semitism led to the destruction of Jewry in so many places and at so many times.

Still, I do not doubt that there is some connection between anti-Semitism and Jewish survival. This connection appears if we consider the survival of Jewry from the internal point of view, and consider the connection between anti-Semitism and the choices and decisions Jews made. An obvious example is the biography of Theodore Herzl, whose belief in assimilation and the disappearance of Jewry ended when he confronted virulent anti-Semitism in France as a journalist covering the Dreyfus Affair. This type of story can be told and retold countless times for countless individuals. The following story is commonplace, and I repeat it only because it is so absolutely typical:

> Albert I Gordon tells the story of a Minneapolis Jewish family of German origin which produced three native-born generations in this country. The grandfather, born in Albany in 1862, moved to Minneapolis in 1883. His 'family associated exclusively with Jewish families. . .'
>
> The son's story is a simple one: on his own evidence, he 'was never interested in Jewish life or Jewish organisations'. If his 'daughter were to marry out of her faith', he would not have 'seriously' objected, and he was even a member of a Christian Science Church 'for about six or seven months'. And yet, when he applied for membership in the Minneapolis Athletic Club, he was told 'that they

> don't want any Jews there'. When 'the same thing happened in the Automobile Club', he was 'very much upset about it', but he still did 'not think that there ought to be Jewish clubs'.
>
> The granddaughter had 'no awareness of. . . Jewishness'. She 'never resented the fact that there was a quota system at school', and 'always had friends among Jews and Christians', predominantly among the latter until her days at the university. At the time she related her story, she found that her real friends were 'in the Jewish group'.[27]

The story is typical, because it demonstrates the way in which anti-Semitism can bring back into Jewry Jews who otherwise, out of sheer indifference, would have left Jewry. Indifferent Jews, like the son and granddaughter of the story, find that they are only fully accepted in their social relations with other Jews. In this way, anti-Semitism affects how they choose to live their lives, e.g., the granddaughter's choosing to have mainly Jewish friends at university, and this means that, looking at anti-Semitism from its internal effects on Jewry alone, there is no doubt that anti-Semitism has affected the choices and decisions Jews make regarding their relationship to Jewry in such a way that it has enhanced the chances of survival of the Jewish way of life. In the case of the father, Jewry had ceased to answer his needs for culture and community altogether, for he seemed perfectly at home in a Christian Science Church. In these kinds of cases, anti-Semitism alone is able to make for the survival of these people as Jews, long after any story about culture and community has become entirely inappropriate.

Sometimes it is said that Jewry survived only because of anti-Semitism. Such a claim is far too strong, and I would like to point out some limitations on the survival-enhancing aspects of anti-Semitism that I conceded above. First, although anti-Semitism has had these survival-enhancing aspects in the modern period, these beneficial effects of anti-Semitism from the point of view of Jewish survival must be temporally restricted. The idea implicit in the story of the Minneapolis family, as indeed in Herzl s biography, is the inability or extreme difficulty a Jew faces in voluntarily disassociating himself or withdrawing from Jewry. Anti-Semitism in this modern sense is a racialist ideology, according to which the race to which one belongs is a fact about a person over which he has no control. This assumption is of course implicit in the Nazis' anti-Jewish legislation, and in the modern phenomenon of individuals who have long ceased to regard themselves as Jews still being so regarded by non-Jews. In the Warsaw ghetto, there was a Catholic Church which functioned only for those individuals considered as Jews by Nazi legislation but who were in fact practising Catholics, and who went to the same gas chambers as the other inmates of the ghetto. But this is entirely a modern phenomenon. It is difficult to date with any precision the change in attitude to the Jews from regarding them as a community from which voluntary departure could be effected to regarding them as a race into which one was born for life, but roughly until the late eighteenth or early nineteenth century, by and large, a Jew could choose to cease being Jewish by conversion. Hellenised Jews could cease being Jews by engaging in emperor worship and, by surgical means, reversing their circumsision. In the Medieval and early modern period, a Jew could leave Jewry through apostasy. There are certain exceptions to this general claim, but in the main it does distinguish the way in which Jewry was regarded differently in the late modern and earlier periods.

It is a necessary condition for anti-Jewish attitudes having a significant beneficial effect on Jewish survival that Jewry not be voluntarily escapable. Had the father's membership in the Christian Science Church made him a non-Jew in the eyes of others, and had he therefore been accepted for membership in the clubs to which he aspired, the story would have had quite a different ending. It is only in the modern period that voluntary egress from Jewry is blocked, and thus it is only in the modern period, say for the last two hundred years out of the two thousand and more history of Diaspora Jewry, that anti-Jewish attitudes have contributed to Jewish survival. Before this period, anti-Jewish attitudes had only a significant negative import for Jewish survival.

Second, even if we restrict the beneficial consequences for Jewry of anti-Semitism to the modern or late modern period, anti-Semitism cannot be a cause of Jewish survival on the same level of importance as the satisfaction of a need for community and way of life. What anti-Semitism usually does, although this is not indicated in the story of the Minneapolis family but is borne out in many of the stories of Jews who have returned to Jewish life from assimilation (I am thinking of examples such as the Bundist Vladimir Medem or the anarchist-socialist Bernard Lazare) is to force individuals to a new appraisal of the values of their own culture and way of life. Jewish assimilationists have often espoused the essentially Enlightenment rationalist ideal that is suspicious of any form of cultural or ethnic particularity; anti-Semitism often pushes an individual into questioning the ethic of universality which submerges the importance of cultural differences between people. This presupposes, however, that there is an existing Jewish way of life which is potentially able to answer these needs in people, and indeed which is actually fulfilling those needs for an existent community. I would put the matter this way: presupposed in this is that the survival of a Jewish heritage and tradition is essentially explained by the satisfaction it brings to the lives of individuals in that tradition, and that anti-Semitism works as a 'reinforcing' cause, which brings it about that more Jews, through a realistic appraisal of their life situation, will find meaning and value as Jews than would have been the case had there been no anti-Semitism.

Finally (and connected to the second point), there is a distinction between Jewish survival and flourishing (the degree to which it survives). It is a fault of Leon s classical account, and is equally a fault in my account, that there has been no attempt to quantify any of the causal effects (which Leon and I have merely referred to as 'survival') of either economic function or need-satisfaction or anti-Semitism. Does 'survival of Jewry' mean as a large international grouping, as a major social force, as a miniscule sect (like the Donmehs of Turkey or the few surviving crypto-Jews of Portugal), or what? What I should like to assert is that satisfaction of cultural needs explains the basic survival of Jewry, but that in the modern period anti-Semitism makes it survive with greater numbers than would have otherwise been the case. What makes me diffident about this assertion is that, in our present state of knowledge of society, we are simply unable to attach any quantitative measure to the extent to which two causes which lead to the same effect contribute to that effect. I would say that we do not have the evidence available to say that in the modern period had there been no anti-Semitism, there would have been no Jewish survival (again, abstracting away from the external effects of anti-Semitism). Nor do we have reason to believe that, in the absence of anti-Semitism under genuine socialism, the satisfaction by the Jewish way of life of the need of Jews for a community and culture will be insufficient for Jewish survival. One simply does not know now whether Jewry will survive or not under socialism, but, as I said earlier, Otto Heller's expectation of the 'Untergang des Judentums' has no justification, and is nothing to which we must be committed on the basis of historical materialism.

I have not intended these three remarks as anything like a comprehensive account of anti-Semitism and its relation to Jewish survival. It should be obvious that I think that anti-Semitism is less important, although still with some importance, in answering the question of Jewish survival than is usually thought. I offer these three points as occasional remarks which should be considered in developing a more complete account of anti-Semitism and its effects on Jewish survival.

The Nature of Jewish Emancipation

I want to conclude this paper with some observations about one possible course of Jewish emancipation. I have argued that the expectation of the disappearance of Jewry is unfounded, because of the inadequacy of the classical account of Jewish survival on which that expectation is based. If Jewry does survive under socialism (and this is an 'if'), in what might its emancipation consist? I am not addressing myself to the problem of Jewish emancipation in pre-socialist conditions; on this question, my views are the conventional Marxist ones. I do not think that Jewish emancipation (like that of women or blacks or the third world) is possible under capitalism, and I find disingenuous calls to oppose a Zionist solution to the contemporary Jewish problem that do not stress this impossibility.[28]

The great tragedy of the Jewish problem today, as Isaac Deutscher so often and so eloquently stressed, is that it is insoluble except by socialism. Yet it is a solution which may come too late, for by then barbarism may have already finished its work as far as the Jewish people is concerned.

Trotsky never developed what one might call a theory of the nature of Jewry and its liberation, but one can detect, in the few remarks he made after the rise of both Stalinist and Hitlerite anti-Semitism, the characteristic maturity of insight of the man. Trotsky speaks of one possible avenue of Jewish emancipation. He did not say that Jewry would or would not disappear under socialism, for who can now know the ways in which people will refashion their lives in conditions of human liberation. But his remarks make it clear that he was not committed to such disappearance of Jewry in the long run, and that he was prepared to speculate about the possibility of non-disappearance; he says that socialists must at least be prepared for the continuance of the Jewish people for an 'epoch'. 'Once socialism has become the master of our planet. . . it will have unimaginable resources in all domains. Human history has witnessed the epoch of great migrations on the basis of barbarism. Socialism will open the possibility of great migrations on the basis of the most developed technique and culture. It goes without saying that what is here involved is not compulsory displacements. . . but displacements freely consented to, or rather demanded by certain nationalities or parts of nationalities. The dispersed Jews who would want to be reassembled in the same community will find a. . . spot. . . The same possibility will be opened for the Arabs, as for all other scattered nations. *National topography will become part* of the planned economy.' 'The establishment of a territorial base for Jewry in Palestine or any other country. . . Only a triumphant socialism can take upon itself such tasks.' 'Are we not correct in saying that a world socialist federation will have to make possible the creation of a Biro-Bidzhan for those Jews who wish to have their own autonomous republic as the arena for their own culture' (TA 4106).[29] There would, for Trotsky, be no more reason to refuse to meet the felt need by Jews, if they were forthcoming, to territorialise their community under socialism than there would be to refuse to meet the needs of anyone else. Of course, Trotsky is thinking of a Soviet Jewry whose involvement in Jewish culture had, before its cultural destruction under Stalin and now his successors, been very deep. Jewry today almost everywhere lacks the same depth of involvement. This might mean that it is less likely that Jews as they are now would ask for territorialisation. But the point is that, whatever the depth of their involvement, if they were to ask for territorialisation, Trotsky appears willing to accede to these demands (assuming of course that they do not lead to the involuntary displacement of others). There is no need to operate a further criterion about the extent of Jewish culture in the lives of those who ask for territorialisation. Territorialisation is one possible path of Jewish emancipation under socialism, one option among many.

I do not extract from this for a moment that Trotsky would have shown any sympathy for Zionism, the attempt to effect a territorialisation of the Jews as a solution to the Jewish question under capitalism, a solution which involves the involuntary displacement of Arabs in order to give a bourgeois national home to the Jews. Trotsky makes his opposition to Zionism clear, although his criticisms are often made in the spirit of sadness that Zionism holds out such false hopes for the solution to the sufferings of a people. Trotsky is speaking of acceding to the possibility of Jewish territorial demands under socialism, not under capitalism. Still, I think that Trotsky's remarks place certain constraints on what can count as an acceptable critique of Zionism from the mouths of Marxists. In particular, his remarks imply that there can be nothing 'racialist' in the desire of any group that feels itself to be sufficiently a unity to want to live together in a common territory. Long and involved discussions about whether the Jews are really a nation, an ethnic group, a people, a race, a religion, or a caste, and as one or the other, have or fail to have an entitlement to territory are irrelevant to this issue of the right of territorialisation.[30] Socialism as planned economy is about answering people's felt needs, assuming that so doing is not detrimental to the satisfaction of the needs of others. Planning to meet needs means, as Trotsky made so clear, planning to let the members of any sort of group live together if they desire this, without any further contorted investigation about whether they can justify those felt needs in terms of 'really' counting as a nationality (whatever precisely this is supposed to mean). If Jews under socialism say that they need or desire to live together in a common territory, Trotsky assumes that such demands would be legitimate. No further question about the correct categorisation of Jewry has to be raised.

What in fact is Jewry? I mentioned some of the obvious choices above, each of which has had its champion. I have not discussed this question, and will only make a few relevant remarks here, having usually taken the prudent path in this paper and used the relatively non-commital expression 'Jewry'. I confess to not being much moved by the question: What are the Jews? On reflection, there is something undialectical about the question, which insists that Jewry must be brought under one category to the exclusion of others. Reality is complex, and the Jews have some of the characteristics of a religion, some of a nationality, some of an ethnic community, and so on. The similarities and analogies are so diverse that the insistence on placing Jews in one category rather than another will distort reality sufficiently to make it useless for scientific purposes. This problem attends the classification of any single phenomenon as of a type or kind, but usually the scientific advantages of finding a general category in which to fit the particular greatly outweigh the disadvantages. They are not outweighed in the case of Jewry. And any general category specially invented for the case of the Jews is likely to have precisely one instance only; whatever one understands by the general category will be entirely related to how one understands the specific case. Thus, it is not at all clear what would be gained by inventing such a uniquely applicable general category, except a kind of pseudo-understanding encouraged by the use of a general label.

What I would insist on, though, is that it is a mistake to argue that Jewry is only a religion, a mistake on which some leftist analyses are grounded. These analyses would find in the 'reduction' of Jewry to Judaism the reason for expecting its disappearance under socialism, since all religions are fated to vanish at that point in history. This is a very large question; it will be obvious that I am not in sympathy with this viewpoint, having spoken throughout of a Jewish way of life, culture, etc. I cannot resolve this debate here, but it might be useful to mention at least the following considerations. First, I think as historical materialists it would be wise to be agnostic about the general claim that all religions will vanish under socialism. I do not mean that we should believe that they will not vanish. Rather, like the question of the survival of Jewry without anti-Semitism, we simply are in no position to know one way or the other. Even though historical materialism gives us a general approach in answering questions, it does not give us any *a priori* knowledge about the causes of specific phenomena. We do not really know what the causes of religious belief are, and certainly vague references to class society and the ideology of ruling classes, or ignorance of natural processes, are inadequate, especially for the theologically sophisticated forms in which religious belief is put today. Second, the point I would stress is the non-identity of Jewish culture with Judaism. Being Jewish and believing in Judaism are not identical, in the way in which being Catholic and believing in Catholicism are. They are not identical, and I have stressed the social and cultural aspects of Jewry rather than the religious aspects. Since they are not identical, I believe that the possibility exists of a secular Jewish culture.

I believe that even in the Diaspora to some extent a Jewish secular culture already exists. I am aware that it is problematic to apply the distinction between the secular and the religious to Judaism,[31] because the distinction is basically a post-Christian Enlightenment distinction. In the Christian sense of 'religion', Judaism, Islam, Buddhism and Hinduism are not religions at all, because they contain the 'secular' in themselves. They *are* as much ways of life as religions in the Christian sense. That said, it is still worth saying that in contemporary Judaism there is an essentially secular culture hidden within a misleading religious form. The religious form that Jewish life usually takes in the Diaspora is misleading; the involvement in Jewish life today by large numbers of Jews, in spite of the fact that it has a religious form, has only a cultural and social significance. My assertion is not based only on speculation. There are certain empirical findings that support my interpretation. Since the end of the last world war, synagogue membership in Britain and America has grown significantly (about 60 per cent of American Jews are affiliated with a synagogue), and in the case of Britain, the steep rise in synagogue membership since the war is in sharp contrast to what has happened in the churches. Both in Britain and America, synagogue affiliation is the greater the further removed the individual is from large Jewish populations. This suggests that synagogues in suburbs and small communities have taken over the social and cultural function of the Jewish 'ghetto' or neighbourhood. This is further demonstrated in what one writer has called the 'secularisation' of the synagogue; the synagogue itself becomes increasingly a natural home for non-religious Jewish activities and organisations. 'Thus, not only have secular activities come to predominate over religious activities, but the religious activities themselves have been secularised.'[32]

I doubt whether most Jews who participate in Jewish life today, at least in western countries of the Diaspora, actually believe what they say when they repeat certain ritual words, or accept the literal theological significance of the customs and ceremonies in which they participate. Some other significance must be attached to what they say and do other than the literal theological meaning, for it is not easy to believe that modern Jews who participate in religious rituals really accept the physical resurrection of the dead, or the coming of the Messiah, or that Moses received the Talmud on Sinai along with the Torah (all of which such participants in rituals *say*). A good comparison is the way in which the same secularisation process can be seen at work in the religious customs and practices of non-Jewish society. The celebration of Christmas, and especially the Christmas dinner, has a social and family significance wholly detached for most people from any theological meaning. The function of the Passover Seder is similar in the lives of many Jews—it is one way in which the individual's bonds with an extended family are strengthened. Jewish life offers many other examples, and I suspect that historical materialists, especially those of Jewish origin, have missed the point because they assume that Jews generally observe as few of the rituals and ceremonies as do they. This is not true—various studies suggest widespread observance of some rituals and ceremonies on a highly selective basis, one of the criteria of that selection appearing to be the ability of the ceremony to 'express Jewish identity'.[33] This process of the secularisation of religion is made even easier for Jews than Christians by the fact that Judaism is not just a 'religion', but already has what one might call the secular within it. Many Jewish holidays have a minimal religious content, since they are celebrations of historical or semi-historical events, or mark points of harvesting in the agricultural year. So, in content, if not in form, there are grounds for believing that Jews already have available, in their dispersed state, a culture or form of life that can in principle be detached from that religious form. As for a Jewry under socialism, if such there is fated to be, there is no reason to believe that it would be any less capable of evolving a strong, non-religious culture than is any other human group.

NOTES

I wish to thank the following for their helpful criticism of the ideas in this paper: G.A. Cohen, Rene Gimpel, Henry Drucker, Michel Löwy, John Bunzl, Ardon Lyon, Hillel Ticktin, Ernest Krausz and Norman Geras.

Almost none of my critics agreed with anything I herein say.

1. Abram Leon, *The Jewish Question: A Marxist Interpretation,* Pathfinder Press, New York, 1972. In order to minimise footnotes, page references to this book are given in the text.
2. A discussion of the state of Prussian Jewry at the time of Marx is given by Julius Carlebach, *Karl Marx and the Radical Critique of Judaism,* Routledge and Kegan Paul, London, 1978, pp. 9–147. For a description of the cultural and philosophical image of the Jew in this period, see Leon Poliakov, *A History of Anti-Semitism,* vol. III, Routledge and Kegan Paul, London, 1975.
3. Toni Oelsner, 'The Place of the Jews in Economic History as Viewed by German Scholars', *Yearbook of the Leo Baeck Institute,* 1962, pp. 183–212.
4. Nathan Weinstock, 'Introduction', in Leon, *op. cit.,* pp. 38–45.
5. Maxime Rodinson, 'Preface', in Leon, *La Conception Materialiste de la Question Juive,* Etudes et Documentation Internationales, Paris, 1968.
6. See Andrew Sharf, *Byzantine Jewry: From Justinian to the Fourth Crusade,* Routledge and Kegan Paul, London, 1971, for an account of the occupations of Byzantine Jewry.
7. Those familiar with the literature on functional explanation will realise my debt to Carl Hempel, *Aspects of Scientific Explanation,* The Free Press, New York and London, 1965, Essay 11. Nothing in my discussion presupposes an acceptance of Hempel's view that in such an explanation there must be a deductive relationship between explanans and explanandum.
8. See Hempel, *ibid.,* pp. 310–4.
9. Hannah Arendt attempts to attribute to Jews a specialised investment function (loans to the State) in nineteenth century capitalism, for example. See her *The Origins of Totalitarianism,* Meridian Books, New York, 1958.
10. As I say later, there are occasions on which the internal and external aspects are inseparable.
11. See Michael Grant, *The Jews in the Roman World,* Weidenfeld and Nicolson, London, 1973, for an account of the occupations of Jews outside Judea in the Roman period.
12. M.I. Finlay, *Aspects of Antiquity,* Penguin, Harmondsworth, 1977, describes Greek and Roman attitudes to trade and commerce. My own views are supported by remarks of Karl Kautsky, *Foundations of Christianity,* Monthly Review Press, New York, 1972, pp. 245–53.
13. James Parkes, *The Jew in the Medieval Community,* Hermon Press, New York, 1976, p. 328.

14. Henri Pirenne, *Economic and Social History of Medieval Europe,* Harcourt, Brace and World, New York, paperback, undated, pp. 131–3.
15. James Parkes, *op. cit.*, p. 307.
16. Maxime Rodinson, *Islam and Capitalism,* Penguin Books, Harmondsworth, 1980, pp. 37–8 and *passim.* provides a general introduction for the position of the Jews in usury under Islam.
17. Simon Dubnow, *History of the Jews: From the Later Middle Ages to the Renaissance,* Vol. III, Thomas Yoseloff, London, 1969, pp. 374–93, pp. 746–99. Salo Baron, *A Social and Religious History of the Jews,* Columbia University Press, New York, Vol. XVI, and especially pp. 214–312.
18. For example, from the fifth to the eighth centuries, the Syrians in western Europe were merchants and bankers at least as important as and perhaps more important than the Jews. This is discussed in James Parkes, *The Conflict of the Church and Synagogue,* Athaneum, New York, 1969, pp. 313–6. Parkes quotes Bréhier: 'It was the Syrians who controlled the whole of economic life' in this period in western Europe.
19. Karl Marx, *Economic and Philosophical Manuscripts of 1844,* Progress Publishers, Moscow, 1967, p. 104. I mention below 'a personal sense of worth'. An interesting account of Marx's views on this is given by Allen Wood, *Karl Marx,* Routledge and Kegan Paul, London, 1981, Chapter II.
20. Isaiah Berlin, 'Benjamin Disraeli, Karl Marx, and the Search for Identity', in *Against the Current,* Oxford University Press, Oxford, 1981, p. 257.
21. See Russell Keat, 'Individualism and Community in Socialist Thought', in Mepham and Ruben, (eds.), *Issues in Marxist Philosophy,* vol. IV, Harvester Press, Brighton, 1981, pp. 127–52.
22. George Simmel, *Soziologie,* Berlin, Duncker and Humblot, Berlin, 1908, pp. 460 ff.
23. Jon Elster, *Logic and Society,* Wiley, Chichester, 1978, p. 141. I would stress the point about sufficient concentration of Jewish population to permit both organisational structure and the possibility of intra-marriage. Conditions of communal reproduction require a threshold level of population density. Both Leon and Rodinson dwell on the virtual assimilation and disappearance of western European Jewry before the influx of eastern European Jews. A factor they fail to mention in the miniscule size of these Jewries until the nineteenth century.
24. Maxime Rodinson, 'Preface', in Leon, *op. cit.*, p. xxxi.
25. See for instance various of the papers in *Jewish Life in Britain 1962–1977,* ed. by Sonia Lipman and Vivian Lipman, K.G. Saur, London, 1981, or S. Sharot, *Judaism: A Sociology,* David and Charles, London, 1976.
26. Maxime Rodinson, 'Preface', p. xli.
27. C. Bezalel Sherman, *The Jew Within American Society,* Wayne State University Press, 1960, pp. 146–7.
28. As Moshe Machover fails to stress it in M. Machover and M. Jafar, *Zionism & War and Peace in the Middle East,* a pamphlet published by the Palestine Solidarity Committee, p. 9: '. . . if you believe that Jews can and should live in freedom and dignity among non-Jews in this country (and elsewhere), that anti-Semitism can be fought and beaten—then you are thinking as a progressive person'. Can be beaten under capitalism? The way in which Machover words his claim, in order to make it appear anodyne, makes it susceptible of a reformist interpretation (I have no doubt that Machover does not intend for it to be given this interpretation).
29. Leon Trotsky, 'On the Jewish Question', Pathfinder Press, New York, 1970. Quotes from pp. 20–1 and p. 18. Quote followed by 'TA 4106' is from the Trotsky Archives, Harvard University.

30. For an example of this essentially irrelevant attempt to demonstrate that the Jews are not a nationality and have no right to territorialisation, see Maxime Rodinson, *Israel: A Colonial-Settler State,* Monad Press, New York, 1973. Part of his argument, which I regard as incontrovertibly correct, is that Jews today cannot trace linear descent to the Jews of Judea. I wonder whether Rodinson supposes that French children today, sons and daughters of Portuguese immigrants or of Germans in Alsace or of Norman invaders, who learn about 'our ancestors the Gauls' can trace linear descent back to them. See especially pp. 79–80. National 'history' is in general something imposed on individuals regardless of actual genealogical lineage. I would stress that my disagreement from Rodinson on this issue does not entail my support for Jewish claims to bourgeois national sovereignty which includes the forcible displacement of others.
31. Cf. Ernest Krausz, 'The Religious Factor in Jewish Identification', *International Social Science Journal,* Vol. XXIX, No. 2, 1977, pp. 250–60.
32. S. Sharot, *op. cit.,* p. 153.
33. Marshall Sklare, *America's Jews,* Random House, New York, 1971, pp. 110–4. See also Sharot, pp. 149–50.

A CRITIQUE OF *THE ETHIOPIAN REVOLUTION*

Paul Kelemen

The Ethiopian military's accession to power in 1974, and their subsequent proclamation of a programme of land reform and nationalisation, evoke a number of parallels in the Third World on which its study could shed light. But the military's claim to espouse socialism and its allegiance to the Soviet Union–however these are interpreted–situate its policies within the even broader context of the struggle for socialism and by reference to what is but an aspect of this struggle, the debate on what constitutes socialism. Halliday and Molyneux's study, *The Ethiopian Revolution*,[1] gives expression to an increasingly influential position in this debate; it both reflects on and represents political forces which are challenging anew the demarcation that Marxism has drawn between itself and reformist currents on the characterisation of socialism.

The political developments that have followed the overthrow of Emperor Haile Selassie, provide a critical vantage point on several of the more contested areas of Marxist analysis; the relation between class and state, the place of national self-determination in the struggle for socialism and the role of the Soviet Union in the Third World. *The Ethiopian Revolution* intervenes in each of these issues.

Halliday and Molyneux embark on their analysis of the current Ethiopian regime by an examination of the social order over which Haile Selassie presided. The contradictions within that order unleashed an urban protest movement that created the conditions in which a radicalised section of the army was able to overthrow the Emperor.[2] Once in power, the military carried out, they argue, a radical social transformation, dismantling the economic basis of the landed aristocracy that had been the mainstay of the Haile Selassie regime. In Halliday and Molyneux's view, the emergence of a centralised state that made this transformation possible, at the same time, brought about the conflict between the state and the nationalist movements based on the Eritrean, Tigray, Oromo and, in the Ogaden, Somali peoples. Since 1974, the military has been in a state of war with these nationalist movements,[3] which see the regime as a continuation of the Amhara domination that was established in the 1880s and 1890s, when the ruling class of the Shoa kingdom subjugated the surrounding kingdoms, forming the basis of the present day Ethiopian political entity. The military's efforts to repress the national struggles is portrayed by Halliday and Molyneux as arising from the formation of a centralised state that was necessary to carry out a policy of social transformation that they see as having taken Ethiopia in a socialist direction. Their central thesis is that the Ethiopian military regime has brought about a 'revolution from above' which could, on condition of overcoming certain obstacles, initiate the transition to socialism.

It is this thesis that is subjected here to a critical examination, both in its general implications for Marxist theory and its specific application to Ethiopia. The analysis through which it is developed rests, as I will try to show, on the theory of non-capitalist development. Although Halliday and Molyneux are apparently anxious to affirm a judicious distance from this theory, advancing its relevance to Ethiopia with some reservations, they diverge from it only on a secondary point and embrace its problematic. I will first indicate those aspects of the problematic of non-capitalist development that will help to illuminate the theoretical underpinning of their study and then discuss how this leads them to abandon Marxist concepts for sociological categories which abstract social developments from the class struggle and imprison their account of post-1974 Ethiopia within the ideology of the Ethiopian state.

The theory of non-capitalist development, as advanced by Soviet writers, contends that the existence of the socialist system gives the opportunity for Third World countries 'to bypass the more advanced forms of class-antagonistic relations, the capitalist socio-economic formation above all' (Andreyev 1977, p. 30).[4] It argues that an alliance between world socialism and national democratic forces which incorporate workers, the peasantry and the urban petty bourgeoisie can lay the basis for socialist development in the Third World.

Soviet writers trace the genesis of the theory to Marx—to his comments on communal property relations in Russia forming the basis of a direct transition to socialism; and to Lenin—to his remarks that the establishment of soviets in Russia opened the possibility of the peasantry rallying to communism in the predominantly agrarian countries of the colonial world. Irrespective of the question of whether these postulates have been borne out by events, they indicate that Marx and Lenin, while holding to the view that the general historical tendency was the emergence of socialism from the contradictions of capitalism, were nevertheless prepared to hypothesise that some societies might proceed directly from the pre-capitalist to the socialist stage. It is only to the extent that the theory of non-capitalist development postulates that societies do not have to pass through capitalist development that the texts of Marx and Lenin referred to can be marshalled in their support. They do not, however, lend weight to the particular economic and political features that are ascribed to the non-capitalist path.

In so far as the theory can lay claim to any classical heritage, it is to the post-revolutionary texts of Lenin on state capitalism. There Lenin appears to suggest a continuity between the nationalised sector in its state capitalist and its socialist forms. As Bettelheim remarks, Lenin's writings on this issue,

> do not make clear whether upon transition to the next stage of the revolution, the apparatuses of State capitalism are destined to play a role also in the building of socialism. . . some of his formulations in that period might suggest that the same apparatuses are destined, without being revolutionised, to play a part in socialist construction.[5]

The limitations of Lenin's thinking on this question stemmed from his exclusive concentration on the task set by the principal contradiction in the immediate aftermath of the revolution: how to reduce the labouring time of the masses to allow them to take control of the affairs of the state. 'At that stage, the centre of gravity of the masses taking power was the state not the process of productive work.'[6] The obstacles presented by the capitalist organisation of the labour process—with its separation between mental and manual labour and the tasks of decision-making from the work of execution to workers forming themselves into the collective masters of the new society—was at the time beyond Lenin's theoretical horizon. The continuity between state capitalism and socialism existed for him by virtue of the proletariat holding state power. He neglected the importance for the advance of socialism of the transformation of the social relations of production in the state sector not because he ignored the need for the proletariat to exercise power but because he considered it purely in its political form, its control of the state. The same cannot be said for the theory of the non-capitalist path of development, in which the continuity between state capitalism and socialism is established without any regard to the issue of working class power either in the form of control of the state or in the form of control of the direct process of production. Ulyanovsky writes:

> Many of the economic principles that lead in the direction of socialism and have been tested by time are being put into practice by these countries. These include nationalisation of the basic industries, expansion and strengthening of the state sector, the introduction of agrarian reforms that favour the peasantry and gradual industrialisation.[7]

The economic evolution towards socialism, 'the socialist orientation', is alleged to take place when 'the state capitalist sector has been transformed into a national democratic sector of socialist orientation'.[8] This comes about not as a result of the transformation of social relations of production but from the character of the state: 'the social nature of the state sector', writes Ulyanovsky, 'is derived from the social nature of the state power, from the class basis of the state, and from its domestic and foreign policy.'[9] While this position is formally analogous to that of Lenin, in essence it is quite different, for here the state sector is situated on a continuum leading to socialism even from the stage when the proletariat does not hold state power.

The social base of the state, the classes which support the 'socialist orientation', consists of the working class, the peasantry, the working intelligentsia, the petty bourgeoisie and in certain instances part of the middle bourgeoisie [10] However, it is not these classes that are in control of the state but radical petty bourgeois leaders, usually army officers, who are, Soviet writers argue, largely autonomous from social classes:

> A characteristic of many of the Afro-Asian countries over the past 15-20 years has been the considerable increase in the independent role of the state superstructure. From 1960 to 1975 there were roughly 90 military coups or attempted coups. By 1975 more than 20 of the 46 African states were under the rule of military regimes. In this sort of situation we usually find that the state apparatus is rarely subjected to direct control of class organisations. . .[11]

Thus, although the social character of the state was held to determine the social character of the nationalised sector of the economy, the state, too—by virtue of its 'independent role'—escapes class determination. Having first discarded the question of the type of relations of production that prevail in the nationalised sector of the economy on the grounds that its social content is determined by the state, the state itself is then detached from any reference to class domination. The state's 'socialist orientation', therefore, cannot be given any other determination than its own volition. The result is, that while the theoreticians of the non-capitalist path take care to mention the need to democratise the state, to strengthen the organisations of the working class and even to develop new state structures, in order to 'firmly secure socialist orientation from encroachments by reaction from home and abroad',[12] they do not identify these transformations with any particular social force. This lacuna is camouflaged by the argument that the transformation of the state depends on strengthening the organisations of the working class, through the raising of its political consciousness which, in turn, depends on the formation of a 'vanguard party'. But the original problem is merely displaced to resurge elsewhere, for in the absence of conceptualising state and class in the context of class struggle, the party is sociologically unanchored, it can emerge for its ideological task out of anywhere, even from the state—a process underway in Ethiopia, reportedly, at the behest of Soviet advisers.

What is absent from the theory of non-capitalist development is the position basic to Marxism that the formation of the working class into an independent political force is the *sine qua non* of the socialist revolution and transition. The failure to take into account the necessity of the proletariat to constitute itself into a historical force in its own right severs the dialectical unity between socialism and democracy. For it is only from the standpoint that 'the emancipation of the working class must be conquered by the working classes themselves',[13] that the struggle for democracy can be seen as inseparable from the struggle for socialism. This is to be understood not only in the sense that democracy provides the best conditions for the self-organisation of the oppressed but, more fundamentally, in the sense that the struggle for democratic rights of the oppressed sections of society is, itself, part of the transformation of the social relations which maintain the disorganisation and subordination of the masses. That is why Lenin argued that 'the proletariat cannot perform the socialist revolution unless it prepares for it by the struggle for democracy.'[14]

The prospects for a socialist transition are assessed by Soviet writers not by developments that enhance the ability of the oppressed classes to seize state power, but by the extent to which the state's policies approximate to a model of socialism of which the main components are nationalisation, land reform and close relations with the Soviet Union. This last criterion is presented as the crucial indicator of a state's orientation and in practice has been the basis of Soviet categorisation of Third World states, as the revisions in successive lists of socialist oriented countries show.

The ideological effects of the failure of the theory of non-capitalist development to render account of social transformation in terms of the struggle of the oppressed classes and, in particular, of the consequent severing of the internal connection between socialism and democracy, can be seen clearly in Halliday and Molyneux's analysis of post-1974 Ethiopia. It leads them, as we shall see, to a conceptualisation of the socio-economic structure on the basis of juridical relations and–as its concomitant–to a statist conception of socialist politics, in which democracy is contingent to socialism.

Halliday and Molyneux develop their main thesis, that a 'revolution from above' has been carried out in Ethiopia, through two lines of argument. First, that the military government that came to power in Ethiopia implemented from above a transformation of class relations that merits the term 'revolution'. Second, that this 'revolution from above' constitutes an advance on the path to the transition to socialism, interpreted by the authors, in line with the theory of non-capitalist development, to mean that it has 'created a state sector–in industry, finance and agriculture–and has through the mass mobilisation and planning system increased its overall ability to direct the economy'.[15] Although Halliday and Molyneux give considerable attention to the first argument, to establish that the Ethiopian revolution was one of 'the most radical from above', it is only by relation to the second, on the basis of determining the class relations that 'the revolution from above' has brought about, that such terms as 'radical' and 'far reaching' can be rendered theoretically and politically meaningful. If the transformations carried out are separated from the question of what type of class relations they established, then the issue of whether they amount to a revolution or not boils down to one of formal definitions. Yet, it is precisely this separation that Halliday and Molyneux operate. After pointing to the fundamental social transformations carried out by the state in Germany and Japan in the second half of the 19th century, they add:

> The concept of revolution from above is therefore one which sparingly used has a valid application: whether such revolutions can be socialist as well as capitalist and whether the Ethiopian revolution can legitimately be included in either category, are separate matters.[16]

In this way the ground is prepared for 'the revolution from above' in Ethiopia to be linked to a social force that is presented as indeterminate in class terms, the military bureaucracy. It comes into being as 'an autonomous and radical sector of the state apparatus'.[17]

The autonomy that Halliday and Molyneux attribute to the military governs their entire analysis of the developments in post-1974 Ethiopia. They attribute its origin to the manner in which the society ruled by Haile Selassie finally exploded in a contradiction within the state apparatus. The structure of the imperial state had not been able 'to transform itself into a functioning modern administration. The Emperor took all the major decisions and his power in the provinces was weak'.[18] In the countryside, the dominant class was made up of the large landowners who retained control of the administrative organs and it is to this fact that Halliday and Molyneux attribute the fragmentation of Ethiopian society, which, they argue, has had a crucial bearing on political developments under the military. The outmoded state apparatus was swelled at the centre by its involvement in the capitalist sector:

> bureaucratic capitalism did denote a tangible phenomenon in the following senses: (a) the state played a significant role in promoting certain capitalist enterprises, investing more heavily than any local bourgeoisie, if less than foreign capital; and (b) these enterprises were organised in part to yield extra benefits to those state employees with access to them.[19]

The imperial state based on an alliance between bureaucratic capitalism and the landowning class, was unable to carry out the agrarian reform that capitalist expansion required. The fundamental cause of the imperial state's overthrow, Halliday and Molyneux conclude, lay 'in the failure of the regime to resolve the agrarian crisis, to develop the country's productive forces in such a way as to improve the population's living standards and even, in the provinces ravaged by famine, maintain previous subsistence levels'.[20]

The state was enmeshed within an insoluble contradiction on the one hand it was the agent of capitalist development, on the other, it was linked to the landowning aristocracy of the provinces, whose existence was antithetical to that development. Emphasising how this contradiction coalesced within the state, the authors write:

> the state apparatus became a partial promoter of capitalist development and, at the same time, the site of a conflict between groups associated with this capitalist development and those associated with the pre-capitalist order. The gulf thus created within the state was to be more than a reflection of the conflicts within the socio-economic formation as a whole; it became the politically most acute contradiction within Ethiopian society, the conflict that was to determine the fall of the *ancien regime* and the nature of the new post-revolutionary system.[21]

The movement that led to the overthrow of Haile Selassie began in the army, in February 1974. A series of mutinies by soldiers over their conditions was followed by a widescale urban protest movement, based largely on the students and white collar workers. 'This ferment was, after a lull, reinvigorated by visibly more permanent politicisation of the armed forces.'[22]

On the relative importance of the mass protest movement and the movement of the armed forces, in the overthrow of the regime, Halliday and Molyneux, comment: 'The attack on the nobility and ultimately on the Emperor came not from the civilian bodies but from the radical junior officers in the armed forces.'[23] When the military finally overthrew the Emperor and seized power in September, only the aristocracy had been dislodged.

> No social revolution had yet occurred. But it was partly because of the imminence of. . . a political counter-revolution that the new government felt pressed to take a series of radical measures designed to undermine the economic and social power of those who might have favoured a return to some version of the previous regime.[24]

Having seized power, the military (the Derg) implemented an economic programme consisting of nationalisation and land reform:

> On February 3 seventy-two industrial and commercial companies were fully nationalised, and the state assumed majority control in twenty-nine others. By late 1976 two-thirds of all manufacturing was under the control of the Ministry of Industry. On March 4th, 1975, the most important reform of all, a land reform, was announced: all rural land was nationalised, tenancy was prohibited, and the peasantry was to have the right to till plots of only ten hectares maximum.[25]

These measures are represented by Halliday and Molyneux, as by the theory of non-capitalist development, as the economic preconditions of socialism. But, since, according to this theory, it is ultimately the policy of the state, its anti-imperialist policy internally and its political alignments externally, which determines the society's socialist orientation, this does not prevent Halliday and Molyneux from identifying the limits of the transformation in the social relations of production brought about by the military.

> Although hiring of labour was henceforth forbidden, the weakness of the state purchasing body, combined with the reliance of the peasantry on their former landlords for their subsistence goods, opened the door to new forms of exploitation of the peasantry by richer peasants and merchants. Overall, the richer peasants were able not only to gain a disproportionate amount of land to continue exploiting the poorer ones, but also to ensure that it was they who controlled the new Peasants' Associations, their credit, equipment and distribution.[26]

A little later they conclude:

> By 1980 there were just forty producer cooperatives in existence, mainly of the initial *malba* variety, and another 130 were under consideration. But state farms and cooperatives combined accounted for only 6 per cent of agricultural output and 20 per cent of marketed production: the Ten Year Plan declared the need for collectivisation, but set no targets for it.[27]

In the nationalised industrial sector, the transformation of the social relations of production similarly did not go beyond the establishment of capitalist relations. 'By 1976, widespread demands were being raised for shop-floor control over production. These were repelled with the appointment of powerful state managers, and with the imposition of a new trade union structure.'[28]

If therefore 'the revolution from above' in Ethiopia laid the preconditions for a socialist transition, as Halliday and Molyneux following the theory of non-capitalist development argue, this is not because the 'radical' transformation the military imposed has gone beyond the establishment of capitalist relations of production but because the policies of the state—what Soviet writers term its 'socialist orientation'—can, on the basis of the nationalised sector, lay the preconditions for the socialist transition. To attribute to the state this capacity to override the balance of class forces, it has not only to be detached from the economic structure —from the class relations on the economic level—but also from the class struggle on the political level or, to be more precise, the struggle of the political forces around the state has to be abstracted from the class struggle.

The terms of this problematic are set in motion by Halliday and Molyneux's discussion of the political forces which is organised around the conceptual couplet, the military-civilian forces. This leads them to trace the history of the military's consolidation in power principally through the relation between the military and the political groups of the left, the Ethiopian People's Revolutionary Party (EPRP), All-Ethiopian Socialist Movement (ME'ISON) and a number of smaller groups all of which were mainly based on the urban petty bourgeoisie. In the process of adjudicating among the policies of these rival groups, the repressive policies of the military are evaluated entirely by reference to these groups. Hence the criticism that Halliday and Molyneux levy against the Derg is the 'abandonment of legality'[29] and the 'violations of legality'.[30] These terms echo the official Soviet criticism of Stalin's rule–they were given currency by Khrushchev at the 20th Party Congress–and they are equally inadequate and mystifying with relation to the Derg. For they abstract repression from its effect in the class struggle, to categorise it instead by relation to law.

The repression of the organisations of the Left took place in the context of the Derg's offensive against the organisations of the working class and of the peasantry. Halliday and Molyneux, themselves, remark that at the same time as the 'red terror' was carried out against the EPRP, the 'working class opposition was crushed'[31] and, similarly, the power of the peasant associations, the *kebeles,* that had been formed to implement the land reform, was emasculated. 'The *kebeles* were taken over by political forces that the Derg had to disown. The result was that by the end of 1978 the power of the *kebeles* had been greatly reduced.'[32]

By divorcing the conflict between the EPRP and the Derg from its wider implications in the class struggle, Halliday and Molyneux obscure the real significance of the division between the two. Although the EPRP was undoubtedly ultra-leftist, as indicated by their policy of urban terrorism which was conducted over the heads of the masses, the principal issue on which they clashed with the Derg was fundamental to the entire course of the struggle in Ethiopia. What Halliday and Molyneux describe as the EPRP's demand for 'immediate civilian rule' was, in fact, a demand for basic democratic rights.

It is also on the issue of democracy that the other main leftist organisation, ME'ISON, diverged from the military, though the former allied with the Derg to work for its objectives from the inside, an endeavour that lasted until 1977, when it, too, was eliminated. The programme of the Derg for the 'National Democratic Revolution' (NDR) was based on that of ME'ISON but, as Lefort notes, it differed on two essential points. It did not recognise the right of self-determination, including the right of secession, to the nationalities within Ethiopia and it did not aim at the destruction of the old state apparatus and its replacement by popular organs of power. ME'ISON demanded that:

> . . . to secure government by the people for the people, the organs of popula administration. . . be placed under the auspices of mass organisations. . . Th bureaucratic apparatus, anti-people and corrupt be dismantled and replaced by revolutionary and democratic apparatus.

Lefort adds: 'There was nothing of this in the NDR. No reform of th state is envisaged in it.'[33] Whether the policies of the EPRP, ME'ISON—or indeed, of the Confederation of Ethiopian Labour Unions (CELU), th leadership of which in 1974 was strongly influenced by the EPRP—wer correct or not, is of secondary importance, what is far more significan for the analysis of the political developments is that these groups, how ever inadequately, gave ideological expression to the struggle for demo cratic rights—for the nationalities and for the Ethiopian masses—and it i that struggle that the Derg crushed.

In September 1975, for example, CELU published a document callin for free speech, free press, freedom of association and union organisation They were demands that had been formulated by the teachers' associatio but it had strong support from sections of the working class and whe some workers were arrested for distributing these demands strikes brok out in a number of factories.[34]

It is the consequence for the socialist struggle of the Derg's repressio of democratic rights that is obscured by Halliday and Molyneux. And thi is a direct consequence of the fact that for them, as for the theoretician of the non-capitalist development, the emergence of the oppressed as a independent political force is not essential for preparing the condition for the socialist transition.

Halliday and Molyneux do not deny the absence of democracy unde the Derg, but they evidently believe that 'autonomous decisions'—a tern used by them—for the oppressed classes and nationalities are no organically related to the realisation of socialism. They are even prepare to concede that 'the non-capitalist path of development' could prepar the ground not for a socialist transition, but for a strengthened capitalis system,[35] but in the case of the Derg, the absence of democratic right under it for the past six years, is assessed by them by criterion devoid o any reference to class forces. The Ethiopian state, they write, has a 'authoritarian' and 'centralised' structure and has a 'novel' and 'pervasive character:

> The new regime's relation to the population as a whole was marked by a numbe of distinctive characteristics. First this was a far more centralised and interven tionist state than the old. . . The second major change was in the relationship t the people. Once the regime was established, few could imagine that Ethiopi was a politically democratic country, in the sense of permitting those at the bas to express their views openly or to take autonomous decisions: this was tru neither for classes nor nationalities nor individuals. But this authoritarian structur

> should not obscure the fact that a new system of mobilisation and communication had been established, through the political organisations of the regime. It was through these mediations that a centralised state was being created, however haltingly. . . Again, recognition of the authoritarian structure of these mechanisms is quite consistent with the assertion of their novel and pervasive character: over seven million people in the Peasant Associations, up to half million in the Trade Unions, several million in the Women's Associations. . .[36]

The characterisation of the state by its formal institutional features rather than by its relation to the oppressed classes–in this case principally by its anti-democratic nature–follows from the analysis of the state having been detached from the question of what class relations it serves to reproduce. Halliday and Molyneux's list of the number of people incorporated into the so-called 'mass organisations', beyond showing the 'novel' and 'pervasive' character of the state, suggests, given the absence of internal democracy, that they are a powerful instrument of domination. 'Politics', the authors defensively add, 'however much it was directed from above, was being brought to the population in a way not previously seen in Ethiopian history'. But politics is not a thing, it is defined by relations of power. The literacy campaign is a case in point. Halliday and Molyneux mention how 'the literacy campaign in particular was designed to bring the people into political life',[37] but they ignore that the literacy campaign is conducted almost entirely in Amharic and as such, within the existing power relations, serves as an instrument for imposing the culture of the dominant nationality on the rest of the population.

The failure to situate the anti-democratic character of the state by relation to the class struggle has particularly far reaching effect on Halliday and Molyneux's understanding of the struggle of the oppressed nationalities and, more especially, of the one that continues to pose the most serious threat to the Ethiopian state, the Eritrean struggle.

Halliday and Molyneux argue that although the Eritrean struggle is justified in principle, it is undermined in practice, in the present historical context, by the fact that it has little prospect of succeeding and by the political nature of the Eritrean movement, which in its strengths and weaknesses mirrors the Derg.

> In its dimensions, both human and political, Eritrea has been a tragedy of great proportions, in which no simple attribution of responsibility or of socialist credentials is possible.[38]

The difficulty that Halliday and Molyneux have in attributing 'socialist credentials' between the oppressors and oppressed stems from their theoretical framework which, as we saw, divorces the struggle for democratic rights from the struggle for socialism. Before returning to this point, it is worth detailing how having detached the Eritrean struggle from the context within which its significance for the class struggle could be evaluated, the authors proceed to establish a symmetry between the two opposed forces, which gives a distorted picture of the Eritrean movement.

The Eritrean liberation movement, they argue, has been characterised by 'factionalism' and 'mutual anathemas' which, 'are merely the public face of feuding that continues invisibly within the fronts themselves and which has periodically to be purged by expulsions, excommunications and liquidations.[39] That the authors characterise the divisions within the Eritrean movement as 'factionalism' follows from their view that there is no substantial difference among the three Eritrean forces.

> The relative strengths and distribution of the three groups indicate that while the claims of all three about their own following must be discounted, none was an insignificant force at that time, and none could be categorised as just being the expression of one confessional-geographical bloc. The cross-currents of Eritrean society were reflected both in their leadership and in the composition of their guerrilla forces. The political programmes of the three indicate further differences, but, again, these are less significant than their own controversies suggest.[40]

In reality, the relative strengths of the three forces are barely comparable. The Eritrean Liberation Front–Popular Liberation Front (ELF–PLF), led by Osman Sabbe Saleh, never a serious rival to the other two fronts, has virtually disintegrated. In 1980, it broke up into two groups and: 'Neither has guerrilla units of any substance inside Eritrea. . .'[41] As to the Eritrean Liberation Front (ELF), during 1981, its main area of operation, the Barka region was taken over by the Eritrean Peoples' Liberation Front (EPLF) and by the time of the Ethiopian 6th offensive, launched in February 1982, it had ceased to exist as an effective military force and took no part in the fighting.[42] It is not merely that Halliday and Molyneux's account has been rapidly surpassed by the events, their account is inadequate for the period they describe and therefore fails to identify tendencies which have been evident for some time. Despite promising a 'materialist and critical analysis of the Eritrean movement,' their discussion does not go beyond locating the regional influences in the origin of the three forces and the differences in their programmes, the significance of which they belittle.

But more serious than the inadequacies of their account of the Eritrean liberation movement, is their assessment of what the Eritrean war reveals of the Ethiopian state. The oppression of the non-Amharic nationalities in Ethiopia—who form approximately three-quarters of the population—and the denial of the right of secession to Eritrea, signifies for them not a particular form of class domination being established but the formal institutional feature of the new state, evidence of its centralised nature:

> Yet, if the pre-revolutionary state has rested upon the disunity of the country and on the balance of its various separate components, the revolutionary state based itself upon a centralised system: in that process of transition, from a centrifugal equilibrium to a new fusion, conflict was inevitable.

The absence of self-determination for the nationalities is referred to as the inevitable result of the transition from one mode of production to another. But whereas the decentralised state, in the Haile Selassie period, had been presented as linked to a particular form of class domination, the new centralism is not linked, even tendentially, to any form of class domination. As we saw before, once the character of the state is disconnected from its relation to class domination, the importance of its democratic or undemocratic character for the struggle for socialism is also obscured. The 'socialist credentials' of the Ethiopian state can then be determined independently of the denial of democratic rights to the nationalities, just as before it was determined independently of the denial of democratic rights to the working class and the peasantry.

The theoretical underpinning of the separation of the characterisation of the state from the relation of class forces in Ethiopia rests on Halliday and Molyneux's interpretation of 'the relative autonomy of the state', through which they weld their analysis to the problematic of non-capitalist development.

The state, argue Halliday and Molyneux, has a degree of relative autonomy 'even in the most settled and developed capitalist societies' but it is 'all the greater in other situations':

> This is so in revolutionary contexts, where the normal controls of social class over the state may be attenuated, and where the very conflicts of the revolutionary period are concentrated on the state—either on gaining control of existing apparatuses or on establishing new institutions capable of replacing those through which the social relations of the old order are reproduced. The autonomy of the state may also be greater in situations of transition from one mode of production to another, where social forces associated with both modes may compete for power not just over the state, but within it, in such a way that the institutions are again released from class controls imposed in situations where one mode and one system of social relations are dominant. Finally, the autonomy of the state may be greater where class relations are themselves less developed, due to the disruption of the social system by external influences or by the predominance of social relations determined by factors other than class, such as ethnic and lineage bonds. . . It will be evident that all three forms of 'autonomy' have pertained in the Ethiopian case: Ethiopia is a society undergoing a revolution, its social relations are transitional and heterogeneous and its class forces are still partially developed.[44]

On the empirical level, the explanation here is circular, making cause and effect reversible. It was the relative autonomy of the state that for Halliday and Molyneux made the revolution from above possible and has continued to be the driving force behind 'the revolutionary period', behind 'the transition from one mode of production to another', and it is presumably this process that has prevented a crystallisation of class forces. Thus it is precisely the conditions which the state, by virtue of its alleged autonomy, brought about, that are then held to account for the autonomy. The state has apparently taken off into self-sustained autonomy, providing the conditions for its own determination.

This is but an effect of Halliday and Molyneux's conceptualisation of the state's autonomy, which situates its functioning exterior to class struggle. Their position breaks with the Marxist point of view that the state is constituted and defined by the relation of domination that is established through class struggle and this is no less the case in situations where the organisation of the subordinate classes is weak and the dominant class is formed largely out of the functionaries of the state apparatus. The state for them is the object of class struggle, it reflects class struggle but it is not the organised form of class domination.

> The state is therefore both a reflection of the conflicts within society, the object of that conflict, and a means by which those concerned to transform society can hope to achieve their aims. If it is to a considerable extent limited by the objective structures of Ethiopian society—it cannot arbitrarily remould the social relations irrespective of the conditions prevailing—it is nevertheless an active agent in the process of consolidating a post-revolutionary order. It reflects to some degree the interests of class forces but it may also play an active role in class formation, in constructing new social relations of which its agents are a part.[45]

The state, for the authors, is a self-determining subject on the Weberian model, limited by the objective situation, subject to pressures from a plurality of forces but not itself internally related to class domination. The concept of relative autonomy refers to a realm of freedom from class determination which permits the state to become the source of its own power. The Marxist terminology is deceptive—this, in fact, is the state as conceived in liberal pluralist theory where classes compete for influence over the institutions of power. The state, and not the balance of forces in the class struggle, as the source of power is the corollary of conceptualising political forces without reference to the class struggle. The relative autonomy of the state, in Halliday and Molyneux's analysis, turns out to be an analytical void, a failure to elucidate how the state functions within the class struggle in Ethiopia, how it organises the relations of domination/subordination, outside of which there can be no understanding of it in a Marxist sense.

In the *Ethiopian Revolution*, instead of class struggle, it is the state theorised as the Subject, acting within a set of objective constraints, that is presented as the motor of history. The action of the Ethiopian state is triggered by the subjectivity of the dominant faction within its personnel.

> Within the state itself, power is concentrated in the hands of a group of radical military officers who have proclaimed their intention to lead Ethiopian society to some form of radical change and their determination to implement what they proclaim is not, by now, in doubt.[46]

In this way, the Ethiopian state's potential for advancing class relations towards the socialist transition is assessed, first of all, by relation to the intentions of its personnel. This sociological reductionist notion of the state is the one to be found in the theory of non-capitalist development, which notwithstanding the claims of Soviet writers, has close affinity not with Marx but with Weber.

As in Weberian sociology where the social actor is the origin of social action and the latter is defined by the meaning the actor attaches to it, the state-Subject's action is defined by the policy through which it interprets its own actions. The divergence of this Weberian type conceptualisation of the state from the Marxist one is not only theoretical. These two conceptions give theoretical effect to contradictory class positions with respect to the state. The Marxist analysis of the state by proceeding from its function within the class struggle, defines its principal aspect by its relation to the oppressed, by how it organises the subordination of those classes and groups.[47] By contrast, the Weberian explanation takes its point of departure from the state's own criterion of operation, the policies which it seeks to implement. This is the point of view of the functionaries of the state, who 'live' the ideology of its practice. That Halliday and Molyneux give expression to the Ethiopian state's own ideology is evident in their assessment of the Derg's policies.

It is on the basis of the military's internal and external policies that the authors talk of the post-1974 regime having 'moved so rapidly and far to the left'.[48] In their view, these policies have attempted to turn the objective constraints on the state–internal to the society and external–in a direction favourable to commencing the socialist transition.

> While there are those in the state who favour a socialist option, the possibility of Ethiopia's attempting a transition to socialism rests upon the fulfilment of all of three conditions: the triumph within the state of those favouring this path; the securing sufficient support from classes within Ethiopia itself; and supportive transnational conditions.[49]

The external conditions to which the policies of the Derg had to orientate are set, according to Halliday and Molyneux, by the Soviet bloc, on the one side, and the West, on the other.

> the conditions for attempting a socialist transition were not given within the confines of Ethiopian society alone: they involve transnational factors, of support (from the USSR and its allies) and of opposition (from the West). Any programme of economic development, a prerequisite for beginning a transition to socialism, involved substantial aid from abroad. Neither the intentions of the major capitalist states, nor the reservations of some of the PMAC leadership about the USSR, were conducive to such an orientation.[50]

While the implication here is that what prevents Soviet aid from assisting towards a socialist transition are 'reservations' on the part of the Derg, subsequently, Halliday and Molyneux point to a number of limitations in the aid itself. Indeed, it is on this point that the authors distance themselves from the theory of non-capitalist development. They cast doubt on its claim that assistance from the Soviet Union plays a decisive part in a country's progression towards the socialist transition. Their overall assessment is that Soviet aid is determined 'primarily by a given country's foreign policy'. In some cases it contributes to the transition to socialism, in others it can aid 'the consolidation of overtly capitalist regimes'.[51]

After these general remarks one might expect an examination, however cursory, of the impact of Soviet aid on Ethiopia's prospects for socialist development but, instead, discussion of Soviet aid is restricted to the supply of arms to the Derg in the Eritrean war, which the authors describe as 'reprehensible'. This moral stricture is an inadequate substitute for a materialist analysis of the Soviet Union's role in Ethiopia. But such an examination is not accessible within the analytical framework of Halliday and Molyneux, which having failed to render account of the class character of the Ethiopian state and of the class relations within the state sector, cannot provide the basis for evaluating the significance of Soviet military support to the suppression of the Eritreans and other nationalities or the impact of Soviet economic support, most of which is channelled to the state sector.

Halliday and Molyneux's discussion of Western strategy towards Ethiopia, since 1977—the year in which the Soviet Union shifted its allegiance from Somalia to the Derg—is even more vitiated by silences. The 'opposition from the West' to the Derg's policies appears to consist, in their account, of the US's reduction of aid to Ethiopia:

> Under Congressional amendments on this issue, on the compensation claims of US firms for nationalisations, the USA was not only prevented from supplying aid, but was also enjoined to vote against aid to Ethiopia in international agencies such as the World Bank. In the fiscal year 1979, the USA provided only $10 million in development assistance, plus $30 million in commodity assistance.[52]

And contrasting Western hostility to the regime with Soviet support, they write:

> Internationally, the PMAC [the Derg] can rely on the support, military, ideological and in some degree economic, of the USSR and its allies. By improving relations with the Arab states, it may at least prevent them and also the West from giving substantial support to groups overtly opposed to the new Ethiopian regime.[53]

This picture of Western hostility to the Derg can only be sustained by ignoring the growing involvement of European interests in Ethiopia. Western, principally European, loans to Ethiopia have increased more than five-fold since 1974. Under the Lomé Treaty, Ethiopia is the largest single recipient of EEC aid.[54] For the fiscal year that ended in July 1981, the EEC allocated $213 million in 'soft' loans and grants, mainly for agriculture and agro-industry.[55] The combined value of EEC economic assistance and emergency relief pledged to Ethiopia is estimated to be $650 million.[56] Of all this Halliday and Molyneux say not a word.

The portrayal of the Ethiopian state as largely cut off from Western 'aid' and capital as a result of its political orientation, conforms to the image of a state struggling for socialism that the Derg itself likes to foster. But it is in relation to the military regime's internal policies that the extent to which Halliday and Molyneux remain prisoners of the state's ideology is most evident. They assess the Derg's internal policies on the basis of a model of socialism that, while it can doubtlessly lay claim to a long history within the international communist movement, nevertheless constitutes a distortion of Marxism. It leads Halliday and Molyneux to determine the socialist content of the Derg's policies–hence of the state's 'socialist orientation'–not by relation to the class struggle in Ethiopia, to the developments that are likely to favour the political forces of the oppressed–the workers, peasants, urban petty bourgeoisie, women, the oppressed nationalities–but by their correspondence to the juridical relations through which the state controls the reproduction of social relations.

The Derg's domestic policies are evaluated by Halliday and Molyneux on the basis of its intervention in the socio-economic structure, in which the principal contradiction is conceptualised as the opposition between two juridical forms, the state owned sector and the private sector. The authors write:

> . . . there is a basis for development towards socialism, given the fact that the 1974 revolution has also created a state sector–in industry, finance and agriculture–and has, through the mass mobilisations and the planning system increased its overall ability to direct the economy. Any further progress on the path to a transition to socialism would involve expanding the state's control over the economy and in particular, substantial transformation of agrarian relations. Here, the most important internal obstacle to a socialist transition remains: the

> predominance of pre-capitalist, petty commodity and capitalist social relations and the inevitability of clashes with the classes benefiting from these relations.[57]

This formulation would put, indiscriminately, in the same category of 'obstacles to a socialist transition', capitalists and poor peasants, merchants and petty traders—it is incapable of identifying the specific class alliances that are necessary to realise a favourable balance of class forces for a socialist revolution and transition. Instead of proceeding from a concrete analysis of the social relations of production, the socio-economic structure is dichotomised on the basis of juridical relations and the nationalised sector is equated with the economic basis of socialism. The sociological reductionist and voluntarist conception of the state here reveals its accomplice: a juridical conception of class relations.

This is not a chance alliance in theory but an organic unity established within an ideology that is linked to a specific form of state practice. It is the ideology of state capitalism which, in the guise of socialism, asserts the state to be the motor of social transformation and perceives in all that escapes its administrative control as 'non-socialist', as 'obstacles' or even as 'bandits' (as the Derg describes the Eritrean resistance).[58] We should not be surprised to find that an analysis—whether of Stalin or of the Derg—that remains within the confines of this ideology is able to provide a critique only of its method of treating these 'obstacles'—its 'violations of legality'—but not of the class nature of the state itself, which define the 'obstacles'. Halliday and Molyneux's book gives a theoretical expression to the ideology of the Ethiopian state, it does not provide an instrument for its understanding.

'Revolution from above', write Halliday and Molyneux, 'is not so much an alternative to revolution from below as an extension or fulfilment of a mass movement from below, where the latter is for a variety of reasons, unable to go beyond the stage of creating an atmosphere of national dissidence and to overthrow the established regime.'[59] Through its silences and misinterpretations, catalogued above, *The Ethiopian Revolution* suggests a contrary lesson: the lesson that the Eritrean and Tigrayan struggles continue to demonstrate in practice—the masses cannot be substituted for in history.

NOTES

1. Fred Halliday and Maxine Molyneux, *The Ethiopian Revolution*, Verso Editions, 1981, London.
2. For an account of Haile Selassie's overthrow and the coming to power of the military cf. J. Markakis and N. Ayele, *Class and Revolution in Ethiopia*, Spokesman, 1978, Nottingham.

   On the military's consolidation in power cf. J. Valdelin, 'Ethiopia 1974–7; from anti-feudal revolution to consolidation of the bourgeois state'. *Race and*

Class No. 4 Spring 1978 and J. Markakis, 'Garrison Socialism in Ethiopia' *MERIP Reports* No. 79. While these texts provide much useful information on the military regime, they give little attention to the national struggles which have come to dominate the politics of the Ethiopian state.
3. An overall picture of the different national struggles and of the involvement of foreign powers in the Horn of Africa is provided by Bereket Habte Selassie, *Conflict and Intervention in the Horn of Africa,* Monthly Review Press, 1980, New York and London. On the Eritrean movement, specifically, cf. L. Cliffe, B. Davidson, B. Habte Selassie (eds), *Behind the War in Eritrea,* Spokesman, 1980, London and D. Pool, 'Revolutionary Vanguard in Eritrea' *Review of African Political Economy* No. 19 September–December 1980. On the Tigrayan movement cf. Solomon Inquai, 'The Hidden Revolution Triumphs in Tigray', *Horn of Africa* vol. IV No. 3, 1981.
4. I. Andreyev, *The Non-Capitalist Way,* Progress Publishers, 1977, Moscow, p. 30.
5. Ch. Bettelheim, *The Class Struggle in the USSR,* Vol. 1, Harvester Press, 1977, Sussex, p. 472.
6. R. Linhart, *Lenine, les paysans, Taylor,* Seuil, 1976, Paris, p. 94.
7. R. Ulyanovsky, *Present-Day Problems in Asia and Africa,* Progress Publishers, 1978, p. 33.
8. *Ibid.*, p. 159.
9. *Ibid.*
10. *Ibid.*, p. 69.
11. *Ibid.*, p. 47.
12. *Ibid.*, p. 87.
13. K. Marx and F. Engels, *Selected Works* vol. 2, Progress Publishers, 1969, p. 19.
14. V.I. Lenin, 'A Caricature of Marxism and Imperialist Economism', *Collected Works,* Vol. 23, Progress Publishers, 1964, p. 74.
15. Halliday and Molyneux, *op. cit.*, p. 271.
16. *Ibid.*, p. 27.
17. *Ibid.*, p. 29.
18. *Ibid.*, p. 59.
19. *Ibid.*, p. 73.
20. *Ibid.*, p. 83.
21. *Ibid.*, p. 69.
22. *Ibid.*, p. 85.
23. *Ibid.*, p. 90.
24. *Ibid.*, p. 95.
25. *Ibid.*, p. 99.
26. *Ibid.*, p. 108.
27. *Ibid.*, p. 109.
28. *Ibid.*, p. 111.
29. *Ibid.*, p. 127.
30. *Ibid.*, p. 37.
31. *Ibid.*, p. 121.
32. *Ibid.*, p. 112.
33. R. Lefort, *Ethiopie: la révolution hérétique,* Maspero, 1981, Paris, p. 232.
34. *Africa Confidential,* Vol. 16, No. 20, 10.10.1975.
35. Halliday and Molyneux, *op. cit.*, p. 158.
36. *Ibid.*, p. 152.
37. *Ibid.*
38. *Ibid.*, p. 172.
39. *Ibid.*, p. 189.
40. *Ibid.*, p. 184.
41. *Africa Confidential,* Vol. 21, No. 10, 7.5.1980.

42. *The Middle East,* No. 90, April 1982.
43. Halliday and Molyneux, *op. cit.,* p. 158.
44. *Ibid.,* p. 146.
45. *Ibid.,* p. 147.
46. *Ibid.,* p. 270.
47. E. Balibar, *On the Dictatorship of the Proletariat,* NLB, 1977, London, p. 231.
48. Halliday and Molyneux, *op. cit.,* p. 154.
49. *Ibid.,* p. 155.
50. *Ibid.*
51. *Ibid.,* p. 282.
52. *Ibid.,* p. 231.
53. *Ibid.,* p. 270.
54. P. Wiles (ed), *The New Communist Third World: An Essay in Political Economy* Croom Helm, 1982, London and Canberra, p. 111.
55. *African Research Bulletin* (Economical, Financial and Technical Series), 15.4.1981.
56. *The Horn of Africa,* Vol. 4, No. 1, 1981.
57. Halliday and Molyneux, *op. cit.,* p. 271.
58. cf. Ch. Bettelheim and B. Chavance, 'Stalinism and the Ideology of State Capitalism', *The Review of Radical Political Economy,* Vol. 13, No. 13, Spring 1981, New York.
59. Halliday and Molyneux, *op. cit.,* p. 31.

THE ETHICAL DANCE—A REVIEW OF ALASDAIR MacINTYRE'S *AFTER VIRTUE*

Peter Sedgwick

The appearance of this book* during 1981 marked the resumption of a public position by a figure who, after making a particularly striking impression in the British New Left in the ten years up to 1968, withdrew both his energies and his person from the nexus of causes and comradeships to which he had contributed a mercurial and generous vitality. Emerging from a Christian (and then Christian-Marxist) background into the turbulent debates of the post-1956 far left, an analytic philosopher with a gift for passionate, resonant expression in both the written and spoken word, a militant owing successive loyalties to Trotskyist, syndicalist or semi-Leninist groups and parties but at the same time respected by and responsive to a wider and less affiliated left: MacIntyre was one of the outstanding socialist intellectuals of that fertile period in British intellectual and political life which saw the rise of CND and its civil-disobedience wing, the expansion of working-class direct action through the shop stewards' movement, the thriving of early vanguard forms of theatre and rock protest, and the beginnings of those long, large waves of popular dissensus (or, in Ralph Miliband's useful term 'de-subordination') which have proven, in the seventies and early eighties, signally resistant to any organised channel of political activity.

I write of Alasdair MacIntyre as an intellectual rather than solely as an academic: and would justify this characterisation partly by observing that, while his style of argument draws much of its force from a particular professional training (analytic philosophy in the British tradition of enquiry), its strengths are hard to locate as proceeding from any one academic area. There are elements of sociological theory here, and some attention to historical or anthropological enquiry (the latter having at an earlier phase come rather unstuck in the fierce debate between him and another philosopher on the significance of the cattle-rearing practices of the Azande, an exchange which continued with unperturbed momentum even when it was pointed out that the Azande had never possessed cattle). There are also many references to the social organisation of literature (the saga and epic as well as the novel) as well as of other arts, musical

***After Virtue: a Study in Moral Theory*, by Alasdair MacIntyre (Duckworth, London).

and visual, which are often seen as less social. While MacIntyre's philosophical identity is securely anchored in his long, often polemical involvement with the great ethical works of the past (and with modern systematic writers on moral questions), the power of his writings derives largely from his enviable capacity to take selected themes from the technical, professionalised debates among philosophers and social scientists and re-fashion them as material for the urgent attention of a non-specialised public, often using dramatic, poetic and prophetic devices in the casting of his arguments. From the earlier articles for the New Left and further-left press in Britain down to the ringing, compelling pages of *After Virtue*, MacIntyre writes in a voice and a vein appropriate to the composure of a most experienced director, producer and stockist of moral silhouettes: shadow-figures from the ethical and political dramas of past centuries, each with a limited circle of possible postures and movements (which may be displayed, for a paragraph or two, upon the lit screen of MacIntyre's elucidatory text) each shortly doomed to pass from a constricted slow-motion to a strangled no-motion, on account of the seizure in their strings and the inefficiency of their logical joints and sockets, all proceeding from some crucial inner vice of their construction that MacIntyre, as shadow-master, collector and doctor to these effigies, will shortly point out after he has given them a turn or so to display their paces and poses for us the readers.

One by one they step out, from the master's vast and compendious travelling-trunk of moral concepts where they sit, filed in well-ordered rows, between public appearances. Out come the sophists, fencing again against Socrates before falling flat on their backs before his witty shafts. Then comes Aristotle, pacing away in a high soliloquy of mime that sorts and re-sorts the basic terms of right action: a tremendous sequence this, such that the maestro cannot bear to put the figure back, or to let his script of logical moves rest unrevised. Out come the flaccid, comfortable agonists, making their measured and obviously limited points: David Hume, Adam Smith, the modern linguistic formalists of morals. The scene then revolves to the display of the well and truly agonised: Soren Kierkegaard's tormented solo, Nietzsche's defiant rejection of moral claims, the Sartrean existentialist's bleak formulation of ineluctable yet impossible choice. As we watch their exercises in unconditioned moral free-wheeling, a sudden blaze of light is cast across the screen in a few well-chosen words from MacIntyre: at once we see that these apparently individualist mavericks have been operated by well-concealed strings linked with quite conservative and staid ethical routines. They are replaced in the trunk, and for our special delectation MacIntyre gives us the triumphal ballet of the epic or tragic Greek heroes, whose noble and courageous gestures are in no whit lessened in effect—on the contrary, their significance is heightened—by the visibility of the ligaments that attach their awesome limbs to the codes and conventions of their tribe or *polis*.

A recurrent feature of the MacIntyre vivarium of shadows is a trope of presentation whereby, often with exceptional clarity and force, a pair of radically opposed, fiercely locked moral antagonists are shown to be engaging in common procedures and presuppositions. Thus, in the various sections of *After Virtue*, we find the role-playing self of Erving Goffman's theorising uncannily related to the self of early Sartre, even though role-playing is anathema for the latter; or the bureaucratic apologists for the managerial ethic are credited with essentially the same theoretical agenda as the anti-bureaucratic critical theorists deriving from the Frankfurt School; or the social-democratic, redistributionist case developed by John Rawls is shown to be consorting, in matters regarded as vital by MacIntyre, with the anti-distributionist, private-property liberalism of Robert Nozick. Even Marxism is adjudged now to be the ethical bed-fellow of the radical individualism offered by bourgeois thinkers, either on the Kantian model of unargued abstract principle or in the utilitarian mould of effects and consequences we owe to Bentham and Mill. Most importantly, the whole of modern philosophical theory about the basis of moral choice is ranked by MacIntyre as one or other expression, overt or indirect, of 'emotivism': the doctrine that all assertions of ethical principle, all statements about what is good or right, all sentences with an 'ought', 'should', or 'should not' in them, are no more than arbitrary expressions of personal preference lacking any possible rational justification. And the rivalry that exists among present-day moral outlooks and principles is not simply the outcome of the ordinary disagreement about what is right or wrong that can be expected even among people with some common set of values. In our age, moral disagreement is a chaos: it is the contest of incommensurables, of different bedrock personal commitments which cannot be argued or adjudicated. The divergence among fundamental ethical positions only reinforces for MacIntyre their cardinal convergence and even identity as exemplars of an emotivist 'Here I stand: I can no other'.

MacIntyre's persuasive sense of a contemporary moral fragmentation is conveyed in all his phases of theoretical writing since 1958. The obverse of a fragmented, dislocated moral discourse would of course be an integrated and ordered one: and the theme of a possible recentring of morals, around one or other focus of shared human community, has been an uninterrupted concern of Alasdair MacIntyre ever since his New Left writings. In his cry 'From the Moral Wilderness' (written for the *New Reasoner* of John Saville and E.P. Thompson in 1959) the sundering of moral purposes in contemporary society is seen as arising because of a long-standing separation between the language of moral choice and the language of desires and wants. To close the gap between unconditioned, purposeless choice and anarchic, individualised desire, a Marxian conception of social human nature is offered, along with the first of MacIntyre's historico-anthropological compendiums of morality in relation to given cultural contexts and idioms. The stock of silhouettes is being prepared: those who witnessed their first performances, in such mesmerising tableaux as that of the Immoral Stalinist and the Moral Anti-Stalinist (whom, by a quick shift in the lighting and an inspired swivel of the stage, MacIntyre showed to be complementary partners rather than antagonists), were in at the beginning of that encyclopaedic montage of morals given us in *After Virtue.*

A Short History of Ethics, published in 1967, develops MacIntyre's critique of the sovereignty of individual choice, whether as the grounding of particular good and right decisions, or as the prime element in philosophers' more general accounting of what it means to decide well and rightly. References to the fatal split between morality and desire appear in the *Short History:* but the main organising frame for what is now a full and heterogeneous survey of past moralising appears to lie in some elusive but attractive musing about certain epochs of history which offered a genuine moral community and a unified language of choice and wish. When this fortunate culture actually existed and when it expired are both fleetingly dated in the *Short History*'s genealogy. There were, it seems, certain peaks of moral integration and commonalty, one in pre-classical Greece before moral aims and social roles become separated in a growing complexity of labour-division, and another in medieval society before capitalism and Protestantism have done their worst in individualising human destinies. MacIntyre is less interested in these ethical Edens than in the philosophical consequences of man's self-expulsion from moral community: the *Short History* is a review of the successive impasses and gyrations of trapped and alienated thinkers, each spinning and then sticking in a mess of incoherently individual intentions or inexplicably benign intuitions.

With MacIntyre's latest projection of the evolving matter of moral thought, the panorama becomes even richer: and much more ordered. What structures *After Virtue* is no longer the chronological constraint of recounting and reinterpreting the major ethical strands in literature and philosophy since Homer: here the central point is the attempt to persuade us that a loss of moral community typical of the distinctly modern ages is both a real event and a real catastrophe. The communitarian MacIntyre is no longer a communist: no hope is posed for a future re-integrated society. The bludgeon to beat down moral individualism is no longer to be found in Marx but—and this will surprise many of his old readers—Aristotle. The devotees of *A Short History of Ethics* will recall the devastating put-down of Aristotle contained in that work: the *Nicomachean Ethics* is a priggish, parochial, complacent book, and its author a class-bound conservative. In *After Virtue* the same book and the same author are dealt with much more patiently, indeed eulogistically, as the source of the major integrative concepts that will restore moral reasoning to its proper coherence and stature.

As with MacIntyre's previous analyses, confusion over moral criteria is held to originate in an inability by modern thinkers to work with a particular conception of goal-directed human nature. But the missing master-code for all the fragmented sub-codes of moral choice is no longer an agreed view of human wants or desires. Why, indeed, should any concept of what we desire or want assist us in clarifying ethical questions? As MacIntyre puts it in *After Virtue* (p. 46): '. . . the question of precisely which of our desires are to be acknowledged as legitimate guides to action. . . cannot be answered by trying to use our desires themselves as some kind of criterion.' With the exit of desire as an ordering focus for morality, MacIntyre now appeals to an Aristotelian concept of virtue (or rather, of The Virtues) to help us to order our ethical preferences in the light of certain high-level individual and group goals. In our barbarised, managerial modern epoch the tradition of the virtues has been lost, and we can never hope again to discover the agreed-on forms of community, citizenship and civically-inspired friendship which were the necessary contextual embedding for the construction of a virtuous life. All the same, there are some local loyalties to certain institutions of communal purpose—one's family, perhaps, or one's profession—and in these a morality of virtue can still be encouraged as a healthy alternative to the manipulative, utilitarian ethos of our dreadful age.

So crude a summary does no justice at all to the nuances, or even to the main lines, of MacIntyre's argument. One of the central merits of *After Virtue* is that it faces key objections to its own main themes in a fair-minded and sensitive manner and accepts them on board as fellow-passengers rather than shoving them away in a glib polemical response. It is clear, for instance, from MacIntyre's account of medieval moralising (Chapter 13) that the middle ages, despite the Aristotelian heritage transmitted through theologians, were a conflict-ridden epoch lacking in a consensual position about what constituted the referent community for the validation of moral choices. This qualification of his earlier claim that medievaldom was an ethically consensual period of course renders MacIntyre's periodisation of moral crisis all that much more problematic. Just when—as several reviewers have already asked—was the point of collapse, from secure values in 'the predecessor culture' to the present endless doubt about the very basis of right and wrong?

Other than in fairly simple societies too poor to maintain a class of intellectuals to scrutinise the direction of their progress, history is likely to offer few if any examples of the simplistic predecessor-ethic whose passing MacIntyre notes and mourns even as he generates doubt whether it has ever lived. Nor does the argument convince where it suggests that an Aristotelian table of the virtues, suitably arranged within a purposive account of social and civil life, makes it easier for those who accept it to find an unproblematic set of moral criteria. The very listing of what is to count as an important virtue is problematic and even contentious: MacIntyre himself has to revise Aristotle's own canon of what is virtuous (adding, for example, some intellectual virtues like a sense of history, downgrading the virtues of the Athenian gentlemen such as magnificence of character); and in regard to MacIntyre's own attempt to convey the logical specialness of virtue—which replaces Aristotle's appeal to a metaphysical 'human nature' by an intricate and absorbing account of the socially-grounded practices which are said to summon forth virtue—it becomes immediately clear that we are, once again, landed in a disputatious moral terrain where competing practices, and their associated benefits or costs, make apparently final and total claims upon the individual conscience. MacIntyre eventually offers the language of the virtues as a more faithful medium for the statement of moral dilemmas rather than as a means of reducing the arbitrariness of basic moral decisions. His rejigged figure of Aristotle thus emerges as a thoroughly modern muppet, contorted in an existentialist or Kantian croak of unconditioned and unreasoning choice.

It is clear, nevertheless, that our impresario of the ethical dance has done a superb job in oiling and repairing that classical figurine which once gave us the *Nicomachean Ethics* and which, with some sandpapering at old and awkward edges and some new choreography for a sociologically-inclined audience, performs with such poise and brilliance in *After Virtue*. And yet the very wizardry of Alasdair MacIntyre's art, when applied with such creative, committed zeal to the re-furnishing of crusty old Aristotle, raises certain doubts as to the limitations which he has always so assiduously revealed in those other moral manikins from his larger repertoire. He has brought out the best in the Aristotelian structure, tending and extending its dialectical powers and respectfully replacing what was outmoded or insupportable for contemporary discussion. Has he not sometimes been a little over-quick in sweeping other philosophical characters off the stage and back into storage once he has caught them out in some elementary pratfall? If he can make Aristotle dance so well, could not he flick Kant, or Hare, or John Stuart Mill, through some rather more flexible and advanced routines than he has hitherto allowed them? One is left wondering whether all those snarled-up, rigid figures from MacIntyre's past moral confrontations had to be shown as quite so static and incapable: and whether his famous display of the Identity of Antagonists did not perhaps occasionally depend on his own very personal selection of an angle of the lighting and a moment when the participants' action is frozen out of later sequence and development. Only in a certain light, and at a certain halting-point in the argument, can the pro-managerial theoriser be rendered similar to the opponent of bureaucratic rationality, the solitary Sartrean choice to the universal Kantian duty, the liberal anti-Stalinist to the Stalinoid authoritarian, and the Marxist revolutionary to the bourgeois moralist.

MacIntyre's life has been a long polemical itinerary, battling against massive and deliberately-chosen odds with the weapons of a ruthless honesty and an intellect of diamond acuity and toughness. His stance remains, in relation to the dominant power-structures of both West and East, irreconcilably oppositional, anti-managerial and hostile to the claims of private property. But the very intensity and rigour of his adversary role has, over the long series of battles in and outside the political left, tended to isolate him from any base in a collective endeavour. His chain of fraternisations while in Britain seems to have followed a common pattern of serious and warm comradeship followed by recoil and disengagement. In a metaphor of personal distance written during his Trotskyist years, MacIntyre commented: 'All of us will pass through phases in which both rightly and wrongly we sharpen the line between ourselves and others. This self-imposed isolation is a feature of every normal adolescence. It is also a normal experience in political organisations in which the first experience of membership and friendship may give way dialectically to a consciousness of distance between oneself and others' ('Freedom and Revolution', *Labour Review,* February–March 1960). These sentences even then conveyed a powerful psychological truth which accorded somewhat oddly with MacIntyre's insistence, then as now, on the necessity for a common disciplinary and collegial structure in which individual selfhood could be realised.

To the personal toll wrought by successive recoil there has now been added the more literal distance of Alasdair MacIntyre's move to live and work in the United States. Not for him the customary options of a displaced left in search of a supportive militant structure. He rejected the possibility of a renewed socialism in the Labour Party—an eloquent critique of Labour's inner collapse, broadcast by MacIntyre in 1968 in his own valediction to the British arena, is reprinted in David Widgery's Penguin collection *The Left in Britain.* Marxism is now no longer a vital core within the fragile, discarded shells of Leninist or Trotskyist group membership, but itself a shell, splintered and devoid of any real ethical nucleus. That radical tendency in ideas which in a number of related lines approximates to MacIntyre's present position—the school of European 'critical theory' with its complex involvement in the critical heritage of the ancients, the modern world of manipulated mass opinion, the methodology of social knowledge and the nature of artistic production—is never referred to in *After Virtue,* except in the surly amalgam we have noted between the Frankfurt School and managerial conformity. The prophet of allegiance and community, MacIntyre has argued himself into a corner where he can find no allies to realise a common project of criticism and change. Rejecting existent and past traditions of common socialist work—though he constantly evokes the imagery of socialist individual lives, of Trotsky or the Marx family, to fortify us in the exercise of virtue—he has taken on the task of singlehandedly constructing the basis for a critical morality and, in the long run, a re-shaped political order through nothing other than the re-centring of his long-running and marvellous marionette-show of ideators around the one sage-figure of antiquity who lived and wrote as a slob, a snob, a prick, an utter fink. Can MacIntyre really accept the Aristotelian view that friendship is a blessing not because we are enabled through it to meet warm, sensitive and funny people but because it helps to cement the social ties of our less attractive fellow-citizens? Can he take so seriously the dictum that it is the function of good government to help make its citizens virtuous—or would he not react as angrily as any bourgeois-liberal or individualist-Marxist to an attempt by government to implant virtues by legislation? Could he actually tolerate a governmental initiative to allocate resources according to the 'just deserts' of individual claimants, particularly when the fluid social teleology he has devised to replace Aristotle's fixed human nature gives no clue to what a just desert might be; nor is it imaginable that a consensual programme of unequal treatment according to desert would go unchallenged (particularly by so rigorous and restless a critic as MacIntyre)? More fundamentally: the virtues, as MacIntyre clearly shows, are a *within-system* ordering of our actions. They need not glorify the actual social and political system that we have, but they can be used to criticise it only from within another system of recognised and established practices. They cannot help us in getting along from one system to another whose practices have yet to be defined. This is why political activism is not a virtue either in Aristotle's or, apparently, in MacIntyre's scheme, and perhaps why activists are so seldom virtuous though they may be useful.

I am tempted, in pondering on Alasdair MacIntyre's journey through polemic, to recall the words of an old American socialist ballad:

> Bill Bailey belonged to every radical party
> That ever came to be
> Till one day he decided
> To start his own party
> So he wouldn't disagree.

In his permanent search for a communitarian focus of moral consensus and allegiance MacIntyre has moved past the narrow terms of the party or sect. He poses rather the construction of larger, even perhaps total forms of social organisation within which practical, moral and political purposes may at last make sense. In the closing paragraphs of *After Virtue* we are bidden to consider that, in the darkness of the present era, the only possible way forward in the immediate future may be in the foundation of 'local forms of community within which civility and the intellectual and moral life can be sustained'. This seems a remarkably good proposal, even though MacIntyre's insistence on a shared basis for moral evaluation will exclude from the membership of these communes a great many utilitarians, existentialists, Marxists, Kantians, Platonists, and plain agnostics or sceptics. Whether after all these bans and proscriptions civility will reign within the walls of such foundations is a matter for conjecture. None but Aristotelians need apply, and even they had better be careful, lest the founder of their virtuous order slopes off at some point of agonised intellectual dissatisfaction.

The reviewer warmly thanks Justin Grossman for his enlivening discussion on certain key points.

SAVILLE'S ROW WITH *THE PENGUIN BOOK OF SPANISH CIVIL WAR VERSE*

Valentine Cunningham

Hostile notices—however maliciously lopsided and carefully wounding—are normally not worth the bother of a reply. Fair-minded readers can be left to arbitrate between the text and the reviewer for themselves. But in the case of John Saville's curiously crude mishandling and venomously wilful misjudging in the last number of the *Socialist Register 1981*, of my 1980 *Penguin Book of Spanish Civil War Verse* some riposte is called for. The more personal insults that Saville feels licensed liberally to sprinkle around —about my so-called paranoia, gormlessness, nasty schoolboyishness, bumbling, ignorance of life, and the rest—I ignore because they are as much beyond rational debate as they are beneath contempt. But Saville does also make serious allegations about careless and/or deliberate distortions of historical fact: and enough of them as to make any standing on dignity in these matters look like an acknowledgement by me that he's proved his points. What's more, the sorts of point about facts and interpretations of fact that Saville raises are also more generally interesting because of what they reveal about the way Thirties' issues are still alive and continuing and about the way ideological assumptions, prejudices, preferences and prescriptions penetrate deeply into all reading and writing of history—even such sturdily confident data-wielding and prejudice-rebutting reading as Saville purports to go in for on this occasion.

One reason, of course, for hesitating to reply to hostile critics is that every sane writer knows full well that his stuff is far from perfect. My Anthology is not spared from being annoyingly shot through with misprints and errors of all sorts that escaped detection at every stage of correction and checking. How on earth, one wonders, did the consistent mis-spelling of MacNeice's name slip through? Or that mis-dating of the battle of Brunete by a year? Or that absurdly wrong assignment to the *Communist Manifesto* of Marx's famous passage about religion as the heart of a heartless world that was quoted in both Auden's and Cornford's poetry? Furthermore, my Introduction carries a number of suggested readings of events that I would now no longer stand by. After all, the Introduction, published with the Anthology in 1980, was actually written in 1975–6, quite a long time ago (the book was an unconscionable time in the printing), which is why I'm not much moved by Saville quoting at me books published thereafter nor uncheerful about admitting I've changed my mind on some issues. I no longer think it even possible, for instance, that Auden paid *two* visits to Spain: Cyril Connolly, I now accept, got his dates mixed up. But there are other speculations, other speculative and slanting readings that I do stand by. And I defend the right to make suggestions, to seek to fill in gaps in the data, to try to detect possibilities between the given lines. Anyway, readers of the past do these things all the time, whether they admit it or not. Saville dislikes flexibility; he wishes to deny the virtue of speculation; he refuses to recognise the possibility of variant readings. So he's particularly irked by my array of 'perhaps', 'not inconceivable', 'one wonders'. He is the kind of historian who claims to know, and believes that the facts, and if not the facts then the implications, are clear. In Cornford's case, he declares, my 'allegations' can be 'disproved by fact', and where the 'facts' are less obvious, as in the case of Pollitt, then 'context' will provide the certitude Saville craves. And being a certitude seeker, Saville can't stand rival readings to his own. When they're offered, he can't bear to discuss them temperately.

Which is odd. For it surely cannot be that Saville is really unaware of how much his own position is only one among several possible, of how his readings are under ideological constraint, nor unaware of the extent to which many of the events and meanings of the Spanish Civil War are open to readings from divergent ideological stances and also frequently subjected to such variant readings. Certainly, after the extraordinary range of political reactions to my Anthology I am left in no doubt that tangling with this war, even if only with the poetry its British participants produced, is to be pushed out into a dangerous ideological cross-fire.

'Although this is supposed to be an anthology of Civil War Verse, every single item is from the left with the exception of an isolated stodgy chunk from Campbell—which is instantly followed by a would-be debunking review of it by Spender.' That is rightist sympathiser Hilary Corke—who even believes 'that the weight of factual evidence is heavily against the supposed nationalist bombing of Guernica'—in the *Listener* (11 September 1980), studiously avoiding defining, naturally, where all the missing rightist poetry might be magicked from. From further right still comes a letter from a Francoist volunteer who fought with Eoin O'Duffy's Irish Christian Front: 'Once again I see a cheap snide remark about O'Duffy's Brigade. I am fed up of these sneers against the men and boys of the brigade. . . I was one of them, an ex-Franciscan Capuchin novice, a boy. . . My religious fervour was strengthened by the sight of churches burned and pillaged. By the sight of destroyed altars, organ lofts, statues and religious paintings. Straw, billies and excrement covered the floor, graffiti marred the walls. Graves of Religious were dug up and the coffins strewn about. . . we were paid Legion rates, fifteen pesetas every five days, about four and five pence. The Reds were drawing between 150 and 200 pesetas a week. Idealism, how are you. . . I am sick to death of the romantic heroes on the Red side and I feel better now I've got this off my chest.' On the other hand, and about as far away politically as you can get from that outburst, Alan Albon warms in the *Anarchist Fortnightly* (1 May, 1981) to what he detects as overlaps between his political preferences and my own:

> In the Autumn of 1980 I came across this book in a bookshop and bought it because I recognised someone on the cover. This man stayed at our house just before he went to Spain as an ambulance driver. He went a Communist sympathiser and had to flee for his life, not from the fascists but the Communists.
>
> From an anarchist point of view the most interesting part of this book is the introduction. . . It is a story of deception and falsification with which we are only too familiar. . . as a history, and to get the feel of the times it is worth reading with a bit of nostalgia for us ageing anarchists with our ageless philosophy.

At least Albon recognises that my Introduction's sympathies lie emphatically with George Orwell, with the POUM and other non-Communist sectaries of the Spanish revolution with whom Orwell fought and sympathised, and on whose behalf *Homage to Catalonia* and the great spate of reviews and letters that accompany it make a polemic—that has never been, in my view, effectively rebutted—for the truth and against persistently lying Stalinist propaganda.

For his part, Saville won't come quite clean. My Introduction manifests a 'Cold War approach', and so it 'ought not to be confused with Orwell's position'. So Orwell's position is worth defending? Well, not quite: 'for the immense scholarly work on Spain and the Civil War in the past quarter of a century has now taken our analysis and our understanding far beyond Orwell's interpretation'. And what that means in practice is that Saville feels enabled—though without actually specifying how and why, and keeping his voice quite low because of the immense prestige Orwell has rightly earned—feels enabled to go right on disbelieving and discrediting the Orwell line on the POUM and Communist dirty-trickery that my Introduction supports. But you can't make approving noises about Orwell in general whilst also defending to the hilt the thirties Communist parties, their leaders like Harry Pollitt, their activists like John Cornford, who supported the arrests and executions of Orwell's kind of friend and who would doubtless have felt little remorse had Orwell himself ended up among the OGPU hit-men's victims. '[E]very night splits, unpopular bosses, and known Fascists are taken for a ride': so John Cornford, writing to Margot Heinemann in August 1936. Only by good luck did Orwell escape with his skin intact when Cornford's Party's definition of 'fascist' widened publicly and violently to embrace the POUM. Saville should make up his mind between Pollitt/Cornford and Orwell.

Because I agree with Orwell and not with his enemies, Saville would like, if possible, in the first place, to prevent me from commenting on any historical events at all. Curiously, for a supposed Marxist, he complains like an old-fashioned bourgeois literateur about the shortage of 'literary discussion', 'literary commentary on the poems themselves' in my Introduction. Pure 'literary commentary', 'literary discussion' solus, 'the poems themselves': my critical theory and practice recognise no such entities, and I'm surprised John Saville should toy with such notions. My Introduction is concerned with the poems, the writings, in context; it is an effort to grant the texts that I print and reprint their necessary historical and political contexts. Saville can't see this. He refuses to admit that every historical and political point made relates directly and continually to writers and the problems of writing in the Thirties and in and about the Spanish Civil War. This helps him repeatedly travesty my analyses. It is obvious to the most casual reader that I'm not trying to write a general history of the Thirties or of the Civil War. But not obvious to Saville. 'His essay', Saville gibes, 'is not a discussion of the impact of the war upon the consciousness, or the conscience, of the British people, or why, when the war broke out in mid-July 1936, it immediately brought together all the fears and the hopes of the anti-fascist movement.' But of course it isn't! It's a discussion of the impact of the war on the minds and hearts of British *writers,* and the way the hopes and fears of anti-fascist *writers* were focused by the war. Saville's phrase 'the fears and the hopes' is lifted, unacknowledged, from my quotation from the autobiography of John Lehmann, novelist, poet and editor of the key literary magazine *New Writing:* 'everything, all our fears, our confused hopes and beliefs. . . veered and converged towards its testing and its opportunity'. That it's the like of John Lehmann I'm concerned with is unevident only to John Saville.

'Cunningham', Saville goes on, 'is mostly concerned with the British Communist Party during the Civil War years and with the attitudes and behaviour of its members.' But, again, no I am not. My Introduction discusses the British Communist Party, but only as its actions touched the lives, deaths and reputations of British writers at the time of the war. It discusses the CP membership, but only insofar as it involved the authors I discuss. Saville's unwillingness to recognise these obvious facts is an important part of his deliberately false picture of me as someone seeking out every last bit of scurrilous gossip and rumour in order to do dirt on Communism. It helps colour his allegation that the witnesses I produce don't count. When, for instance, I bring forward writers who have professed themselves disillusioned politically by their Spanish experiences Saville calls this 'no serious evidence' ('he scrapes up a half dozen or so examples'), because the 'overwhelming majority' of British volunteers, working-men and not writers, didn't get disillusioned.

I actually have my doubts about this kept-up enthusiasm among the majority of volunteers, and Saville would speak less confidently had he actually read Judith Cook's valuable *Apprentices of Freedom* (1979) that he cites in a footnote, shot through as that fine piece of oral history is with disillusioned statements about the conduct of the war, and with notes on volunteers who left the Party after the war. But not for a second do I suggest that the writers I cite stand for all the volunteers. On the contrary, the 'poets' war' myth is one I spend a good deal of space refuting (and not 'in the end', as Saville puts it with his usual misrepresentation, but right at the beginning of my Introduction). But in any discussion like mine, concerned with writers and the war, the professed disillusionments of Orwell, Auden, Spender, Ewart Milne, Miles Tomalin and Jack Lindsay matter immensely. For they, though Saville is the only one blind to this, are the sort of people my Introduction is all about.

I needn't labour the point, but it applies widely to Saville's complaints. So that when he takes me to task in the matter of 'a long discussion of the attitudes to war in general in the 1930s' he's complaining about something that isn't there. I'm only discussing the attitudes prevailing among the young intellectuals and writers that concern my Introduction. And when Saville declares that I 'denigrate the memory of those who fought on the side of the Republic ("many volunteers did have fairly muddy motivations". . .)' he again fails to distinguish the well-documented case that I'm making about intellectuals from a more general case I'm far from making. (Like the editor of *John Cornford: A Memoir,* who cut out Cornford's father's claim that his son was escaping from 'personal responsibilities' in Spain, Saville thus seeks also to blur uncomfortable realities about the intellectuals he cares for.)

It has to be said that Saville does grant, as of course he should, albeit he grants it grudgingly, that 'A literary anthology of the present kind demands a political as well as a literary evaluation' [his old-fashioned 'literary' at work again, one notes]. But Saville quickly makes it clear that any such evaluation must not dare to run on Orwellian lines; it certainly mustn't go counter to Saville's own particular orthodoxies. The CP, Harry Pollitt, the *Daily Worker,* John Cornford, members of the International Brigade, the Stalinist version of the war, must be defended at all costs; no shadow of criticism must ever fall on any part of their memory. Everything must fit Saville's view of the war as the simple, clear-cut anti-fascist crusade that the *Daily Worker* said it was. Nothing, it seems, has detracted, or must detract, from this picture of a simply heroic event. 'Nobility. . . heroism. . . heroism' Saville intones, even though this question of soldierly heroism was exactly the one that troubled thinking socialists in the Twenties and Thirties, and lies at the very centre of unresolved debate among leftist commentators, critics, and writers before, during and after the Spanish war.

At the heart of my Introduction is the major argument that CP propaganda worked, assiduously but misleadingly, to keep the war issues as simple as Saville wants them. Truth, I argue, was cynically wrenched and distorted to suit the CP version of events, on the one hand to make the war look respectable, a bourgeois, writers', artists' and intellectuals' war, and on the other hand to glorify the derring-do of the Communist fighters and the CP-controlled International Brigades at the expense of what looks like the equally undoubted bravery of volunteers and fighters flying non-Communist colours. And Saville fails to meet this argument head on. His efforts at discrediting it merely tinker away futilely at its margins. He has too little to say about my piled-up evidence of the *Daily Worker*'s disregard for accurate reporting. He can only muster a cheap jeer about the style of the opening sentences of my piece 'Neutral? 1930s Writers and Taking Sides', in F. Gloversmith (ed.), *Class Culture and Social Change: A New View of the 1930s* (1980), ignoring the fact that my Anthology's demonstration of the *Daily Worker*'s news manipulation is there followed up by an analysis of how the editors of *Left Review* twisted and wrenched a considerable number of the responses to the *Authors Take Sides on the Spanish War* questionnaire so as to support the desired impression of a massive and cohesive United Front in favour of the Republic among the writers who mattered. Where some manipulation, such as the strange fate of Alex McDade's song 'There's a Valley in Spain', is so obtrusive that even Saville in his role of PR man for the Thirties' CP must comment on it, he tries to laugh it off as of no consequence. The values of the *Daily Worker* he is intent on upholding, however wicked or silly or whatever. When I imply that the CP had little sense of relative literary merits when it disregarded the likes of Cornford and Caudwell but praised Wilfred Macartney as the 'Famous Author', Saville replies that Macartney was indeed 'a well-known author' because his *Walls Have Mouths* was a Left Book Club success. But that was my point. Macartney's sectarian notoriety counted, and counts, for little beside the wider fame of Christopher St John Sprigg's crime stories and air-books, let alone being weighable against the fame of Auden ('Famous Poet to Drive Ambulance in Spain') or of Eric Gill and Henry Moore ('Famous Artists Aid Spain').

And Harry Pollitt, long-time general secretary of the British CP, must be protected from the suggestion—one rooted in a cluster of stories all to the same effect—that he and his Party wanted banner-headline martyrs for the cause (in the words he's said to have said to Spender, 'Go out and get killed, comrade, we need a Byron in the movement'). As my Introduction clearly states, a number of these tales have the ring of apocrypha. Some of them crumble as you probe them. When I wrote to A.L. Rowse, asking him to let me see the evidence that he alleges in *A Cornishman at Oxford* (1965) that he has for his declarations about Ralph Fox's worsening relations with the Party—I was interested too in evidence for Rowse's assertion that Fox 'was ordered to Spain by the Party which wanted martyrs for the cause'—I got no reply. What's more, I'm impressed by what Tom Wintringham's sister, Mrs. M. Penning-Rowsell, has written to me: 'it seems to me that the story of Harry Pollitt suggesting that my brother Tom should go and get killed must really be apocryphal. Harry Pollitt was very fond of Tom, and if there is any foundation for his remark it was probably caused by extreme exasperation with Kitty (not then married to Tom). She certainly had that effect on people, and had been asked to leave Spain by the Republican authorities.' Nonetheless it is the case that Pollitt himself lent a certain life to the stories by his contribution to *Ralph Fox: A Writer in Arms* (1937), ed. John Lehmann, T.A. Jackson and C. Day Lewis, which does (p. 6) actually claim that Fox was a latter-day Byron. 'The great poet Byron went to Greece to fight for liberty; in a later period Comrade Brailsford fought for liberty in Greece; these are the examples our British comrades are following today in the conditions of our time.' 'I recall to you', Pollitt winds up, 'the words of the poet Byron: "Still Freedom yet, thy banner torn but flying. . ." ' Byron twice in a single page! He does seem to have been rather on Pollitt's mind. But this is a piece of my Introduction's evidence Saville just ignores, preferring instead a gush of rhetoric on the subject of my supposed smears.

In any case, whatever I thought of Pollitt and Byron, I myself would not try, as Saville does, to whitewash Pollitt with a sentence of praise garnered from the revised edition of John Gunther's *Inside Europe* (October 1936). To be sure Gunther thought well of Pollitt and the sentence Saville quotes ran through several *Inside Europe* editions until it got abruptly dropped in the February 1940 War Edition. But Gunther also thought well of Stalin and *Inside Europe* provides one of the most embarrassing washes of naive Stalin hagiography to be found anywhere in the Thirties. 'Stalin. . . one of the very greatest. . . In speeches. . . addressed by ordinarily uneffusive folk as "Our Best Collective Farmer Worker", "Our Shockworker", "Our Best of Best", and "Our Darling, Our Guiding Star". . . Guts. Durability. Physique. . . Patience. Tenacity. Concentration. . . Shrewdness. Cunning. Craft. . . Sense of Detail. This is very great. . . Ability to handle men. . . Zeal.' And so on (I quote from the same edition as Saville quotes). It's not the kind of prose to recommend anybody as a percipient judge of political character. (And this regrettable tosh lasted longer than the sentence about Pollitt: Gunther went so far as to polish up the style of this Stalin purple for the War Edition.)

If I were John Saville I'd also dwell on the implications of what Judith Cook's *Apprentices of Freedom* reveals about Harry Pollitt's activities in Spain. What was he after if not another dead hero to the CP's credit when he persuaded Fred Copeman, 'nearly dying in Spain', to join the

Party? 'Harry Pollitt came to see me and said it would be a bloody tragedy if I died without joining' (Cook, p. 26). And what about Pollitt's key role in the British Party's repeated efforts at suppressing and containing what seem now like legitimate protests, foot-draggings and the wish to go home among some of the frequently tired, scared and fed-up International Brigaders? 'Not surprisingly', says Sid Quinn about the Jarama (Cook, p. 74) 'we got some deserters after that battle, and blokes who'd lost morale. There was a wee bit of agitation, and I remember Harry Pollitt came out and, man, were we naive, but he moved us. What we really needed was guns, but he spoke to us, and what a speaker! The best I've bloody heard in my life. He'd bring tears to a glass eye.' Like Will Paynter, kept continually busy in 1937 at the task of making discontented volunteers happy, or Arthur Horner, joining Paynter in the effort to staunch a spate of desertions at Brunete (Cook, pp. 53–55), Pollitt was clearly no simplistic, nor even unjesuitical rhetor. He *was* slippery, as my Introduction alleges.

Saville can't, he says, detect the 'slippery contradictions' in Pollitt's Introduction to *David Guest: A Memoir* (1939). He invites me to explain the slipperiness. Hardly necessary, I'd have thought, since he does give his readers in full the Pollitt passage I was alluding to:

> David Guest and men of similar type would not have us be unmindful of those hundreds of other young men, labourers, dockers, railwaymen, engineers, clerks, seamen, miners and textile workers who have also made the supreme sacrifice. Men whose family circumstances make it impossible for any special Memoirs to be published about them, but who were David's comrades in life, in arms and in death, and to whose immortal memory this volume is as great a tribute as it is to those from the public schools and universities.

Are these words not, Saville asks, 'a principled statement, a reminder to the movement he was addressing that it was the working-class volunteers who were the overwhelming part of the British volunteers, and that most of them would remain unknown and uncommemmorated to later generations?' But I'm afraid I can't read it this way. For a start Saville's 'unknown and uncommemmorated' surprise me: for Pollitt is claiming precisely that the working volunteers *are* being memorialised. But it's the whole movement of the passage's thought that seems to me devious. Pollitt is slippery, in fact, in the extreme, because, whilst he makes those obligatory, warming noises about the merits of the mass of working-class volunteers who are not going to get a special memoir, he (a) gives the Imprimatur of the CP of Great Britain to a volume which for all those professed worries about the 'immortal memory' of the proletarian volunteers is actually largely, if not exclusively, concerned with the immortal memory of the graduate, well-connected volunteer, David Guest, and so shows up his concern for the ordinary volunteer as limited and opportunistically bogus, and (b) because he tries to pretend that this memoir devoted to Guest can, by dint of some manoeuvre, implication, stretch of the imagination too recessive and unclear for me at any rate to spot, manage to be 'as great a tribute' to the poorly-connected, un-bourgeois, socially undistinguished as it is to the likes of Guest (those from the public schools and universities'): which is pathetically misguided and misleading rubbish.

I hope that analysis goes some way towards helping John Saville see what I mean by slippery. I'm not confident it will. For he can't even see what difference the second version of the Jarama Song makes ('what a trivial business it all is, or should be'). The grumbling, the wry discontent, the sly ironies of Alex McDade's song about growing neglectedly old in the Jarama front line—as authentic a soldier's grumble it seems to me as the song G.S. Fraser included in his story 'An Incident of the Campaign', in *Seven*, No. 1 (summer 1938), pp. 11–18; 'O, all you fine rebels, whose guns go rantan, /I am a poor sod of a Government man'—McDade's grousing Saville finds discountable because it's not vehement or crude enough for his taste in soldier's songs (no ' "fuck" and "shit" and "balls" '). And the simplistic hero-mongering ('fought like true sons of the people', 'brave comrades fell', 'our glorious dead') into which the song got revised doesn't offend him because that's just how John Saville himself thinks of the war.

Admittedly, the Jarama Song is a problem. No one appears to know exactly when and by whom and in what stages it was revised. As one who is more persuaded by the unheroic notes sounded by Spanish War participants and observers I certainly experienced something of a shock when I recently watched veteran International Brigaders walking along a Spanish road singing some of the revised version for the benefit of BBC-TV cameras. Clearly one has to defer somewhat to veteran Dave Goodman's witness (in a letter to me)—though I'm still curious as to when the revised version's last verse about standing for our glorious dead 'before we continue this meeting', hardly the sentiments of any kind of marching song, got itself into the picture. Goodman writes:

> It was in January 1938 that I arrived in Spain and February 1939 that I returned home. During that time 'Valley of Jarama' was a song much sung by International Brigaders but the only version I ever heard was the later one. It was much later, after my return to England, and with some surprise, that I encountered the original version. Your explanation of the second version ('. . . transformed by Party hacks into a slogan–laden celebration') is very wide of the mark indeed. . . The fact that by the time of my arrival in Spain a new version was being sung reflected the change in the situation since Jarama. The original version directly related to the experience of those who fought at Jarama, including Alex McDade. The later version, with few exceptions, was sung by those like me for whom the conduct of the International Brigaders at Jarama was an inspiration and part of the tradition inherited by those of us who came later. Who wrote it I do not

know but there is no reason to think that the memory of Alex McDade was in any way traduced by it or that his widow's feelings were callously disregarded.

Goodman also points out—as does Saville—that it is most unfair on the Communist Party that I did not mention that William Rust reprinted the original song in all its 'humorous cynicism' (a phrase Rust borrowed from *The Book of the XV Brigade* whence he derived the Song), and reprinted it in his *Britons in Spain: A History of the British Battalion of the XVth International Brigade* (Lawrence and Wishart, 1939) which was the more or less official CP account (and which, by the way, gives thanks for 'the valuable assistance and advice of Harry Pollitt who. . . for two years devoted himself with unfailing energy and devotion to the needs of the volunteers and the care of their dependents'). I accept the particular criticism. I should have pointed out Rust's reprinting of the Song. Doing so, however, would not have altered my case. When I pursued the matter, which of course began in a reading of Weintraub's *The Last Great Cause* (1968) but, despite Saville's repeated insistence that I've merely quoted Weintraub, goes much further in documentation than Weintraub even begins to, my worries over the Party's preference for the unquestioned heroising of the second version of the song got larger, and so did my hostility towards one more clear set of instances of the *Daily Worker*'s customary slight regard for the truth in its repeated statements that the revised, and in my view damagingly travestied, version was the one McDade himself actually wrote at the Jarama. My annoyance is as strong as ever. I certainly cannot agree with Saville that the affair is of no moment, nor with Dave Goodman that McDade's memory was not being cheerfully traduced.

Likewise, though I'm certainly prompted by Saville's protests into admitting that there may have been occasional overstatements in and about my Introduction's dealing with John Cornford, I stand by the broad outlines of a story that I still think observers less biased than Saville won't be able to help agreeing with. Saville huffs and puffs, but there is plenty of room for my suggestion that the Party was extremely worried about Cornford's passing—of course passing, and I have never suggested otherwise—association with the POUM. I have no doubt that this association of Cornford's *was* disquieting to Pollitt and the Party. Cornford was, after everything that he'd seen of the POUM and despite the political caveats he wasn't chary of spelling out (some of them, in the 'Diary Letter from Aragon', I reprint in my Anthology), still set on returning to fight with his old POUM unit. The crucial letter to his Cambridge tutor—'by the time this reaches you I shall already be on my way to rejoin the unit of the Anti-Fascist Militia with which I have been fighting this summer'—was written on 4 October 1936, the very eve of his departure for Spain, via Paris. The letter shows no knowledge of the new

CP plan for an International Column of foreign volunteers. Cornford had been busily recruiting Communists for the POUM. (How, by the way, can Saville say that I make 'no reference at all' to this 'volunteer group formed by Cornford', when I clearly state that Cornford was aiming to return 'to the same POUM militia, *with others* who would provide an exemplary stiffening in the ranks'?) So I'm not at all surprised that Harry Pollitt appears to have been reluctant to take Cornford entirely into his confidence. The Communist worries about his active POUM associations, associations which only ceased when he arrived in Paris and threw in his lot with the new International Column, are sufficiently manifest in Tom Wintringham's disingenuous efforts in his *English Captain* (1939) to reduce their extent and significance. Saville doesn't refer at all to my evidence from *English Captain*. No wonder, for Wintringham's embarrassing blend of distortion and character assassination stands unrebuttably there, in print. Nor does Saville mention the footnote that Pat Sloan, the Communist, Left Book Club author and Stalinising Russophile who edited *John Cornford: A Memoir*, added to Cornford's report on 'The Situation in Catalonia'. He added it in fact to the passage that Saville quotes, where Cornford is dismissing the political threat of the POUM despite the presence in it of such a magnetic leader as the miner Grossi, 'sincere and courageous revolutionary' ('even brave and intelligent leaders like Grossi are incapable of giving their troops proper political, military, or organisational training'). Sloan's footnote interrupts such reflections sternly: 'The optimism of these remarks concerning the Anarchists and the POUM seem [sic] to be the only particular in which John Cornford's judgment erred. It was precisely the penetration of Fascists into these organisations—noted by J.C.—that made possible the Barcelona uprising of May 1937.'

Evidently what Saville calls Cornford's 'understanding and analysis of POUM' was not sufficiently (in Saville's words) 'abundantly clear' for the Party. Strangely, this footnote is omitted from Jonathan Galassi's reprint of Cornford's Political Report in *Understand the Weapon, Understand the Wound: Selected Writings of John Cornford* (1976). Is that why Saville makes so much of Galassi's volume? ('Cunningham does not appear to know the Galassi volume': not so; it came to hand after I'd written my Introduction, and didn't add anything I wanted—indeed in the case of that footnote it actually left important things out—so I judged it not worth fussing to include.)

Instead, though, of calmly confronting these problems Saville prefers bluster. Characteristically, when I observe that the *Daily Worker* appears to have been slow to report Cornford's death, Saville rants on about my ignorance of battlefield mess, chaos, uncertainty. If he had read a bit more, he might perhaps be less certain about that uncertainty. It is particularly striking to me, not only how tightly organised the

International Brigades were, but also—and this has become even more noticeable since the publication of Judith Cook's book, and Richard Felstead's *No Other Way: Jack Russia and the Spanish Civil War* (Port Talbot, 1981) and *The Road To Spain: Anti-Fascists at War 1936–1939,* ed. D. Corkill and S. Rawnsley (Dunfermline, 1981)—how much the ordinary working-class British volunteers were conscious of the reputation, doings and whereabouts of their more notable and glamorous bourgeois comrades: men like Ralph Fox, 'very dashing' in his 'black beret, black leather coat and large revolver', and Cornford 'a real romantic type, six foot tall. . . like a bloody Greek god' (Cook, p. 43). And it happens that (as Saville adds in a late footnote) Cornford, this most prominent of volunteers, made more prominent still by a white bandage about his head ('he looked like Lord Byron'), was actually seen to die by Walter Greenhalgh. 'We wait and wait and finally John Cornford climbs up to the brow of the hill to look over and the early sun catches his white bandage and that was it. He got one straight through the head' (Cook, p. 41). Knowing that now, helps me keep on wondering why the *Daily Worker* delayed in noticing his death. At any rate, I need more than Saville's free-ranging blah about the battle conditions of Cornford's tragic slaughter to put a stop to my speculations.

But then why, I wonder, this curious intensity of Saville's in his tenacious trawl through my dealings with the Cornford record? It can't be that he really thinks my Introduction 'traduced the memory of a young Communist intellectual', for it's evident that what I was trying to do was rescue Cornford from what I see as his uncomradely traducers in the Communist Party. I can understand, though I cannot altogether sympathise with Saville's efforts on behalf of Harry Pollitt's reputation: they're the patent result of Saville's ideological preference for Thirties' Communism against its critics. But his interventions on behalf of what he believes to be Cornford's good name, interventions made at every possible point, however minor or nearly inconsequential, sound like something more than a simple case of ideology. And, of course, they are. For I've had his package of Cornford objections, down to their last finickingly petty details, made to me before.

There's the objection to my laying stress on the alteration of Cornford's 'party' to 'Party' in the poem 'Full Moon at Tierz' when it appeared in the *Memoir,* and to my wondering whether the 'Anarchist workers' kept Cornford's poem 'A Letter from Aragon' out of Spender and Lehmann's anthology *Poems for Spain* (slight points that become more impressive when set alongside the whole raft of more obvious political doctorings of poems that I refer to in my Introduction in a footnote to the McDade affair, pp. 77–8: evidence like the change of the Donagh MacDonagh's line about Charles Donnelly, 'Something has been gained by this mad missionary' to 'Time will remember this militant visionary', that Saville omits to mention, much as he wrongly declares I haven't informed my readers about the journey of the poem 'A Letter from Aragon', Anarchist worker and all, through the Communist edited pages of the *Left Review* and the Cornford *Memoir*). There's the meal that's made about my re-printing Cornford's 'Diary Letter from Aragon' at a place in my Anthology a few pages after two letters that were actually written after it was ('slap-dash editing', Saville calls it, and confusing to readers: but my Anthology isn't a chronologically arranged gathering of material; the letters are set out unchronologically because I wanted to cluster together material with place-names massively prominent in their titles or contents, Cornford's 'A Letter from Aragon' leading on to his 'Diary Letter from Aragon', which leads into a place-name obsessed portion of H.B. Mallalieu's 'Poem in Spring', leading on to Jacob Bronowski's 'Guadalajara', Cornford's 'Full Moon at Tierz', John Lepper's 'Battle of Jarama 1937', and so on; the letters are unmisleadingly dated; and nothing political is lost or gained by these letters' present positioning). And there's even the objection to including Cornford in a list of Thirties' leftists who shed or altered names with obvious bourgeois connotations when they went over to the workers' side: in this case, Rupert John Cornford's Rupert.

Rupert did undeniably get dropped, Saville agrees, but too early in Cornford's life to count as a politically conscious move: 'everyone knows' he 'was always called John'. But not everyone did know that. I for one did not. I'm glad to be informed. So that while I'm sorry John Saville seems to think the important process of bourgeois socialists seeking to disguise and change their identities by changes of name doesn't matter, and in particular that the pervasive problematic of names among Thirties' writers doesn't touch Cornford (he who published a poem under the name 'Dai Barton' and whose intransigent forename John is made to feature memorably at the beginning of Margot Heinemann's fine poem 'For R.J.C. (Summer, 1936)', a title by the way in which R. if not Rupert still seems to be in play—'No, not the sort of boy for whom one does/Find easily nicknames, Tommy and Bill'), I am nonetheless happy to accept the testimony of Cornford's close friends in this one matter.

It must, though, be stressed that it is the witness of Cornford's close friends; at least of his close friends. For the place where I've seen Saville's Cornford points before, and in almost every particular, large and small, serious and trite, is in the ten pages of notes on my Anthology made by Margot Heinemann, who sent me a xeroxed copy of them. Margot Heinemann is, of course, the beloved whom Cornford sadly left behind him when he was so regrettably cut off in his beginning prime as a poet. Saville's piece is largely, as the repeated coincidences between it and Margot Heinemann's Notes reveals, a put-up job.

One has to respect the natural desire of families and friends to protect the name and memory of a dead loved one. But the record of the protective efforts of dead writers' families and friends is not at all encouraging. They have often been extremely unhelpful. Cassandra Austen destroyed her sister's letters; Mrs. Richard Burton burnt her husband's papers; the second Mrs. George Orwell obstructed Orwell's biographers; the second Mrs. T.S. Eliot has been exceedingly touchy towards critics and over-protective towards her late husband's papers. Relicts have frequently not been the best custodians of the record, nor the best interpreters of it. So when John Saville made use of Margot Heinemann's Notes, especially in such extraordinary detail, he should have done more than acknowledge her help in an isolated footnote. His readers are entitled to know the extent to which his readily detectable set of ideological positions has been afforced by the special pleadings of highly sensitive and necessarily not always objective personal interestedness.

At one point in her annoyed correspondence with me, when she was urging me to get the Cornford letters reprinted 'in their proper order', Margot Heinemann said 'I suppose I could withdraw permission if you didn't'. She did add that 'that seems rather a silly way to resolve the issue': but the threat had slipped out. Thoughts of nobbling cross Saville's mind as well. When he declares that my Anthology is 'a disgrace' to its publishers, he is implying they ought not to keep it in print. So that he writes not only to wound but also with intent to ban; he shoots with, as it were, intent to kill off the author and also his book. This is exactly (comparing small things with great) what the party and/or Party of Margot Heinemann and John Saville tried to do to Orwell and his displeasing Spanish writings. If their party/Party had had its way Orwell would have been shot and his book and articles not written or, once written, not published. Equally, when Saville tries to drive a wedge between my (to him) unacceptable Introduction and the (to him) more acceptable anthologised materials that follow it, he's wielding the same scissors as the leftist critics who persuaded the Left Book Club to lop off the offendingly personal second part of Orwell's *The Road to Wigan Pier.* And when Saville tries to turn my un-Communistic but leftwards-turned Introduction and Anthology into 'Cold-War' anti-socialism he's trying the old Thirties' act, whose treachery Orwell's writings did much to expose, of labelling all critics of Communist orthodoxies 'objectively' Gestapo-fascist or whatever. The result of that, in the Thirties as now, is a loss not just to the cause of truth and of my kind of socialism but to Saville's own cause as well. For we are both, I take it, united against the real traducers of John Cornford, the real detractors from his art, people such as Hilary Corke (in the *Listener* review I cited earlier) who chooses Cornford's 'Full Moon at Tierz' as the basis for a slashing bout of jeers and sneers against Cornford, Cornford's poetry, his politics, that particular poem, people like me who like it, the Spanish resistance to fascism, and ends up praising Francophiliac Evelyn Waugh as the soundest man around in

English Letters of the Thirties. Attacking me, John Saville lets his real opponents get clean away with almost everything.

But so in the Spanish War period did the people Saville tries so utterly to defend. He berates me for implying that the Spanish issues, the Thirties' issues, are over. I agree; I did exaggerate the extent ot which they belong to *Another Country* from our own. One has only to observe his unembarrassed continuation of old Thirties' arguments, his redeployment of the basest Thirties' polemical tactics, to see how right he is: at least in that.

JEREMY SEABROOK AND THE BRITISH WORKING CLASS

Huw Beynon

The subjectivity of the working class forms a central part of all Marxist political economy, and all political groups and parties of the Left claim some access to it; many claim to speak with its voice. Yet the texture of working class experience is something which is rarely questioned. In political and theoretical discourse, working class life is, most often, sloganised or interpreted through highly formalistic and simplified frameworks. These frameworks rarely take issue with the daily lives and felt experience and ideas of people. The value of Jeremy Seabrook's books lies in the access they provide to the complexity of working class life; to the importance of language, nuance and metaphor; to the awareness they demonstrate of historical shift in sensibilities and the importance of this for political and social change. Yet his view is also flawed.

In his most recent book–*Unemployment*[1]–Seabrook is ostensibly concerned to offer direct comparisons of how working people experienced unemployment in two economic recessions–the 1930s and the 1980s. He does this on the basis of visits to Sunderland, Bolton and Birmingham where, by way of several lengthy interviews, the reporting of casual conversation, and observations made on streets, in people's homes and on visits to community and unemployment centres he builds up a powerful and disturbing anthology of sadness and pain. In Bolton, he talked with a Mr Travis who started work in the Worsley Mesnes pit when he was thirteen; and he was soon to experience unemployment for the first time:

> They just stopped the pit, closed it. There was my father, me and my brother working there. We'd all done a full week, and they announced Friday at one o'clock that the pit was closing. They left everything behind, all the machinery, even the coal we'd been cutting that week. They just cut the ropes left it where it was. . . It was my first taste of the dole. You had to go to the chapel to sign on then. On Fridays the dole queue stretched right along the road, five or six deep, and they'd keep up standing there until nine o'clock at night, and even then you wouldn't get paid. You had to start again on Saturday morning.

Adrian Colquhoun lives in the same town and worked as an electric arc welder. A different job from the pits. Working for a big company that recognised trade unions, that had procedures and shop stewards. But in 1980, he too learned about unemployment and the dole:

> A year before we were made redundant, we were all told the jobs were safe. We got an agreement that if there was anybody to go, it'd be through natural wastage; then it became voluntary redundancy; then the last-in-first-out principle. But when it came to it, it really meant getting rid of all those they didn't like. They got rid of the shop stewards first; they do that, then they can do as they like with the rest of the workforce. . . The damage that's being done to skills, the work-people who've done their apprenticeships, who've acquired the experience—what a waste. They blame the workpeople for everything. . . they actually blame the workers for all the inefficiencies of capitalism, and people believe it. People don't usually blame themselves, they blame each other. Work has become so divided, it's the car workers', unless you're a car worker, the miners' fault, unless you work in the pits, the steelworkers' fault if you don't happen to be a steel worker, it's the blue-collar workers if you're a white collar worker and workers in general if you're not one (p. 184).

And for all of them, increasingly, unemployment and a reliance upon 'the dole' is a threat that hangs over them and their way of life.

In 1936, Rowntree did a survey of unemployment which was aimed at establishing the physical 'minimum requirements' for people out of work. His conclusions were frugal by any standards, and have often been contrasted with the more generous principles which underlie the distribution of benefit under the welfare state. In 1981, however, one economist, David Piachaud, returned to Rowntree's statistics. Fifty years earlier, the weekly requirements for a man, woman and three children was priced at forty shillings and five pence; the modern equivalent (given inflation) would be £44.55. Piachaud commented:

> The current supplementary benefit provision for an unemployed family of this size is £56.50 per week. Thus allowing for inflation, the dole now provides. . . only one quarter more than is needed for Rowntree's minimum requirements.[2]

So, in a real way, Mr Travis and Adrian Colquhoun live in the same world still. And in the Midlands, the North East and North West, Seabrook provides ample evidence of this. Through his detailed accounts we hear of women who allow their families the 'luxuries' of streaky bacon and Penguin biscuits and of men who worry more and more as the day arrives to sign on again ('you always get nervous. . .'); of people eating out of dustbins, and of whole families being clothed out of jumble sales; of the havoc that's wrought by the non-arrival of a giro, and the intolerable pressures that unemployment places upon personal relationships, particularly amongst the chronically sick and disadvantaged. Yet if anything, these accounts of material deprivation are understated and subordinated to Seabrook's wider purpose which is to point to a deeper *spiritual* loss accompanying the changes that have taken place since the war. These changes, he insists, are of 'epic' dimensions and have left the poor bereft of social support, with nothing to buffer them from the tyranny of the market place and the bureaucratic insensitivity (near brutality) of the 'caring' agencies of the state. His account is one which tells of 'the deep, hidden price that has been paid for the improvements that working class people have seen' (p. 220). As he puts it: 'nothing can express too strongly the sense of injury that has been done to the people' (p. 64).

The account which *Unemployment* offers of the post-war period is of economic expansion in which workers once 'excluded from the benefits of capitalist production', have emerged in, 'a state of captive dependence upon them' (p. 3). Successive generations have found themselves, 'at the mercy of values and definitions shaped by the market place' (p. 35), and with this has come, 'loss and inconstancy, defection and the breaking of bonds between people' (p. 86). At its worst it has involved, 'the amputated capacity to care' (p. 160), as working class life became little more than the 'strident hymning of commodities' (p. 221). Throughout, the warning issued by Richard Hoggart in 1957 is never far from the surface. In *The Uses of Literacy,*[3] Hoggart remarked that in the post-war period, changes were taking place that were, 'tending to cause the working class to lose culturally much that has been valuable and to gain less than their new situation should have allowed'. In demonstrating the extent of this loss, Seabrook calls upon the evidence of the nineteenth century:

> When E.P. Thompson wrote of the opacity of working class culture, its dense and guarded richness, its well defined complexity and secrecy in the face of capitalist oppression, he might well have been writing about the reverse of what confronts us now. It is the hallucinating display of capitalism that offers an appearance of opaque richness, and the drained working class, transparent as crystal now, gives back increasingly only the reflection of an alien and manufactured diversity. The young see their own reflections in the shop windows, and they haunt the malls and precincts. . . express(ing) the disinheritance of the working class (p. 104).

And we have all connived in this disinheritance. Parents, concerned to give their children a 'good start in life, the best of everything', have 'done something to them which they never anticipated' (p. 144). 'The left' too is culpable. It remained silent, particularly during the sixties, and refused to expand political demands beyond the economic level, thinking that the problem 'could be cured by money, while money is the root cause of it' (p. 101). On top of this there has been a 'collective silence between capital. . . and the representatives of the working class on the price that has been paid' (p. 40). And in Seabrook's mind, in this transaction, 'we have indeed been robbed, and of things beyond price' (p. 92).

This, then, is the 'epic change', a change in which 'the values of the minority. . . have become the norm—the improvident, the self-seeking; while the generosity and the sharing have been eclipsed' (p. 65). And in

Seabrook's view, the consequences are dire indeed for:

> this new condition of the working class is not going to lead to socialism. Socialism could have been an organic expression of the way in which people lived and worked together; why it failed to emerge is a subject of almost infinite conjecture and debate. But one thing is sure: we shan't build socialism out of those values now, out of that endurance and frugality, out of that pride and solidarity. The moment has passed (p. 222–3).

This is powerful stuff, it resonates with talk and discussion in the labour movement especially when old and young meet together. In this, the book belies its title, for is not a treatise on unemployment, but a moral judgment on our time and one which Seabrook has argued for ten years or more. It is one which needs to be thought through and answered.

In attempting this, it is useful to begin with the theme which Seabrook's writings return to repeatedly: that of a working class culture in 'the past', and of a 'sense of loss' which is felt and articulated in lengthy testimony by people who were born before 1930. These testimonies undoubtedly exist, and there is real substance in Seabrook's belief that the very fact that these statements are given at all (that *these* old people at *this* time want to speak) is support in itself for the view that the world of the working class has changed in quite a fundamental way. It is difficult for example, to read through the publications of a group like Centreprise,[4] and escape the feeling that in their accounts of contemporary and pre-war life, we are learning about quite different working classes. In the North East of England too. A more isolated area than the East End of London and perhaps more culturally stable but there the sense of change has also been pronounced. In 1979, for example, the *Strong Words* publishing group produced a collection of accounts of 'changing times on the Durham coalfield'.[5] The booklet was discussed in a meeting at the Town Hall in Crook, a small town in the South West of the country. Before the war several pits had operated in the locality, feeding the local coke works, and coal was a dominant industry in the town through the nineteen sixties. Today the pits remain in memory only, and in pubs old men will crawl under tables and chairs explaining to 'strangers' how they had to work to dig the coal out of the Ballerat seam: 'the best coking coal in the world'. At the meeting, a dialogue developed and during it one young man said this: 'We can see from the way the older ones talk about your lives, that you have something to feel proud of. But what have us younger ones got to be proud of? We've nothing like that.'

All this is grist to Seabrook's mill, and so it's time to introduce a cautionary note, beginning with some of the problems caused by his method of analysis. In talking of 'the past' we are faced with questions of *time* and *place*, and here Seabrook's account is highly generalised and unspecific. He writes, for example, of a working class culture that has existed for 'a couple of centuries or so' and seems unwilling to contemplate other changes over this period when people have expressed equally intense feelings of loss. Furthermore, he presents his account as having *universal* significance. He pays no attention to important regional variations in class experience within Britain (in fact, almost all of Seabrook's work relates to *England*), and more significantly, sees the experience of dispossessed Jamaican peasants 'precisely parallel' to that of the British working class since the war. The story he constructs is of unremitting tragedy. It is an account of near-total cultural decay and as it unfolds (with the religious metaphor always near at hand) it takes on powerful metaphysical qualities. These qualities are given free rein by the nature of the material through which the argument is developed.

Seabrook's work relies entirely upon subjective accounts, and in *Unemployment* he builds his argument around a mixture of carefully worded, tape-recorded testimony and noted observation of spontaneous comment and interaction. Each equally valid, but very different from each other. For example, old men in their homes with their families around them tend not to swear; young men with their mates do so incorrigibly and obscenely. The contrast, in print, is a graphic one, yet only rarely does Seabrook warn the reader of the problem of interpretation. Mostly the accounts are left to stand side by side, heightening (in a way which is not legitimate) the sense of change, and leaving the impression that much of the material is included for its shock qualities. All this raises questions about the *purpose* of the account.

Jeremy Seabrook is, above all else, a child of Richard Hoggart. It is to Hoggart he turns, repeatedly, for his models of class culture and for his politics. It was Hoggart, remember, who argued in 1957 that the reforming minority of political activists had an obligation to the past; an obligation to preserve a culture that was being sold behind the backs of those who were less aware. It is toward this 'active minority' that Seabrook directs his writing. In an earlier book he wrote of Labour Party activists who were 'increasingly isolated from the working class they aim to serve'.[6] These people he feels are 'living in the past', and in *Unemployment*, he criticises their 'defiant optimism', and their insistence upon 'keeping faith' with a vision of social change and the working class which had a place in the nineteenth century but is no more. His accounts of working class life are meant to bring such people down to earth. And here the familiar comparison with Orwell takes an intriguing twist. In the 1930s, Orwell too was concerned to shock the middle class; his aim was to show them how wretched were the lives endured by workers whose energies were at the very foundation of society. Seabrook, in contrast, details how wretched are the workers themselves, and how their lives have come to perpetuate the capitalist order. With such a purpose, it's not surprising that the overwhelming impression created by the book is of *hopelessness.*

Occasionally, in *Unemployment,* the reader is directed beyond the immediate subjective experience and towards the overarching pattern of change. And here the central preoccupation is with 'consumerism' and of a humanity overwhelmed and debased in the shop window. Seabrook quotes an old woman from Sheffield saying: 'working class people used to be proud of how much they could do with very little money; now people feel ashamed of how little they can do without a lot of it' (p. 3), and it is impossible to deny the poignancy of these words. So too with many other of the allusions made to the dominance of consumerism and the market place in the pages of *Unemployment.* The effect of advertising, of branding and the hard sell upon the structure of wants—particularly amongst the young—*is* disturbing; doubly so, given the way in which this abundance exists in a world where the threat of sickness, famine and violent death predominates. But to say this is not to solve the problem. 'Consumerism' (its nature and effects) needs to be outlined and interpreted, and in this Seabrook demonstrates a view of 'culture' and change which is highly mechanical. The new 'consumer culture' is seen as a *direct* product of the market place, obliterating, near totally, all traces of earlier cultural forms. As he puts it: 'The working class has been gutted of most of its substance and a dependence upon commodities has been substituted for it' (p. 8). In an earlier, more affluent time, he had written:

> There is no longer any need to fear the loyalty and commitment of the working class to capitalism because of the spread of consumerism: the middle class moved out great encircling pseudopodia and clutched a substantial part of the working class in its embrace.[7]

Here too Hoggart has a deep influence. As he once wrote of a working class trapped in 'the hypnosis of immature emotional satisfaction'[8] so does Seabrook refer to the market becoming a 'substitute for everything. . . morality, beliefs, philosophy of life, and, above all, a consolation, a soft self-indulgent solace for having no other reason for living'.[9] Viewed in this way (through the severe, near absolute, standards of this English tradition) the mass market and its products (automatic cameras, video, electronic games, calculators. . .) are totally dismissed as 'ugly implants' in people's lives. No attempt is made to consider the possibility of such products facilitating forms of imaginative and cultural development. The fact that story-telling revolves around robots, machines and space exploration (around manufactured and not spiritual/mystical themes) is seen as sufficient evidence to dismiss them as worthless. Nowhere is an attempt made to work with ideas of cultural renewal or with the importance of new inventive forms within the class. While he draws upon Raymond Williams' notion of 'the structure of feeling', the usage is cursory and the influence of Williams ends with this citation.[10] We are left with a view of the working class which gives no place to popular culture as an imminent, dynamic form and this elitist adjudication of cultural practice weighs heavily upon the account.

While Seabrook recognises that many of the 'consumerist' wants are real needs (a part of the new structure of life where council estates have high cost central heating and where public transport—or its absence—made a car a prerequisite for getting to work) he underestimates people's abilities to share his understanding. He underestimates too the extent to which, in these changed and often hostile circumstances, patterns of caring, acts of charity and kindliness still survive. For example, while local collections are taking place all over Britain to subsidise particular or general inadequacies in the National Health Service (providing bionic hands and body scanners. . .) Seabrook expresses surprise that beggars receive money in the poor streets of Birmingham. In all, his antipathy to 'consumerism' produces a view of the working class which is lacking in compassion and borders on contempt. Ten years ago (and with some prophetic quality) he said this:

> If this present generation of consumers become an economic archaism like their grandparents, it is impossible not to wonder if they too will be stranded in old age, croaking like ancient children over the tawdry toys which they have been trained carefully to enjoy.[11]

In *Unemployment* his question is answered:

> The sense of shabbiness in the house of today's poor is different from that shabbiness of the houses of the old poor. . . The Rexine splits and the bright ornaments of only two or three years ago look worn—the opalescent punch set with its coral plastic cups hanging round the bowl, are dyed red grasses, the glass fish, the storm lamp with its panels of frosted plastic. The gauzy runner across the sideboard becomes inextricably dingy; the picture of the Creation of Adam and Eve looking like Tarzan and Jane, she up to her navel in water, seems to lose its colour; the electronic games from Texas don't work; the instrument assembled in Taiwan has fallen to pieces. . . Everything in these poor homes now is provisional and impermanent; not homes at all many of them, but places of brief sojourn in which everybody seems to be on a list waiting for transfer. Places it seems into which violence and cruelty can easily gain admittance; where parents, helpless and impotent can easily strike the screaming child; where the fragility of relationships between adults seems to mirror the lack of durability of all the used-up objects in the house; and people wear out their love for each other as readily as they do last year's fashions. And the story they tell about who moved in with some woman in the next block, whose husband pissed off with some tart he picked up down the club, who left her old man because he was having it off with some bint where he worked. . . (p. 160–1).

The language of these accounts is important. So too is the way that 'consumerism' is seen to be totally corrosive of personal attachments and quite ubiquitous in its influence. While Seabrook writes of the need to clarify the 'overlapping but separate processes' involved in the changes that have taken place, he rarely does, and this weakness becomes clear if we reflect for a moment upon many of his examples. Take the case of a young woman who, shy, afraid and unprepared for her interview at the DHSS is accompanied by her mother, who speaks for her. Seabrook explains:

> What she wanted to say but couldn't, was that she wasn't able to speak for herself, and that it wasn't her fault. Like many others of her generation Karen had no experience of anything very much apart from the commercially created culture in which she has been nurtured with its invitations to fantasy, inertia and unknowingness (p. 73).

But what of the experience of schooling? What of the particular vulnerabilities of a young woman before male authority? Why not discuss these too? Similar questions are prompted by this account of the position of black youngsters:

> The parents have adapted to this new culture where everything depends upon money and the young find they have been shaped by that culture and are then denied the chance to survive in it because they are the new poor, stigmatised by their lack of skills. When this coincides with black skins it looks an even greater discrimination (p. 71).

The fact that 'blackness' appears so late in this account (and then as a matter of coincidence) is significant. It contrasts markedly with what black people themselves have been saying publicly, and in the pages of this book; 'no black is going to get anywhere because they're black' 'The police are there because it's what white people want. . .' It is *racism* and not consumerism that brings the most pain here. And while its growth can be related to the rise of unemployment, as an ideology it has a life of its own, separate from the market and within the working class.

More central to Seabrook's argument is the contrast he draws between the present generation of workers, and an earlier working class involved in 'necessary', 'productive' work. He writes of a time when work had a heroic quality, 'an epic. . . with its demands for the last ounce of human energy and more'. Then, people produced things that were 'directly identifiable with perceived human need as opposed to that of making money' (p. 4), and socialist politics emerged as a 'natural evolution' from this situation. Today, work has changed. Seabrook talks of the 'old structures of work' 'decaying', and of workers being caught up in a 'spiral that distances work from everything that is demonstrably useful or valuable to humanity, and makes the alternative to profit even more remote and unthinkable' (p. 214).

There are many problems with this account. To begin with, it is a feature of capitalism that goods are produced as commodities and sold for money. Under this arrangement it has been the logic of capital which has decided what production is necessary and what is not, and which has determined the subordination of the working class as 'necessary' too. The distinction which Seabrook makes between a time when this subordination was for 'the sake of necessary work' and the situation today when 'subordination (is) for the sake of nothing other than its continued subordination' (p. 11) is not a sound one.[12] His heroic interpretation of work in the earlier period is also unsound. Raphael Samuel has outlined the mindless tedium which was the lot of most manual workers in the nineteenth century, and this, as well as Gareth Stedman-Jones' account of *Outcast London* (where casual labourers lived off the fringes of the aristocratic season), sit uneasily with Seabrook's presentation of the past.[13] If life in this period was 'meaningful' it was made so by the people who lived it. It didn't arrive automatically from 'necessity', nor did politics. Farmers and agricultural workers (to take one of Seabrook's examples of necessary labour) have had a chequered history on the political stage in Europe. Miners too, for while it can be argued that the extractive nature of work in that industry was conducive to radical understandings of exploitation (often, it should be said, via historically derived biblical references to God's earth and the life) this radicalism was expressed through liberalism until comparatively late. Yet in Labour strongholds like Tyneside, skilled men, for generations, worked upon implements of war and destruction. The relationship between economics, work and politics is a much more complex affair than Seabrook allows for, and the historical weakness is mirrored in his contemporary account.

Work and work processes *have* altered in the twentieth century, but there has been much more involved here than decay; more too than a change in the nature of commodities. Mass production is an underpinning theme for much of Seabrook's argument, yet it is rarely analysed. In *Unemployment,* he relies heavily upon quotations from Illich and Schumacher to create an image of the new work processes and their subjective significance. In this way he talks of a 'stripping away of meaning' and of the emergence of 'quite different human beings from the old proletarian type', but it is the market illusion (people 'wrenched from any context of human obligation or commitment')[14] which again dominates. And this is not good enough. As one French commentator has pointed out:

> It is not possible to confine the operative models of a popular culture to the past, the countryside, or to primitive peoples. They exist in the strongholds of the contemporary economy. This is the case with 'ripping off'. This phenomenon spreads everywhere, even if management penalises it or 'looks the other way' in

> order to know nothing of it. . . . workers who 'rip off' subcontract time from the factory (rather than goods, for only scraps are used) with a view of work that is free, creative and precisely without profit.[15]

Considerable evidence exists which illustrates the fact that workers, in even the most 'meaningless' of work situations, find ways of handling monotony and tedium which are often creative and mutually supportive.[16] The worry about Seabrook's account is that it isn't open enough to even consider such evidence. His preoccupation with the market and with moral (absolute) assertions of necessity, blinker his view of working class life, and the changes that have taken place since the war, and this is most clear in his treatment of women and the relationship between the sexes.

In drawing attention to the 'old' working class, Seabrook explicitly mentions four industries: coal, steel, construction and fishing. What these industries have in common is that they have remained for a century or more the exclusive preserve of male manual labour. The 'old' working class in this account is therefore one where the women worked at home. As such the transformation in the culture of the class is linked with the rise of occupations employing female labour. This change is a central issue for any discussion of cultural change (especially one concerned with the 'structure of feeling') and its importance invades the pages of testimony. Seabrook's treatment of the issue is however, cursory in the extreme. Talking with an old man in Sunderland, we learn that: 'in this part of the world the only jobs for women are actresses and prostitutes, and there wasn't much call for either of them' (p. 132). As he speaks, his wife sits and listens. Seabrook comments:

> She nods assent to his account of their life. If she agrees with him it isn't because she is subordinate to him and echoes his ideas, it is because the conditions under which they have lived excluded any other than a shared response of stoicism and endurance (p. 135).

Maybe; maybe not. Certainly it is unlikely that this woman was an actress or a prostitute. More likely than not, she worked as a domestic servant before she married. Then, and particularly in the North East, the woman's place was securely entrenched in domestic labour, and when speaking of those times women there (and in South Wales too) often talk of themselves (or their mothers) as being a 'slave of a slave'. Listen to another account of the family household between the wars:

> There's no doubt about it, the men of that generation were the kingpins of the house. Other people cleaned their shoes. They had a special seat: nobody dared sit in their seat. This kind of thing. My wife's father; nobody dared pass him in case their shadow went on his newspaper. This was a general kind of thing at the time. They were tyrants really in their own way.[17]

Few women today would want to 'put the clock back' to that situation. Few regret the (albeit limited) expansion of employment opportunities for their sex. While some (maybe many) of the older generation might think that young people jump into and out of marriage too easily, few would wish to return to a time when divorce was near impossible, contraception difficult to ensure and abortion a positive danger to life. To say this is not to gloss over problems. One of the women interviewed for the book had been divorced:

> At first just to get out of it, the relief is overwhelming. The sense of freedom. But that doesn't last long; the boredom soon sets in, the sense of futility. It's a different kind of loneliness from what you feel inside a lonely marriage. You achieve what you want, but when you achieve it, it seems so little. You only think of what you're escaping from, not what you're running to (p. 84).

There is a deep and fundamental dilemma here, probably a tragic one.[18] It's a dilemma which touches upon major existential issues (problems of freedom and responsibility) upon which Seabrook is well qualified to comment. He has, after all, written of the policing role of the family within the 'old' culture:

> It was a self-policing community, in which the individuals were constricted at the level of the most basic physiology; you were born, you were married you worked, you had children and you died. Nobody dared affirm anything else.[19]

You want to ask: 'are these the historical options—constriction or excess; self-denial or loneliness?' But here there is no comment. These women's words are left to lie on the page. And this is but one instance.

In *Unemployment,* when Seabrook talks of 'the working class young', he is invariably talking about boys. Perhaps there are all manner of more or less acceptable excuses for this (discussions with girls might have been difficult to arrange etc.), but what is not excusable is the casual and passing reference to women's liberation posters in Community Centres, and the unchecked references to women evoked from the time he spends with the young men. In Sunderland he recounts the dirty stories told by a group of these lads when they were together. He also quotes one lad saying, in private that:

> I can't trust women. I think they're getting at me all the time. The only good women are prossies; it's honest, you pay and that's that (p. 131).

In Lancashire too the stories are of 'getting girls' and there we read of details of a hard pornographic photograph used by one young man during masturbation. In Bolton, Seabrook pays his £2 admission to a home video pornographic show: 'the colour of the film is appalling, and the flesh looks bruised, unnatural violets and reds seem to predominate' (p. 206).

All these accounts are real and believable. Many people will find it disturbing to read them. What is most disturbing however, is the author's *silence.* Seabrook is a man of great literary skill—he has a great talent for dealing with and writing about, the ways in which people think and feel. He constructs a book out of his notes and tape recordings. These accounts were not included by accident. They form a central part of the book's structure. But it is an unspoken part; being barely challenged or interpreted within the book's wider framework.

In the documentary drama *Underage,* film makers Lizzie Lemon and Kim Longinott produce an account of unemployment, based upon three months they spent with fifteen- and sixteen-year-olds in Coventry. The lads are seen fighting, bullying, drinking, swearing and sniffing glue, and, here as David Robins pointed out in *The Times,* 'it is the women who provide the stabilising element'. They also provide a critical perspective on their boy friends.

> He just never shows his feelings and I think that's wrong. . . That time when he pushed his mum—he wanted to say he was sorry but he couldn't 'cos then he'd say 'I've been defeated'. He's *stupid.*[20]

Comments like this are missing in Seabrook's book. It's a sad absence, and one which must be seen as an abiding weakness of the account.

The pages of *Unemployment,* have a haunting quality about them. The accounts go round and around in your head. More than anything else, they perplex you: why, you ask, did a working class with an established way of life of such apparent solidity, cave in so quickly and so easily? We have already noted the way in which mining areas were ravaged in the 1960s. The pits were closed and whole villages and communities transformed. In Durham a Labour council operated the now notorious 'D Village' policy, where villages so categorised were systematically starved of social and industrial capital, forcing people to leave for the 'pools of labour' on the centre of the county. It was the same in the East End of London: one account of how a working class community in Clapton was subject to 'redevelopment' and 'compulsory purchase' is remarkable both for the attachment it reveals people feeling for life in the area, and the absence of any reference to organised action against the move.[21] What accounts like these raise is the question of *politics* and its relation to *culture;* and here there is no denying the central theme of Seabrook's writing, that the socialist movement is in a state of crisis and that 'the work achieved by the Labour movement has to be done all over again' (p. 11).

In writing about this crisis, Gareth Stedman-Jones has noted the need to 'step back from the present apologies offered by Right and Left of the (Labour) Party and take a longer term historical perspective'.[22] Seabrook aids this perspective by his insistence (via Thompson) of the need to investigate the *sub*-political world of the working class and its subterranean *mood.* But such an analysis needs to conjoin, at some point, with politics on the surface, and here Seabrook, careful to avoid simplified notions of 'betrayal', observes that, 'none of what has occurred was done in malice or bad faith'. Rather the problem lay in the fact that:

> While capital didn't rest, labour fell into a kind of stasis, a sort of immobilisation, above all, an absence of imagination. The leaders of labour believed that the gains had been won for all time. They thought the achievements of 1945 inviolable, sacrosanct. They were attached to an optimistic progressivism which in the end became a substitute for moral force; and together these things had a crippling influence on an understanding of just what has happened at a deeper level until it was too late. But it wasn't a defection of love or commitment; at worst a kind of exhaustion, lack of imagination, a certain gullibility.[23]

But surely this 'progressivism', this 'lack of imagination' and 'gullibility' needs to be analysed and located in political *practice.* And here Seabrook's tragic vision could have been leavened with a sense of irony. Many of the areas where the old 'poverty culture' thrived, have been associated with the dominance of Labour Party machines whose crimes in the 1960s were more venal than 'silence' or a 'defection of love'. The corruption scandals in the North East and South Wales (each of which, and successively, reaffirmed a mood of depression amongst working class people, a sense that 'nothing can be done') cannot be seen as yet another example of the corrosive power of consumerism. Labour practices, themselves responded to and influenced the movement of money. For in these areas, where the Aldermanic benches weighed heavily with local Labour dignitaries, Labourism was expressed through the patriarchal and often autocratic, structures of the community. To say this is not to shout 'sell out', or to mock from the privilege of hindsight. Rather it is to assert the presence of deeply conservative and restrictive elements within that political/cultural formation that we term 'Labourism'. It is also to raise, precise and particular questions which Seabrook's highly generalised analysis does not facilitate.

In the 1960s, it was in areas where Labourism had had the least powerful hold (for example, Merseyside and the West Midlands) that resistance took place most openly. Workers in these areas were not, as Seabrook suggests, operating in a 'social vacuum' but were interpreting and developing working class experience and traditions in new contexts. In Liverpool in 1967 one man who worked at the Ford plant at Halewood said this:

> My old fella was a trade unionist. Branch secretary, shop steward and all tha'. He always used to be on about the bosses. . . the capitalists, the General Strike an' tha'. I didn't pay much attention to him. Him and the union caused a lot of trouble in our house. I wanted to be out on the street dancing or having a few bevvies. The old lady used to side with me. But when I came to this place. . . Jesus. . . what a place. It's funny I've remembered all the things my da' said. About the movement an' tha'. I've become as big a unionist as him now. Sometimes I wish I'd listened to him a bit more. He's dead now like and I'd liked to have talked to him. . . I'd like to tell him that I know now.[24]

Accounts like this one can be multiplied many times over and meshed in with struggles and conflicts many of which involved the fight to democratise what were essentially despotic trade union structures. Yet Seabrook's account of those years is of:

> The working class struggle—a phrase which still had meaning in our childhood in the forties—suddenly becom[ing] nothing but an institutionalised ritual.[25]

As with Williams so does Seabrook break with Edward Thompson and that humane tradition within Marxism which stresses the creative aspects of human understanding and struggle. In 1978, Thompson wrote:

> In my view, far too much theoretical attention (much of it plainly a-historical) is paid to 'class' and far too little to 'class struggle'. Indeed class struggle is the prior as well as the most universal concept.[26]

In contrast, Seabrook ignores (or undervalues) the struggles fought through by working class people in the sixties and seventies—and in the eighties too—and his writings consistently neglect them. Given his concern for the changed patterns of caring within the working class, it might have been useful to have walked with the People's March for Jobs. Also, perhaps, to have talked with trade unionists, active in the TGWU's 6–612 Branch for unemployed workers on Merseyside. The occupation organised by the women workers at Plessey's Bathgate plant would be another example of workers facing the issues of unemployment together and in struggle. Instead, he restricts his comments to the riots. Here, where the 'ritual' bursts its seams, he notes:

> the images they produced of looting and destruction do not suggest a resistance to capitalist values, much less the expression of a desire for an alternative. Such reactions are a measure of the growing political impotence of the working class.

To point to the continuance of collective forms of struggle is not to respond with another form of metaphysics, nor is it to underestimate the gravity of the situation for the socialist movement in Britain. Rather it is to make clear that a variety of historical factors (far more various than 'consumerism') have contributed to the present crisis, and that the game is not yet over. Seabrook's comments on the ways in which the politics of Thatcher and the extreme Right ('the only groups that touch the pain') have engaged with the felt experiences of working class people is vitally important; and everything he says about the need for the Left to listen is salutory. But the listening has to be interpreted, and it has to relate to a conception of politics and change which is practical and realisable. It is here that Seabrook's resistance to the potential of new forms of class practice is most destructive. Clear that we cannot go back, he steadfastly (stoically) refuses to imagine a way forward. Refuses too, to take issue with the nature of economic crisis of the 1980s and the ways in which it differs from the one faced by workers in the 1930s. When Adrian Colquhoun spoke of groups of workers separated off from each other (p. 286 above) he was talking about something that is rooted in real processes. So too when workers talk of the *speed* of rundown and closure. Yet Seabrook, firm in his view that the road to socialism is not by expropriating the rich and powerful but 'simply by rendering obsolete the absurd ideological aparatus by which they are maintained' (p. 65) takes no account of the ways in which capital has reconstructed itself via transnational production and the like. Nor of the ways in which the *economic* crisis of British capital (the crisis which has pushed up the rate of unemployment) has conjoined with a political crisis, which has deep implications for the Labour Party. The experience of that party in government (its failure to establish a socialist programme coupled with the direct evidence of many of those reforms which have been implemented—most notably nationalisation), has had its own, independent, effect upon the political culture of the working class. As one shop steward said after the closure of the B.L. plant in Liverpool in 1978:

> I know what Edwardes is. He's a bleeding capitalist. I don't mind him carrying out capitalist kind of decisions. What I object to is people who are supposed to be on our side, being a party to these decisions. Harold Wilson is a local M.P. and he played no part whatsoever in our attempt to save the plant.[27]

As 'decay' is an inappropriate metaphor to illuminate the changes that have taken place in work processes, so too is 'rest' (or the refusal of it) less than helpful in explaining the dynamic of capitalist development since the war. Capital, like rust, never sleeps, but unlike that corrosive agent, it is capable of changing its form. There are limits to this of course, and the task of the socialist movement is to take issue with the changes; understand them and fight back. And in this there are plenty of resources. Seabrook emphasises hopelessness, but deep feelings of resentment and anger exist within the working class which occasionally break through into the pages of *Unemployment.* One man said this:

> They talk about extremism. What about their extremism? Treating people like rubbish, isn't that extremism? (p. 205)

Here, and in the countless other statements like them being made daily, there is hope for a socialist movement. But for that hope to be realised, socialists need to adjust themselves to a capitalist society remarkably different from the one in which the labour movement constructed itself at the turn of the century. There are some signs still that a new movement is possible; 'in the making' even. It has to be fought for, not abdicated.

NOTES

1. *Unemployment,* Quartet Books, 1982. Each quotation followed by a page number is taken from this book.
2. D. Piachaud, *The Times,* 25th June 1982.
3. Richard Hoggart, *The Uses of Literacy,* Chatto and Windus, 1957, p. 17.
4. Most especially, *Working Lives: A People's History of Hackney,* Vols. 1 and 2.
5. The booklet was called *But the World Goes on the Same,* Strong Words, 1979.
6. *What Went Wrong: Working People and the Ideals of the Labour Movement,* Gollancz, 1978, p. 244.
7. Jeremy Seabrook, *The Everlasting Feast,* Allen Lane, 1974, p. 117.
8. *The Uses of Literacy,* p. 323.
9. *The Everlasting Feast.*
10. See, for example, R. Williams, *Materialism and Culture,* New Left Books, 1982. Also the publications of the Centre of Contemporary Culture Studies in the University of Birmingham, especially *Working Class Culture,* Hutchinson, 1979 and *Resistance Through Ritual,* Hutchinson, 1978.
11. *The Everlasting Feast,* p. 17.
12. See, for example, R. Marglin, 'What Do Bosses Do?' in A. Groz (ed.), *The Division of Labour in Society,* Harvester Press, 1975.
13. R. Samuel, 'The Workshop of the World', in *History Workshop Journal* No. 7, 1978, G. Stedman-Jones, *Outcast London,* Oxford University Press, 1971.
14. *What Went Wrong,* p. 76.
15. Michel de Certeau, 'The Oppositional Practices of Everyday Life', in *Social Text,* Vol. 1, No. 3, 1980.
16. The latest comes from an account by another Frenchman, R. Linhart, *The Assembly Line,* John Calder, 1981.
17. T. Monaghan, in K. Armstrong and H. Beynon (eds.), *Hello Are You Working?* Strong Words, 1977.
18. Another way of understanding this dilemma, (and the problem of various interpretations within the socialist movement) can be obtained by reading Seabrook's account of the post-war period, alongside the one offered by Anna Coote and Bea Campbell, *Sweet Freedom,* Picador, 1982.
19. *The Everlasting Feast,* p. 160.
20. *The Times,* August 6th, 1982.
21. *The Island: The Life and Death of an East London Community 1870–1970,* Centreprise, 1979.
22. G. Stedman-Jones, 'March into History', *New Socialist,* January/February, 1982.

23. *The Guardian,* 1st March 1982.
24. Huw Beynon, *Working For Ford,* Penguin Books, 1973, p. 190.
25. *The Everlasting Feast,* p. 117.
26. E.P. Thompson, 'Eighteenth Century English Society: Class Struggle without Class?', *Social History,* Vol. 3, No. 2, May 1978, p. 149.
27. Quoted in *What Happened at Speke?* TGWU, Liverpool 1978. See also the account of the Callaghan government's industrial policy in *State Intervention in Industry: A Workers' Inquiry,* Coventry, Liverpool, Newcastle and N. Shields Trades Council, 1980.

REFLECTIONS ON RECENT LABOUR HISTORIOGRAPHY

John Saville

A rather odd editorial in *History Workshop 12* may serve as a beginning to this selective account of historical and political writing on the contemporary labour movement in Britain. The editorial's main complaint is that in trying to assess the evolution of the Labour Party in the past sixty or seventy years,

> there is so little work to build on, whether as history, theory or politics. Both Marxists and social democrats tend to deal in timeless and specific categories—reformism, parliamentarism, leadership, rank and file. Little attention is paid to either of the major transformations which have taken place within the Labour Party and the trade union movement in various epochs and crises; or at the way in which these might relate, positively or negatively, to changing class formation and party affiliation, changes in the character of central and local government and changes in the place of Britain in the global economy (p. 1).

There is some truth in these generalisations, although the editorial as a whole suggests an ignorance both of the ways in which the historiography of any subject develops, and of what has actually been achieved in published or unpublished work. It must be realised that it is only just over twenty years ago that there began the remarkable expansion of labour-movement studies, but that even today there are still many gaps of a chronological/institutional kind. Institutional history has an old-fashioned sound for many young historians, but the point needs to be made that while the elementary ordering of fact through time is only the beginning of the historian's responsibility, such foundations are required for any intellectual enterprise in the historical field; and that, to quote the most obvious example, straightforward monographs on the history of many trade unions are urgently needed.

It is agreed that much remains to be quarried and then shaped, and that inevitably even in the short space of two decades the kind of questions that historians have asked of their materials have radically altered. But it is mostly incorrect to argue, as this editorial does, that:

> The inspiration for labour history, ever since it began to take off as a movement, has been the search for an alternative non-social democratic tradition. E.P. Thompson's *The Making of the English Working Class* (1963) has evidently

> been one major point of departure, but this book itself was appropriated by a powerful political or sub-political current which has meant that subsequent work has by and large reproduced its biases. Subjects have been chosen for the *dissimilarity* which they offered to the present—heroic periods of struggle, for instance, conceived not so much as forerunners of the present, but rather as examples of what have been lost (p. 3).

Again, there is a quarter-truth embedded in these statements. No-one will deny the enormous influence of Edward Thompson's writings, but whether it has led to an over-emphasis upon the alternative non-reformist tradition is open to question and there is no reference to the critical commentary of *The Making of the English Working Class* which has been slowly building up. And as for the concentration upon the heroic self-sacrifice of the past, it must be understood that any labour movement always incorporates within its own traditions a sense of the past, both the high points and the defeats. So that while no-one today who is a committed socialist can fail to be conscious of the great struggles of the nineteen-thirties—the Hunger Marches, the anti-Mosley demonstrations, the solidarity with Republican Spain—there is also an acute awareness of the 1931 betrayal, and of the miserable performance of the 1929-31 Labour government in general. The more specific analysis of the past, its deeper meaning within the framework of popular history, is surely why historians of the left engage in the study of the labour movement in earlier decades.

The *History Workshop* editorial seems, however, to deny this approach. There is, the editorial notes, a 'lack of curiosity of the Labour left about history and even fear of it—fear during the post-war boom that historical research might prove the Right correct' (p. 3); and these words suggest a lack of knowledge about what has been written or published. Recent studies of the miners in the twentieth century, for example—*The Fed* (1980) by Hywel Francis and David Smith; the excellent essays edited by Martin Bulwer, *Mining and Social Change* (1978) which relate to the North-East coalfield; the symposium on Wales: *A People and a Proletariat* (1980) edited by David Smith—together make an important contribution to our understanding of the labourist, labour-socialist, socialist and trade-union traditions of working-class communities. There is a great deal of relevant material in the journals of the regional labour history societies; and there are studies of working-class communities: *Jutepolis* by W.M. Walker (for example) which have been unduly neglected, at least south of the border. All this is not to suggest complacency. There are many areas of study that remain to be worked, and the nearer we get to our own time the more gaps there are. The impressionistic generalisations that Jeremy Seabrook is publishing (his latest, *Unemployment* (1982)) require, for example, to be tested against more detailed research and commentary on contemporary working-class life and community; and

Seabrook's argument, whatever its merits, that there has taken place a serious erosion of traditional working-class virtues must be incorporated within the debate about sectionalism that Hobsbawm initiated: a matter discussed below.

Alan Warde's *Consensus and Beyond: The Development of Labour Party Strategy Since the Second World War* does not, unfortunately, take us very far to meet the criticisms of the *History Workshop* editorial. The book is an unhappy mixture of rather skimped fact and sociological abstraction, written in an English style that is sometimes meaningless and too often is so anfractuous that meaning is lost, or distorted. Consider this sentence from the concluding chapter; it is not wholly without meaning; but let the reader try rephrasing it in terms that would allow its understanding to be clearly appreciated:

> That minority control over economic production and gross inequalities in distribution are both in contradiction with dominant legitimations in terms of civic or 'politicio-juridicial' equality, is widely recognised as a determinant of political management on capitalism (p. 195).

Dr. Warde's central concern, as his title suggests, is with the different strategies evolved by the Labour Party in the thirty years or so after 1945. The first period which followed the years of the Attlee governments, 1945–51, was dominated by the Social Reformism of Gaitskell, Crosland and Jenkins, providing the basis for bi-partisanship and the politics of consensus. Then, with the growing dissatisfaction with Britain's economic performance in comparison with other advanced countries, by the early 1960s there developed a 'significant change' in Labour strategy. The Wilson governments after 1964 'operated with a very different conception of the political process and of Labour's part in it' (p. 7). This the author describes as Technocratic-Collectivism, 'very much a philosophy of expert *dirigisme*' (p. 102). By the early 1970s, however, Technocratic-Collectivism had 'failed to resolve intra-party conflict or to avert social conflict' (p. 117), and the third strategy that now emerged was the Social Contract: 'A substitute for consensus, this was a political formula which sought peace on the strength of collaboration outside parliamentary channels with the principal functional interests in society—business and unions' (p. 7). For a while successful, the social contract floundered by the late 1970s as a result of developing economic and financial problems and the emergence of an 'oppositional strategy' by the left of the Labour Party. Since economic growth could no longer be guaranteed, the structures of the welfare state were being eroded. Public expenditure began to be cut from 1975, and unemployment levels rose. The social contract finally broke down in the winter of 1978–9, and the Conservative Party won the general election of 1979.

This basic summary of Dr. Warde's argument makes the book sound more reasonable than it is. The problem with it is that there really is nothing more than elementary platitudes, and certain quite crucial parts of the analysis are either too simplistic or wrong. The economic context within which the Labour Party worked out its tactics and strategy is not analysed in any detail; the crucial differences between being in office, or not, in terms of policies, are not considered; and much too sharp a division is made between the 1970s and 1950s, while fully accepting the emergence of a continuing crisis from the mid-sixties on. A much more sophisticated analysis is provided by Keith Middlemas (*Politics in Industrial Society. The Experience of the British System since 1911* (1979)) whose starting point was the recognition of the flexibility and stability of the British political system from the middle of the 1920s, within a world system in which crises have been growing inexorably. Middlemas, to sum up a complex analysis, laid great emphasis upon what he called the 'corporate bias' of British society. The industrial and political crises of the pre-1914 years 'culminated in the manpower and production crises of the First World War, [and] British governments stimulated institutional growth among bodies representing business and labour interests, in order to maintain public consent' (p. 371). It is Middlemas' contention that these interest groups—employers and their organisations, trade unions and their members—became 'governing institutions, existing thereafter as estates of the realm, committed to cooperation with the state, even if they retained the customary habit of opposition to specific party governments' (p. 372). 'Governing institution' was further defined:

> as a description of a body which assumes functions devolved on it by government, shares some or all of the assumptions about national interests held by government, and accepts aims similar to those laid down by government; with the fundamental qualification that this form of association is not compulsory, but voluntary to the extent that it takes place within general limits derived, negatively, from the evidence of what the institution's constituent members will or will not accept (p. 373).

'Corporate bias' is a useful analytical tool, and Middlemas is careful to distinguish it from corporatism. 'Corporate bias which, like the bias of a wood at bowls, is in itself no more than a tendency always to run to one side' (p. 380) rather than a more precise, more clearly defined and coherent pattern of behaviour on the part of either business or trade unions; but while it certainly does not explain everything, it is undoubtedly helpful in proceeding towards an understanding of political and industrial trends in the twentieth century. In this context Middlemas argues that corporate bias worked to a climax of relative success between 1945 and 1965. What Middlemas does not explain—and he would require another volume for the purpose—is how it came about that the leadership of the dominant unions within the TUC accepted the practice of 'corporate bias'—an analysis that cannot be conducted only in terms of ideology, but within the whole complex of limitations imposed on trade unions in bourgeois society. But for Marxist historians there is one further major qualification, that alters fundamentally its meaning, to be made to the thesis in general. As expounded by Middlemas, a rough parity is assumed between 'governing institutions', and there is no sustained theory of the state. The argument that labour is, at the very least, an equal partner in the triangle of government, business and labour underlies the theory of 'corporate bias'; and it has never been true. In 1982, after three years of the most reactionary government in Western Europe, it is palpably not true. And Middlemas, by pushing too hard at his theory, was led into some incautious generalisations about the future. He had emphasised, very properly, the enveloping crisis of British society from the middle sixties, but he could still write, in the year that the Thatcher government came to power:

> it is difficult, on the evidence of the British case, to avoid the conclúsion that trade unions' potential power will eventually predominate over that of management (p. 462)

a statement which it is improbable to expect to come to pass. But he was wholly wrong in his final paragraph, and his error must be largely a failure to appreciate fully the extent and depth of the crisis afflicting the British economy. Given the serious problems that had beset governments in the most recent decade, he wrote—almost his last words:

> Faced with a choice of abandoning at least one of the three desiderata of post-war equilibrium, full employment, rising living standards and stable prices, governments since 1969 have chosen the first (p. 463).

The Thatcher government has in fact abandoned all three, although by continuing a savage deflationary policy they hope to restore some stability to prices. The reason why Middlemas was wrong in his general forecast can only be his failure to plumb the full depth of the crisis of British capitalism, and the desperate remedies which have to be attempted. Moreover, the Thatcher experience has also re-asserted the close interwoven relationships between the Conservative party and multinational business, and the direct ways in which state power can and will be used to curb and constrain the political and industrial weight of trade unionism in crisis situations. What the Thatcher government has also demonstrated much more clearly than for many years is the diminution in the effectiveness of trade-union pressures without vigorous support from its political wing in the Labour Party. The incompetence and ineffectiveness of the Labour Party in opposition since May 1979 may not have had the same quantitative or qualitative consequences as the massive rise in the unemployment figures, but it has been a factor of great significance. Thatcherism has not been supportive to the theory and practice of countervailing power.

The volume by Middlemas remains an important study not to be neglected, but to take analysis further we require both sophisticated methodological studies and hard accounts of how government structures, political parties, business and unions interacted in given situations and historical periods. *History Workshop 13* has published one such analysis of quite extraordinary interest. Brett, Gilliatt and Pope in 'Planned Trade, Labour Party Policy and US Intervention: The Successes and Failures of Post-War Reconstruction' (pp. 130–42) provide the detailed story of the economic policies of the Attlee government 1945–51. The authors have used government records, especially cabinet papers, to great effect, and their conclusions are much sharper and more clearly defined than in any previous account. Moreover, the analysis offers a perspective for the whole period since the war. What was decided in those crucial years immediately following the end of the war against fascism has determined the main lines of economic development of the British economy in the succeeding thirty years, and has imposed strict constraints and limitations upon the Labour governments in this period.

The main conclusion of this study is that the crucial choice for the Attlee government in the years immediately following the war was either to take the 'apparently soft option' presented by American assistance, or to cut back drastically on overseas defence commitments and maintain strict controls on trade, currency levels and capital outflows. In more detailed terms the arguments may be summarised thus:

1. The conditions of the American loan negotiated by Keynes at the end of 1945 were to exert decisive influences upon future economic policy. In the short run, full currency convertibility was insisted upon within one year of the final ratification of the loan agreement. Although the UK was allowed to retain existing external controls, together with wartime domestic controls, the USA was now able continuously to exert conservative pressures upon policies in general. Thus, the UK was not permitted to switch overseas sources of supply away from the USA and the 'dollar gap' therefore became an inescapable fact of Britain's external position. When convertibility was introduced on 15 July 1947, a massive crisis erupted, and in the aftermath of this catastrophe, a major revision followed, of a marked conservative kind, of both home and foreign policies. The only thing that partially saved the position—at least temporarily for the next two years—was the

continued existence of international and domestic controls which made it possible to maintain full employment and expand output. Gaitskell, in a later memorandum of 1950, made the point emphatically that without the retention of physical controls it would not be possible to stem the outflow from the reserves or to preserve full employment as a long-term aim.

2. What Gaitskell argued against, but only in words, was what he described as 'the so-called "liberalisation of European trade".' But the terms of the American loan had ensured a commitment to the International Monetary Fund (IMF) which involved the UK in liberalising trade with Europe in particular: through the OEEC. And this liberalisation did, of course, come about.
3. The post-war arrangements, accepted by the Attlee government, involved the UK with an increasing integration into the American-dominated alliance. The authors quote an illuminating passage from a memorandum of the British government's Economic Development Committee of May 1949. It was decided that 'further investment for health and education might endanger our efforts to achieve viability', not because social investment was reckoned to be less efficient than private investment, but from fears that 'increased investment in the social services might influence Congress in their appropriations from Marshall Aid' (p. 138).
4. The long-term consequences of the American alliance are the history of the past thirty years. The acceptance of very heavy, unproductive defence costs—between 1950 and 1966 the UK spent 4 to 5 per cent of GNP on defence—while in Germany and Japan there were virtually no defence costs, and their rate of investment in productive capital was consequently much higher. By the 1960s their productive investment, capacity and output had far outstripped the levels in the UK. Further, the liberalisation of trade, which came about after 1950, added to the heavy costs of unproductive investment, made the UK vulnerable to balance of payments deficits and capital outflows. Stop-go was the result: the short summary of the unfortunate economic history of the past quarter century, whose critical proportions have steadily grown.

These matters relate to the post-war history of the labour movement and underline the absence of a coherent statement of foreign policy on the part of the left in Britain. Its absence has been a remarkable phenomenon. The ad hoc campaigns against nuclear arms collapsed by the middle sixties and did not re-emerge until fifteen years later; the movement against the war in Vietnam; the political resentment against South Africa; these were never brought together into a single policy. Even more important, the fudging of the issue of NATO—central to the elaboration of any socialist analysis of foreign affairs—meant that there never has been a coherent alternative. And without agreement on a foreign policy, the domestic aims of the left were inevitably limited and severely circumscribed. What has not been sufficiently analysed is the complex inter-relationships between the economics of Britain's international position in the world, her close alliance with America as a centre component of the latter's position on the bastion of world counter-revolution, and the radical alternative on the domestic front in Britain itself.

The most interesting debate of the immediate past has been that begun by Eric Hobsbawm in his 1978 Marx Memorial lecture. The original lecture, which gave rise to a considerable discussion in *Marxism Today*, has now been reprinted with further contributions: *The Forward March of Labour Halted?* (1981). Hobsbawm began by noting the changing social structure of the past half-century: by 1976 about 45 per cent of the occupied population could be classified as non-manual (p. 3); the introduction of women, especially married women, into the labour force has notably altered its overall composition; the decline in the traditional occuaptions of the first half of the century and the improvement in living standards have all contributed substantially to changes in working-class life-styles, and that these changes have markedly quickened during the last thirty years. He went on to note that 35 per cent of the labour force were not in any trade union, and that this proportion has remained unchanged since 1950. His main emphasis was upon the evidence of electoral change; political support for the Labour Party as expressed in general election voting patterns had declined from 49 per cent of the total votes cast in 1951 to under 40 per cent in 1974, and even lower in 1979, when probably about one-third of trade unionists voted for the Conservative Party. Among the trends which provided the background to these changes were the growth of racism and, even more serious, because it represented a further general decline in class solidarity, the spread of economic sectionalism: 'a growing division of workers into sections and groups, each pursuing its own economic interest irrespective of the rest' (p. 14).

What was interesting about the discussion which followed the publication of Hobsbawm's lecture was the narrowness of the arguments to which contributors confined themselves. There was a correct line, it was suggested, which if pursued vigorously would effect the necessary transformation of social consciousness: the correct line being the marriage of political aims and objectives with industrial struggles; and then the forward march would be resumed. There were, it should be noted, some important differences of approach within the group of industrial militants who responded. Two leading members of the Communist Party, for example, Ken Gill and Pete Carter, strongly disagreed on this matter of sectionalism. The former argued that; 'The development of a militant wage *movement* is our first priority. That is the lesson of 1970–74' (p. 22); while Carter put a totally opposed view:

> Too often we substitute, as Gill has done, a certain kind of wishful thinking which says that because we see struggle as political the masses do also. In addition it should be remembered that the wages struggle is only one part of the class struggle and that at certain times some types of wages struggle may be politically self-defeating.
>
> This is why one despairs when Gill says that the restoration of the wages movement is the key area of struggle, without any concrete suggestions as to how it is related to either the political struggle of the left or other areas of struggle like what is the relationship between the fight for wages and the struggle over investment policy, the problems of workers' control, or whether products are socially useful or not (p. 26).

Raymond Williams, whose contribution was the most far-reaching in its long-term implications, commented on the issue of sectionalism and its relationship to the wider aims of the movement:

> Some years ago I described one of the same phenomena as 'militant particularism'; an awkward phrase, but I wanted to get past my simple equation of militancy with *socialism*. Of course almost all labour struggles begin as particularist. People recognise some condition and problem they have in common, and make the effort to work together to change or solve it. But then this is nothing special in the working class. You have only to look at the militancy of stockbrokers or of country landowners or public-school headmasters. The unique and extraordinary character of working-class self-organisation has been that it has tried to connect particular struggles to a general struggle in one quite special way. It has set out, as a movement, to make real what is at first sight the extraordinary claim that defence and advancement of certain particular interests, properly brought together, are in fact in the general interest. That, after all, is the moment of transition to an idea of socialism. And this moment comes not once and for all but many times; is lost and is found again; has to be affirmed and developed, continually, if it is to stay real (pp. 144–5).

The remainder of his contribution was a consideration of the problems of reconciling the particular interests of groups with the general interest of working people as a whole: the theory and practice of socialism. And almost alone among those whose commentaries were published in this volume he noted not only the 'many special and local features' of the British crisis, but that the UK was integrally involved in an international military and political alliance dominated by the United States. The point must be emphasised: that a strategy for the next twenty years that does not have at its centre a socialist foreign policy will be less than coherent, and will fail because its perspectives are parochial rather than international.

At one level, there is an interesting paradox to be confronted. We have witnessed, over the past two decades, a quite remarkable increase in the publication of material about socialism, in the history of labour movements everywhere, in the wide-ranging critique of the non-capitalist societies of Eastern Europe, and in the general sophistication of socialist theory. The bookshelves are filled with exegeses of Marx; educational bodies discuss Marx and Marxism in ways, and to an extent, unknown in the 1950s. There is today a minority socialist culture different from anything we have previously experienced. It is a very small minority; it is affected by affluence; and in this general context there are three aspects of the history of the last decade that are worth remarking on. The first is the decline in numbers and influence of the groups to the left of the Labour Party, especially notable among the former Trotskyist organisations; the second is the emergence of a vigorous popular radicalism within the left of the Labour Party, in part and only in part related to the growth of the Militant tendency, but much broader in its social basis and its influence; the third is the growth of economic sectionalism and the decline in the general appeal of socialist ideas to the majority of the working population outside the committed within the trade unions and the Labour Party. What has to be faced now, Raymond Williams concluded, 'honestly and without recrimination, is that the struggle for that moment–the moment of transition to the *idea* of socialism quite as much as of a transition to socialist practice–has been at least temporarily lost' (p. 145). How and why this has come about must be the central matter for our concern in the coming years.

RUTH FIRST

Ralph Miliband

Ruth First was killed on August 17 last by a letter-bomb sent to her at the Centre of African Studies at the Eduardo Mondlane University in Maputo. She was then the director of research at the Centre and had been in Mozambique for three years. No one seriously doubts that she was murdered by agents of the South African security police. They chose their victim well: for she was one of the most gifted and dedicated South African revolutionaries of our time, and she was, by virtue of her work and her writings, a source of growing influence and inspiration.

Ruth First was born in Johannesburg in 1925 and was the daughter of Jewish left-wing parents who had emigrated to South Africa from Lithuania. She joined the South African Communist Party while a student at Witwatersrand University and became the editor of a series of left-wing newspapers and magazines successively banned by the government. In 1956, she and her husband Joe Slovo were among the defendants in the mass treason trial which ended in the acquittal of all the accused. In the early sixties, she was banned from journalism and was arrested in 1963: the time spent in solitary confinement was the subject of her book *117 Days.* She left South Africa on her release and settled in London with her husband and three daughters.

It was soon after that I came to know her, and the following brief remarks are about her as the person I knew: others who are better qualified will in due course write about her work.

One of the most remarkable things about Ruth First was her ability to combine two very different attitudes. On the one hand, she was totally and irrevocably committed to the cause she had adopted as a student. Her whole personality conveyed an impression of quiet resolve; and it was clear that, whoever else came to be daunted by the hardness and steepness of the road, she would not: for her, the struggle against oppression in South Africa would in one way or another remain her paramount concern in exile as it had been when she was there. On the other hand, her commitment was allied to a sharply critical view of the shortcomings of the left. She was deeply marked by the reflux from Stalinism; and she would get very angry at much that was said and done in the name of socialism and Marxism in many parts of the world. Nor was she sparing in her criticism of the new regimes in Africa, as witness for instance her analysis of many such regimes in *The Barrel of A Gun.* But this made no difference to her commitment. She was the least 'utopian' of revolutionaries: but she was not in the least 'disillusioned'; and she never gave the slightest hint of a doubt about the justice of her cause or about the urgent need to strive for its advancement. She deplored the shortcomings, stupidities and crimes of her own side. But this never dimmed her sense that there was a struggle to be fought against the monstrous tyranny that is South Africa. From her earliest days in political struggle, she had had an exceptionally sharp sense of the concrete meaning of exploitation of black labour, and this remained a special interest of hers. She had in her early days in journalism helped to expose farm labour conditions in South Africa; and her last work in Mozambique was concerned with migrant miners from there into South Africa. Beyond all disappointments and setbacks, it was this sense of the reality of oppression which moved her.

Ruth First was above all a political activist, who became a writer and scholar by force of circumstances and because she had a remarkable talent for social and political analysis. She prized intellectual work but found academic life in Britain lacking in engagement and seriousness; and she looked at her own involvement in academic life with wry amusement, and with a sense that she did not really belong. She was intellectually very tough, direct, precise, unsentimental, impatient with rhetoric and pretentiousness. She had strong opinions, definite perspectives. This might have made her rigid and narrow; but it did not. She remained an intensely questioning person, with a great appetite for learning, with a free mind, an open ear, and a great sense of the ridiculous. When she first came to London, she was very shy about presenting her work to university seminars, and had to be persuaded, rather absurdly, that she was more than competent to do so. She became more confident as time went on, but she remained self-critical, and dismissive about her own achievements and successes. She was very self-demanding, and unassuming. The idea that she could ever become a symbol and an inspiration would have sent her into fits of embarrassed laughter. But her life and her death have made her so. When South Africa has had its revolution, hers will be one of the names in the roll of martyrs which new generations will honour; and she will remain a strong presence in the minds of those who knew her.